S0-BWF-603

For Instructions on How To...

For Instructions on How To...	See Page...
Remove the PC's Cover	95
Put the PC's Case Back On	99
Remove Chips	157
Remove SIMMs	158
Install Chips	160
Install SIMMs	162
Install a Floppy Drive or Tape Drive	192
Remove a Floppy Drive	193
Remove a Hard Drive	217
Install a Hard Drive	219
Install a Second Drive	221
Remove an Expansion Card	259
Install an Expansion Card	260
Replace a Power Supply	277
Install a Video Adapter	301
Add a Monitor	302

For every kind of computer user, there is a SYBEX book.

All computer users learn in their own way. Some need straightforward and methodical explanations. Others are just too busy for this approach. But no matter what camp you fall into, SYBEX has a book that can help you get the most out of your computer and computer software while learning at your own pace.

Beginners generally want to start at the beginning. The **ABC's** series, with its step-by-step lessons in plain language, helps you build basic skills quickly. Or you might try our **Quick & Easy** series, the friendly, full-color guide.

The **Mastering** and **Understanding** series will tell you everything you need to know about a subject. They're perfect for intermediate and advanced computer users, yet they don't make the mistake of leaving beginners behind.

If you're a busy person and are already comfortable with computers, you can choose from two SYBEX series—**Up & Running** and **Running Start**. The **Up & Running** series gets you started in just 20 lessons. Or you can get two books in one, a step-by-step tutorial and an alphabetical reference, with our **Running Start** series.

Everyone who uses computer software can also use a computer software reference. SYBEX offers the gamut—from portable **Instant References** to comprehensive **Encyclopedias**, **Desktop References**, and **Bibles**.

SYBEX even offers special titles on subjects that don't neatly fit a category—like **Tips & Tricks**, the **Shareware Treasure Chests**, and a wide range of books for Macintosh computers and software.

SYBEX books are written by authors who are expert in their subjects. In fact, many make their living as professionals, consultants or teachers in the field of computer software. And their manuscripts are thoroughly reviewed by our technical and editorial staff for accuracy and ease-of-use.

So when you want answers about computers or any popular software package, just help yourself to SYBEX.

For a complete catalog of our publications, please write:

SYBEX Inc.
2021 Challenger Drive
Alameda, CA 94501
Tel: (510) 523-8233/(800) 227-2346 Telex: 336311
Fax: (510) 523-2373

SYBEX is committed to using natural resources wisely to preserve and improve our environment. As a leader in the computer book publishing industry, we are aware that over 40% of America's solid waste is paper. This is why we have been printing the text of books like this one on recycled paper since 1982.

This year our use of recycled paper will result in the saving of more than 15,300 trees. We will lower air pollution effluents by 54,000 pounds, save 6,300,000 gallons of water, and reduce landfill by 2,700 cubic yards.

In choosing a SYBEX book you are not only making a choice for the best in skills and information, you are also choosing to enhance the quality of life for all of us.

The PC Upgrade Guide

for Everybody

THE PC
UPGRADE GUIDE
FOR EVERYBODY

Dan Gookin and
Robert Mullen

San Francisco ◆ Paris ◆ Düsseldorf ◆ Soest

SYBEX®

Acquisitions Editor: Dianne King
Developmental Editor: Sharon Crawford
Editor: Brenda Kienan
Technical Editor: Sheldon M. Dunn
Assistant Editors: Abby Azrael, Michelle Nance
Book Designer: Suzanne Albertson
Illustrations: Van Genderen Studio
Screen Graphics Artist: John Corrigan
Typesetter: Dina F Quan
Production Editor: Carolina Montilla
Production Coordinator/Proofreader: Catherine Mahoney
Proofreader/Production Assistant: Kristin Amlie
Indexer: Ted Laux
Cover Designer: Ingalls + Associates
Cover Photographer: Stephanie O'Shaunessy

Acknowledgments

Special credit goes to Bob Mullen, the writer who revised and expanded this book from its original form to its current, updated incarnation. Thanks, Bob. —D.G.

It's not often that a "new kid on the block" gets to work with one of the kookiest personalities in the computer trade book business. Dan, I thoroughly enjoyed this joint project. I hope it shows between these covers. —R.M.

As always, we value and appreciate the efforts of Matt Wagner and everyone at Waterside Productions for their help with the sometimes-no-fun, business end of this stick.

Books just don't happen overnight. Always there, assisting in the effort to complete this tome, were the following Sybex folk: Sharon Crawford, Brenda Kienan, Sheldon Dunn, Suzanne Albertson, Dina Quan, Catherine Mahoney, Kathleen Lattinville, and David Krassner.

Contents at a Glance

Introduction		**xix**
1	Do It Yourself	**1**
2	Tools and Supplies	**11**
3	Knowing Your PC	**25**
4	Upgrading the PC	**53**
5	Upgrading Software	**101**
6	About Memory	**119**
7	Memory Upgrades	**143**
8	Floppy-Disk Drives	**167**
9	Hard-Disk Drives	**201**
10	Expansion Cards	**235**
11	Power Supply	**265**
12	Monitors and Display Adapters	**281**
13	Maximizing the Printer	**307**
14	The Multimedia PC	**347**
15	Maintenance and Troubleshooting Tips	**371**
A	Diagnostic Error Codes	**399**
B	Drive Types	**415**
Index		**419**

Contents

Introduction   xix

CHAPTER 1
Do It Yourself
1

You Can Do It!   2
   You'll Get to Know More About Your PC   2
   You'll Become a Valued PC Expert   3
Reasons for Doing It Yourself   3
   Because You Can   3
   Your PC Is Modular in Nature   3
   No Change Is Permanent   4
   You'll Save Money and Time   4
   You Don't Have to Be a Hardware Hacker   4
Reasons for Not Doing It Yourself   5
   You're Afraid   5
   You Might Mess Something Up   6
   You're Worried About the Warranty   6
   You Think You Can't Do It   7
Things to Look Out For   7
   Unplug Everything Before You Start   8
   Beware of Static!   8
   Watch Out for Really Cheap Stuff   8
   If It Works, Don't Fix It   9
   Keep a Rein on Yourself   9

CHAPTER 2
Tools and Supplies
11

Tools to Buy	11
Must-Have Tools	12
Good-to-Have Tools	13
Other Tools	15
The Most Important Tool	16
Tool Kits	17
Tools You Should Avoid	17
Using the Various Tools	18
Locating Equipment	18
Where to Find Equipment	19
Types of Equipment to Look For	21
Handling Computer Components	22
General Advice	23

CHAPTER 3
Knowing Your PC
25

How the PC Uses Hardware	25
The Microprocessor	26
The BIOS	26
Temporary Storage—RAM	27
Permanent Storage	28
Support Hardware	28
Power Supply	29
Monitor/Keyboard	29
Peripherals	29
How the PC Uses Software	29
PC/XT, PC/AT, and 386 Class Differences	30
The PC/AT Class Has Extended Memory	31

The PC/AT Class Systems Have 16-Bit Expansion Slots   31

386 Class Systems May Have a Proprietary 32-Bit
Memory Slot   32

386 Class Systems May Also Have a General 32-Bit Slot   32

AT Class Systems Have Battery-Backed-Up RAM   32

Basically, All PCs Are the Same   33

About the PS/2 Line   33

Micro Channel Architecture   33

VGA Graphics   34

PS/2s Are Now Widely Cloned   34

It Is Upgradeable   34

What Happens When You Turn the PC On   35

The Hardware Side   35

The Software Side   38

When Something Goes Wrong   41

POST Errors   44

Strategies   44

DIP Switches and Setup Programs   47

DIP Switches   47

Jumpers   48

Setup Programs   50

Not Everything Is a Problem   51

CHAPTER 4

Upgrading the PC

53

Why You Want to Do This   54

System Overview   56

External Differences   57

Internal Differences   70

Peripheral Differences   85

Committing Surgery   90

General Strategy   91

Taking Your PC's Cover Off   94
Hunting Time   97
Putting Your PC's Cover Back On   98

CHAPTER 5
Upgrading Software
101

The Evil Twins   102
Upgrading Software   102
   Upgrading to Newer Versions of Software   103
   Deciding Not to Upgrade   104
   Some Cautionary Notes   104
   Installing New Software   105
   Working with CONFIG.SYS   107
   Working with AUTOEXEC.BAT   110
   Running Batch Files   112
Upgrading Hardware   113
   Hardware-Prompted Software Upgrades   114

CHAPTER 6
About Memory
119

RAM and the PC   120
   How Memory Is Used   120
   Types of Memory   131
Putting Memory to Work   136
   Smashing the 640K Barrier   136
   Using Extended Memory   139
   Using Expanded Memory   139

CHAPTER 7

Memory Upgrades

143

General Notes on Memory	144
About Chips	144
Where RAM Goes	150
Installing Memory	151
Buying Chips	152
Upgrade Overview	153
Removing Chips	156
Removing SIMMs	158
Plugging in Chips	159
Plugging in SIMMs	161
Troubleshooting and Startup Advice	163
Problems	164

CHAPTER 8

Floppy-Disk Drives

167

General Notes on Disk Drives	168
Background Information	168
Types of Drives	175
Where Floppy Drives Go	176
Floppy Disks	177
Upgrading a Disk Drive	185
Buying a Drive	185
Upgrade Overview	188
Installing a Floppy Drive or Tape-Backup Drive	192
Removing a Drive	193
Replacing a Full-Height Drive	194

Software Considerations	195
Exchanging Disks	195
Formatting	195

CHAPTER 9
Hard-Disk Drives
201

General Notes on Hard-Disk Drives	201
Background Information	202
How a Hard Drive Works	202
The Drive Unit	204
The Controller Card	204
Cables	208
Types of Hard Drives	210
Where They Go	212
Formatting Information	213
Upgrading a Hard Drive	214
Buying a Drive	214
Upgrade Overview	216
Removing a Drive	217
Installing a Drive	219
Installing a Second Drive	220
Software Setup	222
The AT SETUP Program	223
Installing DOS	224
Hard-Disk Management	231
Preventive Maintenance Techniques	232

CHAPTER 10
Expansion Cards
235

General Notes on Expansion Cards   235
   Expansion Cards   236
   Card Types   240
   Expansion Slots   248
Upgrading Expansion Cards   252
   Strategies   252
   Upgrade Overview   254
   Removing an Expansion Card   258
   Installing an Expansion Card   260
Additional Setup   261
   Software Setup   261
   Solving Conflicts   262

CHAPTER 11
Power Supply
265

General Notes on the Power Supply   266
   The Power Supply's Duties   266
   About the Power Supply   267
Replacing a Power Supply   271
   Buying a New Power Supply   272
   Replacement Overview   273
   Removal and Installation   276
Words of Advice   278
   Keeping the PC Power-Healthy   278
   Preventing Mishaps   279

CHAPTER 12
Monitors and Display Adapters
281

General Video Information   282
  PC Graphics   282
  Text and Graphics   284
  Color Graphics Adapters   286
  Monitors   291
Upgrading Monitors and Display Adapters   296
  Strategy   297
  Buying a Display Adapter and Monitor   298
  Upgrade Overview   299
  Upgrading a Video Adapter   300
  Upgrading a Monitor   302
Software Considerations   303
  Companion Diskettes   304
  Changing Your Software   305

CHAPTER 13
Maximizing the Printer
307

About Printers   308
  Printer Description   308
  Printer Types   312
  How Printers Are Judged   317
  Printer Paper   324
Your PC and the Printer   326
  The Printer Port   326
  Your Software and Printers   329
  DOS and the Printer   332

Boosting Printer Performance 337
    Software 337
    Hardware 341

CHAPTER 14
The Multimedia PC
347

A History of Multimedia 347
A Short Survey of What Multimedia Can Do for Your PC 348
Multimedia Hardware Options for Your PC 350
    Audio Upgrades 352
    CD ROM Upgrades 355
    Visual Upgrades 361
    About Device Drivers 365
    Network Considerations 365
Multimedia Software Options for Your Computer 366
    Videographer's Software 367
    Authoring Software 367
    Video Editing Software 368
    Music Creation Software 368
    Karaoke on CD-ROM 369

CHAPTER 15
Maintenance and Troubleshooting Tips
371

Test Driving Equipment 371
    Testing the Warranty 372
    What Might Go Wrong? 372
Identifying Problems 379
    Keep Food, Drink, and Smoke Away from the PC 380
    Use the POST 380
    Evaluation 383

Troubleshooting Tips   384
    External Cables   384
    Floppy Drives   386
    Hard Drives   387
    Internals   389
    Keyboard   390
    Monitor   390
    Power Supply   392
    Printer   392
    Cleaning the Printer   394
    Software   395
Adios   397

APPENDIX A
Diagnostic Error Codes
399

Beeping Errors   399
General POST Error Codes   400
Detailed POST Error Code List   403

APPENDIX B
Drive Types
415

Index   419

Introduction

The personal computer is the most wonderful tool ever invented, enabling you to express your creativity in ways never before possible. Whether you are using a word processor to write a letter or a spreadsheet to analyze the company budget, your PC's hardware and software work together to help meet your computing needs.

The pace of technology is relentless, and it's easy to get left behind. Most people are comfortable with upgrading their software: They read about a new program or a new version of a program they already own, buy the software, and install it. Maybe they also read a few books on how to use it and pick up a few tips from coworkers or a users' group.

Hardware, however, is a different story. Most people fear the inside of their computer. They fail to realize how much more computing power and efficiency they can achieve by upgrading their hardware.

You can expand your system to add more memory, another hard drive, a CD-ROM drive, an S3 accelerated video card, a floptical drive, a new monitor, or an internal FAX/modem. You can give your system a faster microprocessor or upgrade your motherboard to take advantage of the popular VL Local Bus technology to make your Windows applications really fly. The variety of upgrading options is almost endless. I know of no serious computer user who can sit down and say, "Well, there's nothing more I can add to my computer. It's perfect!"

The purpose of this book is to help you get comfortable with the idea of getting inside your computer's case and making changes. Along the way, you'll pick up a lot of useful information about how your computer works and what you can do to make it work better. You'll also have a lot of fun—and you don't have to have a Ph.D. in electrical engineering to do it!

Who You Are

This book was written for the average PC owner. You don't need a degree in computer science, nor do you have to understand Ohm's Law or know how to use a soldering gun. There are no technical readouts, data sheets, or lists of numbers comparing circuitry in different PCs. All you need to follow the upgrading procedures in this book are a few basic tools, patience, and the desire to do it yourself. That's because, for the most part, the modern PC is a plug-and-play machine!

You should have a PC if you want to get the most out of this book. We define a PC as any IBM-compatible computer system. This book does not cover other systems, such as the Apple Macintosh.

Your PC does not have to be broken for you to benefit from the information here. The subject is *upgrading,* not repairing. Though troubleshooting and replacement of parts are covered, the emphasis is on improving your PC.

It helps to know some of the basics of DOS (this book will refer to specific versions when appropriate) and be comfortable with operating your computer. You should know, for example, how to use Ctrl-Alt-Del to reset your system and how to insert a disk in a drive and call up a directory. Nothing advanced. Just basic stuff.

About Your Hardware

There is no single, definitive type of PC. Though most PCs made in the '90s are based on IBM's original design for the AT, each computer is different. To deal with these differences, this book approaches the task of describing computer hardware by using the AT as a generic example. We describe variations in systems when appropriate.

This book assumes that you do not have a laptop PC. If you have a tower model PC (which stands upright on the floor or your working surface), you can also use this book, even though the configuration is different. Finally, you should know what kind of microprocessor your PC has. The microprocessor (sometimes called the CPU, for *central processing unit*) is your computer's brain and is commonly referred to by number: 8088,

80286, 80386, 80486 and so on. PCs are differentiated by the micro-processor they have:

PC/XT	Original IBM PC, PC/XT, or any system with an 8088, 8086, or equivalent microprocessor
AT 286	Any IBM-compatible 80286 system
AT 386	Any IBM-compatible 80386 system
AT 486	Any IBM-compatible 80486 system

In this book, the terms *clone, compatible,* and *PC* are all used interchange-ably. For our purposes, any computer that is compatible with IBM and uses DOS is considered a PC.

How This Book Is Structured

You should read the first four chapters of this book before you begin up-grading your PC. Chapter 1 gives you reasons for doing upgrades yourself, and Chapter 2 tells you the tools and equipment you'll need to get started. In Chapters 3 and 4, you learn everything you need to know about the components of your PC—what they do and where they are located.

Chapter 5 covers upgrading the software on your system. Chapters 6 and 7 cover one of the most useful upgrades you can do, adding memory to give your PC more RAM.

In Chapters 8 and 9, you learn how to upgrade your floppy-disk and hard-disk drives, to give your PC more storage capacity and to increase your computing speed.

Chapter 10 covers the removal and installation of expansion cards, an up-grade that enables you to add all sorts of options to your PC, including a modem and a mouse.

Chapter 11 covers the replacement of the power supply and includes some basic information on electricity.

Chapters 12 and 13 take you outside the system unit and discuss the differ-ent kinds of monitors and printers that are available.

Chapter 14 introduces you to the world of multimedia PC upgrades. Everything from adding a CD-ROM drive to using your PC to work out your Karaoke bit!

Chapter 15 gives you some troubleshooting and maintenance tips.

Generally speaking, the material in this book doesn't need to be read from cover to cover. Only Chapters 1–4 should be read right away. Then feel free to refer to those chapters covering the upgrades you want to do. The bottom line is getting to know your PC's hardware better. Even if you never plan on opening your computer's case, you'll know more about your hardware by reading this book, and from that knowledge, you'll be a better PC user.

Do It
Yourself

A few PC owners naturally want to mess with the guts of their PC—for them, no persuasion is necessary. Everyone else needs a reason to open up a computer, add a component, or make an upgrade. And the reason has to be pretty convincing— after all, people just don't go around upgrading their kitchen appliances all the time. In fact, we're told *not to* mess with the innards of the can opener or the VCR. But computers are different.

This chapter's purpose is to give you reasons for upgrading your PC by yourself. It includes some comforting words and careful explanation of what's required to work on the computer's hardware (which, by the way, is a heckuvalot easier than working on the computer's software).

I'd be kidding you if I said this was child's play—we're still dealing with a complex piece of hardware. But upgrades can be done by just about anyone. There's nothing hard about it at all. "Be careful" is about the only basic rule you need to remember.

● You Can Do It!

Why do this yourself? Because you can. Millions of people monkey with their cars every day. They have no degree in Automobilology, no years of apprenticeship, no authority from Detroit (or Japan) to do so. So why do they mess with a car? Because they can.

Electricity is scary! But, hey, cars are loud and they smell bad. And consider this: you won't get greasy working on a computer.

You save yourself time and money by working on a computer. Say your power supply has blown up—don't worry! When you change a power supply, it doesn't take the rest of the machine with it. You just yank out the old one and replace it with one that works. If you know how to do that, it will cost you maybe $75 (this varies based on what kind of hardware) for parts, and an hour of downtime. Compare that with a cost that includes that $75 for parts *and* a labor cost of at least $50 (probably more), *plus* three days of downtime while the computer's in the shop, not to mention your emotional pain and suffering.

Computers are easier to work on than cars. Nothing is heavy, no jacks or special tools are required, and most of the PC's parts are cheap and widely available. Consider, too, the following advantages.

You'll Get to Know More About Your PC

Lots of people are fluent in DOS. Many are even experts with certain pieces of software; they know all the commands and tricks to get work done effortlessly. That's the payoff if you know PC software. But what about the hardware?

Hardware is the more basic half of your PC equation. While software is important (because it tells the hardware what to do), hardware offers software the potential to do things. If you really know what your PC can do, you'll better be able to match its potential with software that can exploit it.

You'll Become a Valued PC Expert

Knowing about your computer's hardware rounds out your PC experience. And just as you don't need to know programming to use a computer program, you don't need to know engineering basics to learn about PC hardware.

Reasons for Doing It Yourself

As mentioned earlier, some users don't need reasons. They just naturally tinker. But for most of us, there has to be a darn good reason to open something up and look inside.

Our tendency with most electrical appliances is to leave them alone. We remember from childhood, when we innocently put a slice of bread in the toaster and it got stuck, that Mom called the fire department rather than risk pulling it out with a fork. So why, for gosh sakes, would we ever want to stick anything but a floppy diskette into a computer?

There are a number of reasons. In addition to the personal benefits mentioned in the previous section, mull over the following before you decide to do it yourself.

Because You Can

Nothing prevents you from opening your PC and upgrading it yourself. You don't need any specialized tools, the case isn't sealed with epoxy, and the screws aren't threaded wrong. Your computer is designed as a user-serviceable unit, and hardware parts are generally sold off the shelf.

Your PC Is Modular in Nature

The PC, designed originally using off-the-shelf parts, is not one integrated unit. It's built using modular components. Things plug into each other. One item snaps, slides, or screws into another.

This gives you the advantage of being able to plug in or swap certain items without putting your entire system at risk. There may be a few connectors to check, but all the innards of a PC are parts you can install, or remove and replace, with relative ease. Your skills can be as simple as those needed for Tinker Toys or Erector Sets. Modular components mean you can just plug it in and go.

No Change Is Permanent

Breathe easy—you won't be soldering or threading wires, so any change you make to your PC can be undone. In fact, the basic philosophy behind the PC's modular design is: *create your own system*. If you don't like a change, you can always go back. Once you get the hang of upgrading, you'll probably have a closet full of leftover drives and hardware—almost enough to build another computer.

You'll Save Money and Time

When someone else works on your PC, it's done on their time. They come over to fix it at your home or office when it's convenient for them. Until then, your computer sits and your time is wasted. If you take your computer into a shop, even more time is wasted—from one to several days while your computer is away, and your transportation time as well.

The second drawback to having someone else upgrade your system involves money. Sure, sometimes a knowledgeable friend will install your new floppy drive for free. But most of the time repair people are going to do it, and they'll charge you. At the shop, they'll charge you labor *plus* a hiked-up cost for the floppy drive. Why should you pay someone else to do it, when you can do it yourself?

You Don't Have to Be a Hardware Hacker

Hardware hackers walk around with penlights, tiny screwdrivers, soldering irons, and 40,000 pens in their shirt pockets. Hackers know computers inside and out. They know what that tiny little metal spike on the green circuitry board does. They know everything. They could build a working computer out of eight old car radios if they wanted to. But because the PC is modular in nature, you don't need those skills or that inclination.

To upgrade your PC, you need only know how to work a screwdriver, plug something into its proper position, hook it up, and then screw the case back on your PC. Doing it yourself involves no soldering. OK, you can solder if you like. But if you're into that, then you're reaching beyond the scope of this book.

While some people want to *write* programs, others just want to *use* them. Some know just enough to write simple batch files. If you're at that level, then this book is for you—it will tell you exactly what you need to know about hardware. And you won't have to live in fear of hot solder dripping on your arm.

Reasons for Not Doing It Yourself

Along with all the comforting thoughts and nice reasons for upgrading a computer yourself, come a few solid reasons you may have for not wanting to do so. In reality, the computer is scary. You rely on it. It cost a lot of money.

There are justifiable reasons why you would never want to mess with your PC's guts. One of the biggest (in my opinion) is that a good, basic English-language book hasn't been written on the subject (until now). The following may be some concerns you have about doing it yourself.

You're Afraid

There's a lot to be afraid of inside a computer—electricity for one thing. But rest assured, you're fairly insulated from anything dangerous when you're inside the PC. And, this book will show you how to venture in with little risk to life and limb. As long as you take the necessary precautions, you should never have any problems.

Of course, if your fears are too great, then maybe this isn't the subject for you. However, if you have the desire to do it yourself and feel comfortable with that idea, there's no sense in not moving ahead.

You Might Mess Something Up

Within the scope of this book, there's really little you can do to physically damage or mess up your computer. Most of the pieces inside your computer box rely on each other to operate, but if one part is missing, it won't cause other parts to actually *blow up*.

For example, suppose you forget to plug in your hard drive after you install it. The rest of the computer will probably work—you just won't be able to use the hard drive. Or suppose a new hard drive slides off your table and onto your lap. Chances are pretty good it will survive. Preventing those types of accidents, of course, is the first and best policy to take.

Just remember—if you do mess something up beyond all possible repair, you can always take your computer into the PC doctor or local repair outlet—but chances are you'll never need to do this.

You're Worried About the Warranty

Most computers are sold with a 90-day warranty. This means that if the computer or any of its parts fails within that period, you can send it back to the shop for repairs for free.

Electronic equipment does sometimes fail. Chances are (if it does) that it will fail within the first 48 hours of use. After that, mechanical components, such as your disk drives, will usually fail (if they do) within the first two weeks of use. After that, the computer will probably run happily and healthily for a full lifetime—about two to six years, depending on use.

So if you really want to test out the warranty, leave your system on for the first two weeks you own it. Turn the computer off and on once a day to test the power supply. After two weeks, you'll know if the PC is likely to fail.

But turn the monitor off when you're not using it. This avoids "phosphor burn-in," which occurs when an image is displayed too long without change. The image then "etches" itself into the chemicals painted on the inside of the monitor's screen. Over time, it also may cause your monitor to display colors improperly, and in some cases to fail to display images at all.

Some people may feel more comfortable with a dealer-installed upgrade because most dealers will honor the warranty for the parts and the labor without making you go to the parts manufacturer. But this is really a feeble excuse—most manufacturers test their hardware so thoroughly that the parts rarely fail anyway, and most hardware add-ons come with warranties of their own—sometimes as much as five years' worth. It's true that a paid installer might be able to react more quickly than the manufacturer in the event of a part failure, but doubling the cost of the upgrade project for so little return doesn't seem to justify the additional expense for the dealer's security blanket. There's no reason not to install a component yourself and take advantage of the manufacturer's warranty by sending in your hardware registration card.

You Think You Can't Do It

This is the biggest, most unsubstantiated, reason for not doing an upgrade yourself: you think you just can't do it. Maybe you're afraid of everything or lack self confidence. Some people lack experience—not with hardware matters, but with how absolutely easy and painless upgrading your PC can be. Some people just don't know how easy it is to add a hard drive to a system. Some think a color monitor's price range is fine, but they can't do without the computer for six days while (they think) it has to be in the shop.

Others may reason that God and Thomas Edison just don't want plain folk thumbing around inside a PC's case. If that were really true, the PC would have been designed as one integral unit, with no slots or snaps for easy replacement of individual items.

When you look at the big picture, it's scary. But upgrading a PC is easy. There really is no reason why you shouldn't do it yourself.

Things to Look Out For

Upgrading your PC's hardware is easy and fun, but it's not carefree. This subject can be discussed lightly (and it should be, because it's not that hard). But before you get all gung-ho and ready to go, there are some serious things to consider. Keep in mind the following items before you even pick up a screwdriver.

Unplug Everything Before You Start

Electricity is the biggest enemy to upgrading your hardware. It's your personal enemy. If you touch something "live" while working on your computer, it can hurt. You can also hurt the system by doing so. You could even kill yourself. (No kidding.)

The best way to avoid a shock is to unplug your system before you work on it. Since the plug on a PC can be removed at both ends, I recommend that you unplug it from both the computer and wall before you start. (Turn off the computer before you unplug it.)

 You can run the PC with the cover off, and at times this book will recommend you do so. But you don't upgrade it with the cover off and power on. In fact, doing so will damage your system, and it might kill you.

Beware of Static!

The second part of the electrical enemy—static—comes from you. Just as your system could jolt you if you're not careful, you could jolt the system if you collect static electricity (you won't know about it) and then touch something you're not supposed to.

Static has cures and can be prevented. If you hold still (especially your feet), touch some metal to ground yourself, or wear a grounded wrist strap, you don't need to worry about static for a brief time. This will be explained in later chapters. For now, keep in mind that static is something to look out for.

Watch Out for Really Cheap Stuff

Once you get going, you may find that the urge to add new goodies to your computer is unquenchable. Especially with the proliferation of mail order warehouses that seem to make it easy, you may want to pick up cheap, powerful equipment to install in your PC. *Caveat emptor.*

Especially avoid the seemingly endless supply of bargain stuff sold at electronics swap meets. The bozos selling this stuff usually pick up dead inventory from some original equipment manufacturer's warehouse. It's typically second-rate or used crap, which doesn't come with a warranty—and you can bet that the same guy won't be there next week if he does happen to offer some type of "warranty." Just because you can do it yourself doesn't mean you must skimp on quality.

 The other side of the equation is also true: if a component costs a lot, maybe you should have a professional install it.

If It Works, Don't Fix It

Only a few self-made hardware upgraders get the "fix everything" disease. Once these people conquer the interior of the PC, they're always in there. One guy I know even keeps the case off his PC so he can switch monitor cards more easily. That might seem like a fine solution to him, but it's not the answer to his real problem.

"If ain't broke, don't fix it" applies to all computer hardware. If you need a bigger hard drive, add one. If you want to add a 3½" disk drive to your desktop to make it compatible with your laptop, do that. But some other upgrades may only complicate life for you and your PC. If you don't need it, don't buy it.

Keep a Rein on Yourself

Don't go nuts! Since the PC is modular in design, this upgrading stuff is all going to be quite easy to do. After a while, you won't give opening up the PC's case a second thought. You may even do it without sweating (which was a problem I had for years). But keep a serious attitude when you do so. This stuff costs money!

Other ways you can help the situation include modifying some of your *nastier* personal behavior habits—for example, nothing is worse than smoking around a PC. I know smokers. I know they love to smoke. They have the annoying habit of agreeing that it's bad for them, as they continue to puff away their lungs and their pocket money. Minute particles of smoke weave their way into the hermetically-sealed environment of the hard drive, where they can cause a hell of a lot of damage. It's just stupid to smoke around a PC.

Drinking, while not as bad as smoking, can also be hazardous to computing. (This is true whatever the beverage, by the way.) Right now, I have a small, fist-sized bottle of sparkling mineral water by my keyboard. A swipe of my hand to answer the phone could send it tumbling—glup, glup, glupping—into the keyboard.

Worse than that is drinking *anything* while you're working inside the computer. I can't convince enough people not to set their coffee mugs near their PCs! Under no circumstance should you allow liquid, food, or even cats (I could tell stories…) near an open PC.

The point is just to be careful, follow the instructions in this book carefully, and have fun.

Tools and Supplies

Computer hardware uses a very simple assembly technology. You could compare it to an Erector Set, but it's really not even that complex—more like Tinker Toys.

This chapter deals with two subjects: The tools you'll need to work on your PC and the things you're going to install into your PC. You may already have many of the tools mentioned here. You'll have to rush out and buy only a few esoteric ones, and then really only if you want to increase the weight of your tool chest.

Tools to Buy

When you buy a car, they often give you a little package of tools. You get a screwdriver (possibly one of those awkward dual-purpose jobbies), plus a wrench-like thing, and maybe a cheap set of pliers. If you look in the trunk you may also find some type of flimsy "jack" and a lug wrench.

You don't get *any* tools with your computer. Why not? Well, with early machines like the Apple II, you didn't need any tools. The lid just popped off. You could add expansion cards, remove the power supply, or unhook the keyboard without unscrewing anything. (Later models did require some screwdriver use.) The PC was made to be messed with. It features simple twist-type screws, modular parts that park and plug, and quasi-easy access to just about everything in the system. You just need the will to do it yourself—plus a few tools.

Must-Have Tools

The basic tool needed to work on a PC is a screwdriver. They come in various makes, models, and sizes. (See Figure 2.1.) The two models you need for your PC are the plus, or "Phillips," screwdriver, and the minus, or "flathead," screwdriver. Because it's easy to remember, I'll refer to them as plus and minus in this text.

The screwdrivers' sizes are important as well. In this text, four sizes are referred to: tiny, small, medium, and large. A tiny screwdriver is one of those shirt-pocket jobbies, usually with a blade ⅛" to ⅓" wide. The small screwdrivers have a blade between ⅛" and ¼" thick. A medium screwdriver's blade will be from ¼" to ⅜" thick. You won't need any mondo huge screwdrivers to work inside your PC. For the most part, use your best

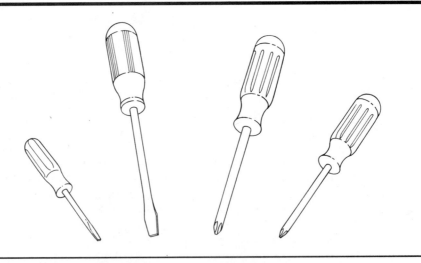

FIGURE 2.1: The upgrader's essential tool kit: tiny minus and medium minus screwdrivers, and medium and small plus screwdrivers

judgment on the size of screwdriver, based on the size of the screws on and inside your PC.

The following four tools will be absolutely necessary to upgrading your PC.

A Tiny Minus Screwdriver This tiny minus, or "flathead," screwdriver is excellent for those tiny screws that come on computer cables. It's really the only way you can anchor the cables securely.

A Small Plus Screwdriver The small-sized plus, or "Phillips," screwdriver will probably be your basic weapon inside the PC. Most of the PC's internal screws are of the plus variety, and are too small for the medium-sized screwdriver.

A Medium Plus Screwdriver A good 90% of computer cases are sealed using plus-type screws. If you ever expect to get in the case, you're going to need a good medium-sized plus screwdriver.

A Medium-Sized Minus Screwdriver This is one of those "just-in-case" tools. Not all PCs are standardized. In fact, most of today's manufacturers of clones and compatibles use a plus screw to seal the case. The original IBM PC used minus screws. So it's a good idea to keep a medium-sized minus screwdriver around in case you encounter any medium-sized minus screws.

That rounds out the basic tool set.

Good-to-Have Tools

The following handy additions will round out your basic tool collection. Compare the descriptions to Figure 2.2.

A Tiny Plus Screwdriver Once in a blue moon you may encounter some peripheral or installable item that has a tiny plus screw in it. Or you might find that your particular small-sized plus screwdriver is just too large. In those cases and others, rounding out your plus screwdriver collection with a third, tiny tool will come in handy.

A Medium Plus Screwdriver with a Long Handle Occasionally you may find a plus screw residing in some deep cavern or crevasse of your PC. The early Tandy 1000s had a screw way-the-heck inside the disk drive bays. The only way to get at that screw was through the side of the

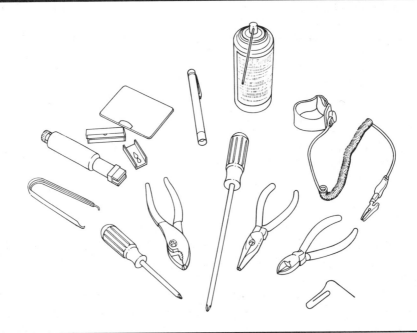

FIGURE 2.2: None of these "good-to-have" tools are really required to upgrade your PC, but they're invaluable to have around for general purposes

computer, about 10" into the center of things. Only a long-handled plus screwdriver could do the job.

Pliers Pliers are one of those universally useful tools any tool chest shouldn't be without. Though I've never used a pair of pliers to fix my PC, I have used them to extract a 3½" diskette from a drive with a broken auto-eject system.

Needle-Nosed Pliers You may find yourself using needle-nosed pliers (as opposed to regular pliers) a lot in the PC. Since computer components are small and human fingers are relatively fat and awkward, you may need needle-nosed pliers to get down into things—where no finger has gone before.

Needle-nosed pliers come in handy for changing things called "jumpers," as well as for rescuing screws that may fall down into the electronic under-growth on your motherboard.

A jumper is a small black plastic rectangle with metal pins jutting up. Jumpers are often called "pin" blocks because they look like little metal pins mounted on non-conductive blocks of black materials and are usually found in some number on those blocks. They're used to complete a connection that enables or disables an option of some sort. You configure these jumper blocks buy adding or removing the actual jumper from across the jumper's pins. More on this later, though.

Wire Cutters Wire cutters are not needed to perform any upgrade mentioned in this book. But if you want to flesh out your PC tool kit, you could include wire cutters.

A Bent Paper Clip This may seem like a silly "tool," but the bent paper clip exists in just about every PC hardware hacker's tool kit. (Some people even charge the US Air Force $600 a piece for them.) The bent paper clip comes in handy for setting "DIP switches," which are often too tiny to set with a finger or screwdriver. (Some people use a pencil, but why mark things up?)

Other Tools

Finally, there are other tools you may want to collect, some really specific to certain tasks, but nonetheless useful when you upgrade your PC.

Chip Puller A chip puller is a specialized set of pliers (more or less) designed to reach around the ends of a computer chip so that you can then safely lift the chip out of its socket without bending any of its little legs. (Some enterprising hackers use a screwdriver to—ugh!—"wedge" the chip out.)

Chip Inserter A chip puller is the opposite of the chip inserter. Most people insert chips simply by eyeballing the chip's legs compared to the socket's holes and then pressing the chip firmly into place with the fingers. But specialized chip inserter tools are available to make the job lots easier.

Pen Light There's a lot of empty space in some PCs, but others are crammed full of add-ins and tangled cables. Sometimes it's really hard to

see the bottom of the case—which you'll need to examine if you're setting DIP switches or reading a serial number. A pen light comes in very handy to illuminate those deep, dark electronic crevasses. It's also one of the few devices you can stick behind the PC when you're hunting for a serial number on the back of the case.

Small Mirror A companion to the pen light is the small, hand held mirror. Sometimes serial numbers and tiny toggle switches are hidden behind printers and PCs. The only way to see them (without rearranging the office) is by using a small mirror.

Can of O^2 O^2 is air, and several companies actually make a living from selling cans of compressed air. You use the air to clean dust and debris that accumulates inside your computer—especially in the printer. (Using O^2 is much safer than blowing; the can doesn't run out of air so quickly and there's no spit intermixed.)

Grounding Wrist Strap One thing to be aware of when working on a PC is static electricity. Later in this chapter you'll see how to avoid static, but sometimes it pays to be extra careful. That's where the grounding wrist strap comes into play. One end of the wrist strap goes (surprisingly) around your wrist. The other end is anchored to the grounding plug on a wall socket, or some other electrically grounded item.

Sticky Labels Finally, some people like to have a sheet full of sticky labels handy as they work on the PC. You use them as you're disassembling to identify and label any cables you may disconnect. On one end of the cable you may put a sticky label "A." On the cable's socket will go another "A." A similar cable and socket will have "B" labels, and so on.

The Most Important Tool

The most important tool you can have, almost invaluable when working on a PC, is patience! Don't be in a hurry. Don't rush things. Relax. Give yourself plenty of time to do the upgrade. Patience is a valuable tool when working on anything, but it really comes in handy when you upgrade your PC.

Tool Kits

Many enterprising, entrepreneurial individuals have seen the need for complete computer hardware upgrading tool sets and have filled the need by providing us with quite a few packages from which to choose.

You can buy simple electronics computer tool kits, computer upgrading tool kits, and complete advanced troubleshooting kits. These range in price from about $29.95 up to several hundred dollars. They also include a variety of tools, ranging from the very basic to some really specific electronic doo-dads that you will never need.

Tools You Should Avoid

There are some tools you definitely won't need for working on your PC. A lot of tool kits will include some of these weird gadgets, and some slimy salespeople may want to sell you some. Anything other than the tools mentioned above should be looked upon with some question. But there are two tools I personally wish you wouldn't get.

A Magnetized Screwdriver The magnetized screwdriver is really a boon to mankind. In addition to its basic screwdriver usefulness, its magnetized head will hold a screw in place as you line up the screwdriver, screw, and hole. If you're clumsy and drop the screw, you can touch it with the magnetized screwdriver to pick it up quickly. Ain't that nifty? Why should you avoid them?

All you need to do is set the magnetic screwdriver on a floppy disk and—poof!—the data is gone. *That's* why you should avoid them, or at least be careful if you use one.

Head-Cleaning Diskettes Some people just love to play computer doctor. One way they do so is by purchasing a head-cleaning diskette, squirting it with cleaning juice, then shoving it into an innocent disk drive.

Head-cleaning diskettes, which are abrasive, do perform the function of removing iron oxide buildup from your drive heads. In some (relatively few) cases, it actually will bring a seemingly dead drive right back to life. But most of the time people use head-cleaning diskettes like voodoo, expecting them to cure any number of a disk drive's ills, none of which are related to iron oxide buildup on the drive head.

Using the Various Tools

It would be really silly to sit down and explain "how to use a screwdriver," though I'm sure a small portion of first-time hardware upgraders may benefit. Just know that there's a business end to each tool; the other end is the end you hold. Beyond that, consider the following words of advice to assist you when using the tools and working on your PC.

Turning a screw can be difficult for some people. It's not like trying to figure out which way to untwist a "twist tie" on a Baggie—there are no rules for that. But for screwing and unscrewing, there *are* two rules:

◆ To tighten a screw, turn it clockwise

◆ To loosen a screw, turn it counterclockwise

This metaphor may help you remember:

To undo something you go *back in time*; to unscrew something you go *counterclockwise*.

You should also follow these two rules that have nothing to do with tools:

◆ Work in a well-lit area

◆ Give yourself lots of desk space

Most people compute in caves. They dim the lights, or turn them off, and close the windows—assuming they have windows. This is because it's easier to see a computer screen in dim light. A cave, however, is not the type of environment you want to be in when you work on your PC hardware. Even a pen light isn't going to help you if it's too dark to see.

You need about three times the amount of desk space your computer occupies to work successfully on PC hardware. People always forget this. Once you get the lid off and set a few things aside, you'll quickly be out of room. And it's an extremely poor idea to work on the PC on the floor.

Locating Equipment

Once you have tools in hand, you're going to need something on which to use them. You have your PC, and you could go ahead and take it all apart and put it back together. But that isn't upgrading. (It isn't really anything but a waste of time.) So you're eventually going to have to hunt down those items you want to put in your PC for upgrading.

Where to Find Equipment

There are lots of places to find the equipment necessary to upgrade your PC. Before you go hunting, though, you should know what it is you're hunting for. This section covers the different options you have for locating equipment, but you really need to know what it is you need before you set out to buy it.

Once you do know what you want, you have your choice of the four following general places to get it:

◆ The original equipment manufacturer

◆ Local dealers

◆ Mail order houses

◆ Used parts suppliers

There are advantages and disadvantages to each of these.

The Original Equipment Manufacturer

The original equipment manufacturer, or "OEM," is the logical source for whatever upgrade part you're buying. After all, your computer dealer doesn't make his own hard drives, he buys them from manufacturers.

The only major drawback to buying from OEMs is that they often don't sell items to individual users. OK, if you wanted to buy 100 of the thing, then they'd sell it to you. But for one power supply or one memory board, forget it.

Local Dealers

Local dealers are often the most reliable and consistent source of computer parts. These dealers could be national computer sales chains, locally owned and operated outfits, or electronics warehouses.

There are only two disadvantages to a local dealer as your computer equipment source. The first is that it's not the cheapest option you can go with. The dealer has to pay employees, local taxes, and overhead to keep the store open. This is cost added to your hardware upgrade (but it's often returned in the form of personal service and support).

The second disadvantage is that dealers, especially in the national chains, would much rather install the equipment themselves. In fact, some chains include the installation cost in the purchase price. When that happens, you might as well have them do it because you're already paying them to.

Mail Order Houses

Mail order used to be the creepy, seedy way to get computer parts. Only the most experienced (or foolhardy) ever ventured to try it. Imagine ordering delicate electronic equipment through the mail! After all, how many times did Aunt Velma's cookies survive the trip from Vermilion all intact?

The advantage to mail order is, primarily, that it's the cheapest way to buy computer equipment. There's no showroom overhead, so the cost and savings can be passed on to you. Many mail order houses offer full warranties on what they sell, and some even add their own warranty extensions. You get a full refund (minus, maybe, a restocking fee) if you're dissatisfied. Mail order is truly the best way to go if you know exactly what it is you want.

Disadvantages of mail order include that the mail system can be slow and sloppy, and that the distance involved makes shipping things back for repair a nightmare (when you compare it to throwing something dead into your trunk and driving across town to get another one). Also, keep in mind that the mail order warehouse's service and support is done long distance. The ordering line may be toll-free, but support usually will cost you.

Used Parts Suppliers

One option that eventually comes up, especially in the eyes of beginners, is to buy used equipment, or worse, buy at an electronics swap meet. In my humble opinion, these are absolutely the worst ways to get started with upgrading your PC's hardware. It's just too risky.

If you want to *try* buying used stuff, here are the advantages and disadvantages:

The advantage to going with used equipment is that it's cheap. You'll probably be able to pick up a used or refurbished piece of hardware for less than 1/10 of what it cost new.

The disadvantages to buying used or questionable equipment are many. But primarily, the disadvantage is that you get no warranty and it's just a bad idea. Even if Electronic Earl seems like a nice guy and says you can return the hard drive at next week's swap meet, don't count on it. A lot of vultures prey upon unsuspecting PC owners.

Suggestions for Finding Equipment

If you're just starting out, the best place to go is a local dealer. But first, shop around. Check out prices, quality, and especially service and support.

After you get comfortable with buying equipment in a store and installing it yourself, you should look into mail order. Remember, mail order is the cheapest way to go, but only if you know exactly what you want. In fact, the way some hardware upgraders operate is to cruise by a local store and check out video cards. Then, when they find what they want, they'll call up a mail order warehouse and order the same card for less. It happens all the time.

Types of Equipment to Look For

Although all DOS computers are called PCs and everything is compatible, there are subtle differences between the makes and models of PCs. You should be aware of these differences when hunting down parts for your PC. After all, buying the wrong thing is embarrassing for someone who really wants to do it themselves.

The most major difference in PCs is between the design of the original PC/XT and the AT—the latter model upon which all of our PCs today are based. When buying hardware for either, you must know which type you have and which type of hardware you need for it.

For example, PC/XTs and ATs may use different types of hard drive controllers. Make sure you get the right controller and hard drive combination for your system.

The PC/XTs also have 8-bit expansion slots. AT systems use 16-bit expansion slots. While you can plug the 8-bit cards into a 16-bit slot, most 16-bit cards will not plug in (and work with) the PC/XT's 8-bit slots. Exceptions are some memory boards and some video adapters. But be careful: only get the type of expansion card that goes with your system.

Once you know what equipment you want, which types you'll need, and where to buy it, then go for it: buy that equipment!

Handling Computer Components

There are certain precautions you should take when you handle computer components, especially those of an electronic nature (such as circuitry boards and expansion cards). Most parts are fairly robust (well made), but if you've never done this sort of thing before, it helps to keep the following items in mind when handling computer components.

Always Handle Electronic Circuitry by the Edge When you pick up an expansion card or any type of circuitry, handle it by the edge. Never hold electronic circuitry like a sandwich; it's just to risky to snap or break something or, if you generate any static, to short something out.

Be Gentle Don't force anything into the computer. Everything should fit snugly, but without any extra effort on your part.

Ground Yourself To avoid discharging static onto computer components, you should ground yourself. Do this by keeping still (not rubbing your feet on the carpet), and touching metal with one hand you're working. For example, keep one hand touching a computer's power supply case while you're working—that's probably grounding enough to avoid a static discharge.

When It Says "No User-Serviceable Parts Inside," It Means It
Avoid the temptation to open up and fix something you weren't meant to open up and fix. The most dangerous components inside a PC are in the power supply—and *that's* in a sealed metal case. Don't open up the power supply or even try to.

Computer monitors also store a lot of voltage— sometimes up to 10,000 volts—that can enter your body though your thumbnail. Monitors are meant for professionals to fix. For your personal hardware upgrading, you can buy a monitor and install it's graphic adapter card into your PC, but don't venture inside the monitor.

Also all hard disks come in a hermetically-sealed hard drive unit. This unit is riveted shut. There is absolutely nothing you can do inside there, nor is there any reason for opening it up. Yet you'd be surprised how many idiots do open them up.

Treat It Like a Baby Though computer parts are robust, you should still treat them gently and with care, like a baby. This really isn't something I need to remind you of. The natural tendency for working inside a computer is to be careful anyway. (Only the "experienced" hardware hackers get really sloppy.) Keep your work environment clean of bottles or cups full of spillable liquid, food, cats, and other objects that may wander into or disrupt your baby while you're working on it.

Take Your Time You're not a short order cook when you upgrade your PC. You don't need to "wrap and slap" to get the job done. Remember your patience tool. Also, that things can be *un*done. If you get stuck, you can work backwards through a procedure to solve your problem.

General Advice

Here are some general words of advice to help you use your tools, equipment and supplies to successfully upgrade your computer.

Know What You're Going To Do Before You Do It Just setting out to "install a memory board" isn't enough. You need to know:

- ◆ What type of memory your PC requires
- ◆ How much memory your software needs to function
- ◆ Where you're going to put the memory
- ◆ Where you're going to buy it
- ◆ And how you're going to install it

This book will help with all those facets of installing memory, and with upgrading anything on your PC. But from your end, you have to make the individual decisions on what's best for you. You have to go…shopping!

You also should lay down an attack plan before you actually attack.

Do Only One Upgrade at a Time If possible, do only one thing to your computer at a time. Few of us, even the hardware hackers, venture inside the PC more than three times a year, so there's a tendency to say, "Well, as long as I'm adding a new hard disk I might as well upgrade my RAM at the same time."

You should develop a strategy. For example, install your memory first. Then, without putting the case on, start the computer and make sure everything works. Be certain the memory upgrade was successful, and *then* turn off and unplug the machine to proceed with the hard drive upgrade.

If you must attempt to upgrade more than one item at a time, develop your own strategy for tracking each of the issues. Why? Because it will be easier to narrow down a problem if you do things step-by-step. If you add memory, a new video card, and a hard drive all at once—and the computer comes up with a blank screen—where did you go wrong? Keep things simple by doing one thing at a time, and it'll be easier to isolate a problem if you have to.

Keep a Bookshelf If you're not already in the habit, you should have a computer bookshelf somewhere near your PC. In your office, there should be a separate computer library or file cabinet. In it you should store all the manuals and documents for your computer and its peripherals. Keep everything organized for reference purposes.

Keep Your Old Boxes This is something you should do in a careful manner so others won't accuse you of being "junky." All computer hardware comes in boxes. Often those boxes contain special Styrofoam designed to fit around the hardware and hold it carefully for shipping and handling. Keep those boxes! They're the best way to pack and move the computer and all its components.

Have Fun! That's the bottom line. Upgrading will save you time and money and let you know more about your computer system, *and* you'll be having fun while you do it. So set out with that in mind. Relax and enjoy yourself as you upgrade your PC. Have a *good* time!

Knowing Your PC

This chapter is about the unexplored territory inside your PC, and what makes it work. This is hardware stuff. It ranges from the early beginnings of the PC, to what today's hardware has to offer you. The nuts-and-bolts, assembly instructions are offered in the next chapter. The material here is primarily background information, stuff that will make you more familiar with your PC and how it works.

You're probably familiar with some of this. Most of your knowledge is likely to be based on DOS and the software side of your PC. But lurking under the careful control of that software is hardware territory. And if the decent folks of this town ever expect any law and order, the sheriff has got to know his (or her!) way around. This chapter is your territorial map.

How the PC Uses Hardware

Breaking down your PC into its describable parts could be a complex job. When you look at it, your computer probably has three main parts: the console, which contains the disk drives, motherboard, expansion cards, and power supply; the monitor; and the keyboard. We could get really scary by deconstructing your PC down to the chip-and-resistor level. In that case, a discussion of how the PC uses hardware would involve thousands of subcategories.

You'll be getting more intimate with hardware later in this book. But for now, the following five areas have been targeted for discussion.

◆ The microprocessor

◆ The BIOS

◆ Temporary storage

◆ Permanent storage

◆ Support hardware

These items aren't so much individual *objects* within the computer as they are *concepts* that play a role in how your PC uses its hardware.

The Microprocessor

The microprocessor is your computer's brain. It's basically a very fast calculator and a storage device. But its storage is limited, so it must have additional storage for the information it manipulates. (In the form of temporary and permanent storage, which will be covered on the next few pages.)

By itself, the microprocessor is really a rather stupid device. It must be told *exactly* what to do. It carries out those instructions (known as *software*) diligently, to the letter. That's really what makes the microprocessor—and the computer—a worthwhile thing. The software is written to tell the microprocessor what to do. That's why the microprocessor is so central to the operation of the computer.

The BIOS

BIOS stands for Basic Input/Output System. It's software that's been encoded on a computer memory chip. Since the chip is "read only," meaning that you can't "write" to it, the chip is known as a *ROM* (Read Only Memory) chip. In a PC, the term BIOS is used instead of ROM (or sometimes it's called ROM BIOS to make everyone happy).

A ROM chip is a memory chip on which information is stored permanently.

RAM (Random Access Memory) chips store information temporarily. Programs, applications, and other kinds of software that you don't need to keep saving to disk are stored temporarily in RAM while you are using them. We'll talk about that more in an upcoming section.

The BIOS is responsible for the following.

The Power-On Self Test   The BIOS's first duty, when the PC is initially turned on, is to perform a system check-out known as the Power-On Self Test, or *POST*. The POST checks out the system, doing an inventory of the various parts inside the PC, counting the disk drives, serial ports, parallel ports, and eventually counting and checking the memory. The POST's job is to make sure the PC's house is in order before the computer officially starts. The POST is covered in detail in the latter half of this chapter.

Bootstrap Loader   The secondary responsibility of the BIOS, after checking out the system via the POST, is to load an operating system from the disk drives. This is known as *bootstrapping* because the computer is "pulling itself up by its bootstraps." It's also where we get the term *"booting"* the computer (although most people think that means to *kick* the thing).

Low-Level Interfaces   The BIOS is also responsible for the low-level interfaces in your computer. It provides communication links between your keyboard, video display, and serial and printer ports for the microprocessor.

Temporary Storage—RAM

The third major part of your PC's hardware is temporary storage—your computer's RAM or memory. The microprocessor itself can store information. But it has a limited amount of space in which to do that. Rather than burden itself with information storage, your computer is populated with RAM chips that provide temporary storage for the information the microprocessor manipulates.

Temporary storage is the microprocessor's scratch pad, its workspace. Into that area will go programs and the information or data created by the

programs. All the action takes place in the microprocessor itself, but the action usually deals with data, which is stored in your system's memory. This is why memory is important, and why the more memory you have the more your software, the microprocessor, and the computer can do for you. (We all know how painful those "out of memory" errors can be.)

Permanent Storage

Permanent storage is memory storage, just like RAM. But unlike RAM, this memory doesn't disappear when you turn off the power. "Permanent storage" takes place on your disk drives, or any other storage device you hook up to the PC (floppy disk and hard disk drives are the most common and popular forms). Using the operating system, you can transfer information from temporary storage to permanent storage. Then you can turn off the PC, knowing that your data has been saved.

Support Hardware

Finally, your computer contains a lot of support hardware like your disk controller cards and your video card, various items that aren't directly related to manipulating information or dealing with the microprocessor, but help your computer do everything it needs to run your software properly. These items include the following.

Support Circuitry There will always be chips, resistors, and other doo-dads in your computer, often resembling some exotic party snack spilled on a green Fiberglas sheet. This circuitry supports the microprocessor, BIOS, RAM, and disk drives, making sure that everything works together, in time and on cue.

Expansion Cards Expansion cards are plug-in options that become part of your total computer system. Sound cards and modems are expansion cards, for example. These and other types of expansion cards plug into another hardware item known as the *bus*, which is a direct line of communication between the microprocessor and the expansion cards. Your computer's bus will look to you like a set of side-by-side black rectangles called *slots*, which accept the edge connectors that are on the bottom edge of expansion cards.

Power Supply

Giving everything juice is the power supply. Power supplies draw electricity from the wall, conditioning it for use inside the PC and dividing it up between the various parts.

Monitor/Keyboard

Outside of the main system unit are the monitor and keyboard, your lines of communications with the PC. The keyboard is where you provide your input; the monitor is where you see the computer's result.

Peripherals

Finally, also outside the system unit but not as central as the monitor and keyboard, are any additional, external items used by the computer. The first of these is probably the printer, where you can get a permanent record of your computing results. Beyond the printer, devices such as modems, plotters, scanners, computer mice, video digitizers, music synthesizers, and other equipment can be plugged into the computer. These truly do make the computer the most flexible tool you can have.

How the PC Uses Software

Software in a computer is far more important than hardware. Without it, the hardware just sits there. A microprocessor can be a brilliant piece of human engineering, but without software instructions to guide it, it's just an expensive work of art.

The PC uses software to get the work done. As far the PC's software is concerned, the most important *piece* of software you have on your computer is DOS.

Yes, that's right, DOS is a piece of software. It's your computer's main piece of software, the one that controls and orchestrates everything that goes on in the computer system. As the Program in Charge, DOS has three major responsibilities.

It Controls the Disk Drives Obviously, since DOS is the *disk* operating system, its main function is to interface your computer's hardware with

disk drives—both hard and floppy. DOS is the control program that organizes and maintains information on the floppy drives, and it assists in loading, saving, and transferring information to and from permanent and temporary storage.

It Interfaces Software with the BIOS DOS also provides high-level links to the BIOS's low-level communications to the rest of the computer. Since the BIOS is customized for each individual PC, DOS gives some applications a common bridge to cross when dealing with unknown computer hardware.

It Interfaces You with the Computer DOS is the main program you use when you operate your PC. It's the "friendly" interface (though some may argue that point) that allows you to have control over the complexity and power the PC has to offer. It also lets you run software that is stored on the floppy diskettes. DOS is your human-to-computer communications link.

PC/XT, PC/AT, and 386 Class Differences

While we all like to think of any computer that runs DOS as a "PC," there are really three different types of machines, each with its own personality, advantages, and quirks. These three machines are separated by which type of microprocessor they use. They are:

◆ The PC/XT class, which uses the 8088 or 8086 CPU

◆ The PC/AT class, which uses the 80286 CPU

◆ The 386 class, which uses the 386 or later CPU

All of these systems run DOS, and most of them will run the same software, but there are differences between them. As a future hardware upgrade guru, you should be aware of these differences.

The AT class is rapidly becoming a thing of the past, and the PC/XT class has long since moved off the store shelves. (This doesn't mean, however, that the products are worthless, or that they'll be ignored in this book.)

PCs are different mainly in the additions to PC architecture that were made with the introduction of the PC/AT and its 80286 microprocessor. Since IBM wasn't the first to come out with a 386 system, the differences between 386s and PC/ATs aren't as great.

 All of the differences between PC/ATs and earlier systems that are described here also apply to 386 systems.

The PC/AT Class Has Extended Memory

The PC/XT class 8086 can only deal with one megabyte of RAM. Thanks to the PC/AT's advanced microprocessor, it can address megabytes of memory.

The extra memory in the PC/AT is referred to as *extended memory*. This memory isn't used by DOS, which simply runs the PC/AT's 80286 in its DOS-compatible 8086 mode, also called the "Real Mode." In the 80286's native mode, the "Protected Mode," it can use megabytes of extended memory to run programs specifically written for that mode.

Only advanced operating systems presently use extended memory—Windows, OS/2, and UNIX all require extended memory to do their stuff. DOS, a Real-Mode-only operating system, cannot access that memory. But to make extended memory useful to DOS, programs can be used to convert extended memory into a form that DOS can use. The subject of special programs that convert extended memory into memory that can be used by DOS is really beyond the scope of this book—that job has to be done when the DOS program is created. For now, just know that the PC/AT and 386 class systems can have megabytes of extended memory installed, whereas PC/XT class systems cannot.

The PC/AT Class Systems Have 16-Bit Expansion Slots

The original IBM PC had 8-bit expansion slots into which various option cards and expansion boards could be plugged. The PC/AT was introduced

with a true 16-bit microprocessor. To take advantage of the situation, IBM added a small extension to the end of the old 8-bit expansion slot. This extension created the 16-bit expansion slot.

You can plug 8-bit cards right into 16-bit expansion slots and everything works fine. If any problems occur, they'll happen when you accidentally buy a 16-bit card and you have a PC/XT with only 8-bit slots.

386 Class Systems May Have a Proprietary 32-Bit Memory Slot

Many 386 systems will have their own memory expansion system, different from the 16-bit expansion slots used in PC/AT systems. Why? Because to get the most from memory, the 386 should use it in its full 32-bit mode. To make this happen, many 386 developers install their own, proprietary 32-bit memory slot.

386 Class Systems May Also Have a General 32-Bit Slot

Another new item on 386 class systems is the 32-bit *processor direct* or *local bus* slot. This slot is used for plugging in other specialty items that, like memory, need the full 32-bit power of the CPU.

AT Class Systems Have Battery-Backed-Up RAM

Some basic parts of the PC/XT's configuration were determined by setting a tiny row of switches inside the computer. These DIP switches would tell the PC about its memory configuration, video display, and so on. When the AT came out, IBM thought they'd give their corporate customers a break and put all that information into a special program. They reasoned that you could then run the program to configure and set up the PC without opening the case.

To keep the AT's setup, information is stored inside the computer by means of special battery-backed-up RAM, often called CMOS. This special area of memory keeps track of the AT's configuration, and it can be changed via a setup program that configures your ROM BIOS. ROM BIOS setup programs are usually built into the AT.

Basically, All PCs Are the Same

Keep in mind that, although the AT class systems have extended memory, 16-bit expansion slots, and battery-backed-up RAM (and 386 systems have their own proprietary memory slot), all PCs are basically the same inside. There are only a few subtle differences between them. Working on one or another doesn't involve any special training.

This book will point out any subtle differences that do exist as we encounter them.

About the PS/2 Line

In 1987, IBM wanted to shock the world with its introduction of the PS/2 (Personal System/2) line of microcomputers. Granted, they were designed with excellence. But the line lacks any clones. Most people bothered only to imitate the PS/2's new VGA graphics standards. The PS/2 had (and has) many great features—like advanced VGA display capabilities—and the ability to identify each expansion card and its configuration details without opening up the PS/2's case. These and other advanced features made the PS/2 rather pricey when compared to the AT. Otherwise, PS/2s are just another type of PC on which you can run DOS software.

The following features are worth noting in IBM's PS/2 line of PC computers.

Micro Channel Architecture

Gone are 8- and 16-bit expansion slots of the mainstream PCs. With the PS/2, IBM introduced the Micro Channel Architecture, or MCA, type of expansion slots. These are really "smart" expansion slots, compared to the older expansion slots, that aren't as capable.

Another weird fact: Not all PS/2 machines use the MCA. Since it's not that popular, IBM fitted some of its line of PCs with the older style 16-bit slots. This is only an issue if you buy an IBM PS/2 system.

VGA Graphics

When the MCA expansion bus bombed in the PC community, nearly everyone noticed IBM's splashy new graphics standard, the VGA (for Video Graphics Array). VGA is quite well established outside of IBM's PS/2 line.

VGA graphics are built-in to nearly all the PS/2s (some low-end models lack the full VGA standard), and you can buy VGA clone cards to plug into your PC. This is about the most important contribution by IBM's PS/2 line to the development of other systems.

PS/2s Are Now Widely Cloned

Rumor had it that when IBM introduced their PS/2 line, the rest of the PC computer community would be doomed. But the PS/2 line was too expensive and remote to do any damage, so the PC clone industry survived.

Although the PS/2 is a good computer design, in fact, one of the best types of PC you can buy today, it wasn't copied 1/100 as much as the original IBM PC or PC/AT. Why? For one thing, IBM wanted a huge licensing fee for cloning, as well as back payment on any other PC clones sold by the same company. That price was too high to pay. So both the PS/2 and its MCA expansion slots were left alone in the PC computing arena.

It Is Upgradeable

As with the first PCs, IBM published a wealth of technical information on their PS/2s. The information is available from IBM, allowing you to discover more about your computer, or to develop your own hardware add-ons. (In fact, some authors make their books real fat by republishing IBM's PS/2 technical specs.) Hardware add-ons and upgrades are supposedly available if you own a PS/2. But that's really not true.

You *can* do it yourself on IBM's equipment. Plenty of parts exist, and there are lots of options from which to choose. But IBM PS/2 owners might just be better off having IBM do the upgrades themselves.

What Happens When You Turn the PC On

"How the PC works" can really be asked, "How does the computer get up in the morning? How does it know what to do, and how does it do that once it knows?" This is central to knowing your PC.

The Hardware Side

The hardware side of the PC works through orchestration of three main elements:

- The computer's microprocessor
- The BIOS
- DOS

BIOS and DOS control communications between your software and micro-processor. The microprocessor has direct control over your computer's RAM, or temporary storage. And DOS provides the interface between the microprocessor and permanent storage. To get your work done, all three of these items work in harmony with your computer's hardware, with the software, and with you.

When you flip the PC's power switch, it sends a surge of electricity through the computer. All the parts are powered up, the hard drive starts to spin, and the power supply's fan begins to whir. The PC comes to life.

When the microprocessor first receives juice, it begins to execute instructions in its memory. The very first instructions it runs are known as the Power-On Self Test, or POST.

The Power-On Self Test

The Power-On Self Test is what happens each time you turn on your PC. It includes any messages you see displayed, any beeping that occurs, and the

memory count most PCs show when they first warm up. All that—in fact nearly everything that happens before your disk drives fire up and load DOS—is the POST working.

The POST does two things:

◆ It checks and verifies the configuration of your PC

◆ It tests for any errors and alerts you to them

The POST compares the actual configuration of your PC/XT with the way you have your system's DIP switches set. (The DIP switches are your own manual way of telling the PC what's installed.) On PC/AT and 386 class systems, the POST compares your battery-backed-up CMOS information against what it finds in the computer. If everything goes well, and the system checks out, then the POST passes control over to the program in your BIOS that boots the PC.

When the POST detects an error, the error is displayed as a visible number or an audible beep. You can use the charts in Appendix A to see what the error actually means. This will come in handy when you're testing and troubleshooting new equipment.

While the memory check at boot-up may seem like a pain, it's really a handy thing to have—as is the rest of the POST. Early computers had no POST, so you really didn't know what items were installed or whether memory was working. Often you had to load BASIC and check the memory size to see if the value fluctuated. Needless to say, that tedious checking wouldn't cut the mustard in a sophisticated business computer.

The POST—a handy thing to have—mainly goes unnoticed during the day-to-day booting of your PC. If anything bad happened, you'd be alerted via a message or beeping. (The worst case scenario, of course, is that you throw the switch to turn on your machine and absolutely nothing happens.)

The POST in Detail

As someone who will be installing a hardware upgrade and may experience difficulty, it's good for you to know exactly what the POST does. The exact function of the POST is listed in step-by-step detail in this section.

When the system won't start, you know that either it's not plugged in, or that there's a problem with your power supply. Beyond that, the POST takes over by checking out the following items in this order.

The System Test The basic elements of your computer system are tested. This includes an extensive microprocessor test, plus a test on the POST itself. (The error checking program must be free of errors, you know.) It also checks the system unit to make sure all parts of the PC are getting enough power and communicating with each other, and establishes the internal memory locations for your serial and printer ports.

The Extended System Test Here the POST will test the computer's timer chip, as well as other aspects of the "extended system." These include the BIOS and control programs of special controllers and adapters that may have their own individual POST programs.

The Display Test The POST will check your display adapter, sometimes just passing control over to a secondary POST. For example, the EGA and VGA controllers have their own POST to check the video subsystem. If everything there checks out, control returns to the main POST for more tests.

The Memory Test This is where you see the tumbling memory figures; the count from 0K up through however many K of RAM your system has— plus extended memory on AT systems. Most BIOSs use a POST that checks memory twice. Some computers have no memory display; in that case the long pause (the longest part of the POST) is the memory test.

The Keyboard Test The keyboard is tested in this step. In case you didn't know this, your PC's keyboard contains its own microprocessor— it's its own computer! In this stage, the POST checks for the keyboard and makes certain everything's OK. If you've ever neglected to plug in your keyboard when your PC starts, then you may know that the POST error you'd see (typically 301) means you need to plug in your keyboard for the computer to start.

The Disk Drive Test In this test, the POST checks your floppy drives. It doesn't really read from them, it just checks to see if they're present. If they aren't, then you're not going to be able to boot the machine. In the original PC, the POST would next load the BASIC program in ROM, allowing you to program in BASIC and use the cassette tape to save and load your programs. Since that time, the disk drive test also includes a knock on the door of the hard-disk controller, causing the hard drive to warm up. From that point, the POST is completed. Your system will beep once, signaling that everything has passed its test and that your computer is fully functional—it's ready to run!

At this point, the POST ends and the BIOS's bootstrap loader program takes over. It first tries to load information from a diskette in your A drive. If none is found, the bootstrap loader attempts to load information from your hard drive. At that point, DOS and your PC software take over.

The Software Side

Installing or upgrading hardware doesn't stop when you shut the case, and there are aspects of software you should be aware of. These things all happen when the PC starts. It's important to be familiar with them if you expect success in your upgrading endeavors.

Once the bootstrap loader locates a diskette in drive A—or, if that's missing, drive C—it loads the first sector, or "boot sector," from that diskette. That sector is transferred into memory, where the microprocessor will start executing the instructions stored there.

The instructions found in the boot sector do two things: If the disk has an operating system (or even a game), the instructions in the boot sector direct the loading of additional information from disk.

Normally, the boot sector directs the loading of additional information from disk. In the case of a bootable DOS diskette, that additional information is found in the file IO.SYS. If a diskette is a non-bootable diskette, the program simply displays a message along the lines of:

```
Non-System disk or disk error
Replace and strike any key when ready
```

If the diskette has been organized as a boot diskette and contains the proper boot files, IO.SYS is found and loaded. If something goes wrong, replace the diskette with one that you know is bootable and start over.

You should always have at least two bootable DOS diskettes available in case one of them is damaged inadvertently.

IO.SYS provides low-level interfaces for DOS with your PC's hardware. The main program communicates instructions to the computer's BIOS or directly to the microprocessor. Once it's set itself up, IO.SYS loads a special startup program (that's transparent to the user) called SYSINIT. It's SYSINIT's job to load the rest of DOS into your system.

SYSINIT first loads the second basic DOS file, MSDOS.SYS into memory. This is the "DOS kernel," or the main cluster of routines and functions that comprise DOS. These include DOS's basic file management, memory management, character input and output, support for the time and date, and the system environment and configuration.

Next, SYSINIT looks for a CONFIG.SYS file in the root directory of your boot disk. If found, SYSINIT will execute any instructions found there, configuring the system according to your CONFIG.SYS commands, or loading any specified device drivers or initialization programs.

The CONFIG.SYS stage is particularly important when you add hardware to your PC. Computer mice, extra memory, and other special software typically come with software drivers you can load into CONFIG.SYS. Until you do that, and until you've installed both the hardware and its driver into CONFIG.SYS, the upgrade or add-on will not function.

After CONFIG.SYS, SYSINIT will look for a COMMAND.COM file and load it. COMMAND.COM is DOS's command line interpreter. It supplies that ugly C:\ prompt from which you can enter DOS commands or run your own applications.

COMMAND.COM is loaded after CONFIG.SYS. This is because CONFIG.SYS allows you to specify a location for COMMAND.COM other than the root directory—or to specify a completely different command interpreter (something other than COMMAND.COM). Instructions for using CONFIG.SYS and relocating COMMAND.COM can be found in any good book on DOS or hard disk management.

Finally, COMMAND.COM will look for a special file called AUTO-EXEC.BAT and run that as well. AUTOEXEC.BAT is a *batch file*, actually a text file that contains various DOS commands, plus special DOS batch file commands, that make it work like a mini-programming language.

AUTOEXEC.BAT is important to anyone who upgrades PC hardware. Like CONFIG.SYS, AUTOEXEC.BAT is one of the five crucial DOS boot programs over which you have direct control. When you install some types of new hardware, or when you upgrade, you may need to add commands to either AUTOEXEC.BAT or CONFIG.SYS to make your new hardware work properly.

The five crucial DOS boot programs are:

◆ IO.SYS

◆ MSDOS.SYS

◆ CONFIG.SYS

◆ COMMAND.COM

◆ AUTOEXEC.BAT

After all the loading, booting, and SYSINITing is done, you're left at your DOS prompt, ready to use your PC.

Where Trouble Can Occur

Most of the time, everything will proceed nicely. As long as you follow the general instructions in this chapter and the specific instructions in the upgrade part of this book, you should experience the sequence of events in the following list when you power-up or reboot your computer:

1. You turn the PC on.

2. A BIOS/startup message appears (or you'll see the flashing cursor).

3. The POST system checkout will occur, usually faster than you can even think about it.

4. The memory test indicators will fly by (or you'll get to skip them with a keystroke).

5. The floppy disk will kick up.

6. The POST will sound a single beep, indicating that everything's OK.

7. DOS will boot.

You may see other messages. For example, some device drivers in CONFIG.SYS will display messages like:

```
Microsoft (R) Mouse Driver Version Vx.xx
Copyright (C) Microsoft Corp. 1983-1993. All rights reserved.
```

If you have an AUTOEXEC.BAT file, it may display messages as well, eventually leaving you at the DOS prompt—though some AUTOEXEC.BAT files end with a special menu program or load you immediately into your favorite software application.

When Something Goes Wrong

When there's trouble in PC city, you'll know about it through a POST error. There are two general types of POST errors. (The individual errors are more specific about what's not working in your PC.) First, there are the audible error messages—when the speaker beeps. There are also visual error messages, usually in the form of cryptic numbers.

Audio errors will occur during the first few moments when the PC is booting, during the Power-On Self Tests that are done before the monitor is checked out. There are numerous patterns to the number of beeps, timings, and all that. Table 3.1 describes some of the more popular beep patterns.

TABLE 3.1: Audio POST Error Codes

BEEP PATTERN	MEANING
No beep	Power supply or motherboard bad
Unremitting beep	Power supply bad
Short, repetitive beeps	Power supply bad
Long beep, short beep	Motherboard bad
Long beep, two short beeps	Video bad
Long beep, three short beeps	Video bad
Two short beeps	Video bad (an error code may be displayed)
Short beep	Video, disk drive, controller, cable bad
No beep	Speaker bad or missing
Short beep	Everything's Okay

Beeping is usually a sign of trouble. You can use Table 3.1 to narrow down the problem, but not every PC is consistent in its beeping pattern. Some AT systems play really bizarre tunes to clue you in to what's wrong.

It is important to recognize video failure. If the video is working and the machine still beeps, then you probably have some type of disk drive failure. And if you never hear a beep at all, then the speaker is busted.

 Remember that one solitary beep after the memory count is to be expected.

After the video checks out, you may be treated to one of the POST's notorious visual error messages. These usually seem to be random numbers, yet if you have the proper tables you can look up the codes and see what they represent. Table 3.2 contains a list of the basic error codes produced by the POST. These typically will tell you which area the error occurred in during the initial tests.

TABLE 3.2: Visual POST Error Codes

CODE, VALUE	DEVICE THAT FAILED THE POST
2x	Power supply
1xx	Motherboard
2xx	Memory (specific location also listed)
3xx	Keyboard (specific key may also be listed)
4xx	Monochrome video
5xx	Color video
6xx	Floppy drive
7xx	Math coprocessor
8xx	Not currently used
9xx	Printer adapter card
10xx	Secondary printer adapter card
11xx	Serial (RS 232) adapter card
12xx	Secondary serial adapter card
13xx	Game, A/D, controller card
14xx	IBM Graphics printer
15xx	SDLC communications
16xx	Not currently used
17xx	Hard drive or controller
18xx	Expansion unit
19xx	Not currently used
20xx	Binary synchronous communications adapter
21xx	Alternate binary synchronous communications adapter

NOTE: Other error codes, from 22xx through 39xx are used by various adapters and later IBM peripherals. The complete list of POST error code values can be found in Appendix A.

POST Errors

The little "xx"s shown adjacent to numbers in the left column in Table 3.2 will actually appear as numbers when your computer displays these codes. These codes which will allow you to narrow down the error possibilities. The most common error codes you might see are as follows.

201 A 201 error is a memory failure. This could happen right after you install memory into a PC, either because a chip is dead, or because you plugged it in wrong or didn't set a DIP switch correctly.

xx 201 Sometimes the 201 will be preceded by a value, represented by "xx" here. This will give you an approximate location of where to hunt for the errant chip.

301 You'll usually see a 301 error when you forget to plug in your keyboard when you start the PC. Sometimes other 3xx errors occur if something (like your elbow) is resting on the keyboard, pressing down a key. These errors usually aren't fatal; just plug in the keyboard or take your elbow off it and reset.

1701 A 1701 is a common hard drive error. It generally means "something is wrong," though what could be wrong really isn't specified. Sometimes, just plugging in the cables a second time will rid you of the 1701 error. Other times you have to really troubleshoot to track down the problem.

Strategies

When something does go wrong, you have a number of options in trying to remedy the situation. First, you can check installation of the hardware. If the error message indicates some piece of hardware isn't functioning— and you've just installed it new—you should check the job you've done.

These errors may not be limited to the POST, by the way. For example, you may install a modem, and it may pass the POST, but then it might happen that your faxing or communications software can't find it. In that case, you'll see a special message stating that loaded software can't find the hardware it's supposed to interact with. Check the equipment's documentation for ways to deal with this problem...you'll probably have to reinstall the software when this problem occurs.

Second, you can run self-diagnostics on the upgradeable item. Some modems come with built-in diagnostic programs. Many VGA video cards also have a diagnostic program you can run from the DOS prompt. Try these out to make sure everything is functioning—even if you never see an error message.

Third, some computers come with a special, self-booting diagnostics diskette. Others may have special diagnostic software you run from DOS. Still other machines may have a diagnostic ROM program you can call up when the computer first starts or by pressing a special key combination. These diagnostic programs can be run to examine your memory and system configuration in more detail than the POST offers. Nearly every IBM computer, from the first PC to the latest PS/2, has a special diagnostic diskette for troubleshooting.

Fourth, you can try any of the following general strategies to make sure everything is working properly:

◆ Turn the system off, wait a few moments, then turn it on again. Sometimes this will do the trick. (Be sure to wait at least 5 seconds before turning it on again.)

◆ Check or change your system configuration. You may have to deal with any DIP switches found on expansion cards or disk drives, plus an AT or 386's setup program.

◆ Check all cables and connectors, both inside and outside of the PC.

◆ Check the disk drives. Disk drives are the only moving part (next to the power supply) in your PC. Because of that, they'll probably break before anything else.

◆ Check the display. If you're not seeing anything, maybe the monitor isn't plugged in. Maybe the brightness knob is turned all the way down. Or the monitor may be completely turned off. Check all of that.

◆ Check expansion card connections. Especially after moving a PC, some cards may wiggle loose.

Check List

In addition to the above troubleshooting strategies, here is a check list of some items you may want to look over. Check out all of these items before you become totally frustrated or give up.

Is it plugged in? Is the power switch on? A lot of consultants make a quick $50 by showing up at a client's office and plugging in a "broken" computer—this could be embarrassing.

Are there any missing pieces? Who knows where they go, but look for missing cables, loose cables; a printer without any paper, ribbon, or toner; a modem not plugged into the phone system (wall jack); or anything that should be there and isn't.

Are any internal cables loose? Some computers have a ganglia of cables inside. When you shut the lid too fast, the cables could be pulled from their sockets. All internal cables should be properly connected, and the lid should be closed carefully.

Is the PC running too hot? Sometimes computers don't get proper ventilation. If they're butt-up against a wall, or if something is blocking the front vent, the system can heat up and become nonfunctional in less than an hour.

And finally, though it's a sad question:

Is the operator stupid? Sometimes users will sit and look for the "*any* key." Sometimes it says to press the Arrow key, but they find something like 13 arrows on their keyboard, six of which are pointing up. And which key is the "Control" key, anyway?—it doesn't say "Control" on any of them.

Be patient if you're troubleshooting for someone else. Though this may all be second nature to you, a lot of people are intimidated and easily frustrated by computers.

DIP Switches and Setup Programs

We've talked a lot about DIP switches and the AT's setup program. You might well wonder: What are these? Why are they important?

Both the DIP switches and setup programs are used by the PC/XT and PC/AT computers, as well as certain expansion cards and peripherals, for hardware configuration. It's a way of setting certain options of preparing and configuring the computer for operation. When you upgrade your computer, you may have to set a DIP switch or run your AT's setup program to configure the computer for the new hardware.

DIP Switches

DIP switches are a row of tiny "slide" or "rocker" type switches. They're usually numbered, 1 through 8 (or however many) on the "switch block." An indicator on one side of the switch block shows which position is ON. You can assume that the other position is OFF.

Figure 3.1 shows a typical DIP switch block. The switches are numbered 1 through 8, and the ON position is indicated by the ↑. The black squares in the picture indicate the position of the DIP slide switches. Switches 1, 2, 4, and 7 are off. Switches 3, 5, 6, and 8 are on.

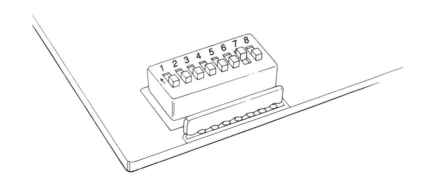

FIGURE 3.1: A typical DIP switch block

You set a switch by sliding it to the on or off position. You can slide them with a pen or pencil, but as a hardware upgrading professional, you'll probably want to use your bent paper clip tool.

The following list shows the items most often set by DIP switches in a PC/XT. (For specifics, refer to your own PC/XT's manual.)

◆ Number of floppy drives installed

◆ Presence of a math coprocessor

◆ Amount of memory installed

◆ Type of display: monochrome or color

The individual positions of these switches and their settings may vary from PC to PC, though nearly all of them are based on the original IBM PC's design.

 If you don't have a PC/XT, note that some expansion cards also have DIP switches on them for configuration purposes. Printers also are famous for having DIP switches. In fact, if your printer is double-spacing when you don't want it to, or malfunctioning in some other way, it probably means you have to read the manual and set one of its DIP switches properly.

Also note that some AT-class systems will have a small set of DIP switches to determine the type of video adapter installed. Normally, AT systems use a setup program in the BIOS to set the video adapter, but this isn't always the case.

Jumpers

Another form of switch that might appear on your system's motherboard is a *jumper*. A jumper looks like a small black box, no bigger than ¼" square. It sits over two little metal poles sticking out of the motherboard, or jutting out from an expansion card.

To set the jumper, you locate the two pins you wish to place the jumper over. The pins will usually have a label, something like "J1" or "J9" or some J-number. You position the black box over the pins and press down. The box makes the connection between the pins and you're all set.

Figure 3.2 shows a typical jumper setup. There are four pins in a row, labeled "J1" and "J2." The jumper is the black box over "J2." It's considered to be "set" to position "J2."

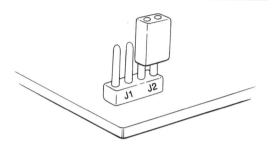

FIGURE 3.2:   A typical jumper setup

You can also remove jumpers. Because they're so tiny, you might have to pull them off with a set of needle-nosed pliers, but your fingers can do the job most of the time. Normally you don't set aside the black box. You simply put it over one of the pins instead of both, as shown in Figure 3.3.

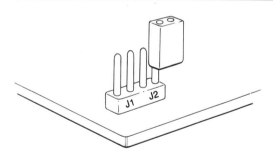

FIGURE 3.3:   A jumper turned off

Setting a jumper over one pin doesn't "set" anything, it just keeps you from losing the jumpers.

Jumpers can be found on various motherboards, but especially on some expansion cards. Like DIP switches, they serve to let the hardware know of its internal configuration.

Setup Programs

Instead of DIP switches, most AT-class systems (which includes all 386 systems) have what's known as CMOS memory, which is constantly saved in the computer by a battery. (It's also called your battery-backed-up RAM.) Into this memory is stored all the basic information about an AT's configuration—the stuff that was normally set by DIP switches on a PC/XT's motherboard.

 In addition to basic system configurations, the AT's CMOS memory also keeps track of the time and date. You have to manually enter those for a PC/XT, or buy a clock card that has its own battery.

To get at the CMOS memory, to change or examine its contents, you must run a special setup program. Most of the time, this program is internal—as part of your system's BIOS. You access it at boot time by pressing certain keys. (The specific key combination differs from PC to PC; Ctrl-Alt-Enter is popular.)

Once the setup program runs, you can change or modify the configuration of your system. The items controlled from setup include the following.

◆ The system date and time

◆ The number and types of disk drives (both hard and floppy)

◆ The system memory, both main motherboard memory and extended memory

◆ The type of display

◆ The type of keyboard

◆ The system's speed

◆ The presence of a math coprocessor

◆ Other, various system optimization options

Because the setup program and its contents are so important, you should check your AT's manual for how to bring it up. Then, once it's on the screen, press the Print Screen key to get a hard copy of it. Keep that hard copy with your system's manuals. You do this for three reasons:

◆ If you ever upgrade again, you'll have a copy of the original from which to take notes. If you make any modifications, be sure to create yet another hard copy of the setup program's screen for the next time you change something.

◆ If anything ever happens to the CMOS RAM, you should have a copy of your original so you can reset its values.

◆ Batteries don't last forever. At some point in the future, your AT's battery will die and your computer won't boot right. At that point in time, you should buy a new battery, then use your hard copy of the setup program to reset the values.

Not Everything Is a Problem

This chapter dealt a lot with some of the problems that can occur when you first start your computer. Before moving on, note that not everything is a problem. The PC will normally start right up with no hitch whatsoever. Even when you upgrade, a good 90% of the time everything will work as planned.

Your upgrades should be successful, provided you're careful and follow the instructions detailed in this book.

Upgrading the PC

The PC is full of potential. IBM made it that way by designing their personal computer systems with open architecture. They probably never thought people like you and I would be venturing inside our computers, but with easy access to the computer's hardware and with the wide availability of upgrade options, this stuff isn't that hard to do. First you need some basic training, though, so now it's time to get your hands dirty. (Not quite!)

This chapter is about opening your computer and looking inside. The emphasis here is on your *computer*. There are diagrams and figures in this chapter, but what's important here is that you take the plunge and look inside your own PC—it's time to *do it*!

Before you pop the lid off your PC case, read this chapter for background information. It starts off with an overview of the upgrade process, giving you reasons to upgrade. Next comes an overview of all internal, external, and peripheral parts of your computer. Finally—the surgery. This is actually the briefest and easiest part, but you need to know the other, background information to get the most out of it.

Nothing described in this chapter is a dangerous or difficult thing to do. As long as you follow the instructions, set everything up properly, and use the recommended tools (not forgetting the patience tool), everything will come out fine and you'll have a lot of fun.

Why You Want to Do This

There are more than enough reasons for wanting to upgrade your PC yourself. A lot of them were listed back in Chapter 1. But the best overall reason for wanting to upgrade your own PC is because you can.

You can change just about anything in your computer. Thanks to its modular design, you can plug in or replace any component without affecting the overall machine. In fact, if any effect takes place, it will probably be that your system runs faster.

To Expand Your System

You can expand your system with more memory, a hard drive, a faster hard drive, a larger-capacity floppy drive, a new video standard, an internal modem, or any of a number of options that put more stuff into your computer. You can replace older parts—take out a slow hard disk and put in a faster, high-capacity one, for example.

Computers are infinitely upgradeable. PC owners who know a lot about their computers are never totally happy with what they have. I don't know of a single user who says, "Well, there's nothing more I can add to my computer. It's perfect."

To Make Your Computer Run Faster

Making a computer faster involves both the hardware and software. Sometimes it's one, sometimes the other, and sometimes both. For example, database programs rely almost completely on fast disk access to get their job done, so buying a faster computer really wouldn't help a database application, while buying a faster hard drive would.

If you're happy with the software you've installed, your reason for upgrading may be to make the system run *faster*. You may be interested in moving into a whole new world of computing performance, with a newer and faster microprocessor. This next section is about upgrading the heart of your PC.

To Elevate Your System to a New Platform

You could upgrade your system to give it a new microprocessor. That would benefit most of the work you might do with your PC, in that your applications will run faster.

You could add accelerator cards to a PC/XT to turn it into a 286, 386 or 486 system. Or you could perform what's known as a "motherboard swap" to completely replace your system's circuitry with newer, faster hardware. Recent advances in motherboard design can improve your computer's overall performance up to 600%! If you replace your 286 motherboard with a VESA local bus motherboard with a 486 processor, you'll get at least a 600% improvement in performance—especially if you're using Windows.

There is significant overlap between the three reasons for upgrading mentioned. And there are dozens more reasons beyond these, most of which are specific to the needs of a certain user.

You don't want to work on your PC's hardware every day, though, and you shouldn't have to. Unlike obsessed car freaks who are out there under the hood every Saturday morning, you will only open your PC's case for upgrade purposes three times a year, on the average.

Just as you don't do hard disk (software) maintenance or install new applications every day, you don't upgrade your PC all too often. Nonetheless—knowing DOS, good hard disk management, hardware information, and how to upgrade by yourself are all important aspects to becoming a better PC user.

System Overview

A book about DOS—or hard disk management—covers a lot of different machines. Whether the reader of that book is using an IBM PS/2 or one of Fred's Discount Mondo Clones, both machines run DOS, and the differences between PC-DOS and MS-DOS are just too slight to mention. So a DOS book would apply to everyone. That isn't true of a PC hardware book. All PCs are different. There are thousands of models out there, and trying to document them all in this book would be ludicrous. Instead, a solution has been devised.

Figure 4.1 shows what I call the "Generic PC." It's a typical PC computer which has the three basic parts of all PCs: a monitor, console, and keyboard. Any other detail in this PC isn't important. Basically, it's to be accepted as the general model that looks the way most of our computers

FIGURE 4.1: The generic PC

would if you squinted. (Some people, including myself, keep the monitor and keyboard beside the PC.)

As we've said, the general layout of each PC is similar, and this book can't get into detail on everything, including the specifics of whichever PC system you own, so we're taking the generic PC approach. It's up to you to locate the items and individual options on and in your computer. This book will tell you where to look, and what terms to apply to those options when you find them.

To help you in understanding all the variations and parts, the following sections break down the generic PC into three general areas:

◆ External Differences

◆ Internal Differences

◆ Peripheral Differences

After you read through this material, you'll be able to recognize parts quickly and know you way around just about any PC.

External Differences

All PCs look similar on the outside. This is because most clones and compatibles followed IBM's original design. Some clone cases are stylized, but most follow the same pattern as the original PC or PC/AT, with a few subtle variations. (In fact, they're almost all the same boring shade of gray.)

The external differences of a PC are described here in four sections:

◆ Model differences

◆ The system unit

◆ Keyboards

◆ Monitors

This covers the major external options on all PCs. Anything else that's outside of the case is considered a peripheral here, and is covered in a later section.

Model Differences

There are two classes of PC models: The PC/XT-style and the AT-style. These aren't dependent upon what computer you have, or which microprocessor it sports. Instead, it's just a different case design. The most popular at present is the AT-style, but there are still plenty of PC/XT-style models floating around.

Figure 4.2 shows a typical PC/XT-style case. This case design had two full-height disk drives sitting side by side on the right side of the machine. The case is generally not as tall nor as wide as the AT-style cases. In fact, one of the reasons the PC/XT design lost popularity was that there wasn't enough internal space for expansion cards. (Most PC/XT-style cases could barely squeeze in five expansion slots.)

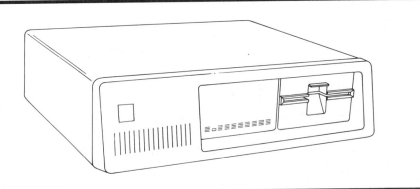

FIGURE 4.2: A typical PC/XT-style case

Figure 4.3 shows a typical PC/AT-style case. Since disk drive technology allows for smaller-sized drives than existed when the original PC came out, the AT-style case makes better use of half-height drives than did the XT case. The same number of drives can be stacked vertically on the right side of the case, as seen in Figure 4.3. There is even room for a third drive, and internal space for more drives. (Height and internal arrangement of disk drives is covered later in this chapter.)

Because the AT-style case takes advantage of smaller disk drives, there's more room in the case for expansion cards. The typical AT-style case can have up to five slots (or sometimes more) for expansion options.

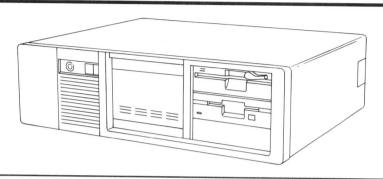

FIGURE 4.3: A typical PC/AT-style case

Keep in mind that an AT-style case can have an 8086, 286, 386, 486 (or even higher) system inside. This case design has proven to be more flexible and useful and has become the standard PC case. Although smaller versions exist, and there are variations, the AT-style case is now the most popular PC case. (Heck, even the modular Macintoshes use a similar arrangement.)

AT-style cases sport a variety of front panel features, but the front panel is always located on the left side of the case, toward the top. It usually has any combination of the following items.

Key and Lock The key and lock (part of the PC/AT's original design) allow you to lock up your PC, freezing the keyboard and preventing others from using the computer. On some locked PCs, you can't even open the case. Most people simply leave their keys dangling in the lock. But those who are more security conscious can lock their PCs to prevent unauthorized access.

Power Light The first PCs had no power light. You could turn off the monitor, and other than the hum of the fan, you wouldn't know whether or not the thing was on. With a power light on your computer's front panel, you can always tell the machine is up and running, just by glancing across the room.

Disk Activity Light The disk activity light tells you when a disk is being accessed. Both hard drives and floppy drives have lights on their front panels—the light flashes when the drive is being accessed by the computer. In an AT-style case, most hard drives are internal, behind the system unit's

front plate, so the hard disk activity light on the front panel is connected to the hard drive controller and helps you "see" the real hard disk light, which is inside the case.

Turbo Mode Light The turbo mode light on some dual-speed PCs lets you know when the system is running in the faster, "turbo" mode. (*Turbo* means "two speeds.") Most PC microprocessors have two speeds: A fast speed and a slower, "compatibility" speed. Why a slower speed? Because most PC software can handle the faster speed of today's microprocessors, but some software, particularly games, time themselves more slowly.

Unless you're playing a game, you'll probably want to use your two-speed PC in the faster turbo mode.

Reset Switch All IBM systems, and a good hunk of the compatibles out there, lack a reset switch. Yet, if your software crashes (or for some reason your system dies), and Control-Alt-Delete doesn't reset, a reset switch is a great boon. It saves you the trouble of turning the PC off, waiting the required 15 seconds, and then turning the thing on again.

Turbo Shift Switch A turbo shift switch is also found on the front panel of many PCs. It's the control for changing your microprocessor's speed from compatible (slow) to turbo (fast). Some switches may have more than one position.

Some PCs use keyboard key combinations (such as Ctrl+Alt++/–) as switches rather than, or in addition to, a front panel device.

Figure 4.4 shows some typical arrangements of the PC's front panel. Three options are illustrated (A, B, and C), but there really is a fourth—option D is "no panel," which may occur on some AT-style cases. But you'll usually find your AT-style case has a front panel like A, B or C in the illustration.

The main difference between A and B in Figure 4.4 is in the use of graphic icons to represent the power, hard disk, and turbo lights, and the Open and Lock key positions. Different AT systems may use different icons—

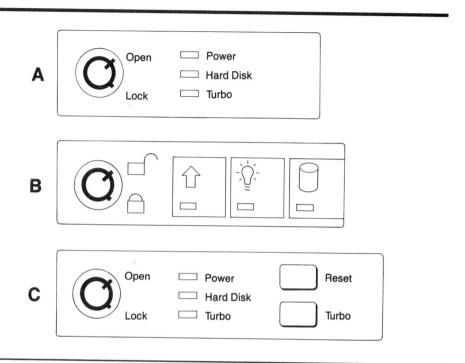

FIGURE 4.4: Front panel configurations

though the lock, light bulb, cylinder and arrow are quite popular—or they may use text *and* icons…it really varies.

Panel C in Figure 4.4 is a variation of Panel A, with the reset and turbo buttons included. These buttons may appear in any arrangement. The reset button is best when it's recessed so you won't accidentally press it. The buttons may also be identified by icons. So…mix and match and take your pick. Somewhere within these variations is bound to be your front panel design. They're all generally the same thing.

Before we go on to describe the system unit in detail, note that there are some other popular case variations available in addition to the popular AT-style case and the older PC/XT-style. These are as follows:

Tower Configuration Floor-standing computers are often called "tower models." They're the same basic design as the AT-style case, with the disk drives oriented for use in an up-and-down manner as opposed to right-to-left.

Figure 4.5 shows a typical tower configuration PC, in which the disk drives are at the top of a vertical system. If the tower were standing on the floor, then this would be the most convenient place for them; you could simply bend over and stick a diskette in the drive.

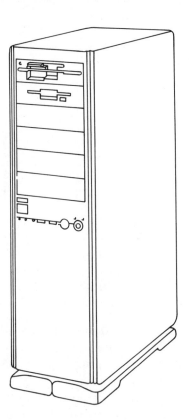

FIGURE 4.5: The tower configuration

Tower systems provide for more room to add several disk drives—more than the AT-style case. Why? Because a standing computer can be taller than a desktop model can be wide. You only have so much desk space. A small portion of the tower configuration's case touches the floor, but it has a lot of room inside.

The PS/2 System Some manufacturers attempted to borrow designs from the IBM PS/2 system's case, but stopped after they found out how small the cases really are. The PS/2 series uses a case smaller than the original PC's case. Why? Because the components got smaller.

The PS/2 has an internal and external arrangement similar to most popular PCs. On the whole it is a new design, too small to be readily cloned and useful, but with enough real estate for the PS/2 to do its job. (See Figure 4.6.)

Small-Footprint Machines A computer's "footprint" is the amount of desk space occupied by its bottom. This isn't the amount of desktop the computer uses; that usually includes the keyboard, cables, mouse, and elbow room—typically twice the footprint size.

Laptops This book doesn't cover laptops. For the most part they're not upgradeable. Some allow you to plug in extra memory chips and options, and one or two expansion cards. But they're really nonstandard, both internally and externally. Because of this (and because laptops are usually your second machine), this book doesn't deal with them.

The Console or System Unit

The *console*, which is also called the *system unit*, is the main box of your PC. All PC's have the same items on their system unit, with varying locations. Especially if you're working on a number of systems, you should know and recognize these items and where to find them.

Not every PC is going to have all of these items. So the emphasis here is on finding and recognizing those things your own PC has. Take a minute to locate and identify the items on your PC's console in Figure 4.7, which represents a generic configuration.

FIGURE 4.6: A PS/2 system computer

The Front Panel Try to locate any lights (LEDs) and what they represent, the key switch, turbo buttons, and any reset button.

The Disk Drive Bays These should be on the right side of the case, in an opening.

Air Vents The air vents will be a pattern of slits on the front of the case. Through these vents, the power supply's fan draws in air to cool the computer's components.

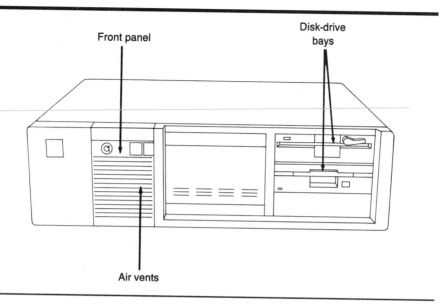

FIGURE 4.7: Front view

The Power Switch The power switch is where you turn your PC on and off. It's generally located in the right rear of the PC. Sometimes the power switch is on the front of the machine (which is convenient and makes sense).

On power switches, "1" is used to represent "On" and "O" is used to represent "Off." You may not even see the words "On" and "Off." (It was that way on the first PC and has been so ever since.) Figure 4.8 illustrates the back of a computer case showing the on/off switch, fan, and expansion card area.

Power Connectors The typical power supply on a PC has two connectors, one for the main cable to the wall (from which the PC draws its juice), and another into which you can plug the monitor. Each connector has either three prongs or three holes—the monitor connector is the one with three holes.

Fan Output Your power supply contains a fan (sometimes two) that draws air in through the vents in front of the PC and forces it out through

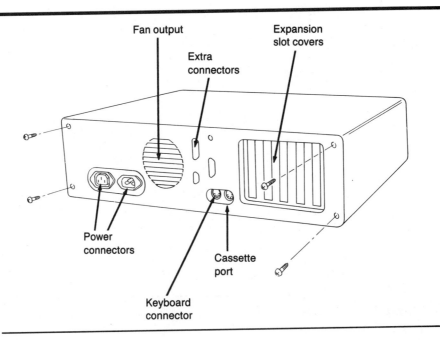

Fan output

Extra
connectors

Expansion
slot covers

Power
connectors

Cassette
port

Keyboard
connector

FIGURE 4.8: The back of a computer case

the fan output in the back of the PC. (This explains that black mark on the wall behind your computer.)

Make sure the fan output vent isn't obstructed. If it's caked with dust (which happens after a time), use a can of air to blow the dust off—but be careful not to blow the dust back into the PC.

Extra Connectors Some systems may have extra connectors, or holes for connectors, between the power supply's fan and the expansion slot covers. If your system has a built-in parallel or serial port, those connectors may be located on the back of your PC.

Some systems may have covers over serial or mouse ports. These plates are often referred to as "knock-outs." You should use a screwdriver and a pair of needle-nosed pliers to remove knock-outs or plate covers, and avoid damaging your computer with sharp blows.

Keyboard Connector The keyboard connector is a round device into which you plug your keyboard cable. The holes in the connector are spread out so there's only one way to connect the cable, but the connector is notched at the top which should help.

Expansion Slot Covers If you look at the back of your PC, on the right side you'll find an area composed of expansion slot covers. In this area lies your motherboard's expansion slots, into which you can plug various expansion cards and options. When you look at your expansion slot area from the back view, you see the back mounting plate of those cards—or—if the slot is unoccupied, the metal slot covers that fill in the holes when no expansion cards are plugged-in.

Some expansion cards may have cable connectors on the part of the card that can be seen from the rear view of the computer. In that case, you'll see the connectors and any cables that may be hanging from them.

Case Screws When you look at the rear of your PC's case, you see several screws that are used to fasten the case to the PCs chassis. Between two and six screws close up your computer's case. Four of the screws are located in the back corners: lower-left, upper-left, lower-right, and upper-right. One is located in the top center, and in a few rare instances you'll find a screw in the bottom center.

The original IBM PC had only two (minus) screws, at the lower-left and lower-right corners of the back of the case. Most of today's PCs have five (plus) screws at the rear of the case, one in each of the four corners and one in the top center back.

Power Supply Screws The power supply is anchored to the back plate of your PC by four screws. These screws are usually smaller than the main case screws.

Figure 4.8 shows the four power supply screws evenly spaced in a rectangle, just inside the rectangle created by the main case screws.

Keyboards

There are many different types of PC keyboards. This has been one of the more humorous aspects of PC computing for a decade—IBM, the company that patented the touch typist's dream, the IBM Selectric typewriter, just can't make up its mind what keyboard to use for its PC line.

There is no such thing as fixing a keyboard, at least not at a do-it-yourself level. But you can use your air can or a special vacuum cleaner with a tiny

nozzle to blow or suck out crud in the keyboard. Otherwise, just replace an errant keyboard, and when you do, choose one of the following three major PC keyboard variations.

The Original PC/XT Keyboard The original PC's keyboard had a lot of funkiness—the keys were marked with arrows and symbols, for example, instead of the words "Tab" or "Enter." The Enter key was too far to the right, so most people kept hitting the accent grave key (`) by mistake. And the backslash key was where the left shift key should be. (See Figure 4.9.)

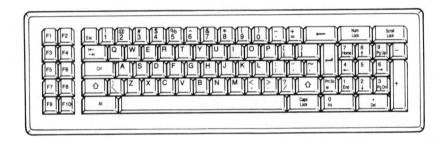

FIGURE 4.9: The original PC/XT keyboard

Variations of this keyboard proliferated. Each newer version still had trouble with the backslash key location. In fact, backslash continues to be one of the most transient keys on the keyboard, which wouldn't be so bad if DOS didn't rely upon backslash so much.

The PC/AT Keyboard The PC/AT keyboard's biggest improvement was in moving the numeric keypad away, separating it from the standard typewriter keyboard. (See Figure 4.10.) The Enter key situation was also improved when it was sized like a Selectric's Enter/Return key. And (this is no small matter) all keys were labeled with words in addition to those cryptic arrows and symbols.

The Enhanced PC Keyboard The enhanced PC keyboard shown in Figure 4.11 is what we're supposed to be using today. It has a smaller Enter key than the AT keyboard, but Enter is still within reach. It finally names the Tab key instead of marking it with a symbol, and it puts Esc back

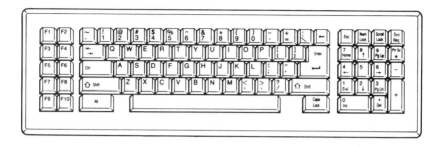

FIGURE 4.10:   The PC/AT keyboard

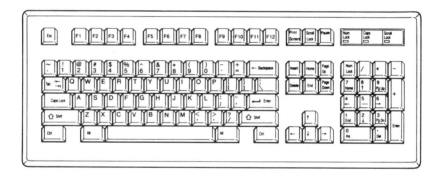

FIGURE 4.11:   The enhanced PC keyboard

where it belongs. There is now a key pad for the cursor arrows, that is separate from the numeric key pad, which makes working with spreadsheets easier. The function keys migrated to the top of the keyboard. And the Control (Ctrl) and Caps Lock keys are backwards from the way they used to be. But humans can get used to anything. As long as you don't have to switch back and forth between too many keyboards, these changes shouldn't drive you nuts.

Monitors

The monitor, the final basic PC external that we'll talk about, never has to be taken apart, so there are only a few things to note about it.

There are two major types of monitors: color and monochrome. A color monitor gives you graphics abilities, and monochrome gives you outstandingly crisp text. You must have a corresponding adapter card inside the PC to drive any monitor.

 If you find you must run your monitor with the brightness "all the way up," there may be a power supply problem within the monitor. If this is the case, you should have a professional look at the monitor. In fact, have a professional look at any monitor that seems to need to be fixed. A computer's monitor is nothing for a do-it-yourselfer to mess with.

Internal Differences

Again, the information here is of a general nature—just pay attention to the examples and illustrations here. Eventually, toward the end of this chapter, you will be asked to open your PC and locate some more important items on the motherboard. But for now, you don't have to pry open your PC to look at these things. Just follow along.

Figure 4.12, illustrating a generic AT-style case, shows the general location of each item that will be discussed in this section.

The Disk Drives

Disk drives are usually located in the front-right side of your computer's case. They're either stacked top-to-bottom, shown in Figure 4.12, or left-to-right in a PC/XT-style case, as shown in Figure 4.13. Some clones mix both vertical and horizontal drive bays on their cases. It's best to avoid cases that use vertical 5¼" drive bays because you can't put a CD-ROM drive in a vertical drive bay—limiting your upgrade to a multimedia PC sometime in the future.

You'll note that the PC/XT-style case doesn't allow much room for expansion cards inside the computer. The hard drive, usually on the left, sits over part of the motherboard, and partially blocks what might be room for some expansion slots. This scenario might occur also in some AT-style cases, where the hard drive sits inside the case with no open access through the front of the system unit.

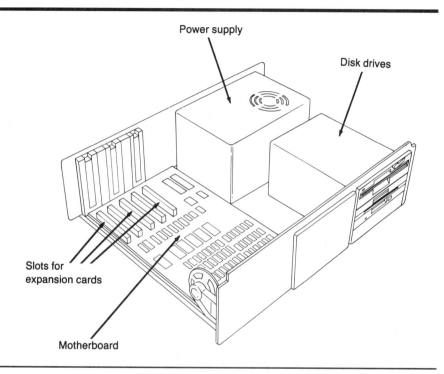

Power supply

Disk drives

Slots for
expansion cards

Motherboard

FIGURE 4.12: Inside a generic PC

Every drive has at least two cables. The first is a *power supply cable*, a multi-colored grouping of four wires that originates from the left side of the power supply and plugs into the back of the drive. Both hard disk drives and floppy drives use the same type of connector. Because of the way the connector is made, you're forced to plug it in correctly! It doesn't matter which cable you plug in (virtually all extra power supply cables provide the same voltages), as long as the drive is plugged into the power supply. Many modern clone power supplies provide up to four extra sets of drive power cables and connectors. If that's not enough (and your power supply can handle more drives) you can buy a Y adapter to split one power cable into two power cables that will each power one drive.

In addition to the power supply cables, every drive has a *controller/data cable*. For floppy drives, this is a 34-wire ribbon cable that connects to the back of the drive. The other end of the cable connects to a floppy disk controller or hard/floppy (combination) disk controller expansion card, or

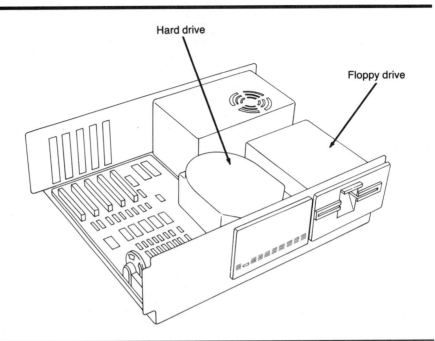

Hard drive

Floppy drive

FIGURE 4.13: Disk drives inside a PC/XT-style case

plugs directly into the motherboard. If you have two floppy drives, they both use the same cable.

 Remember, this is background information. The details of disk drives and cables are covered in Chapters 6 and 7.

IDE Hard drives have just one ribbon cable. MFM, RLL, ESDI drives have two cables each. If your PC has one of these latter drive types, the first cable on your drive will be a 34-wire ribbon cable, similar to the floppy's cable (don't confuse them!), which is used to send control information to the hard drive. A second, narrow, 20-wire ribbon cable—the data line—transfers data to and from the drive. Both of these cables connect to the hard disk controller located either on your motherboard or in an expansion slot.

The hard disk controller and floppy controllers may be located on the same expansion card. Also, you should note that most modern IDE (AT) disk controllers can generally handle two floppy drives and two hard drives. The two floppy drives will use but one cable. Two IDE hard drives can also use a single ribbon cable. Two MFM, RLL, or ESDI hard drives require two cables each.

The Power Supply

The power supply (see Figure 4.14) is located in the right-rear corner of your system unit, directly behind the disk drives. In fact, there's usually less than one finger's worth of space between the power supply and disk drives—just enough room to bend a few cables into. This means that if you have to swap power supplies, you often have to unscrew and slide out your disk drives as well.

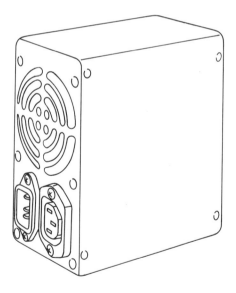

FIGURE 4.14:   The power supply

On the left side of the power supply will be a whole ganglia of cables. There are two types:

◆ The disk drive power cables are a group of four wires—two black, one red, and one yellow. This ends with a white box-like connector that's plugged into the drive's rump. Older power supplies had only two disk drive power cables, modern power supplies have four —or more—drive cables.

◆ There are two motherboard power-supply cables, each including six wires of various colors, which attach to the motherboard, plugging into two adjacent sockets.

 All power-supply cables are notched, so that you can't plug them in backwards. You can, however, plug the motherboard's power cables in bottom-to-top instead of top-to-bottom. Later, in the chapter on power supplies, you'll learn a handy mnemonic for the right way to plug the power into the motherboard.

On top of each PC power supply is a rating that lists both voltage and watts. The watts value is important—it indicates your power supply's actual power output. Nearly every PC/XT should have at least a 150 watt power supply. That's also OK for AT systems and 386s, but it would be better for them to have at least a 200 watt power supply.

The Motherboard

The motherboard is located within your PC's case, on the bottom left side. It's usually a sheet of green fiberglass, covered with silicon chips, resistors, and a virtual snack bowl of electronic circuitry. (The motherboard may be hard to see, especially if it's hidden behind lots of expansion cards and other electronic chop suey.)

The basic motherboard is shown in Figure 4.13. In Figure 4.15, you'll find it pulled out of the system unit for closer inspection.

Again, this illustration is meant to make it easy to see parts. No motherboard is going to have *all* of the parts described below and shown in the figure. You'll also find that there are different sizes and geometric shapes for motherboards. The example shown should help you to locate the parts

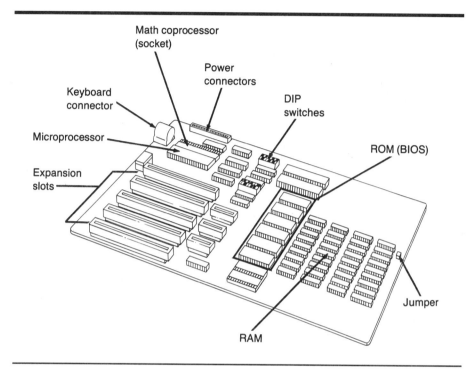

FIGURE 4.15: The motherboard

your motherboard does have, and to recognize some parts you may not have seen before.

The Microprocessor The microprocessor—your computer's CPU or main brain—will appear to be a long wide chip, or a large square chip, located somewhere on the right side of the motherboard, possibly but not always near the middle.

This chip, like all chips, can be identified by an inscription on it's top, listing the chip's number, which might be any of the following:

8088

8086

80C86

V20

V30

V40

80286

386

486

Some of these numbers will be followed by other numbers—values which typically indicate the chip's speed (in megahertz). Just look for the basic number, if it's there, then you've found your computer's microprocessor.

 Sometimes the microprocessor will be hidden under the hard drive or the power supply. If you can't find it, but see that the motherboard extends under the hard drive, that's probably where the microprocessor is located.

The Math Coprocessor The math coprocessor would be located adjacent to the microprocessor. It's usually the same size as the microprocessor, though sometimes it's smaller. The chip's number also will be nearly the same, but it will end in a "7" instead of a "6."

Since a math coprocessor is optional, its location usually just looks like a blank socket, sometimes with a stenciled label on the motherboard that says "math," or "coprocessor," or sometimes just a number.

The Expansion Slots Expansion slots are located side-by-side on the motherboard, along the back. There can be any number of expansion slots; a slot count of anywhere from one to three is common in low-profile desktop cases, with eight being common in a full-size desktop or tower case. You can plug your expansion cards into these slots.

The expansion slots are also referred to as the "system bus" or just the "bus." The slots themselves aren't the bus, but if you look carefully, you'll see tiny rows of wire traces running from left to right, perpendicular to the expansion slots. Those wires, plus some support chips located nearby, constitute your system's *bus*. The bus is a direct line of communications between your microprocessor and the expansion cards.

 Some slots have one or two small extensions on them. These extensions are there to make the slot work as an 8, 16 or 32 bit slot. Slots without the extension are 8-bit slots—the only types of slots found in PC/XT compatibles. Slots with one extension are 16-bit. Slots with two extensions will accept up to a 32-bit card, like a local bus video or drive controller card.

All expansion slots are labeled, usually with a small stenciled number on the motherboard. The number has no meaning as far as which card gets plugged into which slot, except that *one special slot is number 8*. If you have a slot 8, on your motherboard, you should only plug into it special "slot 8" adapter cards. (This, and more information on expansion cards and slots, is covered in Chapter 10.)

The BIOS   The BIOS is your computer's ROM, its personality. Between one and several chips compose your system's BIOS—two is a popular number. It's also hard to pin-point your BIOS' location, though the left center portion of the motherboard is popular. If you know who makes your PC's BIOS, their name on the chip will clue you that you've found it. (Look for names like IBM, COMPAQ, Phoenix, AMI, and so on.)

RAM   One of your motherboard's main residents is RAM, your computer's memory. Memory chips are usually found in the bottom center portion of the motherboard. They're easy to spot because typically they consist of several rows of chips that all look alike.

Unlike older computers that use RAM chips, most computers made in the late '80s and early '90s also have tiny slots for SIMM (Single Inline Memory Module) memory—a number of memory chips on a tiny expansion-card-like holder. SIMM memory plugs into a socket on the motherboard, but is not considered an expansion card.

The Proprietary RAM Connector   A special 32-bit memory slot is often included on 386 systems. This allows the 386 (or higher) system to have full 32-bit memory mounted on an add-on memory card. Otherwise, if memory were added in an expansion slot, the 32-bit microprocessor could only access the memory 16 bits at a time—this would severely slow things down.

 Since most slots intended for memory expansion accept only expansion cards made by the motherboard's manufacturer, you may be able to get the correct memory expansion card only from your dealer. Some motherboards use one of these proprietary cards as your only memory expansion option, and others offer you the use of SIMMs and a proprietary memory expansion card. DTK Computers, for example, made motherboards that used SIMMs (on 386DX motherboards) to handle up to 8MB of RAM, and an optional expansion card that plugged into a special slot to handle added RAM up to 32MB. In the late '80s (when most PCs were limited to 8MB of RAM) this expansion card was popular with network administrators who needed more than 8MB of RAM to support several Windows users. These days, most PCs offer a RAM capacity (in SIMMs) of at least 8MB (and more often 16MB or 32MB) as a general standard.

Other Support Chips   In addition to the parts marked in Figure 4.15, there are several smaller, ubiquitous chips that serve support functions for the motherboard. These chips control such things as the keyboard, the computer's timing, interfaces, and other miscellaneous jobs, most of which are beyond the scope of this book.

It's a good sign if your motherboard has as few of these chips as possible. A good motherboard, made out of parts such as the Chips & Technology chip set, for example, will have fewer and larger chips than a "discrete" motherboard, with dozens of support chips.

DIP Switches   PC/XT systems (and some ATs) have DIP switches located on their motherboards. DIP switches are used to set your system's configuration, number of disk drives, and memory.

The original PC—and most PC clones—have two sets of DIP switches.

The second one will either be toward the rear of the computer, or (most likely) a few chips to the left of the first. Use your manual to distinguish between the two, most DIP switches are marked poorly. Some AT clones will have a smaller DIP switch, which is used to set the display if the display controller is built into the mother board. This is yet a third DIP switch. (Most AT and 386 systems now use the CMOS RAM and the Setup program, instead.)

The two sets of DIP switch blocks are labeled differently—one is SW-1, the other is SW-2. Your PC's manual should give you the approximate locations and relative positions of each, and the SW-1 or SW-2 labels will be stenciled on the motherboard next to the switch.

Jumpers Most recently-made computers may have jumpers instead of DIP switches. Jumpers are found on nearly every PC, from the first to the latest 486.

On XTs, jumpers and DIP switches do such things as determine the type of video adapter you have, your hard drive configuration, memory on the motherboard, and which speed (turbo or slow) the computer starts in. On most ATs, these same settings are now done with BIOS instructions that can be configured when you start your computer.

The Power Connectors The two cables from the power supply to the motherboard plug in somewhere on the motherboard. Just where you'll find them on your motherboard will vary. Look for two cable connectors that are placed inline and adjacent to each other. Each cable has at least four conductors. Your motherboard's manual will show you the exact location.

The Keyboard Connector The keyboard connector is usually located in the right rear portion of the motherboard, just above the power connectors. It sits up off the motherboard a bit, and the keyboard cable passes out through a hole in the back of the case.

LED Connectors Finally, the motherboard will utilize tiny prongs into which you plug cables for your speaker, the reset and turbo switches, and any LEDs on the front panel. The number, location and variety of these cabled connectors depend upon whether you have these options displayed on the outside of your PCs case...though all PCs have a plug and wires for the speaker.

Remember that you won't be able to find most of this stuff on every PC—there are variations. And some motherboards will be greatly obscured by the hard drive and power supply (not to mention any expansion cards you may have). If you need to get access to the motherboard, you may have to yank out a few components. But don't worry, it's not that tough to remove components, and it will make working on the system easier.

Expansion Cards Any expansion cards plug into the slots on the rear of the motherboard. These cards range in length—from those that are very short to those that run the entire depth of your PC. Expansion cards that run the entire depth of your PC are called *full-length* cards. Cards that run only halfway across the PC are called *half-cards*. Cards that are not as tall as conventional cards, called *low-profile cards*, are designed to be installed in cases where case height is limited.

One chip takes a lot less space than a whole card of any currently available size, and the result of this is that expansion cards are shrinking as the years go by. Figure 4.16 shows the locations of an expansion card relative to other items in the PC.

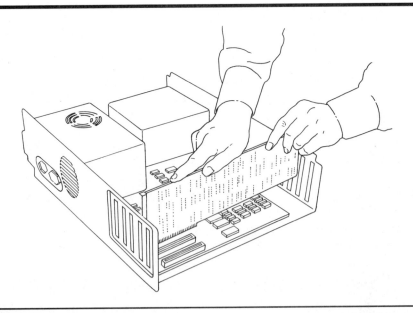

FIGURE 4.16: Inserting an expansion card

The most important element holding a card in place is the slot in the motherboard into which it is plugged. This slot also serves as the card's power source and its line of communication to the PC.

The card is also held in place via its mounting bracket, which attaches to the back of the PC with a screw, and replaces the expansion slot cover on the system unit. Additional connectors for cables may be on the mounting bracket. Through these cables, the card communicates to the outside world.

Nearly every PC has at least two expansion cards. The first is for the video adapter, the second is a combination hard disk/floppy disk controller. Some modern computers actually have the hard disk and video controllers built onto the motherboard to free up slots and improve performance. Local Bus Video controller circuitry, for example, is designed into the motherboard to increase video performance.

The locations of specific cards is not crucial, except that if you have a "slot 8" in your system, you should only put special slot 8 cards into it. And it's a good idea to put 8-bit-only cards into 8-bit slots, rather than waste a 16-bit slot on an 8-bit card.

The hard disk and floppy disk controllers are usually put in the furthest slot to the right—that slot will accommodate the card but not interfere in the space taken up by the hard drive. (If it's a short card, it can go in the far-right slot.) Again, there's no real reason for this, other than that it avoids a long stretch of cables to the disk drives. There's nothing wrong with stringing cables all over, except that it gets messy.

Miscellaneous Parts

There are some miscellaneous items inside your system unit. They're not on the motherboard, they're not part of anything else, and they're not trivial. Several of them are illustrated in Figure 4.17.

The Speaker Computers beep. This means that there has been a connection for the speaker in every PC since day one.

The LED Connectors The LED connectors on your front panel, which originate from the motherboard, indicate that whether power and turbo speed are on, plus whatever else the manufacture may deem important.

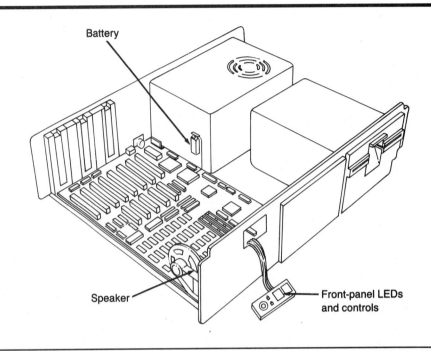

Battery

Speaker

Front-panel LEDs
and controls

FIGURE 4.17: Some miscellaneous parts

In the illustration, the LED connector for your hard drive light comes from the hard disk controller, but it may come from your motherboard depending on your own system's arrangement.

The System's Battery The system battery keeps alive the AT's internal clock, and all the setup information saved in the CMOS memory, when the computer is turned off. The location of the battery varies by manufacturer—often it's stuck just inside the front of the computer case. Sometimes it's clipped on to the motherboard. In a few rare instances the battery might even be soldered to the motherboard.

Anything Else These last several sections have covered all the major tourist attractions inside your PC. But there are other optional things you might find. Anything you see that is not mentioned above is probably particular to your brand of PC.

Tower Configurations

Our discussion of parts has been limited to the desktop configuration that's common to most PCs. There are also floor-standing *tower* models out there. The parts are the same, but the internal arrangement of tower models is a little different from what you might expect. Again, to work on them and upgrade them, you should know what you're looking for and where to find it.

Figure 4.18 shows the major ticket items in a tower-configuration PC. This generic tower model points out the four main items in the PC. Other than those items, everything else, especially the items on the motherboard, will located as it is in desktop PCs.

The Disk Drives The disk drives in a tower model PC are usually located in the upper-front of the tower case, which gives you easy access to them without even bending over. Sometimes a hard drive may be stuck in the middle-center of the back, which is not so easy, but still OK.

The Power Supply The tower PC's power supply is often located in the upper-back of the case. Sometimes it will extend along the entire top of the case if it's a mini-tower case. The On/Off switch extends out through the case wall.

The Motherboard The motherboard is in the lower-rear of the tower case, in the same basic orientation as in a desktop PC. A tower-configuration motherboard may be a lot longer, though, to allow it to fit into the case. Major items on the motherboard are also located in a similar way. (I'll let you in on a secret: it's basically the same motherboard you find in a desktop model, just plugged into a tower case.)

The Expansion Cards The expansion cards are usually located on the motherboard, toward the bottom of the tower PC.

The power supply in a tower model PC is always at the top. This is to ensure the best possible air flow. Heat rises. The air vents in a tower model PC are on the bottom. The heat from the components and air from the vents will rise through the case, drawn up and out by the fan in the power supply.

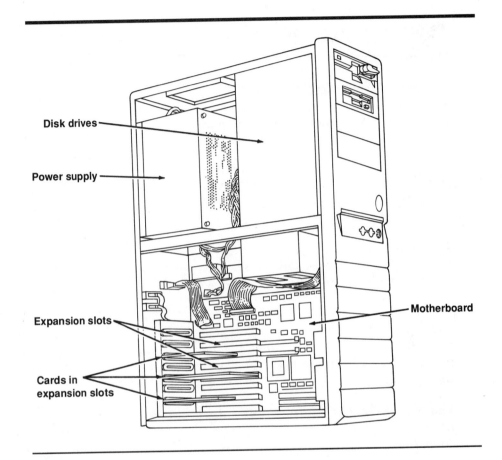

FIGURE 4.18: The tower PC's innards

It is possible to put your desktop model on its side, making it a sort-of home-brew tower model. Purchased floor-mounting brackets will stabilize a desktop model in a tower position. When you place your desktop model on its side, be sure to attend to the following:

◆ Make sure the power supply is at the top of the case, allowing for proper airflow up through the computer.

◆ Some experts say you should have no hard disk problems, or any floppy disk drive problems with your PC
mounted vertically. Others recommend that you format
your hard drive while it's in the vertical position. Still others say you should have the hard drive mounted horizon-
tally (as it is in most tower cases).

My own advice is that if you want a tower model floor-standing
PC, buy one in the first place.

Peripheral Differences

Peripherals are those devices that exist *outside* of your basic system unit,
monitor, and keyboard. Common peripherals include printers and modems; there are other devices you can hook into a PC as well. Thanks to
the PC's open architecture and expansion slots, you can hook up a variety
of devices.

The primary peripheral, your printer, is covered in the following section.
Other peripherals, as well as certain expansion devices, are covered in the
section that immediately follows.

Printers

A printer makes your computer complete. Without it, you'd never be able
to get that valuable "hard copy" printed proof of your electronic efforts—
the permanent copy.

As an upgrade item, the printer is gone over in detail in Chapter 13.
Here, we'll cover background information only. There are five main
printer types:

Dot matrix printers are the most popular and least expensive computer printers. They're rugged and proven, but their text quality is poor.
For basic printing and home use, they can be great bargains.

Impact printers, which are also called daisywheel printers, are basically
typewriters without a keyboard. The daisywheel is a flat circle of characters, like petals on a flower. The printer uses a hammer mechanism to
pound each daisywheel letter through a ribbon to create an image on
paper.

Impact printers used to be popular in the office place. They gave business correspondence a real typewritten look, but they were very expensive, slow, and way too noisy (they sounded as if a small guerrilla war was going on inside the printer). Impact printers became obsolete when inexpensive laser printers became available.

Laser printers are the current leading edge in computer printing technology. Like copy machines, they use a laser beam to create a magnetically charged image on a drum. The drum collects ink in the form of "toner," which sticks to the charged image on the drum. Then the toner is heat-fused to the paper, to create a crisp, near-typeset image of quality.

Plotters aren't really printers, but I've lumped them in here because there's no other place to put them. A plotter makes a hard copy, but does so with a pen and mechanical arm. The mechanical arm moves the pen about, tracing an image onto paper. Instead of a series of dots, you get a smooth line. Some plotters even have more than one pen, allowing for multicolored lines on a page.

Black and color **ink jet printers** represent two special forms of printers. Both squirt ink from a reservoir onto paper. (That's not as messy as it sounds.) The ink printers typically use is one color, and their image is precise—not as good as the new generation of 600 dpi laser printers, but better than most dot matrix printers. They're also just about the quietest printers you can buy.

The Printer Unit Inside of the printer unit (the main "body" of the printer) will be the printing mechanism and the gears that pull the paper through the printer. In addition, ROMs and controls are used for creating the printed image, RAM for storing characters and fonts, and other electrical items.

Inside the printer, or sometimes on the back of its case, you may find a tiny row of DIP switches that are used to configure the printer for different computer environments. (You can hook up a printer to virtually any type of computer.) The DIP switches also set such things as the communications rate and the basic printer mode.

 There are no user-serviceable parts inside the printer. If there are any expansion options, they usually plug into easily accessible ports or slots on the outside of the printer.

The Control Panel Every printer has a control panel, through which some of its features are accessed. The basic control, which sets the printer either to ready-to-print or to a special off-line control mode, is the On-Line control. Other controls may include a Form Feed and Line Feed to advance the paper through printer. More advanced printers may have controls to set the pitch, character size, and font, or to perform diagnostics. Lights and LEDs on the control panel will indicate the printer's status and any errors.

The Feeding Mechanism In a dot matrix printer, the feeding mechanism usually brings paper into the printer, lines up the paper for printing, and then gets the paper out of the printer. The various types of feeding mechanisms include: pin feeds, which push the paper through the printer; tractor feeds, which pull the paper through the printer; a platen knob, which works like a typewriter's platen to hold the paper in place (very obsolete these days); and sheet feeders, which hold a bin of sheet-sized paper and feed each sheet individually. Bin sheet feeders allow you to use typing paper if you can get away with that paper quality, so sheet feeding printers are becoming popular.

Ribbons, Toners, or Ink Packs Ribbons, toners, or ink packs are basic printer supplies—you'll use one or another of these, depending on the type of printer you have. Dot matrix and impact printers require ribbon cartridges that you drop into your printer. Handy (but expensive) toner cartridges slide into a laser printer's gut. Ink packs hold a reservoir of ink for use by black and color ink jet printers.

The printer is an invaluable device, but one that isn't readily upgraded. You can (and should), however, perform routine maintenance on your printer if you expect it to live a long and happy life. Maintenance, minor repair, and troubleshooting tips are offered in Chapter 13 of this book, which covers the printer.

Other Peripherals

In addition to the big ticket peripheral, your printer, there are dozens of devices you can hook up to your computer. We'll just talk about a few here.

Mouse A mouse is a pointing device, popularized by the Macintosh computer. It slides around on your desktop and its movements are mimicked

on the screen. The mouse has buttons, which you use to select items on the screen. Generally this offers superior control over graphics programs and in special computer environments.

The mouse plugs into one of your PC's serial ports, with a specific "mouse card" that plugs into its own expansion slot or a built-in port similar to the keyboard connector. Other mouse-like devices include light pens, and graphics tablets that allow the user to use a stylus to "write" on the screen.

Modem A modem allows you to use the phone system to dial up another computer—one that also has a modem—which answers the phone. Modems can be an external peripheral, in which case they're connected to your PC via the serial port. Otherwise, modems are internal, plugged into an expansion slot.

Scanners A scanner is a handy device that "reads" a page of text or graphics and sends that information to your computer. Scanners often come with software that allows you to manipulate and use the graphics in your desktop publishing or design applications. Scanners that read text require special character-recognition software to translate the scanned text into "real" text that you can manipulate in your computer.

Scanners either plug into their own special adapter card, or an SCSI interface card. The SCSI interface card allows you to connect a variety of peripherals to your PC, including hard drives and printers.

Full-Motion Video Full-motion video cards are used to bring NTSC (cable-TV quality) graphics and sound into your PC. A full-motion video card takes data from your hard drive, or from an NTSC source like a VCR or video camera, and displays it on your computer's screen. You can even buy and install a small card in your computer that will allow you to watch cable TV in its own window on your screen for about $200.

Synthesizers Using a special interface card called a MIDI (Musical Instrument Digital Interface), you can hook up a synthesizer and a number of electronic instruments to your PC, giving you the electronic equivalent of a full orchestra.

Computers have been used for years in the music industry. But now the technology is available more widely, allowing many home users to write their own musical compositions.

Sound Cards The 1990s have brought us a great selection of sound resources, beginning with 16-bit audio cards for playing CD-quality sound through our PCs and ending who-knows-where! Sound cards often come with MIDI software, display-based graphical sound-source-mixing software, and the ability to send sound through an external set of speakers or your stereo. A sound card is also a *must* for any serious computer game player.

Joysticks The joystick, an age-old favorite for the computer-game-playing public, can be hooked into a PC using what's called an A/D (Analog-to-Digital) port. IBM's original documentation listed the A/D port as designed for "scientific" and real-world hardware applications. But the only thing ever plugged into it has been a joystick for playing games.

Networks Hooking up a PC network seems to be a popular thing to do, especially now with the advent of peer-to-peer networking with software products like Windows for Workgroups and LANtastic. In a busy office where the sharing of computer information is important, having network communications between PCs really makes things run more easily. In order to support the network—which is in itself one big computer—you need to install a network adapter card into your PC, plus a lot of extra cables outside the back.

Other Devices It would be impossible to name here *all* of the devices peripheral to a computer—a few more are covered in Chapter 10, which deals with expansion cards.

Expansion Items

Some "peripherals" aren't really peripherals. Instead, they're extensions of what you already have in your PC. Though these are really rather odd-ball items, occasionally you may come across a PC that has one of the following—or you may want to upgrade to using one of these peripherals.

A Second Monitor or a Large-Screen Monitor The PC's hardware has always been able to support two monitors, though few users install two. In PC/XT systems, there are DIP switch settings for installing two monitors. For AT systems, you have to consult your video hardware manual to see what must be done if you want to use two monitors.

About the biggest hassle in having two monitors is knowing where on your desk to place the second one.

External Drives Some older PCs had a problem in that the case and the power supply were too small to allow you to upgrade at all. Even today, PC users with demanding hard-drive-storage needs will sometimes have to add drives outside of the case, each drive having its own power supply.

Both floppy drives and hard drives can be mounted externally. The mounting kit for an external drive holds the drive, plus its power supply. A connecting cable hooks the drive to a controller card inside the PC.

An Expansion Unit Since the first PC had only five expansion slots, quite a few people ran out of slots when they upgraded their system. One solution was to buy an expansion unit, which was basically shaped like a system unit without the motherboard and disk drives.

Expansion units contain a row of expansion slots plus a power supply. One of the expansion slots connects to a card in the main system unit. Via that card, the PC treats the expansion unit as if it were more slots in the PC. You can add cards, more disk drives, and what-have-you in the expansion unit.

You don't see expansion units much any more. Today's PCs include more than enough room for internal disk drives and expansion cards.

● Committing Surgery

There's nothing scary here. In fact, the primary purpose of this section is to tell you how to remove your PC's cover. You will not be taking your entire computer apart now. While that might be fun, there's little practicality in it now. Just getting the lid off and back on again is enough.

You're going to be doing some work in this section, so set out your tools and get ready for hands-on adventure.

Before you get started, note the following:

◆ This is a demonstration. You'll be making no permanent changes to your system, and nothing you do here is going to affect the way your computer works. As long as you follow the instructions, you'll be OK.

◆ To avoid trouble, you'll unplug your PC from the wall before you even lift a screwdriver. If there's no possibility of power coming into your PC, then you won't mess anything up—including yourself. You will be in no danger.

◆ You should really follow along. You may be tempted to "read only" this material. While reading-before-doing is always highly recommended, you should actually take the steps outlined here to remove your PC's case. You'll learn more if you do.

General Strategy

As we take the basic steps for each of the upgrades described in this package, it will be assumed that you've already removed the cover of your PC (which is what we're describing) and are ready to work.

You'll need a general strategy—a plan involving a series of events and a mental checklist—to use as you upgrade, install, or remove something from your computer.

Here are eleven strategic points in a checklist, which represents the basic steps for performing surgery on your PC:

1. Read before doing

2. Power down

3. Unplug the computer

4. Create a work space

5. Get your tools

6. Take the PC's cover off

7. Install/upgrade/remove the item in question

8. Test the PC's configuration (optional)

9. Put the PC's cover back on

10. Plug it in

11. Boot

Read Before Doing

Before you even think about lifting a screwdriver, check out the related section in this book on what it is you're about to do. From the diagrams in this chapter and elsewhere, you should get a rough idea of where everything is and how to find things. *Always read over a description of what you're going to do before trying it.* Familiarity with instructions is very important.

Power Down

Powering down your system involves more than just shutting off the power switch. Before you perform a hardware upgrade, you should do each of the following:

1. Save any data in any programs you're working on.

2. Back up important data, or the entire hard drive.

3. Park the heads on your hard drive if necessary

4. Turn off any peripherals, printers, monitors, modems, etc.

5. Unplug the PC.

Consider the above to be a checklist. Make sure you've taken each step—especially Step 2. Should anything happen to the hard drive, you want to have a duplicate sitting around.

Even if the upgrade you're going to do involves memory or something seemingly unrelated to the hard drive, BACK IT UP. This doesn't have to be an entire hard disk backup; you can back up just the most important data files (at your own risk, of course).

Unplug the Computer

This is a separate step because it's so important. Unplug the computer from the wall. Then unplug the cord from the power supply. This will save you if some bozo sees the cord unplugged and decides to "do you a favor" by plugging it in. (This has happened to me more than once.)

Create a Work Space

You're going to need some elbow room to work on your PC. Clean away that pile of papers that naturally accumulates around all computers. Move the monitor and keyboard to one side, or move some peripherals, if you have to.

Get Your Tools

Each upgrade in this book requires little more than a screwdriver. But in some cases, specific tools are required. You should set out all your tools (you'll be told which tools you'll need in the section of this book dedicated to doing the job) and get them ready for work.

Take the PC's Cover Off

After you unplug the system (and provide yourself with some elbow room) remove the PC's lid. Once that's off, you're ready to work on your computer's innards.

Install/Upgrade/Remove the Item in Question

This is where you make the change. Everything inside the PC screws, snaps, or slides in place, but you may still have some work to do. Some PCs are jammed full of stuff, so getting to where you want to go will take time. This is where you use your "patience" tool.

Test the PC's Configuration (Optional)

One recommended step is to plug in the PC and test it with the lid off. You power up and make sure the new hardware device is working properly *before* you put the lid back on. This is a completely safe thing to do *as long as you're careful*. It saves the hassle of repeating steps if you notice something isn't working right.

If everything checks out, you power off again, unplug the system, and re-place the lid. If there's a problem, the computer is open and ready for you to troubleshoot.

Put the PC's Cover Back On

You should reassemble any internal items you've removed, and eventually put the lid back on the PC, screwing it on snugly. You should also reconnect any cables you disconnected when you first took the lid off.

Plug It In

Plug the computer back into the wall socket.

Boot

Turn the power on and watch your computer boot. You've just successfully upgraded your PC!

There's nothing wimpy about calling your dealer, developer, or hardware OEM if you get stuck—the pros do it all the time. Most hardware manufacturers have support lines. Feel free to call a manufacturer if you think you need help.

Taking Your PC's Cover Off

Keeping in mind all the steps outlined in the previous section, here are the instructions for taking your PC apart. Remember, we're only removing the lid at this stage. It's not necessary to plunge into tearing down your entire system at this point.

Remember the other, more general steps we've discussed. Create a work space, move peripherals aside, and so on.... Do these things each time you work on your PC.

HOW TO REMOVE THE PC'S COVER

Procedure: To remove the system unit case

Tools Needed: Screwdriver (matching the screws on the back of your case)

Steps:

1. Power down your PC.

2. Turn off all peripherals.

3. Unplug your computer from both the power supply on the back and the wall socket.

4. Remove the screws on the back of the PC's case. There will be as few as two and as many as six screws. As you remove each screw, set it aside in a convenient yet safe location. Use a small dish if you have one. The point is to not spill and lose the screws into the rug.

5. Remove the PC's lid. The lid slides forward. You'll want to do this slowly and gently, by first grabbing the rear of the lid on the sides of the system unit, and then sliding it forward. Be careful that the top of the lid doesn't snag anything inside the PC. And don't press on the disk drives to push the lid forward.

Once the lid is far enough forward, lift it up and off, as shown in Figure 4.19. The sides of the lid might hook under a metal lip, so you may have to wiggle the lid's sides to bring it free of the PC. Once it's off, set it aside.

 If you notice that the lid still doesn't come off, that may be because your key is locked. That's happened more than once. Be sure the key is in the open position before you slide off the PC's top.

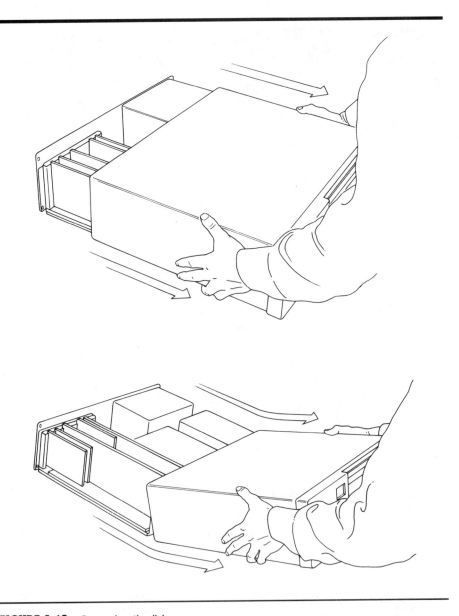

FIGURE 4.19: Removing the lid

That's all there is to taking the lid off your PC. Now let's continue on to bigger and better things.

Hunting Time

Now you have the lid off your PC. (And it wasn't that hard, was it?) Time to scope out the interior and get to know where things are. First, you should find and locate the four major parts of your system unit:

◆ The power supply

◆ The disk drives

◆ The motherboard

◆ Any expansion cards

Next, after hunting down the four biggies, you should take the time to locate the following items on your motherboard:

◆ The microprocessor

◆ The math coprocessor, or an empty socket for one

◆ The BIOS

◆ The expansion slots

◆ RAM

◆ Any proprietary RAM connectors

◆ Various support chips and electrical doo-dads

◆ Any DIP switches

◆ Any jumpers

◆ The power connectors

◆ The keyboard connector

◆ Any LED connectors to the front panel

◆ The speaker

◆ The battery (if you have an AT or 386 system)

◆ Dust

After you're done looking around, put the lid back on your PC.

At this point, it is possible to fire up the PC and use it, although the FCC wouldn't approve. There's nothing in the case that will leap out and shock you; all the dangerous stuff is carefully contained inside the power supply's case. You can even touch the chips while the computer is running. (This is normally done only as an interim step to make sure everything is working properly.)

 If you plug your PC back into the wall and power it up, don't do any of the following:

◆ Spill anything inside the PC

◆ Touch an expansion slot or use a tool on anything metal

◆ Install something with the power on

Other than that, turn off the computer, unplug the power cable and get ready to put the lid on. Remember, PCs are designed to draw in air through a set of intake vents, across the computer's components and then out the fan in the rear of the case. If you run your PC with the case *off*, you may shorten the computer's life or cause premature failure due to heat (and dust) buildup.

Putting Your PC's Cover Back On

Putting the lid back on your PC is the scary part. That's usually when you can encounter a snag—the case will grab and pull a cable from its socket if you're not careful.

 Keep an eye on the right side of the case, where the power supply's On/Off switch is.

HOW TO PUT THE PC'S CASE BACK ON

Procedure: To put the system unit case back on

Tools Needed: Screwdriver, matching the screws on the back of your case

Steps:

1. Position the lid over the case, and line everything up.

2. Gently push the case back. The sides of the case will usually fit under a lip on the bottom of the system unit. Make sure the sides of the case are positioned properly before you push the case back. If you notice the sides bowing a bit, then you probably don't have it on correctly. As you push back, keep an eye on the cables and expansion cards. You don't want to snag one and tear it out. The case should go back nearly all the way. A gentle push on the front of the lid will move it within distance for the screws.

3. Line up the screws with the holes and tighten them back into position. You might want to start with the top center screw, though it's best to start with whichever screw hole is lined up properly.

4. Once all the screws are back in position, reassemble the PC.

5. Put away your tools. (My dad always told me to do this. After I lost five hammers, I learned.)

Put the monitor back on top, rearrange your desk, and get ready to flip the power switch—your surgery is over!

 If the lid doesn't go back all the way— if it stops ½" to 1" short—then the key has probably flopped into the locked position. Make sure it's open and try again.

For some reason, computer case lids don't slide back all the way. You always have to push them a bit to get back that final $\frac{1}{8}$" to the screw holes.

That's really all there is to it. Taking the lid on and off turns out to be simple, which is good because it's the first step in other procedures. For the other hardware upgrades in this book you'll have to perform this step over and over. That's OK, because it's really not that hard.

Now you're ready to roll.

Upgrading Software

This book is about more than just adding new hardware to your system. Upgrading your hardware is only half the equation. Beyond that lies software. After all, it's the software that controls your hardware.

This chapter is about upgrading software, the second half of the PC upgrade equation. There are really two times you'll be upgrading software: 1) when you upgrade it directly, perhaps by installing a newer, improved version of the software or by adding a new software package to your system; and 2) when you upgrade your software to deal with some new piece of hardware you've installed. Both of these are important.

The nice thing about these upgrades is that you don't need a screwdriver. In fact, screwdriving is only a small part of upgrading your PC. Most books just leave you with this knowledge: "Here, pop in these chips and—voilà—your computer has more memory!" Wrong. You still need to configure your PC to deal with the extra memory (which is covered in Chapter 6 on memory). But more importantly, you need to upgrade your software to deal with the memory—or with any other hardware you may add to your PC. That's the subject covered here.

The Evil Twins

We call hardware and software upgrades the "evil twins" here because they play off each other. You just can't ignore the need for a software upgrade following a hardware upgrade—and vice versa. Hardware upgrades prompt software upgrades, and software upgrades prompt hardware upgrades. It's a vicious cycle.

One example concerns memory. You can never be too rich, too thin, or have enough RAM in your PC. Back in the early '80s, having 512K in a PC was ridiculous. Who needed all that memory? But programs quickly swelled to gargantuan proportions, taking advantage of all the RAM—and more—that your PC could hold. So memory upgrades are popular on everyone's PC upgrade list.

New software needs more memory. Even though DOS's "conventional memory" is capped off at 640K, programs still require more. Often the extra memory is configured as extended or expanded memory. (Usually it's expanded memory under DOS.)

Upgrading software and hardware is an interdependent proposition, which is why this chapter on software upgrades is important. Conversely, throughout Part II of this book, you'll see the software side of each hardware upgrade. This is especially true of Chapter 6 on memory. Memory is a major issue in the PC world at present. So having the memory and knowing how to use it are both important parts of upgrading your PC.

Upgrading Software

Upgrading software sounds easy—if not easy, then easier than upgrading hardware. People think nothing about sticking a new program on their hard drive, or typing the famous Microsoft SETUP command at the A:\ prompt, or the equally famous INSTALL command (used by everyone else). But pick up a wrench and install hardware? Forget it!

Software upgrades are the silent half of upgrading your PC. Unlike hardware upgrades, upgrading software isn't as clean cut. There are no common designs, guaranteed-you-can-find-them screw holes, or easily marked slots and sockets for installing software. It's totally up to you to decide where to put the software and how to integrate it into your computer system. Manuals are usually fuzzy on the subject.

While reading through the following sections, keep in mind that DOS makes no rules about software upgrades. Especially with regard to files on a hard drive, all the organization and file maintenance is left up to you. If you'd like to look deeper into the subject, then check out a good book on hard disk management.

Upgrading to Newer Versions of Software

New versions of software come out for several reasons, as detailed here.

Fixed Bugs

Though all software should be bug-free when released, there are always a few things that don't work right. Eventually, through in-house testing or from user complaints, the software developer will track down bugs, fix them, and upgrade the software.

Added Features

Software is an ongoing process. Programmers are always tinkering, adding new features that they didn't have time for in the original release.

Improvements

Improvements to the basic software package also come from program-mers' tinkering. After a while, they think of new ways to do things in the program, better presentation, or just ways of making the application run faster. These are all improvements that make looking into an upgrade worthwhile. And the clue to finding out how dated your software is, or the degree to which it's been upgraded, is via the version number.

Software version numbers have two parts, indicating the major release and the minor release, or update. The major release is listed first, followed by a period, and then the minor release. Increases in the minor release value, such as from 3.6 to 3.7, usually reflect bug fixes, the addition of new features, mouse support, and so on. Major releases, such as from 4.5 to 5.0 to 6.0, typically reflect complete overhauls and major updates (or an attempt by the marketing department to be on a version number par with the competition).

To know whether or not to update, keep an eye on the version numbers. Will any of the fixed bugs help you get work done better? Are the added features things that you really need? And are the improvements worth buying the upgrade? Does the upgrade product maker support current versions of their product for free versus charging for supporting obsolete versions of their software? If so, order the upgrade.

Deciding Not to Upgrade

Before you get all excited and ready to update your software to the latest version, note that updating is an entirely optional thing. You don't have to upgrade, and here are some reasons why.

The Software Does the Job

If you're happy with your application, then great! Keep it and use it. Don't let anyone pressure you into buying more than you use.

You Pay for Features You Don't Need

Suppose the new version/release adds features you don't need. For example, you're a home user and the new version offers network support. Who cares! Maybe the new feature offers improved communications with their GonzoSoft database. If you don't need that, why pay for it?

You Don't Have the Hardware to Support It

New versions of software may want to use memory you don't have. Or they may demand a color display to do the job. Suppose you have a monochrome display and the new version offers support for color printing. Who needs it! Or maybe version 23.7 requires eight megabytes more disk space than you have. If so, fine. Skip it.

Some Cautionary Notes

Now that I have you in a rebellious mood, I want to remind you that at some point, you may be forced into an upgrade. Imagine that you buy a new printer. Unfortunately, your older software was written while the printer's design engineer was a freshman at Cornell. You'll need to up-grade if you want to support that printer. The same holds true for graphics standards. If you're into graphic design and you've just upgraded to the latest graphics display, then you'll need the software to drive it. (It's the old "evil twin" thing again.)

The new software will also give you better integration with other prod-ucts. Sure, this may not seem important now. But consider the benefits of exchanging data: Say you'd like to paste a picture in the middle of your spreadsheet. Or suppose you get into desktop publishing and the package can't read the documents created by your primitive word processor. These are things you may miss when you skip upgrading.

Also, upgrading software keeps you on a par with other users of the soft-ware. Generally speaking, most people do upgrade. If everyone at the of-fice is using GonzoWrite 4.2 and you're still on version 3.5 at home, there are going to be problems. (The opposite is also true: If you upgrade and no one else does, you're the odd duck out.) You should standardize on one common version. And if that means updating, then do it.

Installing New Software

If you're just upgrading older software you own, or if you're installing new applications, you have to take certain steps. These are almost the same steps taken when you disassemble a computer on the hardware side. The only difference is, you keep your computer plugged in and the power on when you install new or updated software.

When you're installing new software, there really are no additional hints you can get other than those provided in the manual. Those hints used to be fairly detailed, letting you know exactly what was happening, about all the files that would be installed or created, and so on. But today, the trend seems to be running some sort of INSTALL or SETUP program that does all the work for you. In fact, the manual's only instructions on the subject are often just "Log on to Drive A and type SETUP." That's not very clear.

The problem is worse when you update software. In that scenario, you're either instructed to install the program all over, meaning you may have two versions on your system. Or you're simply asked overwrite the older files with the new ones. But isn't that a bit much to ask?

Installing a second version of the software seems to make sense for most people—providing you have the room on your hard drive. You can then use either version until you get used to the new one. After that, the old one can be deleted and you can free up the space it used. But again, that's a bit much to ask.

Things to Consider

Whenever you update software on your system, there are several things you may want to keep in mind. This is beyond the gut-wrenching decision of whether or not to upgrade, and the decision about how to do the upgrade. Specifically, the things you should keep in mind are the following.

Updating Your Data Files When you move up to a new version of the software, your old data files are usually compatible and readable by the new software. If not, there should be a conversion program. But the reverse isn't necessarily true: The new data files produced by the latest version of the software will probably not be readable by the older software.

Deleting the Old Version Eventually, you're going to have to remove the old version of the software, once you've completely switched over to the update. This will free up disk space, and prevent you from accidentally reusing the old program (undesirable especially if all your data files are incompatible).

Matching Your Software to Your Hardware Finally, remember any hardware modifications you've made to your system when using the upgrade. For example, suppose your old printer was unknown to the old software. The new software may support it directly. So remember to change your printer driver, and other things about your system including the type of display and any expanded memory you have that the software can take advantage of.

New Software

Beyond upgrading software is adding new software to your system. There are several things you should consider when buying new software, the following of which you should know about even before you pick up the package.

Does It Work with Your Hardware? So many people buy games only to find out that the games won't work on their Hercules monochrome system, or that their 386 computer is just too fast for the game. Read the software requirements on the side of the box before taking the package home and learning the hard way.

How Much Disk Space Does It Take? For upgrading as well, how many megabytes of hard disk storage will the software take? Do you have the room for it? And if you don't have a hard disk, will the software run from floppies only? (Note that if the box says "Hard disk recommended," they're not being kind: You need a hard disk to run the software.)

Do You Have Enough Memory? Memory is crucial for some software packages. Most of the major hitters need the full 640K, plus EMS (expanded memory). If you don't have the memory, then the software will run sluggishly—guaranteed.

Where Are You Going to Put It? Hard disk management and file maintenance are important to running a good hard disk system. DOS makes no rules for the locations of files or how you plan out your subdirectories. Only if you're practicing a good plan, have a decent subdirectory structure, and are using practical organizational skills will upgrading be other than a problem.

Most new software will install itself in its own subdirectory off the root directory. But this isn't good enough for most people. Consider a flexible subdirectory organization. And then, when installing the software, know in advance where you want to put the application. Most INSTALL or SETUP programs give you the option of a drive and subdirectory on which to install the program. Think this out carefully before you blindly place an application right off the root directory.

Working with CONFIG.SYS

There are two parts of DOS that also come into play when you upgrade, or just install, new software. This is beyond using DOS commands (if any) to put the software on your drive. Though sometimes it isn't a required step, some programs insist that you modify your system's CONFIG.SYS file. The second part of DOS you may need to modify is your AUTOEXEC.BAT file, which is covered in the following section.

How CONFIG.SYS Fits In

In the grand scheme of things, CONFIG.SYS is a very important file. Its job is to configure your system (as you might guess from its name). But more important than that, CONFIG.SYS is a file you have direct control over.

CONFIG.SYS is loaded before COMMAND.COM. It has to be, because one of CONFIG.SYS's commands (the SHELL command) is used to specify a location for COMMAND.COM, or an alternative type of command interpreter for DOS. In addition, CONFIG.SYS allocates memory space for files and buffers, which is important to some database and disk-intensive applications, and it sets up other aspects of your system.

One of the neat things about DOS 6 is that it will allow you to skip running the CONFIG.SYS and AUTOEXEC.BAT files, let you run each line in the CONFIG.SYS file as it comes up (and then elect to run or not to run the AUTOEXEC.BAT file). This is done by pressing F5 (to skip CONFIG.SYS altogether) or F8 (to skip through CONFIG.SYS) just after the "Starting MS-DOS" message appears. You can also select a file to run from multiple CONFIG.SYS and AUTOEXEC.BAT files.

CONFIG.SYS and Your Hardware

CONFIG.SYS primarily deals with software. It sets aside memory space for DOS to manipulate files and store information, and it does other things, mostly to assist DOS and customize it for your computer. But that's all software stuff.

On the hardware side, CONFIG.SYS is important in that it allows you to install device drivers. Device drivers are special software programs that allow your PC to interface with some alien device, not a normal part of the computer's BIOS or a piece of hardware known by DOS.

For example, one of the most common device drivers found in a CONFIG.SYS file is MOUSE.SYS, the mouse driver. A computer mouse is a new, alien device to most PCs. In order to let your software interface with the mouse, you must load a mouse driver. It's through the driver's software that your applications can locate, monitor, and manipulate the mouse. To make all that happen, the mouse driver is loaded via a DEVICE command in your CONFIG.SYS file, something like:

```
DEVICE = C:\MOUSE\MOUSE.SYS
```

Other drivers are specified in CONFIG.SYS to control other hardware devices: The ANSI.SYS screen driver can be used to give you colorful DOS prompts and text files; the common EMS driver is used to control an expanded memory card in many PCs; a CD-ROM driver is used to interface the computer with a CD-ROM drive; and the list goes on.

Note that some drivers also have a .COM version. This is a memory-resident version of the device driver, usually loaded via AUTOEXEC.BAT rather than CONFIG.SYS. The choice of using the .SYS or .COM driver in CONFIG.SYS or AUTOEXEC.BAT is up to you, though it's recommended you use the .SYS version because it's automatic, loads the driver into conventional memory (or optional upper memory) and generally uses less memory than the .COM version.

The Software Side

CONFIG.SYS's DEVICE and DEVICEHIGH commands are geared toward certain hardware upgrades. But aside from that, everything else that goes on in CONFIG.SYS is designed to customize DOS to your computer system. CONFIG.SYS can be used to load memory-resident programs (DOS version 4 only), and it can also set up RAM disks and print spoolers, using the proper commands. But that's still basic DOS, not really related to any software upgrade you may perform.

If you're installing hardware and it comes with a software INSTALL program, it may make changes to CONFIG.SYS, primarily to install the device driver with some optional parameters. Other times, the hardware installation procedure may only contain instructions in the manual for modifying CONFIG.SYS. (This is covered below.)

Some INSTALL programs will modify CONFIG.SYS to comply with the application's appetite. The smarter of these INSTALL programs will check your CONFIG.SYS to see if you already have enough FILES and BUFFERS allocated. If not, the program will make the adjustments itself. Other programs may simply suggest the FILES and BUFFERS sizes, leaving it up to you to allocate them.

Making Changes to CONFIG.SYS

Sometimes the manual will request that you yourself make changes to CONFIG.SYS, either to change the FILES and BUFFERS values, or to add a DEVICE driver.

Some INSTALL programs will modify CONFIG.SYS. A lot of people, power users mostly, really hate that. They want to do it themselves. After all, IN-STALL programs aren't the most intelligent software applications on the planet. They could botch up the order of a carefully created CONFIG.SYS file, leaving you to patch it up later. If (or when) that happens, or if you're forced to do it yourself, you'll need to modify your CONFIG.SYS file.

CONFIG.SYS, with all its power and priority, is only a text file. It's kept in the root directory of your boot disk. You can make changes to it using a word processor or text editor. But in order for the changes to have effect, you need to reset the system.

If CONFIG.SYS already exists, you can edit it using a plain text editor (like DOS's EDLIN) or your word processor in the text or ASCII mode. This is also the way you can create CONFIG.SYS if your system currently lacks it. Just remember to save the file in the plain text (or ASCII) mode if you're using your word processor.

As long as you know in advance what it is you want to change, altering CONFIG.SYS isn't a problem. It normally sits there and does its job without you needing to perform constant adjustment. Only when you add new hardware or software that requires a CONFIG.SYS modification will you need to change anything. And then remember to reboot to make the changes take effect.

Working with AUTOEXEC.BAT

In the normal scheme of things, AUTOEXEC.BAT is used to run initialization programs and commands that you'd normally type each time you start your computer. AUTOEXEC.BAT does them automatically.

AUTOEXEC.BAT is a batch file, as noted by its .BAT file name extension. A batch file is a text file on disk that contains a list of DOS commands, plus special batch file directives. When you type the name of the batch file at the DOS prompt, the commands in the batch file are executed—exactly as if you had entered the commands yourself.

Quite a few software packages may make modifications to your AUTO-EXEC.BAT file when they install. The most common modification is putting the application's subdirectory on your search path. (The search path is set by the PATH command and contains a list subdirectories in which you'd like DOS to search for programs.)

If you're running a good hard disk system, then your path is probably well thought out and doesn't need every new application tacking itself onto it. In fact, having more than three subdirectories on your path is a bad idea; it slows down the system as DOS searches through each subdirectory on the path for whatever you type at the command prompt.

Other items you might want to set in AUTOEXEC.BAT when installing software are as follows.

Memory-Resident Software

Some applications are memory resident, meaning they're loaded into memory and stay there until you "pop" them up. Memory-resident programs are typically loaded by AUTOEXEC.BAT. So to take advantage of any memory-resident software you may install, you should modify AUTO-EXEC.BAT to load it for you automatically.

Setting Environment Variables

Some software relies upon environment variables to function. These variables are created using the SET command. For example, if the GonzoCom communications package needs to have the WHERE variable set to GonzoCom's subdirectory, you could put the following in your AUTO-EXEC.BAT file:

```
SET WHERE=C:\COMM\GONZO
```

Running Software Directly

A final way to end your AUTOEXEC.BAT file is to have it automatically run whatever software you normally run first thing in the morning. For example, if you constantly log to your WordPerfect subdirectory and run WordPerfect first thing in the morning, you can put those commands at the tail end of AUTOEXEC.BAT, letting the computer do it for you:

```
CD \WP
WP
```

Another item to stick into AUTOEXEC.BAT may be some type of calendar or schedule program. The program could pop-up and remind you of important appointments and necessary phone calls for the day—even before dumping you out to the DOS prompt.

All this can be put into an AUTOEXEC.BAT file, which makes it one of the handiest files you can have on your PC. Like CONFIG.SYS, you can create or edit AUTOEXEC.BAT using a text editor or word processor. If you use a word processor, remember to save AUTOEXEC.BAT back to disk in the text or ASCII mode.

Running Batch Files

AUTOEXEC.BAT isn't the only batch file that can assist you with new—or any—software on your system. Batch files, which are basically a series of DOS commands stored in a text file, can help you run all your software. They provide assistance in the following ways:

◆ Setting environment variables

◆ Changing to the proper subdirectories

◆ Specifying command line options

Running Programs in a Certain Order

Some applications are quite straightforward to run. You simply type the name of the program on the DOS command line and there it is. But other applications require additional setup, such as mentioned in the steps above. When that's the case, you can combine all those setup steps into a batch file for convenient execution.

Like AUTOEXEC.BAT, all batch files are plain vanilla text files on disk—but with a .BAT file name extension. To create them, you can use a text editor, such as DOS's EDLIN, or a word processor in the text mode. You then type all the commands you normally use to start a program, and save it off to disk.

For example, suppose you always enter the following when you start your word processor:

```
CD \WP
WP
```

Those two commands can be placed into a batch file, WP.BAT. Typing WP.BAT is a single step that replaces the two steps above. Any additional setup required could also be specified in the WP.BAT file. Here is an example:

```
CD \MEMRES\GRAMMAR
GRAMPOP  /TSR
CD \WP
WP
CD \MEMRES\GRAMMAR
GRAMPOP  /REMOVE
```

This fictitious batch file first logs to the subdirectory \MEMRES\GRAM-MAR where the GRAMPOP program is loaded. Assume GRAMPOP is a memory-resident grammar-checking utility, and the /TSR switch loads it into memory. From there, your word processing program is run as normal. But once you quit the word processor, you return to GRAMPOP's subdirectory to unload it from memory. All these steps are accomplished via one batch file.

To make this system truly effective, the name of the batch file subdirectory is placed on the system's search path. When you type the name of a program or file at the command line, DOS will first look for the file in the current directory, and then it will look in the directories listed in the search path. If all your applications are run via batch files and those batch files are in a subdirectory on the search path, then you can run any application from any subdirectory simply by typing its batch file name.

Upgrading Hardware

Upgrading your hardware has a more limited impact than software upgrades. The hardware upgrade usually only requires you to change your CONFIG.SYS or AUTOEXEC.BAT file. A minor adjustment to some of your software may be in order to recognize the new hardware. But it's nothing major.

Software, on the other hand, usually demands a lot from the hardware. If you were to make every hardware upgrade possible to get the most from your software, you'd be maxing out your credit card every day of the year. So consider that these hardware-prompted software upgrades are little tamer than upgrading software directly.

Hardware-Prompted Software Upgrades

There are times when you'll want to fix up your software to match the capabilities of your new hardware. These upgrades can be broken down into five categories:

◆ Taking advantage of extra memory

◆ New video standards

◆ New printers

◆ Disk drives

◆ Other stuff

This just about covers it. Only esoteric things such as the power supply or keyboard require no attention on the software side of the equation. But for all the major stuff, there are software tunes and tweaks you may have to perform. The reason for all this is to get the most out of your hardware and your investment in the computer. (Remember, it's the software that controls the hardware—not the other way around.)

Taking Advantage of Extra Memory

Memory is on everyone's mind, including your computer's. To find out how much you need memory, consider life without it. It's common for today's word processors to contain spell checkers, document proofreaders, an online thesaurus, support for math, columns, graphics, and on and on. That wasn't possible a few years ago. And it isn't possible today without enough memory. Things such as networking, laser printers, and advanced graphics were all considered impossible on personal computers years ago. But thanks to heaps of memory (and the microprocessors that can take advantage of it), all of that is considered commonplace today.

Setting Up a RAM Disk, Print Spooler, or Disk Cache Extra memory can be put to use in the form of a RAM disk, print spooler, or disk cache. These three handy devices expand the capabilities of your system and use that extra memory.

The RAM disk is an electronic version of a floppy drive. It's a lot faster than a floppy (or hard) drive, and it takes advantage of any extra memory you may have in your system. To set one up, install the RAM disk's device driver either in CONFIG.SYS or AUTOEXEC.BAT. DOS comes with a RAM disk driver called RAMDRIVE (sometimes called VDISK), though other, faster RAM disk device drivers are available.

A print spooler is an area of memory designed to store characters you send to the printer. The printer is the slowest part of any computer system. Normally when you print, you and the PC sit around and wait for the printer. But with a print spooler installed, characters go to the spooler's memory rather than wait for the printer. The spooler is usually memory resident and feeds characters off to the printer while you're doing something else. Kiss waiting for the printer good-bye!

Finally, a disk cache is a large data buffer (a storage area) for your hard drive. Information read from disk is duplicated and saved in memory (the cache). If you need to read that same information again, it's read from the cache memory instead of disk. This greatly speeds things up, especially since some 60 to 90% of all disk activity is rereading the same information.

Other Uses for Extra Memory If you've just installed extra memory in your system, especially in the form of EMS memory, then you should go back and recheck all your applications' manuals to see if any of them support EMS. You may be surprised to find that quite a few do.

For most programs, they'll automatically detect the extra memory and immediately put it to use. Other programs may require you to set an optional switch, or run a SETUP program (or install it all over again) to use the extra memory. Remember that you can use a batch file to run the application if all it requires to recognize extra memory is an optional switch.

Disk Drives

Upgrading disk drives is a popular upgrade, but it lacks some of the software implications found in upgrading memory. The PC can support two floppy drives innately. If you add any more, such as external drives, you

might need to specify a software driver for them in your CONFIG.SYS file. This is usually done by the DRIVER.SYS device driver.

DRIVER.SYS was written to support external drives. Sometimes you can get away with having extra drives simply by tossing the right DIP switches, or setting jumpers on a multiple floppy drive controller card. But if DOS doesn't recognize the drive, or if it only formats the drive to 360K, then DRIVER.SYS can be used.

What DRIVER.SYS does is give a drive letter and specifications for the floppy drive to DOS. The format, as it sits in your CONFIG.SYS file, is:

```
DEVICE=pathname\DRIVER.SYS /D:ddd
[/T:ttt][/S:ss][/H:hh][/C][/N][/F:f]
```

Pathname is the drive and subdirectory location of the DRIVER.SYS file. DRIVER.SYS itself must be followed by the /D switch and the number of the drive (as *ddd* above). The drive number ranges from 0 through 255 and it indicates the physical location of the drive. Drive 0 is really your A drive, and drive 1 is drive B.

The remaining values for DRIVER.SYS are optional. But they can be used in certain circumstances to force DOS into recognizing a drive's full formatted capacity.

For example, if you install a 720K 3½" drive as your drive B in a PC/XT, DOS will only recognize it as a 360K drive. Why? Because it expects drive B to be 360K. (AT and 386 users can specify the size via the SETUP program.) To remedy the situation, the DEVICE command is used in CONFIG.SYS as follows:

```
DEVICE=\DRIVER.SYS /D:1 /T:80 /S:9 /H:2 /F:2
```

This command tells DOS that drive B (/D:1) is really a 720K drive. The /T:80 switch tells DOS that the drive supports 80 tracks (double that of a 360K drive, hence 720K); /S:9 tells DOS the drive supports nine sector tracks; /H:2 indicates the drive has two drive heads; and /F:2 tells DOS that the drive is a 720K device type.

The only drawback to this trick is that DOS still thinks drive B is a 360K 3½" drive. However, a logical "external" drive D is a 720K drive. Just as a single floppy system can have both drive A and drive B in the same place, the logical drive D is your B drive accessed in the 720K mode. I know, it's silly. But it's one of the few ways you can get a 720K drive on a PC/XT.

Other than external drives, the only thing you'll need to worry about when adding drives is formatting and using them. When you add a new hard drive to your system, you'll need to format it using DOS's FORMAT command (since most hard drives come already low-level formatted from their makers). Check out Chapter 9 for more on hard drive upgrades.

Once you get the hard drive formatted, you'll need to concern yourself with subdirectory organization. If you're practicing good hard disk management skills, you should already know how you want to organize your files into subdirectories. Otherwise, the subdirectories should be created as you add new software to the disk.

Others

Any hardware upgrade you do could require that some changes be made on the software side of your PC. For some upgrades or additions, adding a device driver to CONFIG.SYS will do the trick. Other upgrades may require extensive changes to your software, and still others may not affect software at all (superficially).

Keep in mind that the basic task here is to match your software to the hardware in your system. You buy a computer to run software. But when you upgrade, you open up a whole new world of software compatibility. Be sure to check your manuals to see if the new hardware device you've installed is usable by any software you own. If so, then you're really getting your money's worth out of the upgrade. And that's the only good reason for making the upgrade in the first place.

About Memory

If one of the fellows Dorothy met on the Yellow Brick Road had been a personal computer, he might have sung "If I only had more RAM." Of course, the Wizard of Oz would have then handed him a package of SIMMs and this book, and there'd be no story.

This chapter is the first of two about upgrading memory. Why two chapters? Because plugging in chips isn't all there is to a RAM upgrade. What's more important is to know what to do with the memory—how to use it.

What to do with your computer's memory is covered in this chapter. Upgrade instructions follow in the next chapter.

The first part of the chapter deals with general memory concepts, bytes and Ks, how DOS uses memory, and the different types of memory in a PC. The second part tells you how to use software to get the most from the RAM in your computer, even if you're not plugging in chips or SIMMs.

Remember, the nuts-and-bolts memory installation is in the next chapter. You can take advantage of the items covered in this chapter without ever even opening your PC's case.

RAM and the PC

Computer memory is commonly referred to as RAM, which stands for Random Access Memory. RAM is temporary storage, controlled by the PC's microprocessor and used by software to let you create and manipulate information. It's really quite versatile—the more RAM you have, the more your PC can do.

There are many different aspects to RAM, how it's used, and its potential. This chapter will unravel the mystery for you in two sections:

◆ How Memory is Used

◆ Types of Memory

 The terms "RAM" and "memory" refer to the same thing here— they're interchangeable. Don't be confused, or assume they apply to two different things.

How Memory Is Used

Inside your PC, the brain of the operation is the microprocessor. It helps to think of the microprocessor as a high-speed calculator. A calculator, however, has nowhere to put the results it calculates. So extra storage is needed. That storage comes in two flavors:

◆ Temporary storage

◆ Permanent storage

Both of these types of storage can be referred to as "memory," but one is RAM and the other is disk storage.

RAM is temporary storage—when you turn the power off, the contents of RAM are lost. So to complement RAM, permanent storage on floppy and hard disks is used. Information saved to "disk memory" isn't erased when you turn off the computer's power. It's stored permanently.

Bytes and Kilobytes

When speaking about computer storage, the term "byte" is used as the basic unit of information. To understand memory, you'll need to know that term, as well as two others: *kilobyte* and *megabyte*.

What Is a Byte? All computer memory is measured in bytes—but what *is* a byte? In plain English, you can consider a byte a *character*: a letter of the alphabet, symbol, punctuation mark, or any other single character. The word "byte" is four bytes long—it contains four characters, and so it would be stored in four bytes of computer memory.

The Kilobyte Just as inches are grouped into feet, yards, and miles, bytes are further grouped into kilobytes and megabytes. These are convenient terms used to describe a lot of memory storage. A *kilobyte*, or "K," is 1,024 bytes. Since computers deal with binary digits—base 2—1,024 is the closest power of 2 to 1,000 (2^{10} = 1,024), and K is the common abbreviation for 1,000. So when you say 1K, you're referring to 1,024 bytes, or about half-a-page of written text.

1K = 1,024 bytes.

Megabytes The *megabyte*, abbreviated "MB," represents about one million bytes, or exactly 1,024K. In bytes that's 1,024 x 1,024, or 1,048,576 bytes, or characters, of information. (For comparison purposes, one megabyte is approximately twice the number of characters used in this book.)

1MB = 1,024K or 1,048,576 bytes.

Computer memory storage has blossomed in the past several years. So the terms K (kilobyte) and MB (megabyte) are commonly used to refer to RAM or hard disk storage. Remember, one K is 1,204 bytes, and one MB is 1,024K, or about one million bytes.

Memory Basics

When you speak about memory, there are three basic items you should know:

- ◆ How memory is linked to the design of the microprocessor
- ◆ That memory is contiguous

◆ The differences between RAM and ROM

These three topics are covered in the following sections.

Memory, the Microprocessor, and Address Space The amount of memory a computer can use is related to the design of its microprocessor. The amount of memory a microprocessor can take advantage of is referred to as its *address space*. For example, the 8080 microprocessor, common in many older CP/MB computers, could address 64K.

The first IBM PC used an 8088 microprocessor. It could address up to 1,024K, or 1MB, of RAM. That seemed like a lot, especially when compared to the tiny 64K of the CP/MB computers. But today, it's a joke.

To keep all PCs compatible, they must still abide by the old 8088's 1MB address space. This puts limitations on today's microprocessors, which have far larger address spaces. For example, even though an 80286 microprocessor can address up to 16 megabytes of memory, and an 80386 can address up to 4,096 megabytes, they must still limit themselves to 1MB to be PC- and DOS-compatible.

Contiguous Memory Other than the 1MB limit on a PC's usable RAM under DOS, you should also know that memory in a PC is *contiguous*. That 1MB of RAM goes from address 0 all the way up through 1MB. (Though not all of it is RAM, which will be discussed in a moment.)

You can't have "holes" in a PC's RAM. It must start at memory location 0 and increase from there without skipping any memory locations.

It helps to think of your PC's memory as bricks stacked on top of each other. Each brick is a "bank" of memory. You start on the bottom and work your way up. You can't stack a block on top of air.

Why is this important to know? Because when you upgrade your PC's RAM, you must do so from low memory locations to high. If your PC only has 256K and you want 512K, you must add the extra 256K on top of the first, and so on, until you system will hold no more. *Memory must be placed into the machine in a contiguous manner.* There can be no holes. Likewise, you can't overlap memory—that would lead to conflicts (and POST errors).

RAM and ROM Finally, there are really two types of memory in a computer: RAM and ROM.

RAM stands for Random Access Memory. It's what we commonly refer to as computer memory, used by the microprocessor to both read and write information. RAM is temporary storage.

ROM is Read-Only Memory. It works a lot like RAM, but it cannot be written to—it's permanent. ROM is accessed like RAM. It stores information. But the information can only be read (hence "read-only"). And the contents of ROM are not lost when the power is turned off.

Computers use ROM for a variety of purposes. The PC's BIOS, its innate instructions and low-level routines, are stored on a ROM chip. The video controller for EGA and VGA graphics is stored in a special ROM chip, as is your hard disk controller.

The Memory Map It was the job of the PC's original designers to divide the 8088's address space up into RAM and ROM locations. What they did was to take the 1,024K of address space and divide it up into 16 64K chunks. Each 64K chunk is called a "bank" of memory, and they were numbered bank "0" through "9," and then "A" through "F."

Figure 6.1 shows a PC's memory map, and illustrates the locations of RAM and ROM in a typical IBM compatible computer.

Banks 0 through 9 are designated for RAM. Banks A through F are reserved for special RAM locations, such as video display memory, and ROM (such as your PC's BIOS and the hard drive controller). Other locations, not currently used, are marked "reserved" by IBM. For example, Bank "E" is used for ROM in their PS/2 systems. But most PCs leave these areas untouched.

Upgrading Memory—A History

To add memory to a PC on an expansion card you need to know two things:

♦ How much memory is on the expansion card

♦ Where the memory will start

Remember, the PC's memory can have no holes (it must be contiguous). So if you have 64K on the expansion card, you must add it starting at 64K (the amount on the motherboard). The computer will then have a total of 128K of RAM—contiguous from memory locations 0 through 128K. Of that, 64K is on the motherboard, and 64K is on the expansion card.

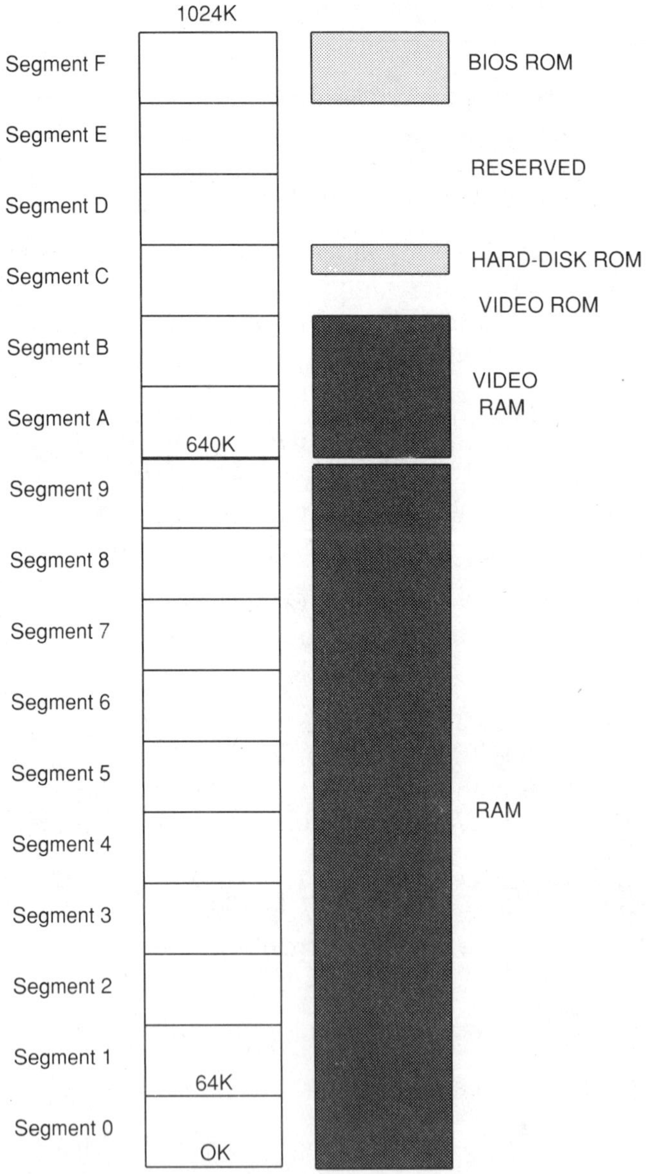

FIGURE 6.1: A PC memory map

There are three things working together to make up RAM in the PC:

- ◆ The RAM on the motherboard
- ◆ Any extra RAM on expansion cards
- ◆ DIP switches

Presently, most PC/ATs come with 1MB of RAM already on the motherboard. If not, you can upgrade by adding chips or changing SIMMs directly on the motherboard. But ATs aren't getting any benefits from that extra RAM under DOS. As a PC-compatible system, AT and 386 computers can use only 640K of their megabyte of RAM for DOS. The rest of memory is either ignored or used as "shadow RAM," which means that the contents of the BIOS and other ROMs (from memory locations 640K to 1,024K) are copied to RAM to make them run faster. These configuration options are usually set via the SETUP program and they can make some systems run a lot faster.

Some AT systems incorporate some type of *proprietary* memory expansion system. This system isn't an expansion card, but rather an extension of the motherboard's memory.

The 80386 and higher microprocessor runs at a full 32-bits, as opposed to the 16-bits of the 80286 and 8088/86 PCs. To take advantage of that, some 386 computer designs have used a special 32-bit memory slot into which fast (and compatible) memory can be installed, rather than arranging for the motherboard to handle the added memory in SIMMs mounted on the motherboard. While you still can use standard expansion cards to boost a 386's memory, it won't run as fast or as well as memory installed in the proprietary slot or in SIMMs on the motherboard.

The current maximum for memory in most AT and 386 systems is between 8MB and 128MB. This is based on the design of the motherboard, and it doesn't reflect the actual memory that can be used by the systems, or the fact that DOS still ignores all memory beyond the 1MB limit of an 8088, and will only run programs in the bottom 640K of that memory. You can buy motherboards that will handle 64MB in 4MB SIMMs. It's really a question of how much you want to spend on the motherboard and the added SIMMs in order to utilize that capacity.

How DOS Uses Memory

DOS uses memory to load programs. Further, programs use memory to store their data. In the normal course of events, DOS itself will use anywhere from 40K to 90K of your basic 640K of RAM. The rest of memory can be used by your programs. Usually, all the memory is used by only one program. However, you can take advantage of memory resident software or "program switchers" to have more than one application in memory at a time. Both programs can't *run* at the same time (not directly under DOS), but you can have access to them.

There are two DOS commands you can use to check on the amount of memory in your system. The first command is CHKDSK, which looks for lost or "busted up" files, and attempts to fix them if any are found. When CHKDSK is done, it also (for some reason) displays the amount of memory in your system. For example, if at the C:\ prompt when you type CHKDSK, you'll see something like:

```
G:\DOS\chkdsk

  124633088 bytes total disk space
       8192 bytes in 1 hidden files
    1105920 bytes in 132 directories
   83460096 bytes in 1872 user files
   40050688 bytes available on disk

       8192 bytes in each allocation unit
      15214 total allocation units on disk
       4889 available allocation units on disk

     655360 total bytes memory
     430112 bytes free
```

Here DOS 6's CHKDSK displays information about the disk—its volume label, the date the disk was formatted, information on the disk space and number of files, and then—at the end of the list—memory information. According to the output, this PC has 655,360 bytes of memory total, of which 430,112 bytes are free. The rest is used by DOS (or any memory resident programs).

The second command to deal with memory is DOS's MEM. Unlike CHKDSK, which displays memory information as an aside, MEM displays all sorts of good information about memory. (MEM is available if you have DOS 4 or higher.)

With DOS 6, at the C:\ prompt, you can type **MEM**, and the MEM utility will produce output like the following:

```
G:\MEM

Memory Type        Total =  Used  +  Free
---------------    ------   ------   ------
Conventional        640K     220K     420K
Upper               155K     155K      0K
Adapter RAM/ROM     384K     384K      0K
Extended (XMS)    15205K   14181K    1024K
---------------   ------   ------   ------
Total memory      16384K   14940K    1444K

Total under 1 MB   795K     375K     420K

Largest executable program size    420K   (429824 bytes)
Largest free upper memory block      0K       (0 bytes)
MS-DOS is resident in the high memory area.
```

This shows you the maximum memory in your system, the amount *free* (available), and the largest program size you can load (which is really the total amount available). Below the Adapter RAM/ROM item are values showing the amount of extended or expanded memory (if any) available.

MEM also has optional switches: The /DEBUG switch lists the same information, but includes additional details describing how memory is used. The following listing shows the output of DOS 6's MEM command with the /DEBUG switch:

```
Conventional Memory Detail:
Segment    Total               Name       Type
-------    --------------      --------   ------
00000        1039    (1K)                 Interrupt Vector 00040
271     (0K)                   ROM Communication Area
00050         527    (1K)                 DOS Communication Area
00070        9960    (3K)                 IO System Data
                                  CON      System Device Driver
                                  AUX      System Device Driver
                                  PRN      System Device Driver
                                  CLOCK$   System Device Driver
                                  A: - F:  System Device Driver
                                  COM1     System Device Driver
                                  LPT1     System Device Driver
                                  LPT2     System Device Driver
                                  LPT3     System Device Driver
```

```
                                COM2        System Device Driver
                                COM3        System Device Driver
                                COM4        System Device Driver
      00129        5168   (5K)   MSDOS       System Data
      0026C       84000  (82K)   IO          System Data
                   1136   (1K)   XMSXXXX0    Installed Device=HIMEM
                   3104   (3K)   $MMXXXX0    Installed Device=EMM386
                  15280  (15K)   MS$MOUSE    Installed Device=MOUSE
                    112   (0K)   PROTMAN$    Installed Device=PROTMAN
                   4352   (4K)   NET$HLP$    Installed Device=WORKGRP
 9136    (9K)   MS2000$     Installed Device=NE2000
                  42528  (42K)   MSCD001     Installed Device=MTMCDD
                   2080   (2K)   FILES=40
                    256   (0K)   FCBS=4
                    512   (1K)   BUFFERS=40
                   2288   (2K)   LASTDRIVE=Z
                   3008   (3K)   STACKS=9,256
      016EE          80   (0K)   MSDOS       System Program
      016F3        2640   (3K)   COMMAND     Program
      01798          80   (0K)   win386      Data
      0179D        1040   (1K)   COMMAND     Environment
      017DE          96   (0K)   win386      Data
      017E4       30816  (30K)   SR          Program
      01F6A       10944  (11K)   CFPI        Program
      02216         272   (0K)   WIN         Environment
      02227       28816  (28K)   SMARTDRV    Program
      02930       27984  (27K)   MSCDEX      Program
      03005        1408   (1K)   WIN         Program
      0305D         304   (0K)   win386      Environment
      03070       22848  (22K)   win386      Program
      03604         288   (0K)   COMMAND     Data
      03616        2640   (3K)   COMMAND     Program 036BB          1040
 (1K)   COMMAND   Environment
      036FC         288   (0K)   MEM         Environment
      0370E       88608  (87K)   MEM         Program
      04CB0      341232 (333K)   MSDOS       — Free —
```

Upper Memory Detail:

Segment	Region	Total		Name	Type
0C93A	1	38688	(38K)	IO	System Data
		37856	(37K)	G: — I:	Installed Device=STACKER
		784	(1K)	SETVERXX	Installed Device=SETVER
0D2AC	1	9168	(9K)	IO	System Data
		9136	(9K)	MVPROAS	Installed Device=MVSOUND

```
0D4E9    1       288    (0K)  CPCKNL    Environment
0D4FB    1      5120    (5K)  CPCKNL    Program
0D63B    1       272    (0K)  TMB        Environment
0D64C    1     33472   (33K)  TMB        Program
0DE78    1       288    (0K)  VOICE     Environment
0DE8A    1     63584   (62K)  VOICE     Program
0EE10    1       272    (0K)  SR        Environment
0EE21    1       288    (0K)  CFPI      Environment 0EE33      1
7376    (7K)  win386    Data
```

Memory Summary:

Type of Memory	Total	=	Used	+	Free
Conventional	655360 (640K)		225520 (220K)		429840 (420K)
Upper	158864 (155K)		158864 (155K)		0 (0K)
Adapter RAM/ROM	393216 (384K)		393216 (384K)		0 (0K)
Extended (XMS)	15569776 (15205K)		14521200 (14181K)		1048576

```
-- -- -- -- -- -- -- -- -- -- -- -- -- -- -- -- -- -- -- -- --
-- -- -- -- -- -- -- -- -- -- -- --
Total memory    16777216 (16384K)  5298800 (14940K) 1478416
Total under 1MB 814224   (795K)     384384  (375K) 429840
Memory accessible using Int 15h          0   (0K)
Largest executable program size     429824  (420K)
Largest free upper memory block          0   (0K)
MS-DOS is resident in the high memory area.
XMS version  2.00; driver version  2.05
```

MEM is an interesting DOS command. It really shows you how DOS is using your PC's memory, but its full details are only of real use to programmers who want to check on the location of certain items in memory.

Using Extra Memory

Not every program you run on your PC will be a bloated memory hog. Some programs run just fine on only 40K of RAM. For the longest time in PC history, it seemed like any program was swimming in 640K of RAM. So a lot of people thought of interesting ways to put "extra memory" in your PC to work. Four of the most popular have been:

◆ Memory resident programs

◆ RAM disks

◆ Disk caches

◆ Print spoolers

Memory Resident Programs The most popular way to take advantage of extra memory is to use *memory resident programs*. These are programs that remain in RAM even when they quit. The term "TSR," often used to describe memory resident software, comes from the DOS function called *Terminate and Stay Resident*—the way memory resident software is created.

Memory resident software usually monitors (and sometimes manages) some state of affairs in your PC. For example, it may monitor the clock, and display the current time on the screen 24-hours-a-day. Or it may monitor the keyboard, waiting for a special key combination to be pressed. When you hit those keys, the program will come alive and "pop up" on screen over whatever you're doing. Other types of memory resident software may modify the way your PC works, emulating a certain printer or graphics adapter, or giving DOS more features.

RAM Disks Another popular use for extra memory is in the form of the RAM disk. A *RAM disk*, also called an electronic disk, or VDISK (for virtual disk), is a disk drive that uses RAM for storage instead of a physical disk. A device driver is loaded by CONFIG.SYS to set aside an area of memory. Then DOS is fooled into thinking that the RAM is actually a disk drive. It proceeds to format the "drive" and assign it a drive letter. From that point onward, you can treat the area of RAM just like a disk drive.

Disk Caches Disk caches are another popular way to put extra memory to work. A *disk cache* is a storage area in memory. It monitors all disk activity and, over the long run, makes all disk access much quicker.

Any time DOS reads information from disk, a copy of it is kept in the cache memory. If the same data needs to be read again, the cache program picks it up from cache memory instead of reading it from disk. Since most disk access is repetitive, this greatly speeds all disk operations. Unlike a RAM disk, the cache only keeps a copy of information already on disk. Information is still written directly to disk, so nothing is lost if the power goes out.

Print Spoolers Finally, extra memory can be put to use in the form of a *print spooler*—an area of memory that stores characters waiting for the printer.

The printer is the slowest device in your computer system. Most of the time, the computer waits for the printer to begin printing before it becomes available for any other use. A print spooler sets aside a small area in memory, and then all characters sent to the printer go to memory instead. They then have to wait in memory while the spooler program dishes them out to the printer a handful at a time. During this time you can continue using the computer. The spooler will only "steal" computer time when the printer is ready to print, so you get your printing done while you're using the computer for something else.

Types of Memory

There are lots of terms used to describe memory in a PC. There's the basic 640K of DOS, then there's memory from 640K to 1,024K that's used for video memory, ROM, and the BIOS. Some PCs have megabytes of expanded or extended memory. The purpose of this section is to define those types of memory and describe how each is used.

DOS Memory

DOS memory refers to the basic 1MB of RAM, common to all PCs. (This is all based on the design and limitations of the first PC, which had an 8088 microprocessor capable of only dealing with 1MB of RAM.) Even though you may have a 386-based system, with 16MB of RAM installed, that first megabyte will be the same under DOS as it is for all PCs.

Not all DOS memory is used for RAM. Instead, DOS memory is divided into two parts:

◆ Conventional DOS memory

◆ The Upper Memory Area

Conventional DOS memory is the basic 640K DOS gives to your run programs and store data. It's also known as Low DOS Memory.

The Upper Memory Area consists of all memory locations in your PC from 640K up through 1,024K or 1MB. Figure 6.2 illustrates the location of Conventional and Upper Memory using a variation of DOS memory map shown earlier.

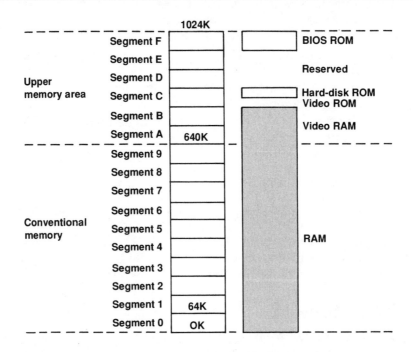

FIGURE 6.2: The locations of conventional and high DOS memory

The difference between conventional and high DOS memory (also called the UMA, for Upper Memory Area)— other than their locations—include that you can load and run programs in conventional DOS Memory, but not high DOS memory. That area is reserved for the BIOS, video RAM, and other future expansion.

But PCs can have more memory installed. That memory comes in two flavors:

◆ Expanded memory

◆ Extended memory

Both of these types of memory exist outside of the DOS memory covered in this section. Of the two, extended memory is more useful under DOS today. But this doesn't necessarily orphan expanded memory.

For those who'd like to know, the HMA (High Memory Area) and the UMA (Upper Memory Area) are two different regions. UMBs (Upper Memory Blocks) are portions of the UMA.

Expanded Memory

The PC memory crunch was first noticed by spreadsheet users. They needed a lot of RAM to store huge spreadsheets, and Conventional DOS Memory just wasn't cutting it. So three companies—Lotus, Intel and Microsoft—got together and developed the Expanded Memory Specification, or EMS. (The full title is LIM EMS, for the Lotus, Intel, and Microsoft Expanded Memory Specification.)

EMS defines what's known as expanded memory. This memory isn't really part of the DOS memory, and it doesn't "start" at address 1,024K on the memory map. Instead, it's a pool of RAM—a storage area that can be up to 8MB in size. (The current version of EMS, LIM 4.0, allows for up to 32MB of expanded memory.)

Figure 6.3 illustrates how LIM 3.2 EMS works. Bank E (in the figure) is called the *page frame*. It contains four 16K windows into EMS memory. those windows contain a copy of some 16K chunk of EMS memory somewhere in the memory pool. To access that memory, a program uses the EMS device driver. (The device driver controls EMS memory and how it's accessed.)

That may sound kind of awkward, accessing up to 8MB of RAM using only four tiny 16K windows. But when you consider that your hard drive is accessed only 512 bytes at a time, and that memory is faster than disk, then you can see the speed involved. And EMS solved the basic problem: it gave spreadsheet users access to larger amounts of memory.

Extended Memory

Expanded memory was developed for the PC/XT. It worked under DOS, which meant that it was limited to operating in a 1MB environment. But the newer 286 and 386 microprocessors are capable of accessing much more memory than that. That memory is called *extended memory*.

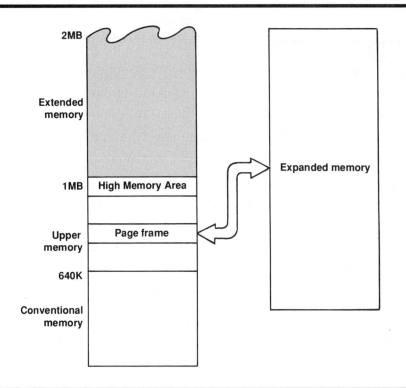

FIGURE 6.3: How EMS works

There is a difference between extended and expanded memory. Right away, expanded memory is what you want under DOS. Extended memory isn't bad, but it has the following qualities.

It's Memory beyond 1MB in a PC/AT 286 or 386 System The 286 and 386 microprocessors are capable of directly accessing megabytes of memory, far more than the 1MB a PC/XT's 8086 can address. Any memory added to a 286 or 386 system beyond the first megabyte is automatically treated as expanded memory. (Refer to Figure 6.4.)

It's Not Used under DOS Extended memory cannot be used by DOS or DOS programs. Extended memory can only be accessed when the 286 or 386 is operating in its *Protected Mode*. That's an advanced mode of the microprocessor, wherein memory is protected and allocated to each program. DOS was written for the *Real Mode*, which is the 8086-compatible

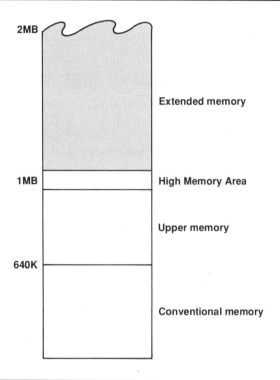

2MB

Extended memory

1MB

High Memory Area

Upper memory

640K

Conventional memory

FIGURE 6.4: Extended memory in a 286 or 386 system is memory beyond 1MB

operating mode of both the 286 and 386. When 286 and 386 processors run DOS, they're in the Real Mode and cannot access or use extended memory.

It Can Be Converted to Expanded Memory Extended memory is, in effect, shut off from use by DOS. However, it is possible to convert extended memory into the more useful expanded memory under DOS. This is done via a software driver that converts the extended memory into LIM-4.0-compatible expanded memory.

The 386 (or higher) systems deal with memory differently than 286 systems. If you have a 386 PC and would like to convert your extended into expanded memory, two programs are recommended: 386MAX from Qualitas; and QEMMB from Quarterdeck Office Systems.

Additional information on using these packages to enhance the memory situation on your PC is covered in the second part of this chapter. But all these conversion programs bring up an interesting question.

What Good Is Extended Memory?

Extended memory is used primarily for Protected Mode operating systems, such as Xenix, UNIX, Windows, and OS/2. In those environments, the 286 and 386 microprocessors operate in their native Protected Mode and can access their megabytes of RAM directly.

Under DOS, the 286 and 386 operate in the real mode—where DOS lives. There the extended memory is either ignored, or converted to expanded memory using one of the previously mentioned device drivers. In that respect, the extended-cum-expanded memory can be used by DOS and DOS programs.

Putting Memory to Work

If you're going to be packing your PC full of RAM, you might as well put it all to use. If you have the full 640K of RAM, then you'll find that a lot of programs will welcome the memory.

For most people, a memory upgrade involves memory beyond 640K, either in the form of expanded or extended memory. That will give you memory above 640K, which you have to put to work.

There are certain secrets to getting the most from memory. The key in DOS is expanded memory under the LIM 4.0 specification. Using that software driver, you can pack quick expanded memory into your system, exploit unused areas of the UMA, and even boost DOS's 640K limit up to 736K—96K above the unbreakable barrier. These techniques for using more memory are covered in the following sections.

Smashing the 640K Barrier

You probably know the saying by heart: DOS is limited to running programs in 640K of RAM—the first ten 64K banks of memory in your PC. Memory above that is used as The UMA, for your video RAM, hard disk controller ROM, and BIOS. And DOS won't access memory beyond 1MB. So that leaves you with 640K of RAM.

Or does it?

Internally, DOS will load only programs in Conventional DOS Memory—your basic 640K of RAM. But the programs themselves could really sit anywhere in that 1MB of DOS memory. After all, there is no brick wall at 640K. To take advantage of the possibility of more memory, you can resort to several interesting tricks:

◆ Stealing video memory

◆ Using the UMA

These are both legitimate ways to sneak in more memory under DOS. The first simply expands DOS's usable memory space. The second allows you to move memory resident software and certain device drivers into the UMA. Once they're out of conventional DOS memory, that makes your basic RAM space larger. Both of these tricks are possible through using DOS 5 or 6.

Stealing Video Memory

Referring back to the PC's memory map (Figure 6.1), you see that video memory starts right after the 640K DOS barrier. Actually, video memory doesn't occupy that full amount of space. Instead, the memory used depends on which display adapter you have. Figure 6.5 shows how each display adapter uses video memory.

Since EGA and VGA are both compatible with CGA, it's possible to run them both in the CGA mode. In that mode, the video display only uses RAM in the upper half of bank B. That's only 32K from the 128K supplied with the card. It leaves 96K of video RAM left over. Using the right software, that 96K can be added right to the basic 640K of RAM in a PC, giving you 736K of usable memory under DOS.

There are quite a few software packages that do this, including some in the public domain. But you must have fully-equipped EGA or VGA graphics in your system to do this. Also, you forego the advanced graphics capabilities of these adapters to run them in the CGA-only mode (which means you can't take advantage of fancy graphics packages with 736K of DOS memory). Finally, not every program will recognize or use the extra RAM. Some will.

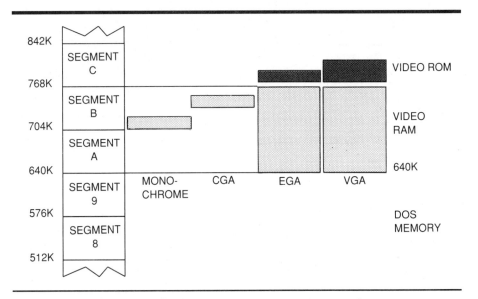

FIGURE 6.5: How the various PC video displays use memory

Using the UMA

There are two popular ways to access and use the region of memory between 640K and 1MB. One of those ways is to use the main benefits of LIM 4.0 and its memory-mapping abilities. Using an LIM 4.0 memory expansion board that has hardware registers in combination with a good EMS device driver, you can do fancy things with memory. (On a 386 you only need a capable memory device driver.) Those memory mapping abilities allow you to squeeze EMS RAM into any part of your PC's basic 1MB. That includes the UMA and the "holes" left there—space unused by ROM or video RAM.

Remember, a 386 PC is also capable of these memory manipulations. You don't need LIM 4.0 EMS hardware on a 386, however, because the 386 microprocessor has more powerful memory management abilities built in. You do need a capable device driver. Two of the best are Quarterdeck's QEMMB and Qualitas' 386MAX. Both offer features similar or identical to QRAM and MOVE'EM, customized for the 386 environment.

The second way to use the region of memory between 640K and 1MB is to use DOS 5 or 6. Both of these versions of DOS allow you to run TSRs and device drivers in the UMA, or Upper Memory Area (also referred to as High DOS). DOS 6 will even help you use the monochrome region of the UMA if you have a 386 or higher. Both of these versions of DOS will also load part of DOS into the first 64K of memory above the 1MB mark, also called the High Memory Area, saving an additional hunk of conventional memory.

Using Extended Memory

Extended memory is a white elephant under DOS, and a boon under Windows. Any time you add memory beyond 1MB to an AT, 286 or 386 system, you're adding extended memory. DOS is a Real Mode operating system. Extended memory can only be used in the 286 and 386's Protected Mode. Under DOS, the memory just sits around wasted.

Not so with Windows—Windows *needs* extended memory, and treats all available memory over the 1MB mark as extended memory. Windows will also use the UMA for its own running, and dole UMA out to Windows applications unless you instruct Windows not to use the UMA for those purposes. Windows uses extended memory. Windows does not use expanded memory.

A few DOS applications can use extended memory directly. RAMDRIVE and other DOS utilities can be loaded into extended memory. Other operating systems than DOS, like OS/2 and UNIX, use (and need) extended memory directly. But under DOS, extended memory is only any good when you convert it into expanded memory.

Using Expanded Memory

Expanded memory was developed to give DOS users more memory storage. From earlier in this chapter, remember that expanded memory is actually a memory storage device—a pool of memory in which data can be stored. You cannot run software in expanded memory.

The computer industry, long a lover of standards but short on following them, has settled on the Lotus-Intel-Microsoft specification version 4.0, abbreviated LIM 4.0. It's a set of rules governing hardware and software that controls expanded memory.

EMS Hardware

On the hardware side, LIM 4.0 is available via LIM-4.0-compatible expansion cards. To get the most from LIM 4.0, you should disable as much of your motherboard memory as possible. Usually this is done in your 286's SETUP program or using the DIP switches on a PC/XT. Simply tell the motherboard that it has only 256K (or less, if possible) of RAM. The rest of your Conventional DOS memory will be supplied via the LIM 4.0 expansion card.

EMS Software

On the software side, if you use a LIM 4.0-compatible add-on memory card, you'll need an LIM 4.0 driver. The driver will come with the card, and it will be called something along the lines of EMS.SYS. You install the driver into your CONFIG.SYS file using the format:

```
DEVICE = EMS.SYS
```

From there, any software you use on your PC that takes advantage of EMS memory can access it. Under LIM 4.0, you can have up to 32MB of EMS RAM in your PC. Though you may not use all of that, any amount you have can greatly improve the performance of some software.

To get the most from all that EMS memory, you really need a superior memory management application. One of the best programs used for managing expanded memory on AT-level systems with a 386 processor or higher is Microsoft's EMM386. EMM386 will even re-map EMS memory into the UMA, as well as load device drivers and memory resident software there.

PCs with a 386 microprocessor already have advanced memory management techniques built into their systems. However, a memory driver is necessary to emulate LIM 4.0, as well as to convert the extended memory into expanded memory. Two of the best packages for that purpose are 386MAX and QEMM, although Microsoft's EMM386 does a great job for no more than the cost of DOS! Additionally, these packages will control the 386's Virtual Mode, allowing you to run multiple DOS applications on a 386 system.

The memory situation under DOS isn't all that bleak. Lots of software supports LIM 4.0, as well as the basic Expanded Memory Specification. The key advantage of LIM 4.0 is its ability to quickly swap out major portions of DOS memory to EMS memory. This comes into play with certain applications known as "program switchers," which allow you to quickly switch between several programs, swapping unused ones out to EMS memory. From the early days, when spreadsheet users needed more room, to today when many people are using advanced graphics applications, you just can't have enough RAM in your PC.

Memory
Upgrades

Adding RAM to your PC isn't that tough to do. It's one of the more basic upgrades, requiring only a bit more skill than plugging in Lego blocks (and a lot more patience). You can buy a "tube" of chips just about anywhere and plug them in yourself. There are no secrets, no tricks, nothing hidden from you. One of the most common upgrades, it's also one of the most beneficial.

This chapter is the second half of our RAM upgrade discussion. Here, we'll talk about plugging chips into sockets. You'll learn how to add the RAM to your PC.

The first part of this chapter discusses basic info on chips and RAM and where they go inside the PC. The second part is the nuts-and-bolts tutorial for upgrading memory. The software side of the RAM upgrade has already been covered in the previous chapter.

● General Notes on Memory

Memory is common. In fact, memory chips are second in popularity only to the microprocessor as something people generally recognize in a PC. Or do they? We'll introduce you to the various external and internal attributes of RAM chips in two sections.

The first section discusses RAM chips, what they look like and what's inside of them. When you purchase a chip, you should be able to read it to find out what type it is. That makes you a good buyer—it's just smart, like thumping a melon before you buy it.

The second section deals with RAM's physical placement inside your PC. Memory's location matters. You have to install it in a specific order or else the PC won't recognize it. These discussions will round out your basic knowledge of RAM and the PC.

About Chips

Upgrading your computer memory involves dealing with RAM chips; plugging them into sockets and throwing the right DIP switches. This section is about those chips specifically. It covers:

◆ Types of Chips

◆ Capacity

◆ Speed

◆ Quantity

◆ Reading Chip Numbers

RAM comes on RAM chips. These chips come in a variety of sizes, hold different amount of memory, run at different speeds, and can be installed in your PC in a number of ways. We've come a long way.

Types of Chips

There are two types of RAM chips: *Static* and *Dynamic*, also abbreviated SRAM and DRAM, respectively. Static RAM (SRAM, pronounced *Ess-RAM*) chips are high-speed and they don't require constant *refreshing*. A Dynamic RAM (DRAM, pronounced *Dee-RAM*) chip is slower than an SRAM chip, and actually has to be written to—refreshed—after it is read in order for it to retain its contents. SRAMs don't, which makes them faster, but they're more expensive. If you have them in your PC, they're probably used for RAM caches to speed up the microprocessor. We are usually referring to DRAM chips when we speak about a PC's RAM.

Inexpensive and widely available, DRAM chips constitute the wide majority of the chips you'll be upgrading in your PC, where you'll find three basic types:

◆ DIPs

◆ SIMMs

◆ SIPs

DIP Chips The most common type of RAM chip used to be the DIP, or *Dual Inline Package*. (This is different from a DIP *switch*, which has a row of switches on top.) DIP refers to the common arrangement of the majority of computer chips: They resemble a flat, black, rectangle with several metal legs on either side—like a bug.

Figure 7.1 shows a typical DIP-style RAM chip. It's a thin black rectangle, a little under 1" long and barely ½" wide. On both long sides of the chip are rows of eight metal legs. Those legs plug the chip into a similar-sized socket—just like Lego blocks.

SIMM Chips SIMM is an abbreviation for *Single Inline Memory Module*. It's actually like a mini memory-expansion card. Figure 7.2 shows a typical SIMM-style RAM chip, which is about ⅓ the size of a playing card. A

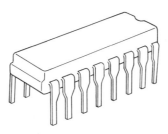

FIGURE 7.1: A typical DIP-style RAM chip

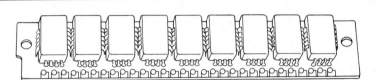

FIGURE 7.2: A typical SIMM

SIMM is fitted with DIP chips. One of the long edges of the SIMM has a row of tiny metal connectors. That edge plugs into one of at least four slots somewhere on the computer's motherboard.

SIMMs came to exist because of the need for convenience. It's just much easier to plug in a sturdy card with DIP chips already on it rather than risk damaging chips individually. Unlike the DIP-style RAM chips, SIMMs don't bend or break easily, and one side is notched so you can't plug them in backwards.

SIP Chips   Finally there are SIP chips—SIP stands for *Single Inline Package*. SIPs are like SIMMs in every way, except for how they're installed. Unlike SIMMs, which use an edge connector to plug into a slot, SIPs have a row of pins that plug into holes. A SIP looks like a mustache comb in that respect. They're nowhere near as common as SIMMs, and they're more fragile.

Capacity

Chips are rated by their capacity and speed. Capacity refers to the number of kilobytes the chip stores, but by itself, a chip really doesn't store any-thing—RAM chips must be grouped into *banks*, and only a number of chips grouped into a bank are capable of storing information.

The capacity of a chip is always measured in bits. For example, the com-mon sizes of RAM chips are $16K \times 1$ bit, $64K \times 1$ bit, $256K \times 1$ bit, and $1,024K \times 1$ bit. So, say when you're buying a 256K chip, you're really buying a 256*Kb* chip. That's Kb for Kilo*bit*. A one-1,204K chip is a one-*megabit* chip, abbreviated 1*Mb*. Note that the lower case B in these refer-ences refers to *bits*, not bytes.

Presently, the two most popular sizes of DRAM chips are the 256Kb and 1Mb chips (only one bit wide). The 16Kb and 64Kb chips still exist, and you can upgrade older PCs with them. An oddball 128Kb chip was used in the original PC/AT, but it has long since ridden off into the sunset.

The two most popular sizes of SIMMs are 1MB and 4MB respectively. Many PCs come through with 1MB or 2MB of SIMM memory made up of 256K SIMMs.

If you have a choice, never buy 256K SIMMs on a new PC. When you are ready to upgrade, you'll have to replace those 256K SIMMs and throw them away...money is wasted. Always specify 1MB SIMMs if you're buying a PC with 4MB of RAM or more.

Speed

The second way a chip is rated is by its speed. The speed of a chip is measured in nanoseconds, abbreviated *ns*. A *nanosecond* is one billionth of a second, or the time it takes a beam of light to travel just under 12". (It's very fast.) The speed of a chip is directly related to the speed of your microprocessor.

When you buy a lot of chips or SIMMs, you'll want to make sure you get the right speed for your system. 150ns or 120ns chips are fine for most plain wrap PCs. But if you have a 386, you will need the faster SIMMs.

You can mix chip speeds in a bank, though its best to mix in only faster chips (for example, putting a 120ns chip in a bank of 80ns chips). There's nothing wrong with sticking a 120ns chip in a bank of 150ns chips, though it's kind of a waste of money. The basic rule of thumb is that the slowest single chip in a bank is the fastest at which the entire bank will perform.

Quantity

If you're upgrading memory via SIMMs (which depends, of course, on having SIMM sockets on your motherboard or memory expansion card), the SIMM will come with all nine (sometimes less) chips installed. In that instance, you'll be buying a 256K SIMM to add 256K to your system, or a 1MB SIMM to add 1 MB. Check your motherboard's documentation for

the increments you must use when upgrading the SIMMs in your own system.

Buy 1MB SIMMs if you will never exceed 8MB of memory in total, and use 4MB SIMMs if you intend to load your computer up past the 8MB point. In the future, wearing a 256K SIMM as a tie clip or using it as a swizzle stick decoration won't be a novelty.

Notches and Dots, and Reading Chip Numbers

A secret code is printed on the top of every RAM chip. This code will tell you what kind of chip you're looking at, its capacity, and its speed. Knowing how to read those values comes in handy, for example, when you find a loose chip or when you're shopping for chips.

Look for two things on each RAM chip:

◆ The notch or dot

◆ The chip number

The notch or dot, which isn't related to the chip's speed, capacity, or number, is an important thing to spot on all RAM chips. It's an orientation guide, designed to assist you when you install the chip. On one end of the chip there will be a notch, or, if the chip isn't notched, one of its top corners will have a dot. That dot indicates "pin one" of the chip, and is used to orient the chip when you install it. For now, just know that the notch or dot exists. (Installing chips is covered in the next part of this chapter.)

The chip's number is your only clue as to the chip's size and capacity.

To weed out important information from lot and vendor numbers, you need to know that there are two values you'll find on all RAM chips:

◆ The chip's capacity

◆ The chip's speed

The chip's capacity is always listed first. It's usually the last part of the first group of numbers on the top row of numbers. Values you'll see commonly are listed in Table 7.1.

TABLE 7.1: The first set of numbers on most RAM chips and what they stand for

NUMBER	MEANING
164	64K × 1 bit
264	64K × 2 bits
1128	128K × 1 bit
2128	128K × 2 bits
1256	256K × 1 bit
2256	256K × 2 bits
4256	256K × 4 bits
11000	1,024K × 1 bit
21000	1,024K × 2 bits
41000	1,024K × 4 bits

Additional numbers may appear on the chip before the numbers listed in the first column of the table. (Usually the first number is a "4".) And letters may follow or precede the number. Typically, the numbers listed in Table 7.1 will be followed by a hyphen and two other numbers. Those numbers after the hyphen—the "suffix" numbers—tell you the chip's speed. For example, the numbers 1 and 2 indicate a speed of 120ns. Other speed values are shown in Table 7.2.

TABLE 7.2: Speed numbers on a chip and their values

NUMBER	MEANING
−15	150ns
−12	120ns
−10	100ns
−80	80ns

An experienced eye can decipher a chip's secret code in no time, which reveals what kind of chip it is and how fast it runs. Table 7.3 lists a few examples, showing the numbers from several different chips and what they mean.

TABLE 7.3: Various numbers from a few chips and their meanings

CHIP NUMBERS	MEANING
8810 8 USA MT 1256-12	256Kb chip, 120ns
KM41C1000AJ-8	1Mb chip, 80ns
53C464S-10	64K × 4 bits, 100ns
4164C-15	64Kb chip, 150ns

In Table 7.3's first example, 1256 refers to a 256K × 1 bit chip. The 9 probably indicates that it's one chip in a bank of nine. Since the numbering scheme comes close to no other value, you can assume it's a 256Kb chip.

Some values are bound to throw you. For example, the early 16Kb chips on the first IBM computers had the following number on them:

AM9016DPC

8132WMP

Those chips didn't follow today's conventions, but you can still make out the 16 in the first number, which is a tip-off that it's a 16Kb chip. You may occasionally stumble across other chips that don't appear to follow any conventions, as well; it's not hard to guess their speed and capacity.

Where RAM Goes

There are three places inside your PC where you'll be installing RAM:

◆ The motherboard

◆ An expansion slot

◆ A proprietary slot

Today, most modern systems have room for megabytes of RAM to be installed on the motherboard. Whatever the case, it's best to pack your motherboard full of RAM before you add a memory card. In fact, the only time that will work against you is if you have a PC or AT system (not a 386) and are using an LIM-4.0-compatible EMS card. (Refer to Chapter 6.)

The last place you can add memory to your system is in a proprietary, or dedicated, memory slot. This slot is actually an extension "cord" for your motherboard's memory. It's called "proprietary" because there are no industry-wide standards for this type of memory card. Each manufacturer will devise its own scheme for the card.

The proprietary slots appear mostly on older 386 systems. That microprocessor works best if the memory it accesses is in full 32-bit mode. Memory on an expansion card can only be accessed in 16-bit mode because you plug it into the PC's bus. Therefore, to get the most from the 386, the special memory slot is used.

386 or higher computers have specific memory upgrade requirements. You must add memory in given increments, usually 2MB or 4MB (or more) at a time. The design of the 386 requires that memory be added in those amounts so that you get the most from the system. It gets expensive, but what you get in performance is worth the cost.

Installing Memory

Upgrading memory is one of the most common and desired upgrades. It's not complicated to do. Plugging in chips or SIMMs is like playing with Tinker Toys or Lego blocks—although it's much more expensive, the parts are less durable, and what you're working on is a valuable computer and not a kid's toy.

Installing memory is covered here in seven sections:

◆ Buying Chips

◆ Upgrade Overview

◆ Removing Chips

◆ Removing SIMMs

◆ Plugging in Chips

◆ Plugging in SIMMs

◆ Problems

Buying Chips

When you buy RAM chips, you should know several things in advance:

◆ The amount of RAM you're going to install

◆ The quantity of chips to expect in the tube or package

◆ The capacity of the chips

◆ The speed of the chips

The amount of RAM you're installing is related to the quantity of chips required, but it might not be a direct relationship. For example, if you've installed 128K of RAM to boost your AT from 512K to 640K on the motherboard, you may need only six chips—four 64K × 4 bits and two 64K × 1 bit chips. (This and any other oddities will be explained in your PC's manual.)

But normally, if you want to add a megabyte of RAM to your PC, you'll be buying one 1MB SIMM, one set of nine 1Mb chips, or four sets of nine 256Kb chips. (Four times 256K is 1MB, and you need nine times four, or 36 chips, to equal 1MB.)

After you determine the amount (total RAM) and quantity (number of chips) needed, you'll have to specify the capacity and speed of the chips. Capacity will be related to the total RAM you're installing and the number of chips that will take. Again, you could have nine 1MB chips or four banks of nine 256Kb chips—this all depends on where you're installing the memory and what types of chips are required. Go with the highest capacity wherever possible.

You can buy chips from a local dealer, a mail order house, or a swap meet. Avoid "pulled chips," which are used chips pulled from older computers. Also, remember that few if any outfits will guarantee chips. If you break one or it doesn't work, don't expect to get your money back.

SIMMs come in anti-static bags that look like tiny versions of the bags expansion cards come in.

DRAM chips come in static-free tubes. You should keep them in the tube until you're ready to do the upgrade. The tubes are transparent, so you can look through to see if you have chips of the proper size and speed.

Remember to count the chips in the tube to make sure you have enough. Nothing is more disappointing than coming home with 16 chips instead of 18. And keep the tube after your upgrade, it will come in handy as the best way to store any chips you may have laying around.

 Remember that you can mix chips of different speeds. But make sure that their minimum speed is compatible with your system. You can stick a 120ns chip in a bank with 150ns chips, but putting a 120ns chip in a bank of 80ns chips will only slow things down.

Upgrade Overview

In most of the upgrade sections in this book, you'll read a detailed overview of each upgrade. Step-by-step instructions will be listed for you to read before you attempt the upgrade. Installing RAM chips is different. The instructions here are generic enough to most situations, but the details will differ slightly depending on your machine.

 Be very careful about grounding yourself while working with chips—sit still!—and before touching a chip, touch your PC's case or the power supply (if it's open). This will drain off any static you have built up. Static could damage the chip. Stay grounded, and don't be in a hurry!

Know Where to Install the Chips

If you're installing the chips on an expansion card or proprietary memory board, then you'll be installing them *before* you put the card in the PC.

If you're installing chips on your motherboard, you may have to remove some expansion cards first. (Expansion cards are covered in Chapter 10.) Putting memory on the motherboard is more difficult than sticking it on

an expansion card. Things might be in the way, your workspace is hindered by the PC's case, and it's hard to inspect your job afterwards to make sure all the chips are seated properly.

One Bank at a Time

When upgrading RAM, you should work one bank at a time. First, locate the bank of RAM you're upgrading. It really doesn't matter in which order you plug in chips, top-to-bottom or left-to-right, but you should work one bank of RAM at a time. For example, if you're installing four banks of 256Kb chips, install each bank as it is numbered consecutively (bank 0 first, then banks 1 and 2, etc.), as opposed to plugging in chips at random. This helps you avoid plugging chips of different capacities into the same bank.

Dispense nine chips from the tube (or one SIMM from the bag) and install them in whichever bank you're working on. Try to keep as many of your new memory devices in the original packaging for as long as you can. This keeps them safe and in one place.

Orient the Chip

Unlike SIMMs, RAM chips can be plugged in wrong. To make it easier to plug them in correctly, each chip has a notch or dot on top. Orient the chip by positioning the notch or dot against a corresponding notch or dot stenciled underneath the socket or on the socket. Figure 7.3 shows how to orient a chip.

If the socket itself lacks a notch, check for a stencil on the actual motherboard. The stencil (usually painted in white around the socket) should have a notch, indicating which way you should orient the chip. If the dot or notch isn't lined up, the chip won't work. It's important to have a chip's orientation set properly.

If a chip has two dots on it, it should also be notched. Don't let the second dot throw you—look for the notch on one side of the chip. Also, SIMMs are notched only on one side (refer to Figure 7.2). You can't plug them in wrong.

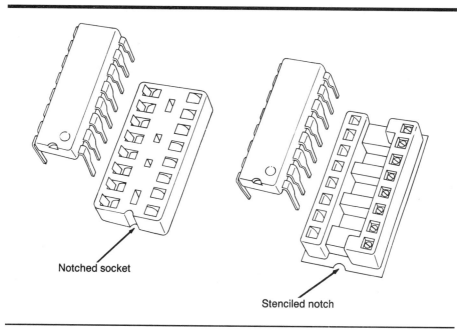

Notched socket

Stenciled notch

FIGURE 7.3: The proper orientation of a RAM chip

Insert the Chip

Once the chip is properly oriented, insert the chip by lining up its legs with the holes in the socket, and then pressing down firmly.

You may need to bend the chip's legs in a bit to make them fit into the socket. If so, put the chip on its side and press it a bit against a flat surface (like a table), angling the legs inward. Don't bend the legs too far, and don't bend them with your fingers. (To avoid this, the best route to take is to buy a chip insertion tool and use it. But it is possible to angle in the legs by gently bending them on a tabletop.)

To insert a SIMM, line it up with the SIMM slot and insert it at an angle. Guide the connector edge of the SIMM into the socket, then move the SIMM into a perpendicular position. There are two holes in the SIMM and two hooks in the SIMM socket. The hooks go through the holes. Sometimes it's necessary to bend the hooks inward to line them up through the holes.

Inspect Your Work

After you install a bank of chips, look over all the chips as they sit in their sockets. You may notice that the bank is uneven, with some chips to the left and others to the right—that's fine, but keep an eye out for chips with their legs out of the sockets.

Finally, make sure all the dots on the all of the chips are lined up. The numbers on top of chips that came from the same manufacturer, and all the little KOREAs and TOSHIBAs should read the same way. The names on chips from different manufacturers, of course, may be different. Check the dots or notches on the all the chips to be sure they're lined up correctly.

Tell the PC About Its New RAM

Your final step in the process of upgrading memory is to let the PC know about the RAM you just installed. If you have a PC/XT level machine, you set DIP switches on the motherboard. For AT type machines, you run the SETUP program.

If you have added RAM to the motherboard, you must tell the PC where the RAM was added and how much you've put in.

Removing Chips

Occasionally, you may need to remove some RAM chips—usually in order to replace 256Kb chips with 1Mb chips. When making a switch, remember to tell the expansion card that now 1Mb chips are installed. Some systems require no other changes and will recognize the newer chips. But check just in case.

HOW TO REMOVE CHIPS

Procedure: Removing chips

Tools Needed: Chip extractor or tiny minus screwdriver

Steps:

1. Power down your PC and remove the lid.

2. Locate the chips you want to remove. If the chips are on an expansion card, remove the card and lay it flat in its own work area. If the chips are on the motherboard, you may need to remove some expansion cards to get at them. It may even make sense to remove the motherboard entirely, if the extra work required will make the replacement of your chips a lot easier.

3. Remove the chips one at a time, and remove all of the chips on one bank at one time. To remove the chip with a chip extractor, position the extractor on the ends of the chip. Gently rock the chip back and forth to loosen it from the socket. Then pull it straight out. Bent legs on a chip will mean harder work when pulling it out. (Legs can be straightened, however.)

   To remove the chip with a minus (flathead) screwdriver, wedge the screwdriver alternately under one side of the chip after another. Each time, twist the blade slightly to raise the chip a fraction of an inch or so. Keep moving around the chip this way, and eventually the chip will lift out of the socket.

4. As you remove the chips, place them into a static-free tube (the best type of storage), or plug them into static-free foam made for that purpose. If any of the chips have bent legs, you may want to straighten them out before storing them.

5. Skip this step if you have an AT. Reset any DIP switches or jumpers to tell the PC that its memory capacity has changed.

6. If you removed any obstructing expansion cards to get at your memory board, re-install them now and put the memory expansion card back into the PC.

7. Put the lid back on the PC and fire it up. AT systems may give you a POST error and require you to run the SETUP program to tell the PC how much RAM it has (or lacks).

Your system now has less RAM, which may be what you want. Most people, however, remove chips in order to install chips with larger capacity in their place. That subject is covered in the upcoming section of this chapter called "Plugging in Chips."

Removing SIMMs

SIMMs are a much handier way of dealing with memory than fumbling with chips. There are fewer mistakes to make, and the mistakes you make are easier to deal with in the long run. You may occasionally have to pull a few 256K SIMMs to replace them with 1MB SIMMs to give your system more memory, however.

HOW TO REMOVE SIMMS

Procedure: Removing SIMMs

Tools Needed: None; screwdriver optional

Steps:

1. Power down your PC and remove the lid.

2. Locate the SIMMs you want to remove. If they're on an expansion card, remove the card from the PC and put it in its own work area. If the SIMMs are on the motherboard, you may need to remove some expansion cards to get at them.

3. Remove the SIMMs. SIMMs are anchored on either side via a hook-and-hole mechanism. Hooks on the SIMM mount go through two tiny holes on either side of the SIMM. You may need a screwdriver to assist you in bending the hooks out of the holes. (Sometimes you can do it with your fingers.)

Once the hooks are free from the holes, tilt the SIMM forward and then pull it up and out. *Handle the SIMM by its edges.*

4. Put the SIMM in a static-free bag for storage.

5. Unless you're replacing the SIMM with one of a higher capacity, after you remove the SIMM(s), you must reset any DIP switches or jumpers, tell the PC or expansion card about the memory you just yanked, and set any necessary DIP switches or jumpers.

6. Re-install any expansion cards that had to be removed to gain access. Put the memory expansion card back into the PC, or re-install any cards that were removed to get at motherboard memory.

7. Put the lid back on the PC and fire it up. If you have an AT system, you'll probably get a POST error. Run the SETUP program to tell the computer how much memory is now installed.

Plugging in Chips

Upgrading RAM means plugging in chips. Whether you're filling an empty bank or swapping for RAM of higher capacity, plugging in chips is a major part of the upgrade. Plugging in chips can be tedious (which is why we now have SIMMs), but it's not something you do every day—and the results will please you, so it's worthwhile.

 During this entire procedure, make sure you're grounded; touch the PC's power supply before handling each chip, and sit still.

HOW TO INSTALL CHIPS

Procedure: Installing chips

Tools Needed: Chip insertion tool (optional)

Steps:

1. Power down your PC and remove the lid.

2. Locate where you want to install the chips. If the chip sockets are on an expansion card, remove the card and lay it flat so you can work on it. If the chips are going on the motherboard, you may need to remove some expansion cards to give you some working room. It may even make some sense to remove the motherboard to gain free access to your chip sockets.

3. Slide out a bank of chips from the static-free tube. You'll need nine chips. If you're upgrading two banks with different capacity chips, make sure all the chips you're installing in one bank are of the same size.

4. Put the chip into the chip insertion tool. If you don't have a chip insertion tool, then move to the next step.

5. Position the chip over its socket. Make sure the dot or notch in the top of the chip lines up with the notch in the socket, or with a stenciled notch on the motherboard/expansion card. If you've already stuck the chip into the insertion tool, you may need to remove it to double-check its orientation.

6. Position the chip so that each of its "legs" fits over a hole in the chip socket. If you're not using a chip insertion tool, you may have to bend the legs in a bit so that they'll fit. To do this, rest the chip on its side on a hard flat surface. With the legs pointing toward you, carefully bend the chip toward you. Repeat this procedure for the other side of the chip. The legs should be then be angled correctly.

7. Press down firmly but gently. The chip will only go down so far; make sure it's down all the way. Once it's positioned, press firmly with your thumb to push it in all the way.

8. Repeat steps 4 through 7 for each chip in the bank.

9. Inspect your work. Always look over each bank after you've installed it. Check to see that each chip is properly oriented and that all pins are in their sockets.

10. You may be upgrading several banks of memory at a time, depending on what you're upgrading and in what size increments you can upgrade it. For example, many expansion cards allow upgrades in 512K or one megabyte increments. Keep installing chips until the job is done.

11. If you're upgrading memory on an expansion card, check it for DIP switches or jumpers. Set them according to the card's manual and the amount of memory you've installed. If you're upgrading memory on the motherboard of a PC/XT type system, it will require that its DIP switches be set. However, upgrading memory on a 386's motherboard or proprietary expansion board requires only modifying your SETUP program.

12. Re-install any expansion cards that you may have removed to gain free access to your memory chip sockets. If you've upgraded motherboard memory and removed expansion cards to do so, re-install them now. If you were installing memory on an expansion card, re-install it now.

13. Put the lid back on the PC and power up. (Refer to the final paragraphs of the section "Troubleshooting and Startup Advice" for troubleshooting and startup advice.)

Plugging in SIMMs

When it became obvious that all PCs required nine chips in a bank for upgrading RAM, some genius developed the SIMM. Not only are they sturdier than single RAM chips, they're easier to install. Most of today's high-end PCs and memory expansion cards are equipped with SIMM sockets.

HOW TO INSTALL SIMMS

Procedure: Installing SIMMs

Tools Needed: None

Steps:

1. Power down your PC and remove the lid.

2. Locate where you want to install the SIMM. If you're installing the SIMM on an expansion card, remove the card and lay it flat to give yourself ample work space. If the SIMM goes on the motherboard, you might have to remove some expansion cards to gain access to it.

3. Slide the SIMM out of its static-free bag.

4. Position the SIMM over its socket. Make sure you have the SIMM in its proper slot. You need to fill your empty SIMM sockets starting with bank 0, then fill bank 1, then 2 and so-on. Refer to your motherboard's manual for details on the SIMM sockets to fill first based on the size of the SIMMs you're installing.

5. Insert the SIMM at an angle, guiding it into the slot. The long edge of the SIMM (with the metal connectors) goes into the slot. One side of the SIMM is notched so that you can't put it in backwards.

   Back the SIMM in, with its chips facing downward. Once the SIMM is in the slot, straighten it up so that the SIMM is perpendicular to your motherboard. Guide the two hooks in the SIMM mount into the holes on either side of the SIMM. You may have some trouble doing this, in which case you can bend the hooks inward slightly using a pair of pliers.

6. Make sure the SIMM is properly seated. SIMMs really do snap into place. They'll sit either perfectly perpendicular or at a given angle to the motherboard. Make sure each SIMM is all the way in and that the edge is fully in the slot.

7. Repeat steps 4 through 6 for each SIMM you're installing.

8. Inspect your work. You don't have to check for bent legs with SIMMs (because they have no "legs") or for SIMMs put in backwards (because you can't put them in backwards), but you might want to touch gently the top of each SIMM and wiggle it to make sure it's sturdy and properly seated.

9. Set any DIP switches or jumpers. Some memory expansion cards may require you to set DIP switches or jumpers to tell it how much RAM you've installed and where the RAM starts in memory. Since SIMMs are rarely used on PC/XTs, you probably won't have to set any DIP switches on the motherboard, but check to be sure.

10. Re-install any expansion cards that were removed because they were in the way. If you added memory to an expansion card, re-install that card at this time.

11. Put the lid back on the PC and power up.

Troubleshooting and Startup Advice

If any chips or SIMMs aren't working, you may get a POST error when you start the computer. The most common error is a "Parity Error," which usually indicates that one chip is dead or, more likely, that some chip has a leg out of the socket. (This is a good argument for powering up with the lid off to make troubleshooting easier.)

On AT-level systems you'll always get a POST error after adding memory. The error will indicate that memory sizes in the system don't match the sizes on record. To fix things, run your SETUP program and tell the computer how much RAM you've installed. (This happens because the AT system's extended memory is tested by the POST.)

Expanded memory boards in a PC/XT don't generally report any errors on power up (the first time). You must install the expanded memory manager in your CONFIG.SYS file, then reboot if any auto-testing is to take place. Some boards will come with diagnostic software to test your RAM; this software may even give you the exact location of an errant chip on the card.

Problems

Upgrading memory carries the potential for rare but numerous problems. When they do occur, it helps to know what to do and how to deal with them. The two most common problems and one peculiar situation you may encounter when you upgrade RAM are:

◆ Parity errors

◆ Improperly installed chips

◆ Left-over parts

Parity errors, the bane of most RAM upgrades, are an indication either of an improperly installed chip or a dead bit in RAM somewhere.

The PC will happily let you know of the parity error, usually via a POST error message. After that, the machine will freeze, and display a message along the lines of "Parity error" with a cryptic number. If you're lucky, the number can be deciphered and you can easily locate the errant chip. If you get one of these POST errors, check the POST table at the end of this book for an explanation of the POST error number.

Bending one leg of a chip up, as shown in Figure 7.4, is a common installation error. It's occasionally hard to spot, especially if you're installing several banks of DIP chips. (This error won't happen on a SIMM, where the chips are pre-soldered into position.)

To correct the problem, carefully pull the chip. Then lay it flat and bend the leg back into position using either needle-pliers or a minus screw-driver to straighten it out. Straighten the leg as best you can and re-install it. Chances are the chip will work normally.

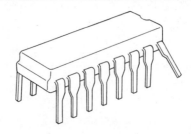

FIGURE 7.4: A chip with one bent leg

 Be careful—the leg is metal and will break off if you bend it back and forth too much. If you break the leg off, the chip is useless.

Another problem you may encounter is left-over parts. As your PC grows, and especially as you upgrade its performance, you'll acquire a lot of extra parts. In the 256Kb-to-1Mb RAM chip upgrade, you'll probably acquire 256Kb chips and SIMMs, for example, and anyone who's had a PC for more than four years probably has a closet full of expansion cards and maybe even an old monochrome monitor.

What can you do with those extra chips? You may be able to sell them as "pulled chips" to someone, but don't expect a quick sell or handsome profit. Some memory chips are usable in some expansion cards, so don't throw those chips away.

Floppy-Disk Drives

Floppy-disk drives are the most "mechanical" things in your computer—everything else is a mixture of electronic circuitry, chips, and cables. Because floppy drives are mechanical, they are the most likely thing to break after you've had your PC for a while. Not to be negative—there are also times when you may just *want* to upgrade or replace a floppy drive. For example, you may want to exchange a 5¼" drive for a 3½" drive to make it compatible with your laptop; you may want to add a drive B to your single-drive system; or you may want to replace your old 360K full-height with two 1.2MB half-height drives.

Whatever your reason, this chapter is about floppy drives and how to upgrade and install them. It isn't really hard to do, but you must keep track of a few different items, so some background information is required before you wrench out an old floppy drive and replace it with the latest model.

Upgrading floppy drives isn't as common a procedure as adding memory; it is, however, something quite a few users with older systems should consider doing. The PC industry has settled on the 1.2MB format for 5¼" disks and the 1.44MB format for 3½" disks. Software is still being distributed on 360K 5¼" disks and 720K 3½" disks, but having a high-capacity floppy drive makes such tasks as data transportation and hard drive backup a heckuvalot easier.

General Notes on Disk Drives

The purpose of this section is to make you familiar with the details of disks and drives. This information is more general than complex; it will provide you with the specific terms for items you may already generally be referring to. Knowing the jargon helps when you're buying new floppy drives.

Background Information

There are two main parts to a floppy drive:

◆ The Drive Unit (there can be more than one)

◆ The Controller Card

Between the drive unit and the controller card is the cable. There is also a power supply cable attached to the back of each drive unit.

The Drive Unit

The disk drive itself is a light, compact unit, which is about 4" to 6" wide, 1½" tall, and 7" deep. The front of the drive—the pretty side—consists of the following parts.

◆ The slot where the disk slides into the drive

◆ The disk activity lamp (LED)

◆ The door latch or eject button

Figure 8.1 shows these three important external items on two generic floppy-drive faceplates.

The locations of the activity lamp and latch/eject button will vary—different drive manufactures have seen fit to put them in different locations—but their function is always the same: The activity lamp always lights up

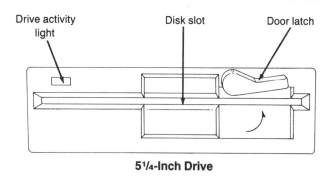

5¼-Inch Drive

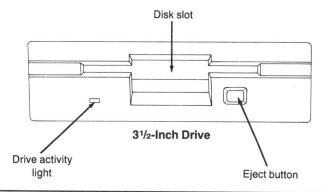

3½-Inch Drive

FIGURE 8.1: Generic floppy-drive faceplates

when the computer is accessing the drive; and the latch is used to "close the door," clamp the floppy disk in place, and touch the read/write heads to the disk. (Older drives actually had a hinged door-like device.)

The eject button on a 3½" drive is used *only* to push the disk from the drive unit. Inserting a 3½" disk into the drive is enough to clamp it into place.

Why Is Orientation Important?

Orientation is important because you're supposed to insert your disks label-up.

If you find that your newly installed drive doesn't read any of your old disks, stick one in upside-down. If it works that way, that means you've installed the drive upside-down. Floppy drives will always have their door-closing buttons or levers on the right side of the drive, so if your button or lever is on the left side of the drive, you've made a boo-boo!

On the drive unit's sides you'll find mounting holes. There are two sets of two holes (four holes in total) on each side. Figure 8.1 shows the mounting holes on one side of a drive.

The back of the drive contains your two vital connectors: The power supply, and the control/data cable connector (which is the drive's "umbilical cord"). The cables that are provided to power your floppy drives can come in two general forms. Both will probably be made of white plastic (actually, nylon).

The connectors provided for 5¼" drives will be the larger of the two. The connector for the 5¼" floppy drive will have visible "male" conductors seen inside the white connector. The connectors provided for 3½" drives look like a very small white plastic box (compared to the size of the connector for 5¼" drives).

Your PC may have up to six of these cables, in a mix of the two types. Each of these two cable connectors will have the same number of wires leading directly into the power supply. Even though both connector types look different, they do the same thing, and the wires carry the same type and amounts of electricity to your floppy drives.

The corners of the connectors are beveled, which prevents you from plugging in the power supply connector upside-down. All you have to do is identify which size connector to use for the drive you're installing. To do that, you can match the jack on the drive to one of the two power cable connectors and plug in the only connector that will fit the drive's particular power jack.

The control/data cables look like a ribbon. This cable attaches to the drive via a 34-pin edge connector. You'll notice that there's a notch at one end of the edge connector. This notch helps you to plug the cable in correctly. In fact, this "polarization" of the control cable connectors prevents incorrect installation.

Inside the drive unit are the guts that make your floppy drive work. It isn't wise to mess with any of this stuff inside the floppy drive. You should know what's what, where it is, and what it does, nonetheless.

The following items within the floppy drive are pointed out in Figure 8.2.

The drive spindle and spindle motor	This device turns the disk around by clamping the disk in the center.
The head assembly	The head assembly contains the read/write heads, which read data from and write data to your disks.

 Most drives contain two heads, for reading both sides of the disk at the same time.

The Stepper Motor The stepper motor moves the head assembly in and out, over the surface of the disk, and the head assembly is mounted on rails, so the whole thing can move in and out. It's the stepper motor that positions the read/write heads over an area of the disk. (DOS controls all of this by dictating commands to your floppy-disk controller.)

The floppy drive unit is one compact package, with a lot of stuff going on in there. 3½" drives are even more confusing because they're usually mounted in a 5¼" drive bracket and then completely sealed inside a metal case. Never mind all that, you need to know only the basics:

◆ Which way is up

◆ Where the mounting screw holes are

◆ Where the power supply connector is

◆ Where the control/data edge connector is

 You might also keep an eye out for any jumpers. You'll read about setting them later in this chapter.

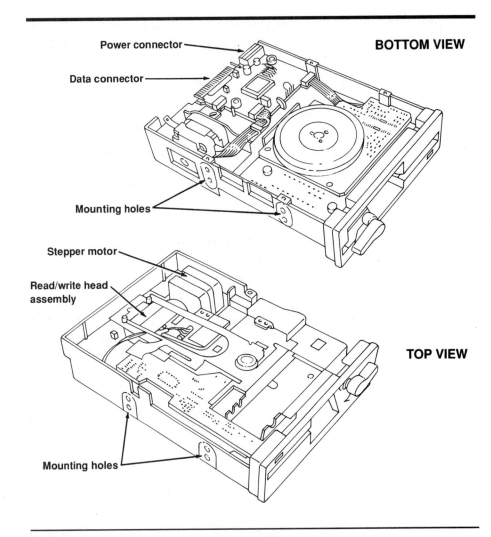

Power connector

Data connector

BOTTOM VIEW

Mounting holes

Stepper motor

Read/write head assembly

TOP VIEW

Mounting holes

FIGURE 8.2: On this disk drive you can see the read/write head assembly, the stepper motor, the mounting holes on the side of the drive unit, and the power supply and data/control connector on the drive's rump

The Controller Card

To interface the floppy drive with your PC, you need a controller—usually an expansion card that plugs into one of the slots on your PC's bus, but in some newer PCs the floppy controller (the circuitry) is built into the motherboard. (In that case, the floppy cable plugs into the motherboard directly.) Other times, the floppy controller will be combined with a hard-disk controller on one card, or it may be part of a multifunction card containing a printer port, mouse port, joystick, and so on.

A floppy-disk controller for our example generic PC is illustrated in Figure 8.3.

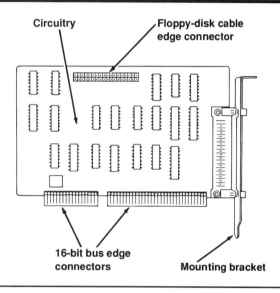

FIGURE 8.3: A generic floppy-disk controller

In the illustration, you should identify the following parts.

The Drive-Cable Edge Connector Located in an unusual place—on the end of the card—so it will stick out, is the 34-pin connector for the drive cable. Note that it may or may not be notched just like the edge connector on the floppy drive unit. If you plug your cable in the wrong way, the drive won't work, or the drive's light will run constantly. In this case, reverse the ribbon cable on the pin connector on the controller card, and the drive should run properly.

The Bus Edge Connector The second edge connector on the drive is for the PC's system bus. This 62-pin edge connector, which plugs into an expansion slot on the motherboard, allows the drive controller to interface directly with your PC's microprocessor (and DOS, and your software, and ultimately you).

Circuitry Of all the expansion cards in your system, the floppy-disk controller is perhaps the most simple (except perhaps the original PC's analog-to-digital port card, into which you plugged a joystick). There really isn't much else to the floppy-disk controller card.

The Cable

One of the few tangles you may encounter when installing a floppy drive is with the cable. The cable connects your drive(s) to the drive controller. The way you hook up the cable, along with a few other items, determines which of your drives is A and which is B.

The controller cable itself is a 34-line ribbon cable. Note that a ribbon cable is flexible; you can bend it. Don't be shy about tweaking it at 90-degree angles to weave the cable through your system unit's internal jungle.

There are three connectors on the cable. Two of them go to drive A and B, the third hooks into your floppy-disk controller.

Here are some easy mnemonics for figuring out the floppy-drive controller cable:

◆ The connectors go **A-B-C**, for drive **A**, drive **B**, and the **C**ontroller

◆ The drive B connector is **B**ackward

Most cables have the drive A and B connectors quite close to one end. Also, you should notice that the cable is switched, twisted in the middle, right before the last connector. So you always plug that end into your first (or only) floppy drive...namely drive A. The other end, the one far away from the other two, goes to the controller card.

Other than remembering which connector on the cable goes where, it's really no sweat to hook things up. Remember, everything is notched. If you have drive A, you plug the A connector on the cable into it, then the power supply, and you're set. Same thing with drive B.

But What If the Connectors Aren't Notched?

If an edge connector isn't notched, then you have to use another method to find out which way to connect it: Look for pin 1. Pin 1 is identified by a stenciled *1* on the edge connector, or somewhere nearby. The gold strips on the edge connector are numbered. For the drive cable, it's numbered 1-33 on the odd side, and 2-34 on the even side.

The cable also has numbers, but they're wire numbers. (Some connectors have wire numbers on them as well.) Wire 1, which corresponds to pin 1, is marked on most cables with a red or blue line. To connect an un-notched cable properly, put wire 1 on the cable on the same side as pin 1 (or pin 2) on the edge connector.

Types of Drives

There are differences between drives, including the following.

- ◆ The drive's formatted capacity
- ◆ The drive height
- ◆ The number of sides and heads
- ◆ The disk size

The drive's formatted capacity is usually all you'll use to describe which floppy drive you want. Currently, there are five standards in PC computing:

360K	$5\frac{1}{4}$"
720K	$3\frac{1}{2}$"
1.2MB	$5\frac{1}{4}$"
1.44MB	$3\frac{1}{2}$"
2.8MB	$3\frac{1}{2}$"

The formatted capacity is an indication of the drive's physical size. 720K, 1.44MB and 2.8MB disks are nearly always 3½", and 360K and 1.2MB disks are always 5¼". So when you refer to a drive, you can pretty much get by with just saying which formatted capacity you want. But there are other considerations as well.

Floptical (21M) drives may use a laser in combination with a holographic imager to read and write to media. These elaborate drives use conventional mechanical head arrangements to read and write to DD and HD disks, and laser technology to read/write to VHD (21M) disks, which are becoming more popular.

The final difference is the physical size of the disk that goes into the drive. The 5¼" square disk has been around since about 1978. At that time, you could only put some 140K on the disk—but that was a lot in those days. Today, a 5¼" disk can be formatted to 1.2MB, depending on the drive and media used.

Where Floppy Drives Go

Disk drives are mounted internally, in your PC's system unit. Most of the drive sits inside the case. But the faceplate is outside and is usually designed to match the color and style of your PC's case.

Floppy drives—and hard drives as well—are mounted into drive bays. the number and size of bays vary from model to model.

Figure 8.4 illustrates the various drive bay combinations for PC, AT, and tower model computers.

There are no hard and fast rules to follow in positioning the drives you install or upgrade. Drive A is traditionally on top of, or to the right of, drive B. But since you can do anything you want (as long as you get the cables right), you can switch the drives. For example, my PC system has drive A on the bottom; my AT system has drive A on the top. (Call me weird.)

External drives are mounted outside the PC in their own case and often with their own power supply. A cable connects them to your floppy-disk controller—or to a proprietary controller of their own. A second cable may plug them into a wall socket, or they may draw juice directly from the computer.

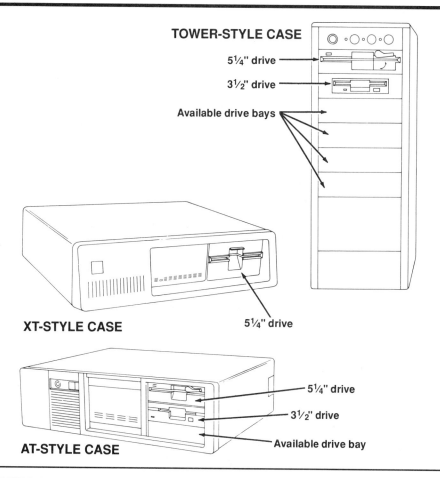

FIGURE 8.4: Drive bay combinations

Floppy Disks

Normally you might not think of floppy disks when you upgrade—the subject is rather tangential to the other topics covered in this chapter. You probably know which type of disk drive you want based on the size of the floppy disks you use. You should know a few things about disks before moving on.

Parts of a Disk

There are two main types of floppy disks used by all types of PCs: The 5¼" floppy disk, and the 3½" disk, (often called a flexy-disk or micro disk, although I personally hate the terms). Other formats also exist: IBM once introduced an 8" disk (which didn't receive much acceptance from manufacturers) for the PC, and there are 3¼" disks and 2½" disks for some laptops. But the biggies, in terms of popular use, are the 5¼- and 3½-inchers, and even the floptical 21MB, 3½" disk looks just like a DD or HD 3½" floppy disk.

Jacket and Media The jacket may also be called a sleeve. Be careful not to confuse it with the paper envelope used to hold the disk. The jacket contains the *media*, which is a mylar material coated with magnetic oxide. Basically, the disk media is the same as found on a cassette tape, but mushed flat like a pancake, and of a much higher quality than that used for cassettes.

Label The manufacturer's label—usually on the upper-left corner of the top side of a disk—is mentioned here because it's a vital clue to inserting the disk into a drive correctly. You can also add your own label to the disk. You can write the current contents of the diskette onto any label you choose to use.

Drive-Hub Hole The drive-hub hole is the main hole in the middle of the disk. It's where the disk drive's spindle will clamp onto the disk and spin it around. 360K disks with have a reinforcement ring, slightly thicker than the disk media, just around the hole. Diskettes with a capacity of more than 360K will not have this hub.

Index Hole The index hole is a small hole, which if you were looking at a clock, would be located at about 3:30, next to the drive-hub hole. The index hole is used to locate sector 0 on the disk as the disk spins.

Read/Write Window In the read/write window you can see the disk's media. This is where the floppy drive's read/write heads will make physical contact with the disk to read and write your data.

Don't put your fingers or anything else inside the read/write window—you'll damage the disk.

Exposed Media In the case of a 21M floppy disk, the exposed media is an amber color and is transparent, but otherwise appears to be much like that of a DD or HD 3½" floppy disk. Again, *don't touch the media*, you'll leave skin oils and dirt on the media.

Write-Enable Notch The write-enable notch appears on all 5¼" disk-ettes. The write-enable notch allows you to write to the disk and read from it. If you place a write-protect tab over the notch, you can only read from the disk.

Protective Shutter A protective metal shutter covers the read/write window and protects the media on 3½" disks. You can slide the window to one side with your fingers to reveal the read/write media.

Spindle Connector On the back (bottom) of the 3½" disk is a spe-cial connector by which the drive spins the disk. Note that there is no index hole.

Write-Protect Hole The write-protect hole mechanism on 3½" disks is a sliding tile covering or uncovering a small hole. When the tile covers the hole, the disk can be written to (it is write-enabled). If you can see through the hole, the disk cannot be written to (it is write-protected).

High-Density-Media Detection Hole The high-density 1.44MB disks have a second hole in them, on the opposite side of the disk from the write-protect hole. This media-detection hole is used by high-density drives to help detect a 1.44MB disk.

 You cannot magically transform a 720K disk into a 1.44MB disk by punching a hole in it. (This subject is dealt with in more de-tail toward the end of this chapter.)

The 2.8MB disks also have a special hole in them, but it's not level on the disk with the write-enable hole; instead, it's almost one notch lower, and on the opposite side of the disk.

Notches and Groves There are some additional notches and grooves on the 3½" disk, which ensure that the disk is properly inserted in the drive and hold it in position.

On the whole, the 3½" disk is a tremendous improvement over the 5¼" model. This improvement is of particular importance to the owners of laptop PCs because those systems, like many desktop PCs (including IBM's PS/2 line), use 3½" disks. This means upgrading to a 3½" floppy drive would maintain compatibility with your laptop or PS/2 units.

How Disks Work

Disks are used to store information. The information is put on the disk in the form of magnetic impulses, created by the drive's read/write head, which arrange iron oxide particles on the surface of the disk.

The read/write heads move in and out over the surface of the disk at preset *stops*, which are positioned exactly using the head assembly's stepper motor, which is used to move the head assembly in the preset increments. This, combined with the spinning of the disk, means that the read/write head can access just about any area of the disk in a given range.

 There are two read/write heads for each side of the disk. They move together.

The way information is stored on the disk is covered in the following section on Formatting Information. Before we move on, you should note that there are a few flaws with the way floppy disks work.

Your Floppy Drive Is Slow Floppy disks aren't always spinning, so there's a lag in between the request for information and the point when the drive gets up to speed. Sometimes the disk starts to flutter if it spins too fast. Today's floppy disks run at about 150ms, which, compared to your hard drive's speed of 80ms or less, is pretty darn slow. Floptical drives (21MB) run at about 60ms-70ms, so they're a lot faster than either DD or HD floppy drives. When floptical drives are reading and writing to DD or HD diskettes, they must spin the disk at the speed of a normal floppy drive, so the access time goes up to 150ms.

Your Floppy Drive Doesn't Store Much Information The way a floppy disk is made provides for low-density data storage. The 21MB disk used by the floptical drive is unique in that it is etched with addresses when the disk is made (as opposed to using an electronic addressing system as is done on your DD and HD floppies). Since the addresses are etched into the floptical disk, the floptical disk is more reliable than disk-ettes that use an electronic addressing system.

A Floppy Drive Can Be Abrasive Because the read/write heads are in direct contact with the media in a DD or HD drive, neither the heads nor the media will last forever. Eventually the surface of the disk will become unusable due to a combination of abrasion and magnetic oxide buildup. The beginning of the end becomes evident when your disk starts to sound like you're using it as sandpaper instead of computer storage media. After a time, magnetic oxide builds up on the read/write head. Diskettes should be discarded when they show signs of excessive wear.

A lot has happened to the world of floppy-disk drives. Toshiba has been pushing their new standard 2.8MB floppy disk. So far, the only major inroad into establishing a new standard for removable media is in the floptical 21MB disk drive. Because you can replace your current 3½" drive with a floptical drive and gain the ability to use either DD, HD, or VHD disks in the same drive, the floptical standard may become the upgrade of choice for many users.

Formatting Diskettes

A conventional DD or HD disk must be *formatted* before it can hold infor-mation. Formatting involves the operating system laying out "parking places" in which to store future files and data on the disk. As we said ear-lier, 21MB floppy disks require no formatting because their addressing system is permanent, like that of a CD—you don't have to format a 21MB disk!

DOS formats a disk by dividing it up into *tracks, cylinders, sectors, clusters,* and eventually bytes.

A *track* is a formatted ring of information on one side of the disk. Disks have two sides and drives have a read/write head for each side, so the two matching tracks on either side of the disk are referred to collectively as a *cylinder.*

Tracks are formatted by the read/write head as it moves over the surface of the spinning disk. Tracks are really separate rings, like parking stalls

painted around a stadium—they aren't in a spiral like the long groove in a record album.

Each track is divided into *sectors*. (See Figure 8.5.) Bytes of information are actually stored in these *sectors* on the disk. Tracks are divided into sectors because that creates a more convenient and efficient method for storing information. If you could store information only on tracks, only a handful of files—no matter what their actual size—would fit on a disk.

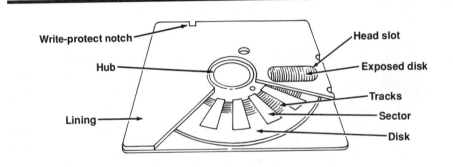

FIGURE 8.5:   Tracks and sectors on a typical disk

Under DOS, each sector typically contains 512 bytes, or about one half-page of text. The sectors are grouped into larger units, called *clusters*, for use with DOS. When allocating space for a file, DOS will assign it by cluster rather than by individual sectors. Why? ...Again, because of convenience.

A cluster on a hard drive usually consists of four or more sectors, usually 2K, or 2,048 bytes. On a floppy drive, clusters are often equal to one sector, or 512 bytes.

As far as the DD and HD disk format is concerned, DOS only cares about tracks and cylinders, plus sectors. There are a number of different combinations of tracks and sectors, depending on the density of the magnetic media and the type of drive involved.

Table 8.1 lists the different cylinder, track, and sector values for four popular PC disk sizes and formats.

TABLE 8.1: Disk formats with cylinders, tracks, sectors, and total bytes of storage

DISK FORMAT	CYLINDERS	TRACKS	SECTORS	TOTAL BYTES
360K	40	80	9	368,640
720K	80	160	9	737,280
1.2MB	80	160	15	1,228,800
1.44MB	80	160	18	1,474,560

Not only can the higher-capacity disks have double the tracks of the 360K format, but they can squeeze more 512K sectors on each track. This explains why special media is required for those higher-capacity disks (and why they cost more).

The typical DOS user won't have to be concerned with all this detail. The FORMAT command senses the maximum capacity of any drive and formats the disk in the drive to its full capacity. When you want to format a disk in a drive for which the disk is not standard, you need to know about tracks and sectors. That information is covered later in this chapter as well as in your DOS manual.

Buying Disks

In addition to choosing from the abundant brand names (and "generics") available, you have to buy the proper disk to go with your disk drive.

This isn't as much of a hassle as it was a few years ago, but there are still peculiarities and things to watch out for. The following attributes describe disks you can buy off the shelf.

Double-Sided Disks The most popular format for disks today is double-sided. This makes sense because disks have two sides. Nearly all disks you buy will be certified as double-sided, meaning the manufacturer has tested both sides of the disk.

Double-Density Disks Double-density disks were the popular standard when the PC was introduced. If a disk is double-sided, you can get 360K of data on the diskette. The standard PC 5¼" floppy is a double-sided,

high-density diskette, which is what you should look for on the box when you buy disks.

At this point the term TPI (for Tracks Per Inch) comes into play. You can gauge the "density" of a disk using the TPI number. The more tracks per inch, the more information the disk can hold. A double-density disk is rated at about 48 TPI. (Note that it still holds only 40 tracks). A 3½" disk has a TPI of 135.

As you'll soon see, the "density" definitions can get out of hand. TPI is always the best gauge to use when comparing the information on the sides of disk boxes.

Quad-Density Disks This oddball format found its way onto a few disk drive systems, but failed to catch on in the marketplace. Basically, it's a 5¼" 720K disk format, double the standard double-sided double-density drive. The quad-density format is rarely heard of today, except when noted in lectures such as this.

High-Density Disks Also known as HD (for High Density), or high-capacity, these disks are basically of the 1.2MB and 1.44MB sizes. The TPI gauge for a 1.2MB disk is 96; for a 1.44MB disk it's 135. Astute readers will note that 720K and 1.44MB disks have the same TPI density—there are other differences in the media that explain why you should not format a 720K rated disk to 1.44MB (lecture forthcoming). Table 8.2 shows you a table of TPI values for the four popular diskette types.

TABLE 8.2: The tracks-per-inch (TPI) values for the four common disk formats

DISK SIZE	TPI	DESCRIPTION
360K, 5½-inches	48	Double-Sided/Double-Density
720K, 3½-inches	135	Double-Sided/Double-Density
1.2MB, 5¼-inches	96	Double-Sided/High-Density
1.44MB, 3½-inches	135	Double-Sided/High-Density

Extended-Density Disks The "ED" disk has a capacity of 2.8MB. This disk comes in the standard 3½" jacket and looks identical to DD and HD 3½" disks.

Pre-Formatted Disks Formatting a box of ten 1.44MB disks takes about 20 minutes. Some clever manufacturers have decided it would be a good idea to pre-format the disks they sell, to save you time. Buying pre-formatted disks will really save you a lot of time, but remember that you'll pay extra for the pre-formatting.

Upgrading a Disk Drive

Now that you're all boned up on everything you need to know about disk drives and disks, here are the carefully plotted instructions for upgrading one on your own.

Installing and removing have been separated in this book because you don't often need to do both. If you're adding a drive B to a machine that had only drive A, there's nothing to remove (except maybe a faceplate) before you install the drive. The same holds true for replacing a full-height drive—that's a specific upgrade that owners of older PCs may attempt.

Buying a Drive

Few people simply remove drives—they usually replace a drive with a higher-density drive (such as a floptical). Buying a drive is probably the hardest part of your upgrade process. There are some choices to make. You should consider the following when you go drive hunting.

Know What You Want

You could be adding a drive B to your system, you could be changing drive A to a 3½" drive to make it compatible with your laptop or PS/2 system, or you could be replacing a dead drive with a new one. First you have to decide your purpose, and what drive will best serve you.

You'll also have to decide what you want to spend. New drives cost between $50 and $250 (for a floptical drive).

Know the Size Remember the five basic formats for the drive:

2.8MB, 3½"

1.2MB, 3½"

1.44MB, 5¼"

720K, 3½"

360K, 5¼"

3½" drives usually come with 5¼" mounting gear that lets you plug them into a standard 5½" drive bay. Some tower units might have 3½" mounting. Be sure to request the correct mounting for your drive when you order it, as well as all the other descriptive statistics.

Tell Them Which Computer You Have You should also tell the salesperson whether you're installing the drive into a PC/XT or AT system. Some older PC/XTs (made prior to 1985) had to have special jumpers set on the controller card. Without the proper setting of these jumpers, the BIOS and the floppy-disk controller couldn't recognize and format the drive to its full capacity, so you should mention the type of machine if the drive you're replacing is a full-height drive.

Brand Names As far as brand names go, take your pick. Just steer clear of unknown names, no-name clones, flea market finds, and anything without a warranty. Most of the time a reputable dealer will stock only what gives him the least amount of hassle. Since buying drives off the shelf isn't something everyone does, don't expect a lot of choice.

Price Cost is a major factor to most people most of the time, but the price difference between drives is so minimal that it boils down to a Ford-vs.-Chevy kind of debate Some people swear by Sony's, others insist upon Teac or even Iomega (if the drive is VHD). These makers charge varying amounts for their version of the same drive.

Color Disk drives come in different colors—nothing your interior decorator would faint at, the colors are usually beige and seldom black (these days)—to match your PC's case.

Drive A or B? It doesn't matter any more if you own an AT. All floppy drives made in the 1990's will run as either drive A or B, depending on where the drive(s) are plugged into the data cable.

If you're buying a used drive for an older PC, try to request a drive that's pre-configured for positioning as drive A or B. If the dealer scratches his head, or mumbles that "all drives are alike," he's probably right in the sense that all PC drives will be configured as drive B, with DS1 set.

Faceplate If you're replacing a full-height drive with a half-height, you're going to need a half-height faceplate to install in the leftover space. Remember to buy one.

Note the Case Style PC/XT-style cases may need a mounting bracket to handle a half-height drive. These cases were designed around full-height drives, so there will be no screw holes for any drives on the top-underside of the drive bays. Be sure to specify a mounting bracket if this is your situation.

If your case is an AT case, you probably won't need any extra hardware unless you want to install a 3 ½" drive in a 5 ¼" bay.

Where to Shop Personally, I've ordered all my drives—both hard and floppy—via mail order. Everything has always arrived on time and in excellent condition.

About Mounting Rails

In a PC/XT style case, the screw holes on the side of the disk drive unit are used to anchor the side of the drive to the drive bay.

The drive is anchored on one side only—the left bay is anchored on the left side, and the right bay on the right side. This will seem more important to you when you install the drive.

Mounting rails are metal or plastic, pontoon-shaped doo-hickeys that screw into the side of your drive. Note that the pointed end, as shown in Figure 8.6, goes to the rear of the drive.

Floppy-Disk Drives

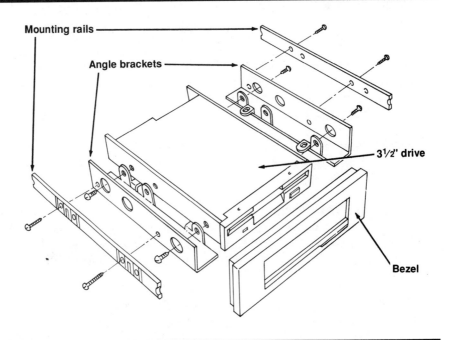

FIGURE 8.6: Mounting rails attached to the side of a floppy drive

You must attach the mounting rail to each side of your drive. The drive bay in an AT-style case doesn't have screw holes. But it does have grooves into which you slide the drive. Mounting rails provide guides for those grooves. You position your drive in front of the bay, line up the grooves with the rails, and slide it back.

Once the drive is in position (and after you've attached the cables), you screw two angle brackets into the front of the case (see Figure 8.6). These brackets keep the drive in position, anchoring it into the system.

This more secure way to anchor a drive is a lot sturdier than the way half-height drives are attached to a PC/XT-style case.

Upgrade Overview

All action for upgrading a floppy drive usually takes place in the drive bay on the right. Of course, this isn't mandatory, it's just that the right bay is usually the exposed bay and you don't want to mount your drive behind the PC's front panel. (On my PC/XT case the floppy drives are mounted in the left bay; it was more convenient in my case.)

The basic steps for upgrading a drive are as follows.

Remove the PC's Lid Remember to power down and unplug the machine before you even lift a screwdriver. Also, ground yourself by touching the power supply before you start touching things inside the computer.

Locate the Drive You Want to Remove Find the floppy drive you want to remove, located in one of the bays. Make a note of which cables connect to it and where the screws are.

Unscrew the Mounting Screws The screws will be on the side. If the screws are on the side, and your drive is in the left bay, you may need to remove some expansion cards to get at them. (This is covered in Chapter 10.) Otherwise the screws will be easily accessible. Set the screws aside to be saved for installing the new drive. If you're dealing with mounting rails, don't lose the angle brackets.

Slide the Drive Forward a Bit The drive is now free and can be slid forward a bit to give you room to remove the cables behind the drive.

Unplug the Power Supply Cable The power supply cable is a four-wire job with a white plastic box on the end. Grab it by the white box and pull firmly to remove it. All power supply connectors are the same, for both floppy and hard drives, so it doesn't matter which one you plug into your drive. Simply bend the connector out of the way.

Unplug the Data Cable The data cable will slide off the edge connector when you pull it. Sometimes sliding the drive forward will cause the connector to slip off. You may want to label the connector A or B, but this isn't necessary. Unless you're doing two floppy drive upgrades at once, there's no need to label the connector. It should be the only connector available in the machine at the time. Go ahead and label it, though, if doing so makes you feel better. Don't remove the data cable from the controller card. Keep all other ends of the floppy cable attached.

Slide the Drive All the Way Forward and Free The drive is now free and you can remove it. All drives, floppy and hard, pull out through the front of the drive bay.

Set the Old Drive Aside You can put the drive anywhere, for example on your tabletop. Don't put it on the carpet, where fibers may join with the circuit board (or you may step on it). The best place to put the drive is in the box your new drive came packaged in. If it's a dead drive, label it "DEAD" or "OBSOLETE" on the box. Otherwise, label the box as to the type of drive you're storing, and put the box into storage. If the drive has mounting rails, you may want to unscrew them at this time, setting the rails and the screws aside.

Locate the Replacement or New Drive Be careful to avoid re-installing your old drive. Most floppy drives look identical to the untrained eye, and it's easy to make that mistake!

If you're putting in a new drive that requires a new controller card, you'll have to upgrade the controller card at this point. Installing a card into the PC is covered in Chapter 9. Remember that you can use the same cable that's already in your PC (unless, of course, the cable is damaged). If you're putting a half-height drive in a PC-style case, you may need to add a mounting bracket to support the half-height drive in the top position. To do so, remove the screws from the lower drive's position, install the bracket, and then put the screws back on the lower drive.

Slide the Drive in from the Front Position the drive in front of the drive bay and push it back. It should slide easily into place.

You shouldn't slide the drive back all the way at this point. Also, be careful that you're not installing the drive upside-down.

Attach the Power Supply Cable Plug the white power supply connector into the white receptacle on the drive's logic board. The connector fits just one way, so don't force it. It does, however, require a bit of pressing to push the connector in all the way.

Attach the Data Cable The data cable should be notched—don't force it! If you can't seem to get it on, or if it attaches only at an angle, flip it over, line up the notch, and try again. If you're adding a new controller at this stage, you would attach the cable to the controller as well.

Slide the Drive in All the Way Once the cables are attached, slide the drive back until the faceplate that bears the slot for inserting diskettes is flush with the front of your computer's case.

Tighten the Screws Match the screw holes on the side of the drive with the holes in the drive bay or mounting bracket. Just four screws are required to anchor the drive—you can use those holes that line up best and allow you to position the drive properly. If you're dealing with mounting rails, put the angle brackets into the drive so they hold the drive into the bay and wrap around to the front of the case over the screw holes. Then tighten the screws.

Make Sure All Connections Are Sound Before firing up the machine or putting the lid back on, make sure that neither the data cable or power supply cable have come off. Reach back with your fingers (or simply look) to make sure everything is still attached.

Put the PC's Lid Back On As an optional step, before putting the lid back on, you can fire up the PC to make sure the drive works. (Just keep your hands out of it.) Otherwise, put the lid back on and you're ready to use your new drive.

All Done Once you're done, turn on your PC and try to access your new drive. If you get a POST error, then you might have forgotten to set your PC/XTs DIP switches or run your AT's SETUP program. If you have an XT, turn the system off and open the case to set the DIP switches. Run SETUP if you have an AT.

 Always power down before you put your hands inside an open computer!

If the computer starts up fine after you've installed a floppy drive, make sure everything was done properly by using the FORMAT command on the drive. If the drive FORMATs out to its given capacity—ta DA!—you've

done it. If not, you'll have to try DRIVER.SYS in your CONFIG.SYS file, or recheck your jumper settings.

Installing a Floppy Drive or Tape-Backup Drive

You install a tape-backup drive as if it were a floppy drive, and then you plug its cable between the existing data cable and the floppy drive controller.

HOW TO INSTALL A FLOPPY DRIVE OR TAPE DRIVE

Procedure: Installing a disk or tape drive

Tools Needed: Medium plus screwdriver

Steps:

1. Power down your PC and remove the lid. (If you've just removed a drive, and your case is already open, you can skip this step.)

2. Remove the old drive if necessary, or the faceplate covering the drive bay, if that's necessary.

3. Slide the drive into position. Drives slide in from the front. Make sure you don't have it upside down.

4. Attach the power supply and umbilical cables to the drive. They go on one way only. If the drive is a tape drive, follow the maker's instructions for installing the cable.

5. Slide the drive into the bay until the front of the drive is flush with the front of the computer's case.

6. Anchor the drive into position by attaching and tightening the four mounting screws. If you're dealing with mounting rails, position the angle brackets and then tighten the screws on both sides of the front of the drive.

7. Recheck your connections.

8. Close up the lid and test the new equipment. (You may first want to fire up the machine to test it with the lid off.)

Removing a Drive

Follow this next set of steps to learn how to remove a floppy drive. If you're simply *adding* a drive to an empty bay, you obviously won't have to remove a drive first.

HOW TO REMOVE A FLOPPY DRIVE

Procedure: Removing a floppy drive

Tools Needed: Medium plus screwdriver

Steps:

1. Power down your PC and remove the lid.

2. Locate the drive and remove its screws. There are four mounting screws. Set the screws and angle brackets (if any) aside, or put them in a baggie and tape them to the drive.

3. Slide the drive forward and detach the power supply cable and data cable. Bend them out of the way.

4. Slide the drive forward and free. At this point you may want to put the drive aside, box it up, or toss it out. Remember to disconnect the mounting rails (if any) if you're going to be putting a new drive in its place.

5. Replace the drive. Or, if you aren't going to replace the drive, install a blank faceplate over the drive bay hole.

If you're changing drive B to drive A you should reposition drive B on the cable. If you have an AT, simply unplug drive B from the middle connector on the data cable and replug it into the end connector on the same data cable. Also, reset any DIP switches or run your AT's SETUP program to let the system know about the new drive A and missing drive B. Otherwise, if you're installing a new drive, you can move on to the next section.

If you install a second 5¼" or 3½" drive that's of a different capacity than your first drive, for example a 720K drive A and a 1.44M drive B, you might want to label the drives using one of those raised-letter marking-tape machines. This should avoid any future confusion, especially when someone else uses the computer.

Replacing a Full-Height Drive

Quite a few disk upgrades involve replacing a full-height drive with two half-heights. If you're going to do this type of upgrade, keep in mind the following.

Identify Drive A and Drive B If you're replacing an old full-height drive A with an A and B, remember which drives are which. Unless you buy one preconfigured as A or B, you may have to set its jumpers, and if it's drive A, put a terminating resistor on it.

If your PC has full-height drives, you should pay particular attention to the jumper and terminating resistor information in this section.

Your Controller Card If you do have full-height disk drives, odds are pretty good that you have an older controller card. Consider getting a new controller card, or a hard/floppy-disk controller combo. You'll find those options more compatible with the newer high-capacity disk drives.

These days, a new HD/FD controller can be had for less than $20, street dinero.

The Mounting Bracket Full-height drive bays have screw holes only on the bottom. To anchor a half-height drive in the top position, you'll need a half-height-drive mounting bracket to give you that extra set of screw holes necessary.

Power Cable Splitter Older PCs with full-height drives had only two drive connectors on the power supply. If so, you'll need a power cable splitter, also called a Y cable. This Y cable simply acts as an extension cord for your power supply…it turns one cable into two.

The Faceplate If you're replacing a full-height drive with a single half-height, you'll need a half-height faceplate to cover the resulting hole.

Software Considerations

The process of upgrading a floppy drive isn't all about hardware. Some software is involved—after all, it's the software that really runs your computer.

On the software side, there are two main issues to deal with:

◆ Exchanging Disks
◆ Formatting

Exchanging Disks

Exchanging data between different older and newer PCs can be a real hassle because the older PC may not be able to recognize and use newer diskette formats. There are a few things to be leery of. These are all covered below.

Formatting

DOS is set up to recognize all types of disk drives and to format (if need be) the disks you use in them to the maximum size allowed by the drive (the *default* size).

The DOS format command is FORMAT, followed by the letter (plus a colon) that names the drive containing the disk to be formatted—for example:

FORMAT A:

to format the floppy in drive A. This is about all you need to know to format a disk. But there is more than one disk format. Three additional formats exist from the early days of DOS 1, and these formats are still supported by DOS 6's FORMAT command. This makes FORMAT very flexible, with a lot of esoteric options and switches.

Most often, you'll use FORMAT's optional switches to format a low-density disk in a height-density drive. For example, you might format a 360K disk in a 1.2MB drive, or a 720K disk in a 1.44MB drive.

To format disks to a capacity other than the default, use the FORMAT command with its optional switches set as shown in Table 8.3.

TABLE 8.3:   Disk sizes and their format command line options

FORMATTED CAPACITY	DRIVE SIZE	FORMAT OPTIONS
160K	1.2MB	/1 /8
360K	1.2MB	/4 /1 /8
180K	1.2MB	/1
360K	1.2MB	/4 /1
320K	1.2MB	/8
360K	1.2MB	/4 /8
360K	1.2MB	/4
720K	1.44MB	/N:9 /T:80

It's Always a Good Idea to Format a Disk at Its Rated Capacity

Format 360K disks to 360K, format 1.44MB disks to 1.44MB. 1.44MB disks should be formatted to 1.44MB, and 720K disks should be formatted to 720K.

When problems arise are when you format a disk for a size other than what it's intended to be.

Don't Format a High-Capacity Disk to Low-Capacity

Sure, you can do it, but it's a waste of media. Few low-capacity disks will be able to read the drive because of the high-capacity media's tighter storage of information.

On Formatting Low-Capacity Disks in a High-Capacity Drive

This can be done. In fact, formatting a 360K disk to 360K in a 1.2MB drive sometimes formats it better than formatting one in a 360K-only drive. They used to say that formatting a 360K disk in a 1.2MB drive rendered the disk unreadable by other 360K drives—this isn't true.

However, you should avoid the temptation to format low-capacity disks to a higher capacity. While this may work initially, the format will not hold and the disk's data will eventually fade away.

On 3½" Drives

There is no problem with formatting a 720K disk in a 1.44MB drive. Moving 3½" disks between different capacity drives isn't a problem either.

On Formatting a Low-Capacity Disk to Make It a High-Capacity Disk

This *can't* be done. The magnetic density of the 1.2MB disk is much greater than the 360K disk. While DOS will proceed as you direct it, the 360K disk will usually come up with more than 50% bad sectors.

Also, the close proximity of the tracks on such a low-density magnetic surface will lead to heinous magnetic migration—after a time, the magnetic particles will slowly corrupt themselves, rendering your data useless.

On Floptical Disks

Floptical (or VHD) disks don't need to be formatted by the user because they don't use a FAT (an electronic file addressing system); they use a

permanent addressing system that's etched or stamped into the disk when it's made.

There are basically two different ways for manufacturers to create floptical (21MB) disks. The cheaper way is by stamping the tracks into the media. Higher-quality disks are addressed (etched) using laser technology. At this time in the evolution of the product, you may want to stick with the maker's own flopticals instead of buying a rogue bargain brand.

Flopticals cost about $16 per disk, which seems bug-eyed high until you consider the per-megabyte cost of a HD disk in comparison. To store the same amount of data, meg-for-meg, a 21MB floptical disk actually costs less. And, as the floptical's popularity increases, its price is sure to drop.

On Formatting a 720K Disk to 1.44MB

This is another thing tried by too many bozos on the bus. They figure that since both formats of 3½" disks are 135 TPI, all they need to do is punch a hole in a 720K disk to make it into a 1.44MB....Think of the money you'd save! (There are even companies that sell tools for this.)

Punching a hole in a 720K disk to make it 1.44MB is just stupid. Don't ever punch a hole in a floptical disk to "see what'll happen." ...The shame!

1.44MB disks have a higher magnetic density than their 720K brothers. That's why they cost more. (Duh!) While punching a hole will fool the drive and DOS into formatting the 720K disk to 1.44MB, and the resulting disk may actually work for a while, eventually magnetic migration will creep in. After anywhere from an hour to two months, a 720K disk formatted to 1.44MB will lose data. Then, especially if you write to the drive again, the data in adjacent tracks will be rendered useless.

It's just a bad thing to do.

To sum up:

◆ Buy the right media for the right drive

◆ Format the media to its full capacity

◆ *Don't* format 720K disks to 1.44MB

If you have any other problems with disks, for example you can't format a disk you could read a moment ago, then bulk erase it. (A VCR-tape bulk eraser will do the job. Some cassette tape erasers, however, are too weak to go through a 3$\frac{1}{2}$" disk's shell. Some places do offer specific computer disk bulk erasers.)

Also, if you've been using a disk "for the longest time" and it suddenly becomes unreadable, the problem probably isn't with your drive—it's age. Disks don't last forever. You should back up your disks—especially those you use often—every once in a while. Otherwise you may suddenly find that a disk you've used every day for the past three years just doesn't work any more.

Hard-Disk Drives

Doing the hard-disk drive upgrade thing is very similar to changing a floppy drive. You should, however, know some background information, and a few things about hard drives in particular.

Nearly every PC sold today comes with an installed hard drive. However, you may want to replace yours with a larger hard disk, or you may have to replace a dying hard disk. There is also room for a second hard drive inside your PC, and in light of today's larger and larger software applications and their burgeoning data files, having more hard-disk storage is tops on just about everyone's list (next to more memory, of course). This chapter will tell you how to install a hard drive.

General Notes on Hard-Disk Drives

Hard drives store information using a lot of the same techniques as floppy-disk drives. There's a spinning disk, magnetic media, read/write heads—it's all very similar. The difference lies in that the hard drive is hermetically sealed—air tight—and the mechanical tolerances of the hard disk are much greater than those of floppies, which allows hard drives to store and retrieve more information more quickly.

This section contains general notes on hard drives and hard disk technology—the hardware side. We'll give you some background information and explain some general terms. The details on hard drives are in the next section, which will give you background information on the physical aspects of a hard-disk drive.

 Additional information on setting up a hard disk in DOS (formatting and so on) is covered in the last part of this book in the section titled "Software Setup."

● Background Information

To most users, the hard-disk drive is a mystery box. It has an access light on its faceplate, just like a floppy drive, but there is no slot in the faceplate for removing or inserting a diskette, and the drive is always humming. Of course, those are only simple observations—there's a lot more to a hard-disk drive than just a humming black faceplate.

How a Hard Drive Works

A hard drive contains a disk like a floppy drive does, though often it holds more than one disk, and each is stacked on top of the other like pancakes. Unlike floppy disks, hard disks are rigid, usually made of aluminum, and coated with a thin film of magnetic oxide.

You can see inside a floppy-disk drive, but a hard-disk drive is hermetically sealed—it's in an air-tight environment, void of dust and other particles that could damage the media or the delicate read/write heads. This is important because in a hard-disk drive, the read/write heads literally float some 10 millionths of an inch above the surface of the rapidly spinning disk. That close distance, along with the density of the magnetic media, allows a hard disk to hold much more information than a floppy.

In your upgrading adventures you'll never be tearing into a hard drive's hermetically sealed bubble. (You can try opening up a "dead" drive, but you'll need a special type of screwdriver.) Figure 9.1 should give you an idea of what's going on inside your hard-disk drive.

The disks in a hard drive spin around a spindle that's powered by a motor on the drive unit itself, just like a floppy drive. Note that the disks are rigid and how they're stacked inside the unit. Each disk is called a *platter*, and like a floppy disk, it has two sides. Because there are so many platters (up to six in some drives), the sides are numbered from top-to-bottom. The typical hard-disk drive, with three platters, has sides 0 through 5, with the even-numbered sides on top of the platters and the odd-numbered sides on the bottom.

For each side of each platter, the drive has a read/write head. Notice in the figure that all the read/write heads are mounted on a single unit, known as the *head assembly*. They move together, each accessing a different track, on all sides of the disk at once. It's the physical locations of all those tracks in space that really gives meaning to the formatting term *cylinder*. Three platters with six sides makes for six circular tracks in space— a cylinder.

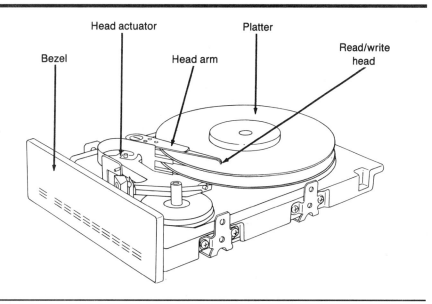

FIGURE 9.1: The inside of a hard drive

The read/write heads move in and out as a unit by the *head actuator mechanism*, a device similar to that which moves the read/write heads in and out over a floppy disk. That's where the similarities end.

The tolerances of the head actuator mechanism are very precise. There are usually two types: *stepper motors* and *voice-coil actuators*.

The Drive Unit

Hard drives come in two sizes: full-height and half-height. The full-height drive still exists, especially for very large capacity hard drives, but for most of the average size drives—even up to 500MB of storage—half-height is the standard size.

The bottom of the drive holds the logic board, which is usually facing up into the drive, so all you see is a green Plexiglas "pincushion." The top of the drive has the metal bubble that contains the sealed disk, read/write heads, and mechanisms.

Most computers have an IDE interface these days. On an IDE interface configuration, there's a single power supply and a single edge connector. You might also see some jumpers. These determine the position of the drive, either as your first disk drive, C, or the second one, D.

Your first disk drive, usually drive C, must have its jumper set so that the computer knows it to be the first (or C) drive on the data cable. If you upgrade and buy a drive D, you will need to change it's jumper so that the computer knows it to be the slave, or second hard drive.

Unlike floppy drives, all hard-disk drives are sold as C. So you must change the jumper on both your C and your new D drive. But changing the jumper isn't always necessary. (That subject is covered in the upcoming section on cables.)

Each connector (both the data cable and the power cable) on the back of a hard-disk drive is notched. There's no way to plug anything in backwards.

The Controller Card

The hard-disk controller interfaces the hard-disks to the PC itself via the bus. In some cases, the hard-disk controller may be on the motherboard of the computer, as is the case with IBM's PS/2 line of computers. In other cases, a system may sport a dual floppy/hard-disk controller. Most of the guts of your controller may be located on your hard drive, as is the case with IDE drives. Whatever the case, a controller is required in the hard-drive setup.

Your drive type and controller card must match. Since drives and controllers are often sold together, the salesperson can help you match them up. But be aware that there are differences in the types of hard drives and controllers. Your choice depends only on the type of drive and the system you're installing it into.

If you have an IDE, ESDI, or SCSI type drive (covered below), reformatting of your drive(s) should not be necessary. If not, then remember to backup your entire hard-disk drive before swapping controllers (if possible). And backing up before operating on a PC is a healthy step to take in any event.

The generic example in Figure 9.2 shows you all the highlights of a hard-disk controller.

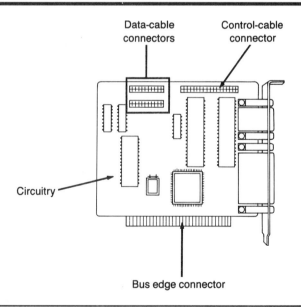

FIGURE 9.2: A generic hard-disk controller

These are key things you need to look for:

◆ Any jumpers or switches

◆ The connector for the floppy drive cable

◆ The connector for the hard drive cable

It may be necessary to set jumpers on some computers (see your documentation). Certain controller cards may conflict with other cards in your system, such as mouse cards. (In that particular instance, you should change the mouse card, *not* the hard-disk controller.)

Conflicts like this are usually caused by HD/FD combo cards that have the ability to provide a mouse and parallel port. For example, some interface cards may have trouble with some internal modem or serial port cards. These problems are resolved by setting the right jumpers. But for the majority, the factory settings are adequate.

Most IDE FD/HD controllers (IDE drive/controller combinations constitute about 95% of those now marketed and used) take a preset *interrupt* so you don't have to worry about conflicts with other hardware devices. Since most modern hard- and floppy-disk controllers are of the IDE type (and most are combo-cards that have the circuitry for both controller cards mounted on a single half-length card), we'll talk about these cards in this section.

The cable connectors used by the hard drive portion of the controller are a little different from those used for the floppy portion. There are two drive cable connectors. One is for floppy drives and one is for hard-disk drives. Each will be marked somewhere nearby with the words "Floppy Drive" or "Hard Drive".

The single 40-pin connector (used for the hard drive portion of the controller card) hooks into a single cable that services both hard-disk drives. Be careful with them: the pins are easy to bend. If you do accidentally bend a pin, gently straighten it out again using needle-nosed pliers. Don't twist it.

Unlike the standard floppy drive controller, there are several types of hard-disk controllers. The correct controller type to be used depends on the drive type. The drive type also prescribes the method by which information will be recorded on the drive.

MFM stands for *Modified Frequency Modulation*, and it refers to the magnetic encoding scheme by which bits are put onto the magnetic media. Of all the controller types, this used to be the least expensive and also the least efficient at storing information.

RLL stands for *Run Length Limited*. It stores information in a much tighter format than MFM, so RLL drives can boast nearly twice the formatted capacity of similar MFM drives. But be warned: these benefits are only drawn when both the drive and controller support the RLL format.

ESDI stands for *Enhanced Small Device Interface*. These drives and controllers are very fast and hold a lot of data. They're typically found on high-end PCs or file servers. Also, because ESDI drives have minds of their own (so to speak), you can run any ESDI drive with any ESDI controller. There's no need to reformat when switching controllers. The popularity of ESDIs has waned, however, with the onset of IDE and the SCSI-2 standards.

SCSI stands for *Small Computer System Interface* (pronounced "scuzzy"). SCSI is actually more than a disk-drive interface. Up to seven devices can be chained together on one SCSI card. So you can run seven hard-disk drives; or one hard-disk drive and a printer, scanner, digitizer; or any number of SCSI-compatible devices; all off of one controller card. Also, like ESDI drives, SCSI drives are smart, fast, and come in a variety of sizes.

IDE stands for *Integrated Drive Electronics*. The IDE drive is by far the most popular drive in existence today. That's because a large part of the controller is built onto the drive itself. (Ever notice how small a modern IDE HD/FD controller is these days?) IDE drives are also about the very cheapest. Because such a large part of the controller is built into the bellies of IDE drives, hard drive vendors don't have to accommodate a whole mix of hard-disk drives. An IDE drive emulates ST-506 when it's talking to a controller that doesn't recognize it, so compatibility problems are truly minimized.

The process of installing the IDE drive is incredibly simple. IDE drives tend to operate at speeds approaching those of SCSI drives and even very large SCSI drives. When an IDE drive has its own memory chips (called a "hard buffer" or "cache buffer" used to speed the access time of the drive, the drive's average access time can be as low as 9ms.

Interleave

The *interleave* factor determines how the information is organized on each track of the hard disk. Some PCs are just too slow to read the information from a spinning drive as it rotates under the read/write head. They need time to digest, so the sectors in each track are laid out in an interleaved pattern. It's measured as a ratio, with 1:1 being the fastest in realized data access speed. (See Figure 9.3.)

A 3:1 interleave means that three sectors of information pass under the read/write head for every one sector the drive, controller, and computer are capable of reading. To make the most efficient use of the drive, the sectors are scattered about each track so that the next sequential sector on disk will be ready to read from once the previous sector has been digested. This interleave means no time is wasted waiting for the next sector to rotate under the read/write head.

Today's powerful and speedy PCs with equally powerful hard drives have the fastest interleave available, 1:1. For example, all ESDI drives have a 1:1 interleave. Virtually all modern IDE drives can use a 1:1 interleave as well. Each sector can be read from disk sequentially, so there really isn't any interleave at all.

The interleave factor is important because a bad interleave can really slow down a disk. It's one thing to use an interleave in favor of a slow PC. But too great an interleave means the computer waits too long for the proper sector to come under the read/write head. All that waiting takes time and slows down the drive.

Cables

There's one set of cables that hook IDE hard drives to the controller card. This cable looks like a ribbon, and it has 40 conductors in it. ESDI, MFM, RLL, and SCSI drives require two ribbon cables per drive.

The edge connector on the drive is usually notched, so installation isn't difficult. But the pins on the controller card may not have a key or an obvious orientation. For that end of the cable, remember to line up pin 1 on the connector with line 1 on the cable. The 40-line controller cable is remarkably similar to the cable used to connect your floppy drives. But it's not the same cable!

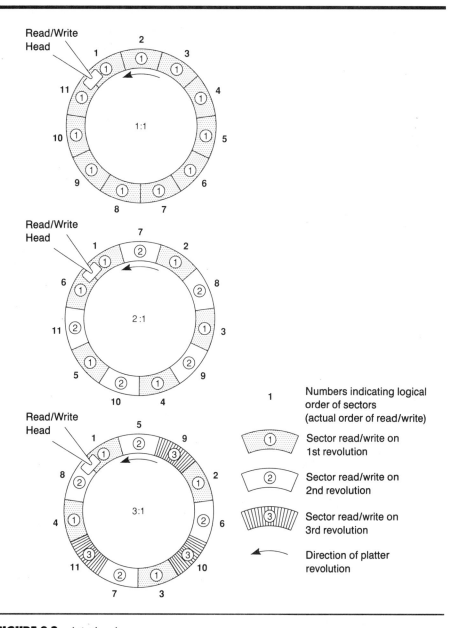

FIGURE 9.3: Interleaving

Like the floppy cable, the typical hard-disk controller cable supports two hard-disks. One end of the cable plugs into the hard-disk controller and the end connector goes to drive your hard drive. Actually, since most hard-disk controller cables connect to the controller card via a pin connector and not an edge connector, you won't go too far with this mistake.

 Some PCs may have a special straight-through cable, without another connector in the middle. When this is the case and you need to add a second hard drive, you'll need to buy a dual-drive cable.

Types of Hard Drives

This chapter focuses on IDE hard-disk drives, primarily because they're the most popular mass storage device and are widely available. But there are other storage devices you may want to consider.

In addition to the standard type of PC hard-disk drive, the following mass storage devices are mentioned in this section:

◆ Hard cards

◆ Removable hard-disk drives

◆ Floptical-disk drives

◆ Tape-backup systems

Standard Hard Drives

There are four types of standard hard-disk drives that you can install into your PC:

◆ A 5¼" full-height drive

◆ A 5¼" half-height drive

◆ A 3½" half-height drive

◆ A 3½" third-height drive

In computer technology, things keep getting physically smaller and smaller. The 3½" drive came about due to shrinking technology, as well as the need for smaller hard-disk drives in laptops. You can still use a

$3^{1}/2''$ drive in a desktop PC; it comes with mounting gear just as the $3^{1}/2''$ floppy drive does.

Most AT drives come with a specified type value. After installation, the POST will detect the drive's presence and notice a mismatch in your battery-backed-up (CMOS) RAM. You'll then be able to assign the correct drive type using your SETUP program and you can continue from there.

Hard Cards

A *hard card* is a great option for adding a hard drive to the system when you're out of empty disk drive bays. A hard card is basically a disk drive that is mounted vertically on the back end of a hard-disk controller card. The original hard cards were put out by Plus Development. They offered a way for older PCs to have a hard drive installed without sacrificing a full-height floppy. (The hard-disk mounts on the card inside the system unit.)

Removable Hard Drives

Ever since people first discovered how fast and easy hard drives are to use, they've looked for ways to make them removable. Why? Because it makes a convenient device even more convenient. Security is enhanced if you can lock up a hard-disk drive in a fire safe. Moving large amounts of information between locations is more convenient if you can just move the hard drive. Unfortunately, technology lagged for the longest time in satisfying users' desires for removable hard-disk drives.

CD-ROM Drives

The current rage in computing is "optical media," in which light beams store information as opposed to magnetic impulses on iron oxide. The advantage to optical disks are that they can last forever (if well kept). The drawback is that both reading and writing to an optical drive is slow—and expensive.

The most common type of optical disk is the CD-ROM. As the name implies, a CD-ROM is a compact disc containing Read Only Memory, or information that's already stored. Though you can store volumes of information on it, you cannot write to a CD-ROM.

The magneto-optical disk is basically a read/write CD-ROM disk. It's removable, transportable, and not terribly expensive. If technology can get

the price down, the magneto-optical disk may offer itself as a replacement for today's hard-disk drive.

Tape-Backup Systems

Storing information on magnetic tape is a method that's been with computers almost since day one. But with today's PCs (and even some of the bigger systems), tape drives are used primarily for backup and long-term data storage. On the larger mainframe computer systems, software is usually distributed on tapes.

Tape backup systems are as popular as they've ever been. Most of them are about the same size as a half-height floppy, and you can usually mount them in one of the half-height floppy drive bays. If you don't have a free drive bay, you can buy a tape drive to be used externally. The more modern drives will store up to 250M of data per tape using file compression techniques built into the tape-backup software. A tape-backup drive is a good upgrade option, but it tends to be expensive if your backup needs aren't that pressing.

Where They Go

Most of the information about placing a hard-disk drive in your system is identical to the information about locating a floppy drive. In fact, the discussion in Chapter 6 can apply to both cases. Be sure to note the following, however, when you're finding a place for a hard-disk drive in your PC.

There Are Full-Height Drives as Well as Half-Height Drives Not all hard drives are half-heights. You'll need two adjacent, free half-height bays if you expect to install a full-height drive into a computer case that's set up to handle half-height bays. If your case is set up to accept internal hard drives, plan on giving them up to a full-height hard drive. Most computer cases made in the '90s accept 3½" hard drives mounted internally, not externally. If your hard drive is the 5¼" size, you may have to install it in external drive bays just because the internal ones in your particular computer case are made to accept 3½" hard drives. Take a look into the inside of your computer case to learn if you have the space to take 5¼" drives internally. In fact, it's wise to determine the size of your available drive bays (and whether the free bay is external or internal) before you shop for that hard drive!

Most Hard Drives Go In the Left-Side Bay This is the traditional way to do it in a desktop case, and the tradition has a purpose. Hard drives go on the left because that side is usually obscured from view by the system unit's front panel. Floppy drives go on the right, in the open bay, to give you access to them. If you have a tower case, look below the floppy drives to locate your hard drive and any free hard-drive bays. These days, hard drives go all over the place inside a tower case. The location of hard-drive bays in a computer's case really depends the case maker—and some of them place drive bays in really weird locations!

There Is Such a Thing as a Hard Card If you're all out of drive bays, remember that you can purchase a *hard card* hard drive. This is certainly less expensive than buying another PC. If you add a hard card to a PC with no free drive bays, you might not have to remove a valued floppy drive just to accommodate it. Even if you have available drive bays, you might want to save them for a tape-backup unit, a CD-ROM drive, or another storage device. Adding a hard drive in the form of a hard card allows you to reserve a free drive bay for future expansion.

Formatting Information

Formatting a hard drive works exactly the same as it does for a floppy. There are tracks, cylinders, sectors, clusters, and eventually bytes. The difference is that with a hard-disk, you're dealing with several tracks per cylinder, as opposed to two. Each track does have a side, or "head number," associated with it. But on the DOS-terminology level, they're still called cylinders.

The total number of cylinders in a hard drive will be greater than in a floppy drive (obviously). A 20MB hard drive, for example, may have 619 cylinders, while a 1.2MB floppy has only 80. If the disk has two platters, that makes for four disk sides. So the actual number of tracks is 619×4, or 2,476. There are also more sectors-per-track on a typical DOS hard-disk drive. An IDE hard-disk drive has a 39-sector track. (ESDI drives use 34 sectors per track.) There are still 512 bytes per sector. So if you continue with the same example, a 619 cylinder hard drive with two platters will have: 619 (cylinders) $\times$ 4 (sides) = 2,476 (tracks). Multiply that by 17 (sectors per track) and 512 (bytes per sector) and you get 21,551,104 bytes. Divide that by 1,204 and you get 21,046K, and divide that by 1,024 —you finally get 20.55 megabytes. (A 20MB hard-disk!)

Note that drives are usually sold in a size value (number) that indicates the *unformatted* size. That number is always greater than the size of the formatted drive. For example, a 90MB drive may actually format out to only 88MB. While the loss of two megs is not that big a deal, you should be aware of this matter when you purchase a drive. The drive's packaging should mention whether the value listed is the "unformatted capacity" or not.

 There are two types of formats you can do to a hard-disk drive:

◆ The low-level format

◆ The DOS format (using the FORMAT command)

These two types of format are covered in the final part of this chapter.

Upgrading a Hard Drive

Upgrading a hard drive is nearly identical to upgrading a floppy drive. Since the drives are the same size, you need only concern yourself with the cable connections. Two of the hard drive's three cables work just like those on a floppy drive—the third cable, the data cable, isn't any big deal, either.

The focus here is on those parts of the upgrade procedure that differ significantly from a floppy disk upgrade. For more information on upgrading drives, check out Chapter 7.

Buying a Drive

There are many more terms used to describe a hard-disk drive than a floppy drive. When you're upgrading, you really have to do your research to find out exactly what you want. Brand names and loyalties aside, the following four considerations are most important when choosing a new hard-disk drive.

◆ The type of PC you have

◆ The size of the hard drive

◆ The drive's speed

◆ The controller card interface

Some hard drives are made specifically for PC/XTs, others for PC/ATs. Make sure you get the proper drive for your system.

Next you'll need to know the size of the hard drive (in megabytes). How much is enough? Figure you need at least three megabytes per application (four or more megabytes per application if the application involves graphics). Total up your guestimates on this, and then double or triple that value. If you're in a business situation, a minimum size to consider is 80 megabytes—which even then may not be enough, especially if you're a Windows user. (Windows applications are normally 2-6 times larger than DOS applications.)

You'll need to know how fast you want your drive to be. Hard-disk drive speeds are measured in milliseconds, abbreviated *ms*. That's also known as the *average access time value*. The lower the number, the faster. A fast hard drive has a speed of 12ms to 20ms. Average hard drives have speeds from 15ms to 40ms. Anything over 60 ms is considered a dog-slow hard drive—even then, though, it's still a better alternative than using floppies.

Finally comes the *controller card interface*. In some instances, this may be determined by the drive. If you select an ESDI drive for your computer, an ESDI controller is in order. If you choose an IDE drive for your AT, an IDE controller is required.

Traditionally, dealers have recommended controllers for their hard drives. But if a controller offers features and performance that you need, find out if it will match your selected hard drive. There's quite a bit of variety available out there, and you can get just about anything you want—for a price.

Other items that play an important role in hard drive selection include:

◆ Whether the drive uses a voice coil or stepper motor

◆ The MTBF rating

If possible, you should select a hard drive that uses a voice coil mechanism to position the read/write heads, as opposed to the stepper motor. The drive with voice coil will be more expensive, but it's a better system. The key advantage is that a voice coil drive automatically *parks* the read/write heads when they're inactive. This avoids the chance of a "head

crash" should the power suddenly go out. (The subjects of parking the heads and head crashes are covered later in this chapter.)

MTBF stands for *Mean Time Between Failure*, a rating (usually given in hours), that indicates the anticipated life span of your hard drive. For example, a MTBF rating of 10,000 hours means the drive should work for ten thousand hours without any problem (that's a little over a year of solid time). As with most ratings, this should be used only for comparison purposes. You'll probably get a lot more time out of your drive than the MTBF value indicates.

You should know the following about your newly-purchased drive.

◆ The total number of cylinders

◆ The number of heads (or platters)

◆ The drive type or "form factor"

Most of this information is for the benefit of your AT system's SETUP program. It may also help when formatting the diskette (refer to the last section of this book). Most manufacturers spare you from these details on the packaging, yet they're good to know.

The hard drive will come with an error map, either in the box or attached in a pouch on top. Nearly every drive has defective (or *bad*) sectors on it. It's nothing to be too upset over.

Normally, those bad sectors will be plotted and avoided in the process of formatting. If the drive is preformatted (as are most IDE drives), it will "know" of the bad sectors. The drive will simply not use those sectors, so any bad sectors will be effectively transparent to you, the user.

Upgrade Overview

The basic steps for upgrading a hard drive are identical to those of the floppy drive upgrade. The drives go in the same location, with hard drives usually placed in the left drive bays. And they're either side mounted, or rail mounted. All this information, covered in the previous chapter on up-grading floppies, applies here as well.

Like the 34-pin edge connector, the 40-pin data cable connector is notched, both on the card and the cable. (If not, match up pin 1 with line 1 and everything will work fine.) There is one cable for the 40-pin edge connector, and it goes directly to the hard-drive controller. If you have two drives, they'll each share a single 40-line cable.

All other details in the upgrade process are the same. The following three sections of this chapter will discuss individual upgrades in a step-by-step manner. If you need any further details, refer to Chapter 8's floppy drive upgrade overview—the information is basically the same.

Removing a Drive

You may need to remove an older hard drive, or a floppy drive, before you can install a new hard drive.

HOW TO REMOVE A HARD DRIVE

Procedure: Removing a hard (or floppy) drive

Tools Needed: Medium plus screwdriver

Steps:

1. Power down your PC and remove the lid.

2. Locate the drive and remove its screws. For a PC- style case, the two mounting screws will be on the side of the drive. Some AT-style cases may have mounting rails on the drive, with screws on either side of the drive's faceplate. Remeber to remove the mounting rails and set them (and all other screws and brackets) aside for installation of the new drive.

3. Slide the drive forward a bit to detach the power supply cable and 40-line data cable. Bend them out of the way. Remember an IDE drive only has one ribbon cable. If you're working with MFM, RLL, or ESDI drives you may have to deal with two cables for each dirve.

4. Slide the drive forward and free. You can now set the drive aside, put it into a box, or throw it away. Remember to keep the moutning rails (if any) for any new drives you may install.

This would be a good time to set the jumpers on your new (replacement) drive to match the ones on the drive you've just removed. IDE drives need to be set to either *slave* or *master* status. IDE drives usually use jumpers located near the cable connectors to establish either slave or master status. Master status means that the computer will look at the master drive for an operating system if your computer is set to boot froom a hard drive. Computers usually boot to the master rather than the slave hard drive. (The master drive will always get the first available drive letter, the slave gets the next free drive letter.)

The easy way to deal with this jumper setting is to match the settings on the drive you've just removed. Always refer to your new drive's manual to confirm the correctness of this approach for your own individual drive before you continue with the upgrade.

5. Replace the drive, or cover the empty drive bay hole with a blank faceplate, and restart your system. (If you're replacing the drive, keep the PC turned off and the case open to allow for the next part of the procedure.)

If you're removing a drive D and leaving just a C drive, then you need to change the jumpers on your C drive to reflect Master status. If you don't do this correctly, the system will not be able to find a hard drive from which to boot. Your drive's manual will tell you how to change these jumpers to establish a single-hard drive environment.

If your next step is to install a new drive in the old one's place, move on to the next section.

Installing a Drive

After removing a drive, your next step is probably to replace it with something. Or you could be installing the first hard-disk in a system that had none. Whatever the case, this section covers installing a hard-disk into your PC.

If you're installing a second hard drive, please refer to the section that follows this one. This section covers installation of your first hard drive, only. This procedure's description assumes that the hard-disk controller has already been installed into the system, and that the cable is already (or still) connected to it.

HOW TO INSTALL A HARD DRIVE

Procedure: Installing a hard-disk drive

Tools Needed: Medium plus screwdriver

Steps:

1. Power down your PC and remove the lid.

2. Remove the old drive (if it's internal) or the faceplate covering the drive bay (if it's in an external drive bay).

3. Check any jumpers on the new drive. Make sure they're set so that the computer will recognize the drive as the only hard drive in the system. See the drive's manual on how to do this. Adding a drive D is covered in the next section. Double-check this item, though the jumpers are bound to be set that way from the factory.

4. Attach the mounting rails to the drive (if you need them at all). If necessary, screw a mounting rail onto each side of the drive.

5. Slide the drive into position. Hard drives slide in from the front if they're located in an external drive bay, and from the rear (from inside the case) it they're mounted in an internal drive bay.

6. Attach the power supply and data cable to the drive. (The power supply and 40-line data cable can go on in only one way.)

7. Slide the drive into the bay all the way.

8. Anchor the drive into position by tightening the screws. Both desktop AT- and tower-style cases will have screws on the side. For using mounting rails, position the angle brackets and then tighten the screws on both sides of the front of the drive.

9. Connect the LED indicator connector (from the LED mounted on your case) to the appropriate pins on your controller card if you wish to use that LED to note hard drive activity.

10. Test the drive before you close the case.

If you have a PC, no additional hardware setup is required. For AT systems, the SETUP program needs to be run to tell DOS what type of drive you've just installed (if the drive type has changed). Your particular IDE hard drive may need to be formatted using DOS. Some drive-makers format each drive with DOS in order to test it for defects before shipment, so your IDE drive may not need formatting at all. Check the drive's manual to learn if it's sold already formatted by DOS.

If everything checks out, you can close the lid on your PC, tighten everything up.

Installing a Second Drive

Since so many people low-ball their storage needs when they select the size of their hard-disk drives, upgrading to a second hard-disk drive is commonly done. Virtually all PC controllers are designed to handle two drives, so adding a second one is simple: You buy the drive, plus any cables you need, and then you install it.

When you buy a second drive, remember to buy one that's compatible with your controller card. If you have an ESDI, IDE or SCSI controller, nearly any hard drive of one of the same drive type will do. If you're unclear, then simply buy a second hard drive that's identical to the first.

The 40-line controller cable you're using may or may not have an additional connector for a second hard drive. To be safe, see if you can get a dual-drive controller cable when you buy your second hard-disk drive. Nothing is more disappointing than being halfway through an upgrade and finding you have to go back to the store to buy a cable. Don't forget to specify the length of the data cable you'll need. Some of them are pretty short, too short for my own computer. Remember to get another pair of mounting rails and screws—if you need them—too.

HOW TO INSTALL A SECOND DRIVE

Procedure: Installing a second hard-disk drive

Tools Needed: Medium plus screwdriver

Steps:

1. Power down your PC and remove the lid.

2. Set the jumpers on the existing C drive to reflect that it's the one that will hold the boot files. This is also known as setting the drive to master status. The existing drive's manual will detail how to make the drive a master drive.

3. Set the jumpers on the drive to be added so that it's recognized as the slave drive by the computer. Check the manual on the drive to be added for instructions on how to do this.

4. If necessary, attach the mounting rails to the drive. If you're installing a second hard drive into a PC-style case, you may need to purchase a mounting bracket to mount the drive. Most modern desktop and tower cases will accept hard drives without mounting brackets.

5. Slide the drive into position. If you're installing an internal drive, it needs to be slid into place from inside the case. External hard drives should be pushed in from outside the case until it's recessed into the front panel of the computer case, leaving room for the faceplate.

6. Attach the power supply and 40-line data cable to the drive. Most new power supplies have four "pigtails," which divide out to two power cables for floppy drives and two for hard drives. If you don't have enough pigtails, you'll need to buy a "Y" splitter. If so, you may find that your power supply is not up-to-snuff to run the new drive for long. Note that both the power supply and controller cable can go on in only one way.

7. Attach the middle connector on the 40-line data cable to the drive. It's notched, just like your power supply cable.

8. Attach the hard drive cable to the hard-disk controller.

9. Slide the drive all the way into the bay.

10. Anchor the drive into position by tightening the screws.

11. Recheck your connections

12. Close up and test.

If you have a PC, the drive should come to life right away—but if it's still unformatted, don't expect it to be "on-line" just yet. For an AT, you'll need to run the SETUP program to tell the computer what type of drive you've just installed. This second hard drive will be designated as the D drive if you have a single hard drive already.

Software Setup

Unlike most other hardware upgrades, adding a hard drive to your system isn't a close-and-play operation—rather, there's a major software side to hard-disk drive upgrades. This can involve formatting the drive to make it readable to DOS, and then using hard-disk management to make the drive and its information more useful to you.

The software setup of a hard drive baffles most people. Unlike a floppy drive, the hard drive has to be *initialized, partitioned, formatted*, and *setup* for use by DOS. Those are steps a lot of people don't know about when they upgrade, so their immediate reaction might be "my new hard drive doesn't work." ...It does, but only after the proper steps have been taken.

The AT SETUP Program

If you don't have an AT-compatible computer, you can skip this step. AT's lack DIP switches, and come with special battery backed-up RAM (or CMOS memory). The RAM contains configuration information about the computer, including information about the disk drives. Because of this, you have to run a SETUP program to alter your battery backed-up RAM, telling it about the changes you've made.

You computer will detect the presence of a hard drive when you boot. This is part of the POST that takes place each time you start your system. Each POST is different, depending on who made your computer and who supplied the BIOS. But when you boot with a new hard-disk drive that's of a different type from the old one, its presence is detected and an error message is displayed on the screen. For example:

```
Invalid configuration information—please run SETUP program
```

The message may be different on your own system. (In fact, it might be something that seems terrifying!) Don't worry. Take whatever steps are necessary to run your computer's SETUP program, as outlined in the manual.

In the SETUP program, you'll have to *select* the hard drive you've installed. For example, if you've just installed a drive C, you may need to select something called "First Hard Drive" or "Fixed Disk 1." For a second hard drive, you'll make a corresponding selection.

After the hard drive is selected, you need to inform your SETUP program of the drive type. This is where the "drive type" or "form factor" value found in the drive's manual comes into play. The terms and statistics for each drive can get confusing, but there should be a matching drive type or form factor somewhere on the list. Once you know it, enter it into the SETUP program according to the instructions supplied with your computer.

After you assign the drive and type in your SETUP program, reboot the system. It should come up as normal (providing installation was up to snuff), in which case you can continue with the software installation.

Installing DOS

A hard-disk has to be prepared for use with DOS. That's done in the following three steps:

◆ Low-level formatting

◆ FDISK-ing, or partitioning

◆ High-level formatting

A final step, installing DOS, is necessary if the new drive is your first drive, drive C. Formatting alone is fine for your second drive.

Low-Level Formatting

If you're installing an IDE drive, you may not need to low-level format the drive at all. Check the drive's manual to learn if the drive has been preformatted (at the low and high levels) by the drive's maker. If it has, then skip the low-level formatting stuff. New IDE drives should really be low-level formatted by the factory.

There are two levels of format for a hard-disk drive: low-level and high-level. (This causes to a lot of confusion for first-time hard-disk owners.) Basically, the low-level format is the true format, defining the tracks and sectors on the drive. The high-level format, done by DOS, simply makes sure that the tracks and sectors are there, in order, readable, and ready for DOS to use.

There are three ways you can get a low-level format on your drive:

◆ It may come from the factory that way

◆ You can do it with a software program like SETUP

◆ You can use a special third-party disk formatting program

Many drives are already formatted and partitioned when they come from the factory. Some may even have DOS installed (though DOS is copyrighted software and selling a drive that way is considered piracy).

Another warning. Some drives (IDE) should be low-level formatted only at the factory. FDISK will tell you if this is so...and you should not low-level format it again!

There are a number of ways you can find out if your drive was low-level formatted at the factory. The first is to use the FDISK utility on the drive. FDISK recognizes only a drive that's been low-level formatted. So if FDISK says you don't have a hard drive (or a drive D), then you know it isn't low-level formatted. (Additional information on FDISK is covered in the next section).

A more convenient way to tell if the hard disk drive is formatted is to try to use it. At the DOS prompt, type **C:/DIR** and press ENTER. (Or **D:\DIR**.) If you get an "Invalid Drive Letter" type of error, then the drive hasn't been formatted.

When the drive hasn't been low-level formatted, it's up to you to do it. The better quality drives, or those purchased through national dealers, will come with a disk containing a low-level formatting program. They're usually called something like HSECT, FSECT, or HDSETUP. Using one of these programs you can low-level format the drive, either directly or by choosing a menu item.

A low-level format is a dangerous thing. No utility, no matter how miraculous it claims to be, can undo a complete low-level format. Low-level formatting will erase everything on the drive (including that special information put there by the drive's maker that denotes where bad sectors are located). So make sure you actually want to low-level format, especially if the drive has data already on it. For many new drives, it's a necessary step—in that case, read carefully any warning messages the low-level formatting program has to offer before you proceed.

If the drive was bought as part of a whole system, it's probably been formatted at both the low and high levels in order to burn-in the system.

Most PCs made in the '90s include the CMOS SETUP program that allows you to specify the equipment in your "box." Those CMOS SETUP programs low-level format hard drives as well. Check your own system's CMOS SETUP program for this utility. It almost certainly will do low-level formatting—you should not need any additional software.

FDISKing, or Partitioning

FDISK is the name of a DOS utility program. Its primary responsibility is to partition your hard drive. Partitioning tells DOS how big the drive is and which part of the drive will host the boot files. This is the second step, after low-level formatting, which each new DOS hard disk drive must go through.

Partitioning is done for two reasons:

◆ To have more than one operating system

◆ To have more than one logical drive

You may want to divide the single hard-disk drive into logical drives C, D, and E, simply to help keep your files organized and safe from File Allocation Table (FAT) failures. This is the first reason for partitioning a hard drive—to divide it into more than one logical drive.

The second reason for partitioning is to put more than one operating system on the drive. For example, you could put DOS and UNIX (or NT and UNIX) on the same hard drive. DOS would exist in separate partitions on the same drive, DOS formatting its partition the way it likes, and UNIX dealing with its partition in the way it likes.

The most common reason for partitioning, however, is to divide a large hard drive into smaller logical drives. For example, a single 90MB drive can be divided into three logical 30MB drives—C, D, and E. An 80MB drive could be divided into two 30MB drives—C and D—and a 20MB drive—E. Or the original 80MB drive could be divided into four 20MB drives—C, D, E, and F. It all depends on how you want to use the space.

Partitioning a Drive

Whether you have to partition a drive into multiple partitions or you wish to format the entire drive in one partition, you still must run FDISK before DOS can use the drive. If the drive was low-level formatted at the factory, running FDISK is still a good way to check that everything's in order. And it's a required step in putting DOS on a drive that hasn't already been high-level formatted using DOS. (You can even run FDISK when a hard-disk drive is already installed, simply to check the partition information.)

To run FDISK, type **FDISK** at the DOS prompt. FDISK is a simple, menu-driven program. Its main screen will look something like that displayed in Figure 9.4. (If you have a second hard drive, you'll see five options instead of four.)

```
                         MS-DOS Version 6
                       Fixed Disk Setup Program
                 (C)Copyright Microsoft Corp. 1983 - 1993

                           FDISK Options

         Current fixed disk drive: 1

         Choose one of the following:

         1. Create DOS partition or Logical DOS Drive
         2. Set active partition
         3. Delete partition or Logical DOS Drive
         4. Display partition information
         5. Change current fixed disk drive


         Enter choice: [1]




         Press Esc to exit FDISK
```

FIGURE 9.4: FDISK's main menu from MS-DOS 6

If you're installing a drive D, then that's the option you would select now.

If you have a new hard drive, your next step is to select option 1, "Create DOS Partition or Logical DOS Drive." After you press 1, FDISK will display a second screen, as shown in Figure 9.5.

```
                    Create DOS Partition or Logical DOS Drive

Current fixed disk drive: 1

Choose one of the following:

1. Create Primary DOS Partition
2. Create Extended DOS Partition
3. Create Logical DOS Drive(s) in the Extended DOS Partition




Enter choice: [1]




Press Esc to return to FDISK Options
```

FIGURE 9.5: The Create DOS Partition or Logical DOS Drive screen

The primary DOS partition is the main, bootable part of your hard disk. It must be created only once, for drive C. The extended DOS partitions will define any additional, "logical" drives in your system. (Since they're not bootable drives, they're referred to as "extended DOS" partitions.)

For a new drive, select option 1 to create the primary DOS partition. Depending on the version of FDISK you're using, a second screen may ask how much of the drive you wish to use for the primary DOS partition. At this point, FDISK tries hard to be very technical, but it's really not. In fact, often times if you press ENTER for each of the menus in FDISK, it will set up your system exactly as you want it.

After FDISK is done, and you've established the primary DOS partition and any extended DOS partitions (for drives D, E, F, etc.), FDISK will re-boot your machine. This is necessary so that the new information FDISK writes to your disk's boot sector will be loaded into memory.

You still don't have DOS on the hard drive. It isn't even formatted. So remember to keep a bootable floppy in Drive A for the next, final step, which will be formatting the hard drive under DOS.

High-Level Formatting

The final software step to installing a hard drive is the high-level format. This is just like the traditional format you've always done on floppies using DOS's FORMAT command.

The high-level format is basically a type of hard-disk verification. Unlike a low-level format, which really does overwrite all information on the drive, a high-level format on a hard drive will rewrite part of the hard-disk's boot sector, establish a root directory, and then verify all the remaining tracks and sectors in that DOS partition.

You format a hard-disk drive just as you would a floppy disk. Type the FORMAT command on the command prompt, followed by the drive letter of the hard-disk drive you want to format. For example (*don't type this* unless you really want to format the drive):

```
A:\ FORMAT D:
```

After you press ENTER, the drive will begin to format. Unless—if the hard drive is already formatted—you see a warning message as follows:

```
WARNING, ALL DATA ON NON-REMOVABLE DISK
DRIVE D: WILL BE LOST!
Proceed with Format (Y/N)?
```

If this happens, press Y to begin formatting, or N to leave the disk (and its data) as is.

 DON'T FORMAT YOUR HARD DRIVE NOW! Wait until this next section, which shows you how to make your hard drive bootable as well as usable by DOS.

For new drives, the formatting should proceed as normal. It takes a while, so get a cup of coffee if you want. Remember to format all the logical drive partitions if you've created them. A hard drive partitioned into drives C, D, and E must have all of its logical drives formatted before you can stick data on any of them.

Installing DOS

If you're installing a drive C, you'll want to put a copy of DOS on the drive, and make it a bootable disk. Do this by specifying the /S switch after the format command as follows:

```
A> FORMAT C: /S
```

The /S switch transfers the system to the hard drive, primarily the two hidden DOS boot files. To complete the boot process, you may have to copy the COMMAND.COM file to your hard drive, like this:

```
A> COPY COMMAND.COM C:
```

This finishes the software setup of drive C, which is the only hard drive you'll need to transfer the system to. (Any additional hard drives will merely serve as huge data disks.) To test the installation, reboot your computer without a floppy disk in drive A (you may have to use SETUP to change the boot drive from A to C). After a few moments, DOS will be loaded from the hard disk, displaying its name and copyright notice and asking you to enter the date and time.

Upgrading your system to include a hard drive is now complete.

Using Disk Compression Software

On-the-fly *disk compression* has come of age, and there are now three major contenders in this arena. Microsoft is offering its *DoubleSpace* program included with DOS 6, Stac Electronics is offering its immensely popular *Stacker* product, and AddStor is putting forth its *SuperStor* compression product as well.

On-the-fly disk compression works like this: You take a hard drive that is currently in service. You then use special software that compresses everything on that drive. The software magically shrinks the programs and files, making them take up less space without losing any of their integrity. In effect, compression squeezes all the hot air out of the files. (One of these would be great for use on the city council, no?)

As additional files are copied to the hard drive, they're compressed as well. Files from the hard drive are quickly decompressed back to their original size when you want to read from them. That way, no information is lost, but overall hard drive storage is increased, as the files take up less space.

These on-the-fly compression products will give you up to twice the hard disk space and you won't have to add a hard drive. The catch is this: the compression/expansion process takes time, so you'll perceive that your hard drive is running more slowly when the disk compression software is working away. Some compression software makers do offer coprocessing expansion cards that speed up the compression/expansion process to the point where you don't notice any decrease in drive performance.

Hard-Disk Management

Hard disks offer a different way to work with computer programs, data files, and information than floppy-disk-only users were used to. You can have hundreds of files on a hard drive—DOS makes no rules or recommendations about keeping them organized or where to put things. So a lot of new hard disk owners will let their hard disks run amok, creating a really messy situation and losing some of the advantages of having a hard disk. The key to avoiding a hard disk mess is to manage your disk.

Hard-disk management is a complete subject unto itself, and the topic of countless books and magazine articles. It's nothing difficult to master, but it involves some DOS knowledge, and suggestions for how to apply that DOS knowledge—something missing in the DOS manual.

Basically, hard-disk management consists of:

◆ Organizing files

◆ Maintaining files

◆ Organizing software

The first step in dealing with a large hard drive is to organize your files and programs. DOS provides a method for you to do this—by means of subdirectories, or individual work areas that are almost like file drawers in a filing cabinet, which allow you to keep related files and programs grouped together.

Maintaining files involves several things: keeping files organized; deleting unnecessary and obsolete files; copying, moving, and renaming files; and so on. It also deals with two crucial program files on your system: AUTO-EXEC.BAT and CONFIG.SYS, and how they play an important role in making life with a hard drive easier.

Finally, keeping a hard-disk drive in tip-top shape means you know what to do with new software when you get it, and where to install that software. As long as you're organized, installing software should be easy. Put if you are poorly organized, installing new software will often require a great deal of tedious file maintenance.

Preventive Maintenance Techniques

Hard drives are robust. They last a long time and perform flawlessly as long as you treat them right. But there are a few things you should do to insure that you and your hard-disk work well together for some time to come. Some of the things you should consider are the following:

◆ Backing up files and programs

◆ Park the heads

◆ Moving the PC using only the proper procedures

Backing Up Files and Programs

Backing up is crucial. It's not that hard drives are unreliable. It's just that having a spare copy of your data "just in case" is very important. Backing up provides you with security, can be used to restore files and subdirectories you accidentally erase, and ensures against disasters such as hard drive failure, theft, and viruses.

The problem most people have with backup is that it's slow, uses a lot of diskettes, and requires you to sit in front of the PC while the agonizingly tedious process takes place. Those people assume that you have to back up the entire hard-disk each time you do a backup. Instead, you should develop a back-up strategy.

For example, back up only those files you've worked on today, each day of the week. At the end of the week—or maybe once a month—back up the entire hard drive.

There are many powerful back-up programs out there, all of which do the job better and faster than DOS's pitiful BACKUP programs. Just remember to keep a pile of diskettes handy for the backup, and do backups on a regular basis. That way, if disaster strikes, you won't be left in the cold with your data lost. Of course, you could install a tape-backup drive to make your life a lot easier. But it always comes down to money, doesn't it?

Park the Heads

Most drives manufactured after 1990 automatically park their own heads, making any special head-parking process unnecessary. Check your drive's documentation for more on whether you need to park the head when you move your PC.

Head crashes can occur for a variety of reasons. A small particle of smoke or even a fingerprint on the surface of the disk is enough to interfere with the read/write head. If you suddenly jar the drive, or if the power goes off while the PC is on, the heads will come into dangerously sudden contact with the disk media (though that's not really a "crash").

IDE drives don't need their heads parked because they use voice coils mechanisms that park their heads automatically. To prevent the read/write heads from damaging the drive media in computers using MFM, RLL, and ESDI drives, you can use software to park the heads. This moves the read/write heads over some non-crucial area of the disk and often it even locks them into position there. Once they're safely out of the way, you can turn off the computer's power or move it without risking damage to the drive media.

Parking is usually accomplished via some PARK program or utility. The command may change depending on which type of drive you have, though PARK is common. To park the drive, (assuming that PARK's the command needed for your machine), you simply type **PARK** at the DOS prompt and the program moves the read/write heads over to a safe area of the disk. After that, you can power down and move the PC safely.

A lot of people panic on the subject of head parking. They might even buy and use special utilities that park the drive heads every five minutes or so. This is unnecessary. Only if you're going to shut down for the day, move the PC, or leave it unattended for a long period of time should you park the drives. And if your drive has a voice coil mechanism, you don't even need to worry about it.

Moving Procedures

The hard drive is the most delicate mechanism in your computer, but it's still pretty hardy. For example, most hard drives can survive an

earthquake (unless the building falls down). Why? Because they're constantly spinning and create a gyro effect, which makes them more stable than other items in the room when the ground shakes. ...But hard-disk drives aren't invincible.

The only time you'll need to take really special care of your MFM, RLL, or ESDI hard drive is when you move the computer. Whether you're moving it across the room or across the country, consider taking the following steps for safety's sake.

Back Up the Files and Programs Back up your entire hard drive before moving the computer. It's just good common sense to have a spare copy of all the hard drive's data—just in case.

Park that Drive Unless you have an IDE drive, make sure you run a PARK program as the last thing you do before turning off the computer. Again—do so only if the drive needs it. Your manual will tell you.

Take good care of your hard drive and it will take care of you. The hard drive may seem one of the most mysterious devices in your PC, but it doesn't have to confuse you. Consider buying and reading a good hard-disk management book to keep the software side of your hardware upgrade in top form. The hard-disk may be the best, most useful upgrade you ever do.

Expansion Cards

This chapter is about installing and upgrading expansion cards. The upgrade process itself is really rather simple. Matters get complex, however, in the sheer volume and variety of expansion cards available. It would be nice to discuss every type of expansion card available for the PC in this chapter, but there are just too many. Instead, we'll take a general approach.

General Notes on Expansion Cards

You'll have to know about the PC's bus as well as expansion cards. The bus question is increasingly important with newer machines. There are three sections here, each dealing with expansion cards or the bus into which you plug the cards.

The first section contains general information common to all expansion cards. The next section discusses the various types of cards available. The final section discusses the bus and why it's important.

Expansion Cards

All expansion cards are basically printed circuit boards. They contain chips and other electronics, an edge connector to plug them into the computer, and a mounting bracket by which the card is anchored to the PC's frame.

Card Description

To illustrate the parts of an expansion card, a generic one is shown in Figure 10.1. This card is a full-length, AT-style card. Other expansion cards may be shorter or narrower, and have one, two, or even three edge connectors on the bottom as well as edge connectors on the top.

The Card The card is a (usually green) sheet. It's quite stiff, but can be slightly bowed. This is sometimes necessary to fit a card in a poorly designed PC case.

Mounting Bracket The card is anchored in two, sometimes three ways. The first is via the edge connector (and the bus). The second is through a metal mounting bracket on the back of the PC. The third, if the card is long enough, is by a special slot on the front of the system unit.

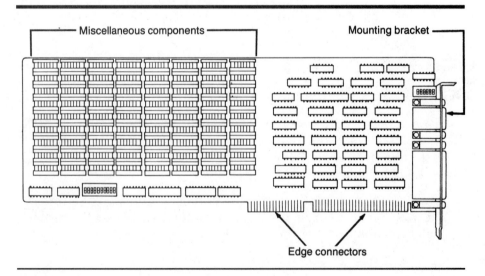

FIGURE 10.1: An expansion card

Edge Connectors A standard PC expansion card comes with one, two, or even three edge connectors, by which the card plugs into the slot and communicates with the PC via the bus. Cards with only one 62-line edge connector are called 8-bit cards (from the PC's 8-bit data bus), and cards with two edge connectors are called 16-bit cards. Likewise, the single slots are called 8-bit slots, and those with the additional 36-line slot are called 16-bit slots. EISA and VESA bus computers can accommodate 32-bit cards which use three edge connectors.

Components All cards have chips, resistors, and other electronic components, almost always on only one side. The other side has rows and rows of tiny pins where the components are soldered on.

Card Size

The physical dimensions of cards vary. Before you buy a card you need to know whether it will fit in your PC. Figure 10.2 shows a few popular expansion card configurations.

Cards are described by their height, length, and whether they have 8-bit, 16-bit, or 32-bit bus connectors. The two heights available are PC/AT and PC/XT. The AT-style case is much taller than the original PC's case. So tall cards, even though they may only be 8-bit, cannot fit in a PC/XT-style case.

The lengths of cards also vary. Full-length cards stretch from the back of the PC's case (where the mounting bracket goes) all the way to the front, a little over 13". There are mid-length cards that are still fairly long. And there are so-called short, or half, cards.

The card's length really depends on the amount of circuitry it needs. Now cards can get quite small. But certain cards, such as those with many megabytes of RAM in SIMMs, are still full-length. Long cards may only fit in certain slots inside the PC.

Finally, most cards are fairly thin, and you can put them right next to one another without having their components touching. But other cards may have a profusion of cables, or secondary "daughterboards," that make them fatter than normal. Some hard disks on a card make the card so wide that it really takes up the space of two cards.

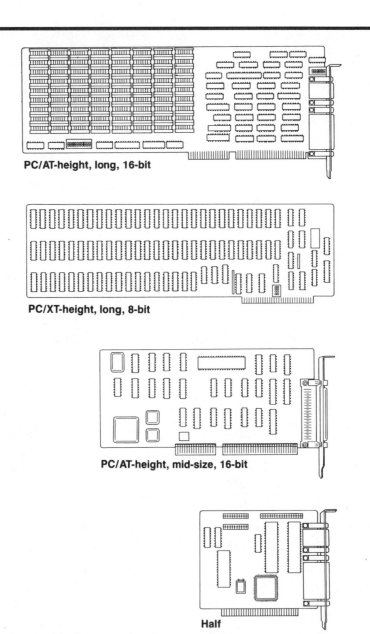

PC/AT-height, long, 16-bit

PC/XT-height, long, 8-bit

PC/AT-height, mid-size, 16-bit

Half

FIGURE 10.2: Common expansion card configurations

Card Contents

Most of the electronic doo-dads on an expansion card will be a mystery to you—unless you have some knowledge of electrical engineering. But for upgrading purposes, there are some things you should recognize and know how to deal with on an expansion card:

◆ Jumpers and DIP switches

◆ Connectors

◆ Piggyback expansion cards and daughterboards

Jumpers and DIP switches are ways of communicating with the expansion card. You set them either according to how the card or your computer is configured. The instructions for setting the jumpers or DIP switches will come with the expansion card's manual.

Expansion cards may also have various connectors. Some will be on the mounting bracket. For example, a card with a printer port may have the port right on the mounting bracket, making it easily accessible from behind the PC. Other connectors may be on the card themselves.

Finally, expansion cards may have special connectors for attaching a daughterboard. These are like expansion cards for an expansion card. A daughterboard (also called piggyback card) is a small expansion card that plugs into another expansion card rather than into one of your computer's system slots. Usually, a piggyback card is found on a memory expansion card. It allows you to add even more RAM to the card after all the RAM sockets on the card are full. Keep in mind that piggyback cards and daughterboards will cost more and that they also make the original card wider.

Today's video cards usually sport a special edge connector that appears on the top edge of the card. This edge connector is provided as part of the VESA standard, to support the interconnection of a second specialized video card. For example, if you want to install a full-motion video card, the use of that extra card may require you to leave your VGA card installed. The new add-on card may come with a ribbon cable with an edge connector on one end intended for attachment to your current VGA card.

Handling Cards

Expansion cards fall in line right behind RAM chips in their handling instructions: *You should always be careful when handling expansion cards*, especially in regard to building up static, which could discharge and harm the card. Always ground yourself before picking up an expansion card. If the PC's case is open, touch the power supply to ground yourself before you pick up the card. Handle all expansion cards by their edges.

Finally, be aware of the backside of most cards. Since expansion cards put their circuitry on only one side of the card, the other side is usually dotted with tiny points (where the chips and what have you are soldered to the card). Those metal points can hurt.

Note that all cards (the good ones, at least) will come in static-free pouches. There are two types of anti-static bags. The pink ones protect from static charges only. The smoky-gray ones protect from static and direct sunlight. Quite a few "hackers" tend to leave cards laying around—maybe to impress their friends. While there's nothing wrong with this, the chances of someone knocking a card off the shelf and stepping on it are too great to risk. Don't be a bozo. Keep loose cards boxed up.

Card Types

This section tries to tackle endless variety by discussing several popular types of expansion cards.

Standard Cards

There are several types of cards that have become the "standards" in the past ten years of PC computing. Primarily, these are cards that supply such necessary parts of the computer as the serial port, printer port, memory, video, and floppy controller.

In any event, the five most common types of expansion cards—the standards—are as follows.

Floppy-Disk Controller This half-card can control up to four floppy disk drives, but will most often control just two. Floppy drives are also controlled from a combo card that controls both the hard drives and the floppy drives...all from a half-length card.

Hard-Disk Controller Starting with the PC/XT, hard drives are more-or-less standard equipment on all PC systems. To interface that hard drive with your PC, you need a hard disk controller card. Sophisticated hard drive controllers are often stand-alone cards, but more often share a half-card with a floppy drive controller.

Memory Today, most PCs accommodate vast amounts of memory in SIMM form directly on the motherboard. Memory mounted on the motherboard can be configured as either EMS or XMS, depending on the need. Motherboard-mounted memory has all but done-in the add-on memory board marketplace. But there are still machines out there that use these cards.

Video The video adapter is the most common card found in a PC, even more so than a memory adapter. Why? Because the typical PC has no built-in video display circuitry. You need a video card if you ever expect to see any video results from the computer. This does, however, give you the advantage of choosing which types of video card, graphics, color, and resolution you want.

Most VGA cards are single-slot solutions. Even the S3 coprocessed, 32-bit video cards with 8M of VRAM get all of their components onto one card. As we said earlier, some special video cards provide services like full-motion video and on-screen TV viewing and require you to hook them up to your VGA card. Plan on your video cards taking up two slots to get these jobs done.

Serial Port An extremely popular addition to many PCs is the extra serial port. Most PCs are using an IDE combo card that sports a FD/HD controller and a serial and parallel port—all on one half-card. A serial port can come on its own card, in which case there are often two serial ports available.

Multifunction and Combination Cards

Finally there are the multifunction cards. These cards combine the functions of a lot of single cards, which will save slots for other purposes.

Mouse Cards

The mouse has been a popular pet for the personal computer since Apple introduced their Macintosh computer with a mouse in 1984. Today dozens of manufacturers make a variety of mice and mouse-like pointing devices, in types ranging from the pen-pointer to the touch-sensitive monitor face. Each of these pointers is essentially a mouse.

More and more PC software is taking advantage of mouse use. Currently, about ⅓ of available packages support a mouse as an option. Some packages *require* a mouse to get work done. So a mouse is a good investment to make, and not that expensive, going for between $15 and $100 (or even less, if you find them discounted).

Mouse Types The mouse itself is usually a palm-sized device with buttons on its top. A cord that extends from the front of the mouse plugs into your PC. It's how the mouse plugs in that determines which of two major types of computer mouse you can have:

◆ Bus

◆ Serial

The bus mouse plugs directly into your PC's expansion bus with its own dedicated controller card. The bus mouse plugs into that expansion card, which plugs into the bus. The expansion card will probably be one of the sparsest, shortest cards in your PC (ideal for use in a short slot, or for the occasional 8-bit slot in an AT-style machine). Sometimes bus mouse ports come on other cards. The ATI VGA Wonder card comes with a bus mouse port as an option.

A *serial mouse*, which plugs into one of your available serial ports, is basically a computer mouse and cable that hooks up like an external modem; you plug it into a serial port.

The Microsoft mouse, and most others, have two buttons, one on the left and one on the right. Some mice have a third button in the middle. Most software that supports a mouse is built to use the Microsoft mouse, so the minimum number of buttons you need is two. However, a few applications do take advantage of the three-button mouse.

There are also alternative pointing devices that work like mice, but often offer either better features or greater ease of use. These include:

Trackballs A trackball is basically a mouse turned upside-down. It has a ball and two buttons. You can move the ball using your fingers to move your mouse pointer and you press the buttons just like you would mouse buttons. Since the trackball doesn't slide around your desk, many people find it easier to use—especially with large screens—than a traditional mouse.

Optical Mice The optical mouse has two infrared lamps that allow it to slide over a special reflective pad while light sensors inside the mouse detect movement. There are no moving parts inside an optical mouse. Unlike the traditional mouse, which can roll on any smooth surface, you need a special reflective pad to use an optical mouse.

Other Variations Also available are variations on the trackball, and mini-joysticks that work like a mouse in an extremely small space.

Mouse Compatibility Since there are a lot of companies that make computer mice, and since IBM didn't lead the way with a standard, the most compatible mouse you can get is Microsoft's. Other mice emulate the Microsoft mouse, but you might as well go with the original.

A computer mouse is controlled (for use under just DOS) via a software driver you install in your CONFIG.SYS file. For example, a line (in your CONFIG.SYS file) like the following will automatically load the mouse driver and activate the mouse each time you start your computer.

```
DEVICEHIGH = C:\MOUSE\MOUSE.SYS
```

A second driver, MOUSE.COM is a memory-resident version of MOUSE.SYS. However, the original purpose of MOUSE.COM was to allow it to be included in batch files that run applications requiring a mouse driver. A reason to avoid putting MOUSE.COM in your AUTOEXEC.BAT file is that it uses up 3K more of RAM that MOUSE.SYS does.

If you're a Windows user who doesn't use DOS software at all, you don't need to load a mouse driver from your CONFIG.SYS or AUTOEXEC.BAT files at all—Windows will drive your mouse.

Modems

Another popular type of expansion card to stick in a PC is the *modem card*. Modems are communications devices that allow your computer to transfer information to another modem-equipped computer using the phone network.

Basically, the modem takes digital signals from your computer (bytes) and translates them into sounds. It can also translate the sounds back into digital bytes. This process is called *mo*dulation/*dem*odulation, from which the word "modem" derives.

There are two types of modems:

◆ Internal

◆ External

An external modem is a peripheral that you plug into a wall socket, a phone jack, and one of your PC's serial ports. An external modem offers the advantage of being visible—you can see its lights flash as its working (which helps to diagnose problems) and you can turn if off when it's not in use. You also can transfer it to any other computer system that has a serial port—including non-PC systems.

Internal modems come on expansion cards. They're generally cheaper than external modems. Because they are designed to plug into a PC's bus, they work only in a PC. However, they don't crowd the top of your desk or add to the tangle of cables behind your PC like external modems do.

One of the more popular combo cards today, the fax/modem, is a combination expansion card that allows the user both to send and receive faxes and to communicate via modem. To function, a fax card must also be a modem card, but not all modem cards include fax capability.

What to Look For in a Modem When you buy a modem, there are two things to look for (in addition to whether it's an internal or external model):

◆ Speed

◆ Compatibility

The speed of a modem is gauged in bits per second, or BPS. (The term "Baud" or "Baud rate" is often incorrectly used.) The higher the BPS, the faster the modem and the greater amount of information you can transmit over a period of time. Currently popular are speeds of 1200, 2400, and 9600 BPS. As with everything, you'll pay a lot more for a fast 9600 BPS modem than you will for a slower 2400 BPS model.

Compatibility is also an important issue, and in the on-line world, Hayes-compatibility is the big thing. Hayes developed and manufactured the original "Smart Modem" in the late '70s. Smart Modem used a series of commands known as AT-commands, and since then all communications software packages have directly supported the Hayes standard. If your modem is Hayes-compatible (or if it supports the Hayes AT-command set) then it, too, will be compatible with a lot of communications software. Adding an internal modem to your system is as easy as plugging in the card and hooking a phone cord between your PC (the back of the modem card) and the wall jack.

The Baker's Dozen (Plus Two)

Here is a list of 15 additional expansion card types. This covers just about every major category of expansion card for the PC, though there are probably dozens more.

Accelerators Accelerators are speed-up devices you can install in your PC. They're like mini-motherboards on a card. You plug them into an expansion slot, then remove your PC's microprocessor and replace it with a cable to the accelerator card. Your system then runs off the faster microprocessor on the accelerator.

Bar-Code Readers Bar-code readers allow you to input bar codes to your PC, which can be useful for reading inventory or other information stored in the form of bar codes.

Coprocessors A coprocessor expansion card (not to be confused with a math coprocessor chip) can be a second microprocessor, or simply some circuitry designed to assist your microprocessor. An example of a coprocessor would be a SCSI-2 controller card, which would do some of the work normally done by the processor in choosing which devices that are

hooked up to the bus get to use the bus…and in what order. Other coprocessor cards are designed to offer advanced video services, and even accept additional microprocessors to help network computers handle high levels of data processing demand.

Debugging Cards Programmers who work on complex software can use debugging cards to snoop around in memory while their software is running. If the software they're testing crashes the system, for example, the debugging card will allow them to sift through the "wreckage" and look for a cause.

Fax Cards Along with the fax boom comes fax capability for your PC. Like internal modems (and in fact *using* a modem), fax cards can transmit and receive directly from the PC. Fax cards are usually sold as fax/modem cards, which allow for both fax and modem functions.

Hard Disk Cards The hard disk on a card is an excellent option for use in PCs with no free drive bays, or older PCs that lack proper upgrade options for a hard drive. The hard disk card is basically a combination hard-disk controller and drive mounted on a heavy-duty expansion card-shaped chassis.

Light Pens A light pen can be used to "draw" on the screen. Light pens have been around for a long time; there are various ways to hook them up to a PC. The original CGA video adapter had a built-in light pen interface.

Mainframe Communications Cards Quite a few PCs (too many) are shackled to mainframes (usually IBM or HP), and used as terminals. Sometimes, to make the proper connections, a dedicated mainframe communications (or terminal emulation) card must be installed. You often hear this type of card referred to as a 3270 emulation card.

MIDI and Sound Cards A computer can be an electronic music system—with you as the conductor—recording, notating, and playing back music generated by MIDI-compatible musical instruments. The MIDI, or Musical Instrument Digital Interface, card can be plugged into a PC, which then allows the computer to orchestrate a variety of electronic instruments.

I love to record excerpts from old sci-fi movies with my sound card and a VCR. I then edit them down and use them as .WAV (sound) files to be played in Windows—just like MACs have been doing for years and years. It's a lot of fun, and costs only the price of the sound board. Some sound boards even have built-in audio amplifiers so you can play your sound "stuff" through your favorite bookshelf speakers!

Network Adapters To hook your PC into a network, you need a network adapter. The network adapter provides the interface between your PC and other computers and peripherals on the network. This, coupled with the networking software, will make your computer "well connected."

Printer Helpers and Rasterizers To speed up operation of some laser printers, special assistant cards can be plugged into your PC. These cards usually come with megabytes of RAM and support circuitry that make the printing job run much faster.

One increasingly popular expansion card is the rasterizer card (intended for use under Windows), which takes over some of the printing tasks normally handled by the system's and the printer's CPUs, and increases the speed of the printing process.

Prototype Cards A prototype card is blank; it's the size and shape of the typical expansion card but contains no circuitry. (The hacker's term for this is "breadboard.") You can wire your own chips onto a prototype card to create your own expansion card.

SCSI A SCSI (Small Computer System Interface, commonly pronounced "scuzzy") is basically a super-fast serial port, into which you can plug up to seven different items. A variety of items—everything from a hard drive to a printer—can be plugged into a single SCSI port. SCSI upgrades are often the order of the day when you decide to add a CD-ROM drive to your system. The latest SCSI-2 standard also does some of the thinking for the system CPU, which increases data-throughput rates dramatically.

Whatever Else There are always more cards out there—voice input, video digitizers, and special purpose cards are available for just about everything under the sun. See Chapter 14 for expansion card upgrade options in the world of multimedia.

Expansion Slots

Bus is a technical term for the direct line of communication between your PC's microprocessor and the devices you plug into expansion slots. The slots are connectors on the bus, so to speak.

You should know about your PC's bus—but it's not something you can upgrade, because the bus is part of your motherboard. Only by buying a new computer system or completely swapping out your motherboard can you get a new bus.

The following items related to the bus are covered in this section:

◆ What is the Bus?

◆ The ISA or AT Bus

◆ The MCA Bus

◆ The EISA Bus

◆ The VESA Bus

What Is the Bus?

The bus, as we said a moment ago, is a line of communications between your PC's microprocessor and the devices plugged into its expansion slots—but the bus is really more than that. The bus also supplies power to all the expansion cards.

Knowing about the bus and its details isn't important to upgrading cards. However, since IBM introduced the PS/2 computers in 1987, there have been a number of different buses for PC owners to contend with.

 Remember, this is nothing you choose; your PC comes with a bus and you can't upgrade it. But the type of bus you have determines which expansion cards you need to look for.

There currently are four popular PC busses:

◆ ISA

◆ MCA

- ◆ EISA
- ◆ VESA Local Bus

The ISA Bus

ISA stands for Industry Standard Architecture, which refers to the bus used in all PCs, ATs, and clones. You also hear the ISA bus referred to as the "classic AT" bus.

There are two types of ISA bus connectors, the 8-bit and the 16-bit (basically an 8-bit slot with an extra 36-line connector). (See Figure 10.3.)

All PC/XT-level systems have 8-bit slots. AT-level systems have 16-bit slots with a couple of 8-bit slots thrown in. You can plug an 8-bit card into a 16-bit slot—the two are compatible—however, that wastes a 16-bit slot that you could use for a 16-bit card. And 16-bit cards can plug into some 8-bit slots, but only those specifically designed to do so (remember also that the PC/XT style case may not be tall enough for 16-bit cards).

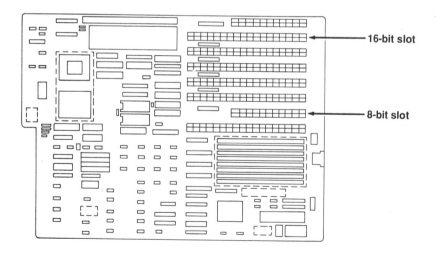

FIGURE 10.3: 8- and 16-bit connectors for the ISA bus

The ISA bus defined the standards for communication and how to resolve conflicts between the various expansion cards. But it does a really poor job of this. The standard is rather loose, and conflicts happen between cards all the time. (This is why you need to set so many jumpers and DIP switches on each card.) Also, the ISA bus only goes out to 16-bits, which is half the width of today's 32-bit 386 and 486 microprocessors.

To resolve the problems of the ISA bus, IBM announced a new bus standard with their PS/2 systems in 1987.

The MCA Bus

MCA stands for Micro Channel Architecture, and it describes the new bus included with IBM's PS/2 computers. (Note that some of the low-end PS/2s still use the old ISA bus.)

MCA is a much better design than ISA. It offers better communications between cards, resolves conflicts in a more civilized manner, and allows you to configure the cards without ever setting a DIP switch. It's smart. But it's also incompatible with the older ISA cards. You cannot plug an ISA board into the MCA slot (nor would you want to). And the MCA cards are physically a lot smaller than the older ISA types.

Currently, MCA is at a disadvantage in the industry. While IBM will license the MCA bus to any clone maker, they require stiff royalties and back payments on all of the licensed clone maker's sales of ISA bus computers. The cost is just too great for most manufacturers, so they've opted to stick with the ISA bus, incorporating 32-bit expansion slots into their ISA motherboards to deal with the demand for improved performance based on the ISA design.

To combat MCA, several developers of PC compatibles got together and came up with their own advanced bus standard.

The EISA Bus

EISA stands for Enhanced Industry Standard Architecture. It's a superset of the old ISA bus, with many of the advanced features of IBM's proprietary MCA bus added.

EISA offers the same features as MCA, including the ability to configure cards without setting DIP switches or jumpers, and faster communications and better resolution of conflicts. EISA is also compatible with the older ISA cards, which you can plug into any EISA slot.

One of the big advantages to the EISA architecture is the ability to plug in an arbitrating SCSI-2 controller and run all of your drives concurrently without waiting for each drive to finish its task before going on with your work. Essentially, the SCSI-2 controller works as a coprocessor expansion card for your system's microprocessor, handling the tasks of deciding which device will get access to the bus next. It frees up the CPU for operations that your software requires and gets data transferred faster because of superior EISA data-transfer rates.

If you're using Windows on an EISA machine, you won't have to wait for the little hourglass to turn back into a mouse pointer while your floppy drive is engaged. Just think of the backups you could do to a floptical drive if you could work while you did your backups! EISA PCs have so far found themselves working for serious power-users, on networks, or for high-end dedicated workstations that require high data-transfer rates.

If you've ever been frustrated with the IRQ assignment thing (especially when an expansion project goes wrong), you should look into the EISA motherboards. If you have an ISA motherboard, you know that devices can duke it out if you make the mistake of assigning an IRQ to more than one expansion card. EISA and VESA slots have an IRQ automatically assigned to each slot. You plug a card into slot 4, and the card gets that slot's dedicated IRQ—simple and elegant.

The VESA Local Bus

This latest adaptation on the ISA bus sports some advanced functionality. The VESA motherboard has at least one standardized 32-bit slot for high-performance video and data transfer purposes. The key word is standardized. This new standard has a shot at becoming the mother of all motherboards, which means that vendors should be lining up to make expansion cards that will utilize the VESA 32-bit local bus. And don't forget—if you buy a VESA motherboard with the video guts mounted right on the motherboard, you have freed up one of the two 32-bit slots for another expansion card that tends to move data slowly—like a scanner, for example.

This video enhancement is called Local Bus Video, where the video card is hooked-up to the CPU via 32-bit connections instead of the 16-bit

connections afforded by a card plugged into an ISA bus. For Windows users, the VESA standard is the way to go. You can use your current ISA video and drive controller cards until you are ready to upgrade to using the 32-bit slots. Of course, you also get all of the benefits of the EISA bus, as described in the earlier section.

The VESA LB seems destined to replace the EISA motherboard as the power-user's motherboard-of-choice.

Upgrading Expansion Cards

Even though there may be dozens of different expansion cards, adding any one of them to your system is a basic operation. It's one of the classic plug-in-and-go PC upgrades. The only way you could conceivably muck it up is if you plug in a card with the PC's power on. So, other than basic installation and possibly resolving some conflicts, there's nothing to it.

The generic approach is taken here again, though a few specific situations are covered in the first section, "Strategies." But for the standard memory, hard-disk/floppy-disk controller, and video card, installing the card is the same.

Strategies

Upgrading an expansion card, like everything you do to your PC, requires a little forethought. You should think about some of the things that follow.

What You Need the Card For

There are a lot of expansion cards and options to choose from. Know in advance what it is you want.

The Type of Card

Remember that expansion cards come in different sizes and are of the 8-bit, 16-bit and 32-bit variety. Make sure you get the right one for your computer. Often there are specific cards for each data path type that do the same thing.

Where It Goes

Do you have room for the card? Nothing is more disconcerting than running out of slots, especially on older PCs. Aside from that, internal placement of the card is up to you. Figure 10.4 will give you some idea of what expansion cards look like when they're plugged in.

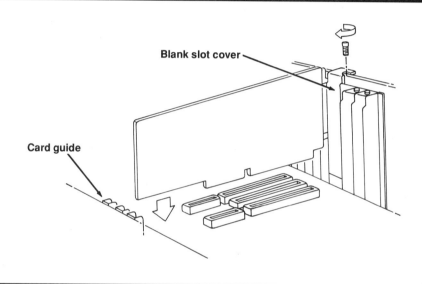

Blank slot cover

Card guide

FIGURE 10.4: Expansion cards inside the PC's case

Use Those Knockouts!

A knockout is a D-shaped hole in your case that hasn't yet been removed. Case makers die-cut holes but don't remove the cut part. You remove the cut part when you want to open a hole for a COM port jack, say, for your mouse to plug into. You simply dislodge the knockout by tapping on it with a screwdriver, then you grasp it with a pair of needle-nosed pliers and twist it to break it free.

Now you have an opening suited to receive an RS232 jack. Some knockouts are sized to take either of a small port jack (good for mice) or the larger size jack (good for external drives, scanners, or other outboard devices).

Many cases (especially tower cases) come with several of these "knock-outs," so you can enable multiple COM ports for external uses. After all, you can only get one full-size COM port onto a card, so if you want a second, you either have to give up another slot opening or use a knockout for the COM port jack.

Consider Cabling

When placing cards inside your PC, consider that a lot of them have a spaghetti bowl of cables springing out of them. Most of the external connectors will be on the back of the card, on its mounting bracket. But sometimes not all the connectors will fit on that thin bracket. An additional bracket can be installed in an empty slot (by removing its slot cover).

How Cards are Mounted

An expansion card slides into place—it's like putting a shelf in a cupboard. Then the card is anchored—on the bottom via the bus and expansion slot, and on the back via the mounting bracket and screw. That keeps the card from wobbling back and forth.

Long cards are also anchored on the front of the PC. Some PCs have a series of grooves on their inside front panel at the same intervals as the expansion slots. If not, most long cards come with a plastic doo-hickey that you can attach to the front of the case and use to further secure the card.

Upgrade Overview

This section covers in detail directions for removing and then installing an expansion card. This is usually done when you're upgrading a video card or replacing two cards of varying types with a single multifunction card. But for most upgrades, you'll simply be installing new cards into the PC—probably until you run out of slots!

If you're removing a card, the following instructions give you an overview. If you just want to read about installing a new card, skip to the heading, "Locate an empty slot," later in this chapter.

Remove the PC's Lid

First, power down the computer and remove its lid.

Locate the Card to Remove

If you've installed the card yourself, you probably know where it is. If not, you may have to look around to find it. The biggest clues are the cables connecting the cards. By tracing cables you can locate the hard- and floppy-drive controllers.

Disconnect Cables

For now, disconnect only those cables on the *back* of the card, if any. You need to remove any externally connected cables so that you can slide the card up and out. Leave the internal cables attached for the time being.

Unscrew the Mounting Bracket

There is a single screw on the top of the mounting bracket. On some PCs with lots of slots, you'll need to be careful to note which screw is holding down the card you want to remove. Set the screw aside.

Ground Yourself

Since you might touch electrical circuitry when you're lifting out the card, ground yourself first. If you're not wearing a grounding wrist strap, touch the PC's power supply for a moment, and stand still.

Lift the Card Straight Up and Out

Grab the card by its edges. The best thing to do is pinch the top two corners of the card and lift. You may have to rock the card end-to-end to release it from the slot. Avoid pinching any chips or electronic parts.

Remove the Card

Once the card is up and out, set it aside. If it doesn't have any cables attached, slide it into a static-free bag or preferably its original packing (which you should always keep). If you're upgrading, you can alternatively "borrow" the new card's packing once it's ready.

Before you put the card away, remove any cables or other items you may want to keep. For example, if you want to swap RAM chips from one card to another, now is the time to unplug them. Put the cables away and try to keep all your PC's cables together.

Cover the Hole

If you're done at this point, you can cover the blank hole left by the card with a spare slot cover. If you don't have any, that's fine.

If you're done, you can close up now, and skip to the heading, "Carefully Slide the Lid Back On." Otherwise you can re-install the card if you just upgraded it (for example, by adding memory), or install a replacement card.

Locate an Empty Slot

Remember everything we talked about in the previous section about the location of cards in a PC. There are 8-bit and 16-bit slots, and you'll want to put the appropriate cards in each.

Remove the Mounting Bracket

Once you've found the slot, unscrew the slot cover's screw and remove the slot cover. Keep the screw.

Move Any Cables Out of the Way

There may be some cables snaked over the slot you're about to put a card into. If so, try to move them out of the way, so your upgrade will be unobstructed.

If you must move cables, you might have to disconnect them from other expansion cards. To remember where a cable goes, label both ends of the cable and its connector.

Install the Front Mount

If your PC's case lacks front mounts for long cards, check the new expansion card's box for a front mount. If it's there, attach it to the inside front of your PC's case. (This is only necessary for long cards.)

Take the Card from Its Package

Note that the card comes in a static-free bag or some other insulated packing material. Be careful when handling the card; ground yourself, and touch the card only by the edges.

Make Adjustments to the Card

You may have to set some cards down in a work area so you can set them up before installation. Setting them up may involve one or more of the following.

◆ Attaching internal cables to the card

◆ Setting DIP switches and jumpers

◆ Installing RAM chips or SIMMs

◆ Other setup

If anything needs to be done to the card, do it now before you stick it into the computer.

Line Up the Card and Slide It Down

Eyeball the card to line it up, positioning the rear mounting bracket over the slot hole and the edge connector over the slot. If it's a long card, you'll also have to line up the front mount.

Lower the card into position, and once the edge connector is over the slot, press the card down firmly. Make sure the card is completely seated in the slot. The rear mounting bracket should be flush with other brackets and slot covers in the system.

Tighten the Screw

Replace the screw on the rear mounting bracket, and tighten it into position. This will help to position the card further.

Attach Any External Cables

Hook up the printer cable, monitor cable, modem cable, or any external connectors. Most modern cables attach by means of thumb-twists, which

are easy to work with when you don't want to pull the PC all the way from the wall. However, some older cables use tiny minus screws. Even so, tighten down all the cables so they won't pull loose.

Double-Check All Your Connections

Make sure everything is properly connected. If you had to remove cables to install the expansion card, reconnect them now. Make sure the card and any cables are all firmly connected. If the card requires any DIP switches on the motherboard to be set, do that now, before you put the lid back on.

Carefully Slide the Lid Back On

If you're done, put the PC's lid back on. Be careful—you don't want to snag any cables and pull them loose. This causes more problems than anything when upgrading. Your next step involves powering up the PC and making sure the card works.

Now comes the question of what to do with leftover cards. Upgrading your PC, especially over a period of time, might mean you wind up with a card collection. Welcome to the club. Seasoned PC owners and upgraders have closets full of expansion cards. You can't sell them, at least not for any profit. But you should keep them around to be used in the event one of your installed cards fails you.

Removing an Expansion Card

Removing an expansion card is easy. You might want to remove an expansion card for any of several reasons: because the card is incompatible with some new installation or the card no longer works, because you want to make room for new cards, because you want to replace a card with a newer version of the same card, or because you want to make modifications (such as adding memory).

HOW TO REMOVE AN EXPANSION CARD

Procedure: Removing an expansion card

Tools Needed: Medium minus or plus screwdriver

Steps:

1. Power down the PC and remove its lid.

2. Locate the expansion card you want to remove. Remember to disconnect any enternal cables from the card and move any obstructing cables out of the way.

3. Unscrew the card from its mounting bracket. This usually involves a small, minus screw, though some PCs may use plus screws instead. Remember to save the screw.

4. Ground yourself first, then pinch the card on both of its top two corners. Lift it up and straight out. (You may have to rock it back and forth to get it loose.)

5. Cover the hole. If you're not replacing the card, install a psare slot cover in its place. Anchor the slot cover using the same screw you removed in step 3.

6. Once the card is free, put it into a static-free bag, preferably the original one it came in, though if you're swapping cards you can store the old card in the new card's bag. Remove any cables from the card before putting it in the bag. Store the cables separately. If removal of the card involved taking something out of your system serial port, memory, etc. remember to reset any DIP switches on the motherboard. (AT-level systems will require the SETUP program to be run.)

7. When you're done, put the lid back on the PC and fire it up. If you have an AT-level system and you've removed some central system component, you may be required to run your SETUP program to instruct the computer of its changes. Also remember that you may have to remove some software dirvers. For example, if you're moving a mouse card to another computer you'll need to remove your MOUSE.SYS driver from CONFIG.SYS.

Installing an Expansion Card

There are three common expansion cards you need in your PC:

◆ The hard-disk controller

◆ The floppy-drive controller

◆ The video adapter

HOW TO INSTALL AN EXPANSION CARD

Procedure: Installing an expansion card

Tools Needed: Medium minus or plus screwdriver

Steps:

1. Power down the PC and remove its lid—or, if you're continuing a replacement or upgrade from the previous section, keep working.

2. Locate an empty slot or use the same slot you just made available. If you're locating a slot, consider cable placement, the length of the card, and the slot 8 issues described earlier.

3. Remove the slot cover. Also, install the front mount if the card you're installing is a long card.

4. Before you put the card into the PC, make sure it's properly configured. Attach any cables, set the DIP switches and jumpers, and add RAM as required for your PC. *Remember to ground yourself before touching the card.*

5. Slide the card into the PC. Press down firmly, making sure it goes all the way into the slot.

6. Tighten the mounting bracket screw. After that, check all your connections. Attach any external cables, then make sure all cables are properly installed. If you have a PC/XT-level system, check to see if any DIP switches on the motherboard need to be set or reset at this time.

7. Carefully slide the top back on your PC, and power up to test it.

AT-level systems will require you to run the SETUP program to tell the PC about its new expansion card. (Usually the POST will error and lead you to the SETUP program automatically.)

Once everything is working, you'll have to setup the software side of the card. Some cards come with diskettes that contain configuration programs. You should run them and make sure the hardware is properly working. Add any software drivers to CONFIG.SYS as necessary.

Additional Setup

After setting DIP switches on the motherboard or card, and working with a SETUP program, there are two other things you may have to deal with following the physical installation of an expansion card:

- ◆ Software setup
- ◆ Solving hardware conflicts

Nothing you add to a PC is quite truly plug-in-and-go (except for the power supply, which is coming up in the next chapter), so keep in mind that after you bolt the lid back on the case, you may still have some work to do.

Software Setup

There is a software side to most hardware upgrades (refer to Chapter 5). For expansion cards, the software setup will vary with each card and what it does. So for more detailed information on the software side of memory cards, hard- and floppy-drive controllers, and video cards, refer to those individual chapters of this book.

Some software will probably be included with any card. This even holds true for memory and video cards. Memory cards, for example, may have drivers for RAM disks and print spoolers, or an EMS driver for an EMS card. Video cards may have sample graphic images and demo programs to

show off the graphics, or they may contain device drivers for CONFIG.SYS or some of your applications.

Whatever the case and whatever the card, there are usually three types of software that come with an expansion card:

◆ Configuration software

◆ Utilities

◆ Fun software

Configuration software comes with some of the more well designed cards, and with all MCA cards.

Utilities come with nearly every expansion card. Multifunction cards and memory cards will come with software drivers for RAM disks, print spoolers, and disk caching programs. Mouse cards come with testing and calibration software, as well as tutorials to help you learn the mouse. And some utilities come in the form of software drivers that let DOS and certain applications get the most from the new hardware.

Finally, some expansion cards come with *fun software*. Music cards might come with sample sound files that make your PC sound like an orchestra, and mouse cards might come with games and puzzles you can play, for example.

Solving Conflicts

Not everything is bright and sunny in the land of adding expansion cards to your systems. That's really the fault of the ISA bus. One of the bus' jobs is to manage what's known as *contention*. (That's the competition between two cards for the same "turf.") The ISA bus just can't deal with contention. The same problem happens with modems, the COM ports, and display adapters that conflict.

The real resolution to these conflicts lies in your careful planning, and the proper settings of the DIP switches and jumpers on a card. If you've added a printer port and suddenly you seem to have none, then you're experiencing printer contention. You must dive into the computer and reset the jumpers on one of the printer cards to make one port LPT1 and the other LPT-something-else.

Another interesting serial communications problem happens when you have two serial ports on two different cards (aside from a modem card). Things can get screwy inside a PC. But most conflicts can be resolved by careful planning. Just don't assign two items to the same port or memory space and your conflicts will be at a minimum.

Power Supply

If the microprocessor is your computer's brain, then the power supply is its heart. The power supply is responsible—as its name implies—for supplying electricity to all parts of your computer. The power supply is an awkward-looking device hidden well out of sight within your computer.

 **DON'T EVER TRY TO DISASSEMBLE THE PC'S POWER SUPPLY.** There's nothing in there you can upgrade or fix yourself. And it's just plain dangerous. Power supply upgrades involve SWAPPING power supplies, not disassembling them.

The power supply is our topic in this chapter. The power supply isn't something you need to know about in any depth. Knowing about memory, the disk drives, and the display adapter is much more important—they play a big role in how you get work done on your PC.

General Notes on the Power Supply

This section contains some background information on power supplies. This isn't technical stuff, though some electronic terms are used (and explained for you). You don't *need* to know about voltage or amps, but the product of the two is watts, and watts are important to know about. There are two sections here to fill you in on all the details of a PC's power supply:

◆ The Power Supply's Duties

◆ About the Power Supply

The Power Supply's Duties

The power supply has three distinct duties:

◆ It supplies the PC with power

◆ It cools the system

◆ It protects the internal components

The power supply also cools your system. It comes with a built-in fan, which is why PCs should make noise when you turn them on (they hum because they don't know the words). That fan draws in air through the slits in the PC's case and the disk drives. The air flows over and cools the motherboard, then flows between and cools the expansion cards, and is finally drawn in through the power supply (which it also cools) and out the exhaust port behind your PC.

The power supply's cooling task explains why most tower PC's have their power supplies on top—heat rises, so to cool the system, the fan must be placed on top of the system where it can draw the rising hot air up away from the components and out of the system. If you're mounting a desktop PC on its side, remember to place it power-supply-side-up.

Finally, the power supply protects the PC. The computer flat-out won't start if, for any reason, the power supply cannot give the PC enough electricity. (This might occur during a "brownout," or as the result of damage to the power supply or wires, for example.)

Also, the power supply is designed so that if it goes *boom*, it won't take the rest of the system with it. When a power supply dies, it pops. You see the famous blue smoke rising from your PC, and you smell ozone (that "dead battery" smell). In that case, replacing the power supply is all you need to do to fix the computer. Its death doesn't spread to other parts of the PC.

Of all the devices in your computer, the power supply is the one you probably need worry about the least. That's for good reason—it does its job.

About the Power Supply

This section covers some details about the power supply itself. There are three topics here:

◆ Location

◆ Examination

◆ Configuration

Location

When you open a PC and look inside, you'll find that it's really tight back there where the power supply lives. Maybe ¼" separates the power supply from the back of the drives. And while the expansion cards aren't close to the power supply's left side, that area is usually filled with cables. So it's pretty snug.

The power supply is anchored to the case in two ways. First, by four screws (one screw for each of the four corners of the power supply) that hold it to the back of your PC. Second, the power supply slides into two clips on the bottom of the case. There are two corresponding holes and slots on the bottom of the power supply. This keeps it secure and stable inside the PC.

Examination

Power supplies are pretty homely to look at—just a metal box with some holes, wires, and plugs in it. They don't need to be pretty—power supplies are internal to the PC. If you have a chance to examine one, you should note the items listed in this section. (Refer to Figure 11.1.)

The *fan intake* is a series of concentric air holes, through which you'll see the PC's fan. There may be one or two fans and intakes, depending on the strength of the power supply and how much air it sucks. Also, the label is important to read, not only because it warns you against taking the power supply apart (which you should never do), but also because it lists the power supply's *rating*. The important thing to look for is *wattage*—how many watts does the power supply give to the PC? (You'll read why this is important in a moment.)

The back of the power supply contains up to four interesting items:

◆ The power connector

◆ The monitor's power connector

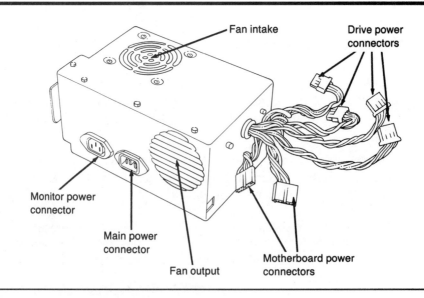

FIGURE 11.1: Parts of the power supply

◆ The fan exhaust port

◆ A power switch

The *power connector* is the three-pronged connector. It's the connector into which you plug the power cable that goes to the wall socket.

The *monitor's power connector* is a matching three-holed connector. Some monitors have special power cables that plug into this connector. If not, you can plug the monitor directly into the wall socket.

The *fan exhaust port* is the hole out of which the power supply blows all the hot air and dust that it has sucked through the PC. (The fan exhaust port usually has a companion black-spot that appears on the wall behind your computer.)

Some power supplies may also have a "European power switch." This is a small, usually red, slide switch that's marked *120V* on one side and *220V* on the other side. In the United States, 120 volts at 60 Hertz is the way utility companies deliver power. In Europe they use 220V at 50 Hertz. (Don't ask me why.) To be compatible across the pond, some power supplies have the switchable selector, allowing the power supply to work on both continents. Other power supplies, called "switchable," don't need the manual switch. They'll automatically detect the change in voltage and cycles (Hertz) and will compensate.

The 6-wire connectors attached to cables coming out of your power supply are used to supply your motherboard with power.

Note that there are two 6-wire connectors and they look dreadfully alike. They are also two of the few unnotched connectors in your PC. If you plug them in wrong, you could fry your motherboard.

To avoid that, note the color of the wires on each connector. The connector that goes toward the rear of the PC will have three black wires, a yellow wire, and a white wire. The connector toward the front of the PC has two black wires, a blue wire, and three red wires.

The important motherboard connector is the one with the single white wire. That wire is called the Power Good line, which has just one job—to supply a signal to the motherboard indicating if there is enough power to start up. That wire is the only white wire and, if you look carefully, you'll notice that there is no wire next to it in the pin 2 position.

An easy way to remember this is black-to-black—put the black wire of one next to the black wire of the other in the center.

The 4-wire connectors are for your disk drives. They're all notched, so you can't plug them in wrong. You'll notice that two of them are longer than the others. Those would be for the drives in your right drive bay. Also, some of the older power supplies will have only two 4-wire connectors. If you add any additional drives, you'll need a power supply splitter, or "Y," cable.

Configuration

Just as RAM or hard disk storage is measured by the kilobyte (K) or megabyte (MB), power supplies are measured in watts.

Electrically speaking, watts measure production, or the amount of *work* done by the electricity. Each electronic part in your computer requires and uses a certain amount of electricity to do its job. That amount is measured in watts. For example, a light bulb's brightness is measured in the number of watts used—brighter bulbs have a higher wattage. And your electric bill is usually based on the total kilowatt-hours of energy you use. (Burning ten 100 watt bulbs for an hour is equivalent to one kilowatt-hour of energy.)

Incidentally, an old rumor used to have it that running a PC 24 hours a day added $40 to your monthly electric bill. This is totally false. A PC consumes anywhere from a couple of kilowatt-hours to 150 kilowatt-hours of juice a month. At most, that may add $12 to your bill.

The power supply is responsible for supplying wattage, which is then divvied up for use by each item in your computer. Since each item in the computer consumes part of the total pie of watts, you need to have a power supply that provides enough watts—otherwise you run into trouble.

Usually your computer will come with a capable power supply. But if you're adding a lot of peripherals, a second hard drive, and/or a couple of megs of RAM, the power consumption gets critical. For example, if you have a PC/XT with only a 135 watt power supply, you should consider an upgrade before things go boom. When it comes to power supplies, more doesn't hurt.

Replacing a Power Supply

Replacing a power supply isn't something you do every day. You may never have to do it. There really are only two reasons for replacing your power supply:

◆ The one you have just died

◆ You want a beefier one to avoid the above

Adding another hard drive, more RAM, or a tape-backup unit to your system can push the amount of watts consumed over the amount the power supply provides—and the power supply will die. Or, one of the enemies of your PC's power supply may fry it. Or, you may just want to take a peek and make sure your power supply is up to snuff.

Replacing a power supply is covered here in three sections:

◆ Buying a New Power Supply

◆ Replacement Overview

◆ Removal and Installation

There are no circumstances in which you'll just be removing a power supply—it would render the PC useless. And no matter how mondo keen your PC is, there's no reason for it to have two power supplies. So we'll concentrate here on replacing the thing.

Buying a New Power Supply

Power supplies are one of the simplest things to buy for a PC. Unlike RAM, which has speeds and capacities, or hard drives with their different capacities and controller cards and whatnot, power supplies are judged by only two qualities:

◆ Wattage

◆ Type

Wattage is the primary thing to look for in a power supply. Though a PC/XT-level system can get by with a 135 watt power supply, 150 watts is better. You can find larger power supplies for that type of system, some with more than one fan and "auto-cooling," which adjusts the fan's rate depending on how hot your PC is. As usual, you'll pay more for that.

For AT-level systems, you'll want a power supply that gives you at least 200 watts. More is better, but don't go overboard. Paying a lot for a big power supply when you don't need the extra wattage is a waste of money.

The second thing to look for in a power supply is its size. PC-style cases have one common configuration for a power supply. No matter who makes it, the power supply will fit into the case. But AT-style systems use a different power supply.

Some PC/XT-level systems are in AT-style cases. They can't use the AT's power supply, because they're really XTs. So get a power supply based on what type of system you have, not what the case looks like.

And then there are the oddballs. Not every computer is a perfect clone of the original PC or PC/AT. For example, the old Leading Edge computers all came with their own proprietary power supplies. You had to order new ones from Leading Edge itself. IBM's PS/2s use a different style of power supply. And COMPAQ computers should only have COMPAQ power supplies installed.

Replacement Overview

Removing an old power supply and installing a new one is perhaps the most involved upgrade procedure. Sometimes you'll have to remove disk drives and expansion cards to get at the power supply. But replacing a power supply is a once-in-a-lifetime thing, so it won't inconvenience you often.

The following steps detail the replacement procedure.

Remove the PC's Lid

Power down the computer (unless the power supply is already kaput) and take off its top.

Disconnect the Power Cables

Remove the monitor's power supply from the back of the PC. The main power cable (to the wall socket) should already be unplugged. If not, unplug it.

Locate the Power Supply

The power supply is the largest single shiny metal box found inside the PC. Note how close it is to the disk drives. This is why you have to slide them forward (but not out) to remove the power supply.

Unscrew the Four Mounting Screws

The power supply is anchored to the case by four mounting screws on the back of the system unit. They're smaller screws than the case's screws, which should already have been removed. Each screw is located in one of the four corners of the back of the power supply. Set them aside after removal.

Slide the Disk Drives Forward

This is potentially the biggest step. For AT-style cases with mounting rails, where the drives screw in on the front of the case, it's no problem—just remove the angle brackets in front of each drive and carefully slide the drives out about three or four inches. You don't need to totally remove them.

If you have a PC-style case, you'll need to unscrew the drives directly from the drive bays. For the right drive bay, that's no problem. But the left drive bay's screws may be obscured by some expansion cards. When that happens, you need to remove some of the longer expansion cards to get at the screws. This makes it a lot of work to remove a power supply, but there's no other way to do it.

Disconnect the Power Connectors from the Drives

As long as you're working with the drives, unpop the white plastic power supply connector from each of the drives. Since you're yanking out the power supply, you need to remove all of its connections.

Disconnect the Power Supply from the Motherboard

The power supply attaches to the motherboard via two 6-wire connectors, somewhat larger than the disk drive connectors

Note how those two connectors go. They're not notched, and if you plug them in wrong, you could damage the system.

The key to remembering which one goes where is to note their color—it's the same for all power supplies. But more reliably, you should note that the connector toward the rear of the PC's case has only five wires. The one to the front of the case has six.

Remove the Power Supply

Slide the power supply toward the front of the PC. Then lift it straight out. You need to slide it forward because the power supply is attached to the bottom of the case via clips. Just slide it back a few inches and it will lift right out.

Once it's out, you can toss the old power supply—especially if it's dead. There's no need for it, no point in repairing it. If it still works, you should think about keeping it around "just in case." But if the closet is already junky enough and the spouse is complaining, toss it.

Place the New Power Supply into the System

From here on, the process reverses itself. Lower the new power supply into the system. Remember the clips. Put the power supply in some 2" from the back of the PC. Then slide it toward the back. Lift it up a bit just to make sure the clips found their holes.

Connect the Motherboard

Attach the two 6-wire power connectors to the motherboard. They're not notched, and it may take some muscle to connect them.

If you have problems attaching these two connectors, then remove the power supply and install them first. Angle in the connector in toward the motherboard and press. Then slide in the power supply.

Connect the Power Connectors to the Drives

Attach each of your drives to the new power supply. There should be four of the plastic connectors, and they're notched so you can't plug them in wrong. Also, note that the power supplies with four connectors will have two of them longer than the others. Those two are for the drives in your right drive bay. There's nothing different about them, they're just longer.

This is where you can make a minor fumble in your upgrading touch-down run. Forgetting to plug in the power connector on a drive is a frustrating mistake, so double-check all your connections.

Screw in the Power Supply

Using the four original screws, tighten the power supply to the back of the PC's case.

Replace the Lid

You're done. Before replacing the lid you may want to double-check all the connections—especially on the drives. And be careful putting the lid back on that you don't snag and detach any cables. Once the lid is bolted back on, hook up the power cables to the wall and monitor and flip the switch.

Under normal circumstances, everything should work just fine. But a few of the following problems may make your heart sink.

Nothing Happens

Don't worry. You could be in a brownout. Or maybe the PC's not plugged in. Or one of the motherboard connectors may be incorrectly installed. Also, the power supply could itself be dead. One way to check it is to plug in the power supply before you install it. Then flip the switch. If the fan comes on, then the power supply itself should be okay.

The PC Beeps

Beeping is what the PC does when the POST hasn't checked the video display. If you hear a long, loud beep, or an endless series of short beeps, then the problem is the power supply. Recheck your connections.

The Disk Drive Doesn't Work

You probably neglected to attach the disk drive's power connector. Also, check to see if any cables were pulled loose during the upgrade.

Normally, everything will go fine. If you're replacing your power supply because it died on you, then you'll notice now that your PC comes up just as it did before the trouble. The power supply's death didn't bring down the rest of the system with it.

Removal and Installation

The following steps can be taken to replace your PC's power supply, whether you want to upgrade to a beefier unit, or remove a dead one.

HOW TO REPLACE A POWER SUPPLY

Procedure: Replacing a power supply

Tools Needed: Medium minus screwdriver, medium plus screwdriver (for the disk drives)

Steps:

1. Power down the PC and remove its lid.

2. Unscrew the power supply from the rear of the system unit. There are four screws, one for each corner of the power supply.

3. Slide the disk drives forward. This will give you working room, and allow you to slide the power supply back, which must be done to remove it.

4. Detach the power supply's cables. Remove the monitor and main power supply cables from the back of the PC. Remove the two connectors from the motherboard (note their positions). And remove any power connectors attached to the disk drives.

5. Remove the power supply. Slide it toward the front of the PC, then lift it out.

6. Position in the new power supply. Lower the new power supply into the case a few inches from the back of the system unit. Slide it forward so the clips on the bottom of the case will slide into the holes on the bottom of the power supply.

7. Reconnect the cables. Attach the power connectors to any disk drives in your system. Attach the two power cables to the motherboard. (Note their placement.)

8. Replace your disk drives. Slide the disk drives back into position, anchoring them to the case.

9. Screw the power supply into position. Replace the four screws that were removed in step 2.

10. Close up and test. To test the power supply, throw the switch. The PC will come up as normal, and that's about all you need to do.

Words of Advice

In most chapters of this book, the final part is devoted to software strategies or upgrades. But nothing further is required in this case. There's nothing to put in your CONFIG.SYS file, no DIP switches or SETUP programs to run. However, there are some words of advice to offer, things that will keep you, your PC, and its power supply working happily for a long time.

Keeping the PC Power-Healthy

There's a mini debate in computerdom about leaving your computer on 24-hours-a-day, all year. Those "in the know" claim that you should leave your PC on all the time. But most users tend to turn their PCs off when they're not in use. What do you do?

It's best if you leave the computer on all the time. Every time you turn a PC off and then on, you subtract one day from its life. The old rumor used to have it that cycling a PC's power (which is the technical term for turning it off and on—no matter how long the duration of downtime) was a "shock" to the system. That extra surge of electricity when the computer is first turned on is bad for the components. Whether that's true or not, who knows?

What's more important about turning a computer off and on is what it does to the temperature of the components. When a PC runs, it gets hot. (If it gets too hot, for example, too hot to touch, then you need a better fan on your power supply.) Warm components are okay, and cool components are okay. But when you turn off the computer and things cool off and then you turn it on and it heats up again, that's what wears and tears on the computer—especially the solder joints.

Say you go to work in the morning and flip on your PC. You work for three hours or so, and the components get warm. Then you turn off the computer for lunch. During that hour (or hour-and-a-half if you're in management), the PC cools. After lunch, you power it on again and it warms up. That's what will do damage to your system.

It's best to leave the PC on all the time—even over the weekends. You may want to turn it off if there's a long holiday or no one will be using the computer for several days, to save the electricity. But for day-to-day use, keep the system on.

When it comes to the on/off issue, the only thing you should concern yourself with is the monitor. Like the system unit, you can keep the monitor on all the time. But the image on the screen may "burn" the picture tube's phosphor, creating a permanent image on the picture tube. This image may even be visible when you turn the monitor off. To avoid burn-in, you can use one of the many "screen-saver" programs out there. That way, you can keep the monitor on, but the image will disappear or be refreshed constantly when the PC's not in use.

As for the printer, as an electronic device it should be on all the time as well if you use it often. However, if printing doesn't take place all the time, you can keep the printer turned off and then turn it on when you have a lot of stuff to print.

Preventing Mishaps

Earlier in this chapter, the six deadly enemies of your power supply were introduced. Rather than await their criminal arrival, you can combat them, just as you might alarm your house in anticipation of a burglary.

There are three items people employ to prevent electrical damage to their PCs:

◆ Power protection strips

◆ Surge and spike protectors

◆ Uninterruptible power supplies

Power protection strips are long devices like household extension cords that are full of electrical sockets. They plug into a single wall socket, which gives them the overall benefit of supplying you with more power outlets. Some of them come with surge suppression and line-noise filtering built in. But beware—not every power strip offers that protection. Some are merely power strips that give you extra outlets and little else. If a spike comes down the line, the fuse in a power strip may save your system—but only if it's designed to do that.

Surge and spike protectors are designed to protect the computer from surges and spikes. They sacrifice themselves to protect your power supply and other items in the PC. Buy one that offers RFI/EMI filtering. (RFI stands for Radio Frequency Interference (line noise), and EMI is ElectroMagnetic

Interference.) They cost more than simple power protection strips, but the cost is worth it.

You should plug everything in your system into these power strips: your monitor (unless it plugs into the PC), printer, modem, fax, and so on. Some power strips come as flat units you can sandwich between your system unit and monitor. Some have switches that turn items in your PC on or off, and a master switch that lets you turn on the entire PC system all at once.

The brutes of the power supply wars are uninterruptible power supplies (UPS). Basically batteries that take over automatically in the event of a power outage or brownout, they are not cheap. Related to the UPS are backup power supplies, which simply run the PC off of a battery that's constantly being recharged, and standby power supplies, which supply you just enough electricity in a blackout or brownout to save your data before you power down the system.

The UPS is ideal for crucial computing (and when the user can afford the high price). Hospitals use UPS systems, not only for their computers but for everything else, for the time until their emergency generators can kick in.

For common office and home use, something like a standby power supply is fine. It gives you enough time to quickly save your data and properly power down the system.

Monitors and
Display Adapters

Of all your computer's components, the *monitor* is the most visible. You can't see 16MB of RAM, and a 150MB hard drive looks like a 40MB model from the outside, but a large colorful monitor is bound to impress. And colorful graphic displays have sold more than one PC in the showroom.

The monitor is only half the equation of graphics and video in the PC, though. The other, far more important, half is the *display adapter* (also called a *video card*), the electronic circuitry that controls the monitor. Since the majority of PCs don't have built-in video, the display adapter is an option. Ideally, you should choose one based on your text, video, and graphics needs, but more often your purchase is based on what impresses you in the showroom and what you can afford. This chapter will help unravel the mysterious acronyms that pertain to PC video technology for you, and make sense of monitors and display adapters for the PC.

The first part of this chapter covers general graphics information, including basic information and decryption of the graphics standards as well as shopping hints (because this stuff is sold by the technical description). The second part covers upgrading your video card. And, finally, we'll wrap up with information on graphics software.

Incidentally, the emphasis here is on upgrading. However, if you're new to PCs or shopping for a second computer, the information provided in this chapter can also help you choose a display adapter and companion monitor. Note also that it is possible to run two monitors simultaneously with one PC, though not all software is friendly to that idea.

General Video Information

PC graphics is a wide but colorful desert to cross. The subject is handled here in four sections:

- ◆ PC Graphics
- ◆ Text and Graphics
- ◆ Color graphics adapters
- ◆ Monitors

You have many options with PC graphics. There are lots of standards, lots of manufacturers, and many ways to put them all together. But when you take into account the software you use, the future, and your budget, your choices usually boil down to one or two. First, some explanation of the options is in order.

PC Graphics

You have two choices for the type of display you use with your PC:

- ◆ Monochrome
- ◆ Color/graphics

We'll cover monochrome and color/graphics generally in the following two sections. More specific information on the makes, models, and modes is covered later in this chapter.

Monochrome

Monochrome video on the PC has always stood for two things:

- ◆ Nice-looking text
- ◆ No graphics

IBM's monochrome display adapter (MDA), which used to hold half the market, offered text-only displays. The characters were nicely formed and the display was crisp. The MDA, however, lacked graphics—circles, lines, boxes, shades, and other computer graphics were impossible on the MDA, because the system was built to handle text characters only. The monochrome text was nice to look at and easy on the eyes.

The Hercules Graphics Card

One way around monochrome's graphics limitations is to install a VGA card that is downward-compatible. Downward-compatible means that your card will work with VGA and all of the "lesser" graphics standards including MDA and the Hercules Graphics standard. Hercules (a company in Hercules, California) developed an MDA "clone" card in the early '80s. The card did everything the original MDA did, but in addition it offered a high-resolution graphics mode. Hercules became an accepted standard for monochrome video because it provided crisp text and graphics for a small amount of money.

Color/Graphics

With color/graphics video on the PC you get:

◆ Clear text

◆ Color text

◆ Graphics

Color/graphics displays for the PC have traditionally been known for their fuzzy, hard-to-read text. This was especially true when they were first introduced. Unlike monochrome, the text characters on a color display are composed of different colored dots or *pixels* (an acronym for *picture elements*).

Colorful text used to be a moot point. To keep compatible with monochrome systems, software developers stuck with white-on-black text for both systems. But slowly, color users were able to assign their own color choices for the programs they used.

The second offering of a color video system is graphics. That's where the graphics adapter card, which controls the monitor, leaves its text character mode.

In graphics mode, a color display gives you lines, circles, colors, and shades. This is color's primary advantage over monochrome displays. Recent advances in color-video hardware have made incredible things possible for PC color graphics. In addition to better looking text, PC displays now offer more sophisticated graphics capabilities. And the price keeps dropping, which is why color systems currently outnumber monochrome systems.

Reasons for Wanting Color/Graphics

The following are reasons why some people prefer a color/graphics video system over monochrome.

Color Text Many people don't care whether their text is in color. But some software packages do look better in color. Certain word processors use color to denote different styles of text on the screen. And color is used in many software packages to identify special text and warning messages.

Graphics If you want graphics, then color is really the only way to go. If you want to use Windows, you want graphics.

Software More and more software is requiring color to get the job done. Graphics applications such as Windows, Excel, painting and drawing programs, CAD, animation, and—yes—games, just look better with color graphics.

Text and Graphics

There are two operating modes for a PC video system:

- ◆ Text mode
- ◆ Graphics mode

In the *text mode*, only text characters are displayed on the screen. This is the normal DOS mode used by many applications. On a color system, the text will be displayed in color; with monochrome you get only black-and-white text.

The *graphics mode* is where the PC draws lines, circles, squares, and dots on the screen. What confuses people is that text can also be displayed in the graphics mode. That text is really graphics, though it looks and behaves like text in the text mode.

Other differences between the two modes are covered in the following two sections.

The Text Mode

The text mode is offered by both monochrome and color systems. The differences between the two are that monochrome text is black-and-white, with a few interesting attributes such as underline and inverse text, and color text is available in 16 foreground and 8 background colors. Both types of text have highlighted, flashing, and inverse text attributes.

The standard PC text screen has a resolution of 80 characters across by 25 characters down. That is, 80 columns by 25 rows of text—on screen. The intersection of each row and column of text contains a character.

For monochrome systems, the 80 × 25 setup is all you get. Color displays have a variety of text modes. For example, all PC color displays support a 40-column mode. This mode was created for the early days of the PC, when IBM thought some people would be using TV sets as monitors.

The *EGA* and *VGA* graphics adapters (we talk about the differences between these graphics adapters later in this chapter) have additional display modes. However, those modes alter the number of rows on the display, not columns. Using those modes, you can get up to 50 rows of text displayed on the PC's screen.

The Graphics Mode

The graphics mode is available on all color video systems. In that mode, each point, or pixel, on the screen is directly controlled by the video-controller card. On monographics systems, the pixel can be turned on or off. Color systems change the color of the pixel (to turn it off its color is changed to black or to the background color).

As with the text mode, graphics modes have resolution. But here, the resolution is measured in pixels. The number of pixels across the screen is the horizontal resolution, the number of pixels up and down is the vertical resolution.

In addition to the resolution, a second attribute is given to graphics screens: the number of colors available. With monographics, you have only two colors: black and white. But color systems can have thousands of different colors available. Each pixel on the display can take on one of those colors.

The number of colors and the resolution a graphics card is capable of producing is dependent on the amount of video memory (RAM) on the card. Each color takes up a certain amount of memory; the more colors, the more memory is required. Memory is also tied to the resolution of the card; higher resolutions require more memory. So a tradeoff is made: At higher resolutions you get fewer colors, but at lower resolutions you get more colors.

One more thing: You often cannot see the total number of colors a graphics card is capable of producing; the on-screen variety is limited by your video memory.

Each graphics card has a maximum number of available colors. For example, the first graphics adapter for the PC had a total of 16 colors available. But in the graphics mode, you could select from only a few of those colors at a time. Even fewer colors could be displayed on the screen at once.

The total number of colors a graphics card can produce is known as its *palette*. And the number of colors the graphics mode can use from that palette is referred to as the *displayable colors*.

For example, the PC's first graphics adapter had a total potential of 16 displayable colors. In its medium-resolution mode, at 320 horizontal by 200 vertical pixels, it could display only four colors from the 16 available. The VGA-graphics adapter has a palette of over 256,000 colors, but can display only 256 on the screen at once in its highest color mode.

This issue of color palettes may sound confusing, but it's merely a memory limitation. 256 out of 256,000-odd colors isn't that bad. But when shopping, remember to clarify the number of *true displayable colors* vs. the total number of colors available in the palette.

Color Graphics Adapters

There are monochrome and color display adapters for the PC. The monochrome side, as you've read so far, is rather plain. There are the MDA and

Hercules adapters. (Yawn.) But things get exciting on the color side of the valley.

The common PC color and graphics options are covered here in three sections:

◆ Type of Adapter

◆ Video RAM

◆ Options

One thing to note about color-graphics adapters is that IBM sets the standard. Other manufacturers design better expansion slots, hard drives, and operating systems for the PC. But IBM still leads the pack with graphics; graphics adapters introduced by others never seem to catch on.

Type of Adapter

There are three popular color-graphics adapters for the PC:

◆ EGA (Enhanced Graphics Adapter)

◆ VGA (Video Graphics Array)

◆ SVGA (Super Video Graphics Adapter)

Others exist, some almost standard (such as PGA and various high-end graphics for computer-assisted design—CAD—and animation). But the three biggies are EGA, VGA, and SVGA.

EGA The *Enhanced Graphics Adapter*, or EGA, became the standard PC graphics adapter starting around 1986—a few years after the card was introduced. IBM originally offered EGA cards with the PC/AT, but the price was too high for most users. CGA cards were cheaper and more widely supported. It took a few years for EGA software to appear, and by then the EGA standard had been supplanted by VGA.

The EGA standard offered up to 64 colors and a variety of high-resolution graphics modes. Table 12.1 shows a few of the more popular graphics modes and colors.

EGA has more modes, resolutions, and colors than those listed in Table 12.1. (That information is really of use only to programmers.) Table 12.1 lists the most colorful values of the highest resolution.

TABLE 12.1: Some EGA graphics modes, resolutions, and colors

MODE	RESOLUTION	COLORS	PALETTE
Low	640H×200V	16	64
Medium	640H×350V	2	2
High	640H×350V	4 or 16	64

When EGA started to take hold and card clones became cheap and plentiful, IBM introduced the PS/2 class of computers and yet another graphics standard, VGA.

VGA VGA stands for *Video Graphics Array*. Why "array" instead of "adapter" is anyone's guess. But it was the new, high-color and high-resolution graphics adapter built into IBM's new line of PS/2 computers, introduced in 1987. And VGA seems to be the only component anyone ever bothered to clone from these computers.

VGA offers more graphics, more colors, and the highest resolution of any common graphics adapter. It has a lot of features and flexibility. In fact, a VGA adapter should be the choice for anyone considering a color adapter for his/her system.

As far as graphics modes go, VGA is very versatile. It's also fully EGA-compatible. A few of the more interesting modes are shown in Table 12.2.

TABLE 12.2: A few VGA graphics modes

MODE	RESOLUTION	COLORS	PALETTE
High Color	320H×200V	256	262,144
Low	640H×200V	16	262,144
Medium	640H×350V	16	262,144
High	640H×480V	2	262,144

VGA cards are widely cloned and cheap. And the clones offer features that IBM's VGA lacks. For example, clone VGA cards also include some of the more common *MCGA* modes. MCGA is a second graphics standard introduced on some PS/2 systems. It offers more colors at a lower resolution than traditional VGA, and most VGA-clone cards offer it as well.

Some VGA clones even offer Hercules graphics emulation and can be used with a monochrome monitor. VGA has its own monochrome, or "shades of gray," mode that looks beautiful on some of the paper-white monitors.

SVGA Finally, the VGA standard was improved upon by several of the clone makers, who have dubbed the new standard *SuperVGA*. This graphics standard offers additional resolutions beyond the upper limit of standard VGA. But note that only a few software packages support SuperVGA. More might in the future, which is why SuperVGA is a good insurance policy against being left behind with an outdated graphics adapter.

The big deal surrounding SVGA is resolution levels. VGA supports resolution levels up to 640×480. SVGA supports resolutions of 800×600 and 1024×768.

Pricing of the SVGA cards depends on which processor is used, how much and what type of memory is on-board, and how well the monitor handles the VESA standard.

Your eyes filter out most of the flicker produced by a monitor, but if you want to do a reality check on your computer, try looking at your PC straight-on, then gradually turn your head until you can just barely see the screen with your peripheral vision. If you have a screen flicker problem, you'll see it then. Consider upgrading to a VESA-compatible monitor if only to save your eyes.

Video RAM

Closely tied to color and resolution is *video memory*. All those pixels are really bits in memory. And the colors the pixels take on are represented by more bits. The more memory you have, the more colors your graphics adapter is capable of displaying, and the greater the resolution.

EGA used from 64K to 128K of RAM, plus 16K of RAM for its BIOS. With VGA, more RAM means more color and more resolution. VGA can use as

much RAM as they can stuff on the card. Today's standard is 1MB, but many high-end cards sport 8MB of dual-ported VRAM.

VGA cards don't necessarily come packed with just 512K of VRAM. You can buy VGA cards with only 256K, 512K, 1MB, or more memory. While the cards with less memory will be cheaper, they'll lack some of the higher resolutions and variety of colors as the fully populated cards. You can upgrade video RAM yourself, and you'll have to if you can't afford the full configuration all at once and want all the colors.

Hardware Acceleration Most Windows users complain about the speed at which their video cards supply their monitors with data. They commonly blame Windows for the slow speed. In fact, Windows will run a lot more quickly than your video card if you have a fast 386 or better. That means that you can beef up the perceived speed of Windows with an *accelerator card*. Hardware-accelerated cards are optimized for Windows, so don't invest in one if you don't use Windows.

An accelerator card usually contains a special processor that focuses on painting screen objects common to Windows, like squares and rectangles. S3 corporation offers a family of accelerator processors for video card makers to buy and install on their cards. There are several other makers, and they all try to do the same thing...speed up the rate in which your monitor shows you things.

The result of using a hardware-accelerated video card is normally a perceived increase of up to 600%. That makes the accelerated video card the best bang-for-the-buck for Windows users when it comes to upgrades vs. budget limitations.

Options

In addition to RAM, PC video adapters often have other goodies on them. The options discussed here are the traditional ones found on many display adapters. With the advent of HD/FD/1S/1P combo cards, additional ports are seen less and less on today's video cards.

The VGA graphics adapter has an optional edge connector on top. Called the *Video Feature Connector* or *VESA Connector*, it provides a way to add some interesting options to your VGA card. IBM was never clear as to what the options would be, however all VGA-clone cards include the same edge connector and optional circuitry on their cards. If you want to add some exotic video stuff to your PC, you may need to leave your current VGA card in the machine and hook it up to the add-on card via this feature connector.

Finally, video cards may have the standard slew of DIP switches and jumpers. VGA and EGA cards may have RAM sockets or daughterboards that allow you to add more video memory. These switches are used to set the card's compatibility, determine the type of monitor attached, and so on. Since they differ with each card, you should carefully read your manual to make sure you're setting the switches correctly. Fortunately, most video cards now have software that either replaces the switches or steps you through the switch-setting process.

Colors Displayed The standard VGA card is a 16-bit card. That term usually refers to the bus or card slot arrangement. But what about the card's ability to display more color information? You can now buy 24-bit video cards for your PC. Ever notice how your VGA card doesn't display a photo quite correctly? It kind of dithers the colors and mottles the display so that it seems that each and every dot stands out. In order for you to see a photo as a photo-quality image, you must use a 24- or 32-bit video card, and many people are moving to 24- and 32-bit cards as the prices drop below $200. After all, don't you want to be able to view images made up from a palette of 1.7 million colors on your screen?

Many 24- and 32-bit video cards are available in hardware-accelerated format as well, though the price is somewhat higher for the added speed benefit. If you're on a budget and you don't usually work with photo-quality images, you may want to opt for the hardware-accelerated 16-bit video card instead of a non- accelerated 24-bit card. This is especially true if you're a Windows user frustrated with the speed at which you're forced to work!

Monitors

Two parts are required for PC screen display: a display-adapter card and a matching monitor. Only the proper combination of both will give you the system you want. This chapter has concentrated on display-adapter cards up to here, so now it's time to bone up on monitors.

Basically your choices boil down to brand name, availability, and price. Certain types of monitors are designed to go with certain cards.

Monitors are covered here in four sections:

◆ Monochrome vs. Color

◆ Monitor Types

◆ Monitor Description

◆ Technical Information

Monochrome vs. Color

Quite honestly, there are only two types of monitors you should look at. Likewise, there are only two display-adapter cards you should consider for a new system or upgrade:

◆ Monochrome

◆ VGA

The monochrome category here includes all MDA, Hercules, and clone monographics cards. They all require a *TTL* (Transistor-Transistor Logic) monitor. You can usually choose between amber and green for the monitor's color, though white is available at a higher price. Amber appears to be the most popular, with green being the traditional color of IBM brand computer screens.

VGA and SuperVGA adapter cards require an *analog* monitor. This is quite different from the digital RGB monitors used by the CGA and EGA graphics adapters. When you have a VGA card, you need a VGA monitor. But note that not all VGA monitors are in color.

There are color VGA monitors and paper-white VGA monitors. The paper-white monitors aren't really "monochrome," but display the VGA colors in shades of gray—up to 64 of them. (It's really quite impressive.)

Monitor Types

There are several terms used to describe the various video displays you can hook up to a PC. Though your choice of a monitor is narrowed by which display adapter you've selected, you should be familiar with these different terms and the types of monitors they describe. Four of the most popular are listed below. (Some of these are listed for historical reference only. But you may still encounter them, which is why you should know what each one is used for.)

Analog   When comparing anything "analog" with "digital," it helps to think of a clock. The standard dial clock is analog, measuring time with constantly moving hands. A digital clock displays numbers, giving you an absolute time as measured by given increments.

All VGA cards should be paired with an analog monitor. Failing to do so will severely damage the monitor. So if you're shopping, make sure your monitor is VGA-compatible.

Multiscanning   A *multiscanning* monitor is capable of changing its frequency to match different display modes. Some multiscanning monitors may even switch from digital to analog input, allowing you to use the same monitor with a CGA, EGA, or VGA system. Note that a multiscanning monitor may also be called a *variable frequency* monitor or a *MultiSync* (which is actually a brand name).

RGB   *RGB* was the first type of color monitor to be popular with CGA systems. It's a digital monitor, so using one with an EGA would limit the EGA's performance, and using an RGB monitor with a VGA adapter would seriously damage the monitor.

RGB stands for *red*, *green*, and *blue*, which are the colors of three electron guns in the back of the monitor. Each gun produces a colored dot on the monitor's screen. You can compare this with the standard TV set, which uses only one electron gun, but fires it at differently colored dots on the TV screen. With an RGB monitor, you get crisply displayed colors.

TTL   The original IBM monochrome monitor was called a *TTL* monitor. TTL stands for Transistor-Transistor Logic. Of course, this now brings up the question of what does Transistor-Transistor Logic actually mean? But that's beside the point here. A TTL monitor is a black-and-white (or amber or green) monitor for use with a monochrome display. You can even hook one up to a VGA system to use VGA in its monochrome mode. Note that a TTL monitor may also be referred to as a direct-drive monitor.

Monitor Description

Monitors are what you look at when you use a PC (assuming you know how to type). There's nothing inside a monitor you need to concern yourself about. Like the power supply (which is also riveted shut), you should never open a monitor. Voltages in there could kill you if you're sloppy. Don't bother.

Outside the monitor, there's the monitor's casing and the display screen. The display is what's facing you when you use the computer, and it's there that the computer (through the video adapter card) displays information.

Monitors may also have anti-glare screens, sometimes in the form of a nylon mesh over the display, sometimes in the form of acid etching on the inside of the monitor's glass screen. This anti-glare screen cuts down on reflections the monitor may make. (Note that glare comes from lights in the room, not the monitor itself.) You can buy anti-glare screens separately and attach them to monitors that lack them, but they increase apparent contrast a lot. Best to see one of these add-on anti-glare screens in action before you buy.

Various controls on the monitor adjust it—they're similar to knobs hidden somewhere on your TV. The adjustment knobs for a monitor may be right up front, on either side, underneath, on the back, or hidden behind some secret panel.

Many state-of-the-art monitors allow the programming of combinations of control settings for special uses, like color mixes and contrast. They achieve this by showing you a digital display that provides the numerical value of your settings. You then save them to presets just like you set the clock on your VCR. —Sorry, I didn't mean to complicate things!

Technical Information

Monitors are often described using baffling technical terms. This section covers some of the more popular terms, explaining them and telling you why they're important. The most common of the technical terms are:

◆ Bandwidth

◆ Dot pitch

◆ Interlacing

- ◆ Resolution
- ◆ Scan rates
- ◆ Size

Bandwidth The speed at which information is sent from the computer to the monitor is known as the *bandwidth*. It's measured in megahertz (MHz), and the higher the value, the better the image.

Dot pitch The distance between each dot (pixel) on the screen is the *dot pitch*. It's measured in millimeters from the center of two neighboring dots. The closer the dots, and smaller the dot pitch value, the finer the resolution of the monitor. Don't accept a monitor with dot pitch of greater than 0.28 millimeters in diameter.

The cheapest VGA monitors have a dot pitch of 0.51mm. Believe you me, this pitch is very bad for your eyes, and not much of a perceived improvement over CGA after you've stared at it for a few hours! Monitors of this quality usually cost one-third to one-half less than monitors with a dot pitch size of 0.28mm and 0.25mm. An hour with Computer Shopper magazine (the mail-order buyer's bible) will convince you that this ratio works, at least in the mail-order channel.

Interlacing Information on a monitor is displayed by an electron gun scanning the phosphor on the inside front of your display. The gun scans from top to bottom, left to right, with each scan displaying a "frame." In essence, the gun works like a thin beam of spray paint coating the inside of your monitor.

To avoid a flickering image, some display adapters will force the monitor to create an *interlaced* image. Instead of the electron gun scanning from top to bottom in a continuous manner, it will skip every other line. On the second pass, it will hit the lines it missed the first time, creating the full image in two scans instead of one. If you're using resolutions of 800 × 600 or higher, you'll want a monitor that displays information at these resolutions in a *non-interlaced* fashion at these resolution levels.

Resolution A monitor's *resolution* describes the number of potential pixels the monitor is capable of displaying. The value is given in horizontal and vertical pixels. For example, a monitor with a resolution of 640 horizontal by 480 vertical pixels is capable of handling many SuperVGA adapters in the extended VGA graphics modes. Many people use SVGA

resolution levels of 800×600 and 1024×768. In truth, you will want at least a 17" monitor to display these resolution levels because everything gets so small, you can't see things clearly.

Scan Rate The *scan rate* is the speed at which the monitor's electron gun passes over the inside surface of the display. It's measured using both horizontal and vertical values given in kilohertz (KHz). Note that the scan rate is composed of these two values, and often referred to separately as both horizontal scan rate and vertical scan rate. (The values will be different.) The higher the scan rate numbers, the better. Make sure that any monitor you purchase has a vertical refresh rate of at least 70Hz.

Size Finally, a more common measure of a monitor is the *size* of its picture tube, measured diagonally in inches. Typical sizes for a monitor are from 13" to 21", though some huge monitors are available, as well as non-standard page-sized and so-called landscape monitors. If you go with an unusual size, make sure your software will support it. Some page-display monitors require a proprietary video card in order to make them work, so be careful if you select that monitor! There are also flat-screen monitors, which some users prefer because they present an undistorted image. (Though the monitor does look concave when compared to the common, curved-screen monitor.)

Upgrading Monitors and Display Adapters

There are only two instances when you'll be working with a display adapter or a monitor:

◆ When you first buy a PC

◆ To upgrade one or the other

Obviously, if you get the first one right, the second one won't be necessary. But there are times when you start out with a monochrome system (they're cheaper and show text better, and they are faster) and then have the pressing need for color. In that instance, you can upgrade. And remember that you can upgrade one or the other; only a monitor or only a display adapter. Just keep them both compatible and you'll be fine.

The hardware side of upgrading is covered here in six sections:

- ◆ Strategy
- ◆ Buying a Monitor and Display Adapter
- ◆ Upgrade Overview
- ◆ Upgrading a Video Adapter
- ◆ Upgrading a Monitor

Strategy

There are three steps you can take to equipping a PC with a new or better video system:

- ◆ Find out what your software requires
- ◆ Pick a graphics adapter and monitor
- ◆ Buy it

Your software will dictate the needs of your hardware. If you're into graphics, your software requires color. Especially if you're into high-powered graphics applications: anything that runs under Microsoft Windows, graphic design, CAD, desktop publishing, and so on (games). If you're only doing data entry, or if the system is delegated to office word processing, then a monochrome system is ideal (and will save money). However, if you have any second thoughts, or consider playing games with the computer, then buy color.

For color, go with VGA, preferably SuperVGA. After you determine your software needs, go graphics-adapter hunting. Since the adapter determines what monitor you need, look for the adapter first. Once that's done, match the adapter with a monitor. Aside from the technical information about a monitor, sit down and *look* at it. If you and your eyeballs can live with it, you move on to the final step: Buy it.

You may be hesitant about buying a monitor/graphic card combination because of new standards. But don't let that hold you back. Graphics standards (if there ever are any new ones), take two or three years to catch on. And VGA takes graphics about as far as the personal computer will need go for some years to come.

If price is holding you back, remember that you can upgrade just the monitor or just the display adapter. You don't have to do everything at once. For example, buy the VGA card first and use it with your EGA monitor. Later on, when you can afford it, buy a decent analog color monitor.

Buying a Display Adapter and Monitor

Shopping tips for buying a monitor and display adapter will vary from store to store, depending on what type of monitor and display you're looking for.

Display Adapter

Generally speaking, for a color-display adapter, look for the following items.

Resolution How high is the resolution? Is it VGA or SuperVGA?

Colors How many colors does the adapter offer? VGA supports a full 262,144—but only 256 can be displayed on the screen at once.

Compatibility Are all IBM's VGA resolutions and colors supported? Does the VGA card offer VESA compatibility? Will they update your card's ROM or video memory if future incompatibilities are discovered?

Price There is a whole range of prices for VGA cards, which makes you wonder why some are more expensive. The reasons aren't obvious, but consider how much video RAM the card has, how many compatible modes it shares, and if it comes with any software drivers to make it work with major applications.

Monitor

For a monitor, consider the following items when shopping:

Compatibility Here the issue isn't compatibility with IBM, it's compatibility with the adapter card you've chosen. Is the bandwidth properly supported? Are the horizontal and vertical scan rates compatible? And is it an analog, multiscanning monitor? Does it conform to the latest safety standards for the protection of your vision and exposure to harmful emissions?

Dot Pitch The dot pitch tells you the crispness of the image, coupled with the monitor's potential resolution. This figure should be used for comparison purposes, however. It's hard to see a dot pitch with the naked eye (unless the differences are very dramatic).

Look Remember to sit down and look into the monitor. Some stores will have several monitors side by side—all running the same demo software. That's fine; pretty pictures look stunning on a PC in the late 20th century. That comparison is OK if you work exclusively with pretty pictures. But boot up some "real" software and look at the text and colors.

Price In addition to shopping price, consider a monitor's warranty. Some monitors have typical TV picture tube warranties of two years, but a few are up to five.

Upgrade Overview

Upgrading to a new video standard on your PC is a fairly basic operation. Adding the monitor is easy, though they are bulky. Adding the display adapter is the same as replacing an expansion card, which was dealt with in Chapter 10. So this section outlines the upgrading steps in a very basic manner.

Install the Graphics-Adapter Card

You may be replacing an older card, or just adding a new card to a PC. Graphics-adapter cards are installed like other expansion cards, and that was detailed in Chapter 10.

Positioning of the graphics adapter card isn't important, though traditionally they go to the left of the system unit. If you have an 8-bit card, try to use an 8-bit slot on an AT-level system. Some 16-bit VGA cards can fit into an 8-bit PC/XT-level system, but make sure the card's skirt doesn't interfere with any motherboard circuitry...like your SIMMs.

Check for DIP switches on the card, and set them as necessary for your system.

Set DIP Switches and Run SETUP

Older PC/XTs have DIP switches that must be changed when you switch from a color monitor to monochrome or vice-versa. For EGA and VGA upgrades, you must tell a PC/XT that it has no video display installed. (Otherwise some of the systems won't boot.)

For AT-level systems, you may have to change your PC's battery-backed-up RAM via the SETUP program. Some computers are "auto-sensing" for the type of display installed. Check your PC's SETUP program anyway, just to be sure.

Install the Monitor

Monitors really need no installation. Simply plug it into the back of your PC (if it has a special adapter) or into a power strip. A second cable from the monitor hooks it up to the display adapter card.

Connect the Two

Plug the monitor into the display adapter card. The connector is a D-shell connector and can go on only one way. Tighten the thumb-twists or use a small screwdriver to anchor the cable in position. The cable may not be long enough for some situations. If that happens, note that you can purchase monitor extension cables. Be sure to specify CGA, EGA, VGA, or monochrome when ordering an extension.

Upgrading a Video Adapter

Whether you're moving up to a VGA system from monochrome, going the other way (which does happen), or adding video to a new PC, it's valuable to know how to upgrade a video adapter. The steps are similar to upgrading an expansion card, with a few additional details to double check.

HOW TO INSTALL A VIDEO ADAPTER

Procedure: Removing/installing a video adapter

Tools Needed: Medium minus screwdriver, tiny minus screwdriver

Steps:

1. Power down the PC and remove its lid. If you're adding a card to a new system (but not removing one first), skip to step 6.

2. Locate the old video adapter. The adapter will be the one connected to your monitor. If not, it may have MDA, Hercules, CGA, EGA, or VGA stenciled on it somewhere. Note that since VGA adapters have that extra-features edge connector on top they're easy to spot.

3. Remove the monitor cable. Unscrew the monitor cable from the back of the card. You may need a tiny minus screwdriver to do this, or the cable may have thumb tighteners on it. If a printer cable is attached, remove it.

4. Unscrew the adapter's mounting bracket from the PC's case. It's usually a small, minus screw, though some PCs may use plus screws. Remember to save the screw.

5. Lift the card up and out. Once the card is free, put it into a static-free bag, preferably the original one it came in or use the new card's bag.

6. Set switches on the new card. Before putting the video adapter into the PC, make sure it's properly configured. Set any DIP switches or jumpers, or add RAM if possible. Remember to touch your PCs case before touching the card to eliminate static charges that could be harmful to circuitry.

7. Slide the card into the PC. If you're adding a new card (as opposed to replacing one), you'll need to remove the expansion slot's mounting bracket. For a replacement card, install it into the same slot you removed the old card from—unless the old slot was 8-bit and the new card is 16-bit. In that case, put the card into a 16-bit slot.

8. Tighten the mounting bracket screw.

9. Check all your connections.

10. Attach the monitor cable.

11. Set any DIP switches. If you have a PC/XT-level system, set the DIP switches on the motherboard to reflect the new video configuration. Remember that EGA or VGA displays in a PC/XT are often referred to as "no video" on the DIP switch settings. For AT systems, you'll need to run your SETUP program *if* there's an error on power-up.

12. Close up. At this point, put the lid back on your PC and power it up—but only if you're done.

If you still need to add a monitor, read the following section. Otherwise, power up the PC and test your new video display.

Upgrading a Monitor

Adding a monitor to your system is as easy as adding a printer; you don't need to take the PC apart to do so. One precaution, though, is to be sure the monitor and display-adapter card match. Other than that, there's nothing to it.

HOW TO ADD A MONITOR

Procedure: Adding a monitor

Tools Needed: None; tiny minus screwdriver

Steps:

1. Power down the PC. You should never plug/unplug anything on a computer with its power running. More than a few people have

ruined keyboards by plugging them into a "hot" keyboard socket. Though you can plug a monitor into an active system, it's best to be safe and power down first.

2. Remove the old monitor. Unhook the monitor's cables from the back of the PC (where they attach to the display adapter card). Lift the monitor up and put it away somewhere, preferably back in its original packing.

3. Set down the new monitor. Put the monitor on top or by the side of your PC.

4. Attach the monitor's cable to the expansion card.

5. Plug the monitor in.

6. Power up the PC.

You may get an POST error if the monitor and display adapter types don't match what your computer already knows about. This can happen if you don't set a DIP switch properly on a PC/XT systems. For AT systems, run your SETUP program to remedy the situation.

If you don't see anything, then make sure the monitor is plugged in and turned on. (Most monitors have their own power switches.) Check to make sure the brightness isn't all the way down, which can create the illusion of a malfunctioning monitor. And recheck all of your connections.

Tell Your PC about Your New Hardware

Some PC/XT and AT-level systems have a DIP switch or SETUP option that specifically states "dual monitors." If you have both color and monochrome systems, flip the switches or run SETUP to tell the PC about it.

● Software Considerations

All hardware upgrades require some software attention, and upgrading your video is no exception. A few years ago that wasn't the case. But with inexpensive, high-quality graphics available to everyone, the hassle of

setting up software to work with the right video display is becoming a fact of life.

There are two areas where software comes into play when upgrading your PC's video. They are:

◆ Companion diskettes

◆ Changing your software

Companion Diskettes

In the old days, you were lucky if you got an instruction booklet with your CGA card. Today, you're lucky if you get only one diskette full of READ.ME files, last-minute documentation, software drivers, and demonstration programs. Graphics have come a long way.

Companion diskettes that come with most graphics adapters contain four or more types of programs, including:

◆ Diagnostics

◆ Utilities

◆ Driver software

◆ Sample programs and demos

The *diagnostics* and *utilities* are good to know about. You should run the diagnostics right after installing the card and monitor. The utilities will come in handy when adjusting the monitor, to automatically dim the monitor after periods of inactivity, or to get those extra graphics modes under DOS.

Driver software is provided to ensure the new video standard works with some popular programs. For example, to get a 132 column by 43 row spreadsheet in 1-2-3, you can run a driver program that came with your VGA card. In the world of Windows, drivers are created for the hardware instead of the software. When you install a new graphics card, you may have to install a new video driver using Windows' Setup utility. One video driver works with all Windows applications.

Finally, the *sample* programs and demos will help show off your new graphics abilities. Some adapters may even come with sample program files to assist programmers in implementing new graphics modes.

Changing Your Software

If your applications are DOS-based, the second half of the software side is updating the software already on your system. Especially for the move up from monochrome to color, you may find yourself re-installing some packages, executing setup programs to set the colors and graphics modes, or re-configuring applications.

In the monochrome world, you have no choices for text appearance. Suddenly, when you toss in 16 foreground and 8 background colors, you'll feel compelled to spend hours selecting the proper combinations for your screen. But don't stop there—white-on-black text on a color monitor is lame. Use some color: try bright white on deep blue, bright yellow on red, purple on brown. Be creative!

Maximizing the Printer

Bizillions of printers are available for the PC family of computers. Most books on upgrading your PC will skip the printers, because there are just too many of them and there aren't any official standards. Though IBM makes printers, there's nothing special about them, nor do their printers have any features you can't find in a Panasonic, Hewlett-Packard, Epson, or Canon model. So printer country is wide open.

After the initial hassle of getting your printer to work with your software, the printer just does its job. Other than occasionally changing a ribbon or toner cartridge, a printer will go unnoticed. So what's there to discuss?

The first part of this chapter is a general discussion of printers, covering different types of printers and how they work. The second part concentrates on the interaction between your PC and the printer. This is one of those unique subjects that no other book or manual will tackle. (If you've ever been there, you know: Your software manual says "refer to the printer manual" and the printer manual says "refer to your software manual.") Finally, there are some hardware and software things you can do to the printer that will really improve its performance. Learning these tricks is truly the only way to upgrade a printer without buying a new one.

● About Printers

Next to a monitor, a printer is the most common computer peripheral. Today, nearly every computer sold goes home with a companion printer. But not much thought is put into the printer purchase—especially with regards to software compatibility. A theme running throughout this chapter will be the lack of printer standards and the numerous things you can do to deal with that.

In the old days, no one worried about printer compatibilities. Just affording a printer was the tough part. Until 1983, printers sold for about $800 each—and those were the cheap ones. Only after the Macintosh came along did PC owners concern themselves with print quality, "looking good on paper." Since that time, PC printers have gotten fancier and more capable, and PC software has become more adept at handling printers.

There are four sections here that discuss general information about PC printers:

◆ Printer Description

◆ Printer Types

◆ How Printers Are Judged

◆ Printer Paper

Some of this information may be familiar to you. Most of it is of importance only if you're shopping for a printer for the first time. All of it applies to nearly every type of printer available for the PC.

Printer Description

Printers come in different sizes and shapes. There is no generic printer, though all dot-matrix printers have a similar boxy shape, and all laser printers look like copy machines that never grew a lid. But with every printer, no matter who makes it, what it looks like, or what type of printer it is, you'll find some or all of the following:

◆ Cables

◆ Front Panel Switches

◆ DIP Switches

◆ A Ribbon or Cartridge

◆ The Printer Manual

You should be able to locate all these items on any printer you use or buy. Further descriptions are provided below.

Cables

Every printer will have at least two cables: a power cable and a printer cable. The *power cable* goes from the printer to the wall socket or power protection strip. The *printer cable* connects the printer to the computer. It's the line through which the PC and printer communicate. This cable can be plugged into either a parallel port or a serial port. That subject is covered later in this chapter, under the section heading *The Printer Port*.

Front Panel Switches

Nearly every printer has a set of switches or buttons on its front panel. The four most common buttons are:

◆ On-line

◆ Line Feed

◆ Form Feed

◆ Power

Some printers may have a whole slew of buttons, knobs, and dials. Some laser printers even have small digital displays and you can watch TV on them if you're handy with electrical parts (just kidding).

The switches on the front panel give you limited control over the printer. The on-line button is used to make the printer available for printing. When the printer is off-line, it won't print. (The button may also be called Select/Deselect.)

Maximizing the Printer

When the printer is off-line, the *Line Feed* and *Form Feed* buttons can be used to adjust the paper in the printer. Line Feed advances a sheet of paper one line at a time through the printer; Form Feed will eject an entire page.

 The buttons can be used for other purposes as well. Sometimes, pressing two or more in combination will change the selected font or print a text pattern. But choosing fonts via a printer's front panel resembles the old days of computing. Today, software does all the work for you.

DIP Switches

In addition to any front panel switches, nearly every type of printer has a row of DIP switches somewhere. For dot-matrix printers, the DIP switches may be internal or on the back of the case. Laser printers usually have their DIP switches on the back of the case, near the printer cable connection.

DIP switches on a printer are used to set the following:

◆ The printer's compatibility mode

◆ A parallel (printer) or serial interface

◆ Communications speeds for a serial interface

◆ Line feeds

◆ Character spacing and style

◆ Page length

Of these items, compatibility, the serial interface, and line feeds are the most important.

A printer's *serial interface*, unlike a parallel (standard printer) interface, must be set to communicate with the PC at a specific speed and format. You configure a printer for use with a serial port by setting the printer's DIP switches.

And finally, there's the question of *line feeds*. In the PC world, a carriage return character is followed by a line feed to create a new line on a page.

The carriage return moves the print head to the left side of the page and the line feed advances the paper through the printer.

Some older computers would send only a carriage return character to the printer. The printed result would then be all on one line of the page; since no line feeds were sent, the paper never advanced. To fix that, the line-feed DIP switch was set, forcing the printer to advance the paper each time it received a carriage return from the computer.

If you set the line feed DIP switch wrong on newer printers, though, your documents will be double-spaced. To fix this problem, locate the "Add LF after CR" or similar DIP switch using your printer's manual and turn it off.

A Ribbon or Cartridge

Printers need ink to make an image on paper. The ink is usually stored in the printer in the form of a *cartridge*.

Most cartridges contain ribbons, which allows you to easily replace a printer's ribbon without getting your fingers inky (that's what the manual says, at least).

Laser printer cartridges contain the toner powder that the laser printer fuses to the paper to create an image. They last longer than standard printer ribbons, but they're more expensive.

Finally, some printers draw ink from reservoirs and spray it directly onto the page. These "ink jet" printers aren't as messy as they sound, and they're the quietest of all computer printers.

The Printer Manual

Be aware of your printer manual. Printer manuals are usually the worst of all the computer manuals, but the most invaluable when you need them. You should always keep your printer manual near your printer.

Printer manuals contain a lot of good stuff. For example, you'll find settings for the printer's DIP switches. And finally, the manual lists information on compatibility, cleaning, and where to send the printer if it needs to be repaired. Unlike other components of your PC, printers are not modular. You should get them professionally serviced if they break.

Printer Types

All printers do the same job, but there are different types of printers that give you different degrees of quality, performance, and price. The two major categories of PC printers are

◆ Dot-Matrix Printers

◆ Laser Printers

There are other categories of printers as well. They're discussed in the section below entitled *Specialty*, but for the most part, the two basic PC printers are the dot-matrix or laser printer.

Dot-Matrix Printers

Dot-matrix printers are the traditional type of computer printer (see Figure 13.1), and they've come a long way from their primitive ancestors of a decade ago.

A dot-matrix printer works by firing a series of metal pins, arranged vertically in a column. These pins press down the printer's ribbon, which then forms a dot on the paper. As the *print head* (the device that contains the

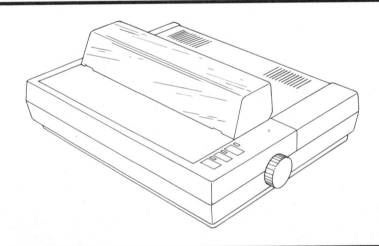

FIGURE 13.1: A dot-matrix printer

pins) moves back and forth across the page, the pins create a pattern—a matrix of dots—in which characters are formed.

Those dots are the tell-tale sign of a computer print out. For years, you could always spot material printed on a dot-matrix printer. The quality wasn't the best. But around 1985 or so, manufacturers upped the number of pins in the print head from 9 to 24. Essentially, they gave you two rows of smaller pins (12 to a row) verses one row of fatter pins. The results were impressive.

A 24-pin dot-matrix printer is capable of producing what the industry calls *NLQ*, or Near Letter Quality text. Letter quality text is of the caliber of characters produced by a typewriter. So in only a handful of years, computer correspondence evolved to the state where it looked more like type-written text than "computer text."

Today, dot-matrix printers are still the most popular type of computer printer. Some of the 9-pin printers can even fake near letter quality by printing text with several passes of the print head. But that's slow when compared to a 24-pin printer.

The prices of dot-matrix printers vary, depending on the print quality, speed, and the printer's carriage width (discussed later in this chapter). But those varying prices and qualities make dot-matrix printers ideal for all computing situations, from home and educational to business uses.

Laser Printers

The *laser printer* is the most versatile printer you can hook up to a PC (see Figure 13.2). It's also the most expensive. Since 1989, though, the price of laser printers has dipped below the $1,000 (street price) mark, making them an affordable option for most small businesses—and even some homes.

Laser printers work similarly to copy machines, though, instead of light reflected off a piece of paper, the image is created by a laser beam (some so-called laser printers use a process that involves LEDs instead of a laser beam). Sophisticated electronics control the beam, positioning it in very tiny increments. The beam paints an image on a drum inside the laser printer. A magnetic charge is created where the beam touches the drum.

That drum then rolls under a toner cartridge, collecting toner on the part of the drum that's magnetically charged. So when the drum then comes

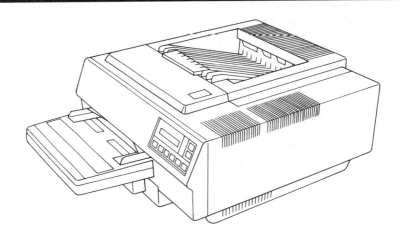

FIGURE 13.2: A laser printer

in contact with the paper, the toner image is transferred to the paper. Heat fuses the toner to the paper.

It's a complex process, but the results are spectacular. While laser printers are more expensive than dot-matrix printers, they're faster. The output is considered near-typeset quality. And though it isn't as nice as the typesetting equipment used to produce this book, a laser printer does give you decent, well-formed text—plus graphics.

Laser printers are also like computers in a way. Some come with sophisticated electronics, their own microprocessor, and often several megabytes of RAM. These smarts are used to save processing time on the PC; the computer hands the printer a set of instructions and information, and then the printer chews on it a while and produces a result. The better the printer's processing power and the more RAM it has, the faster your results.

The advantages of a laser printer over a dot-matrix or other type of PC printer are great. It's the ideal solution for top-quality text, even allowing you to print on your business letterhead. With the laser printer you also get graphics. While dot-matrix printers will create graphics, the process is slow and noisy when compared to the cool efficiency and high quality of a laser printer. Incidentally, this coupling of text and graphics makes the laser printer the ideal output device for desktop publishing. Any other type of printer is second rate.

A real standard has emerged for Laser Printers, called HP LaserJet Series II emulation. Make sure your printer will emulate HPLJ II. If you're going to stick with software created in the 80's, try to buy a laser printer that emulates the IBM Graphics printer as well. If your printer emulates both of these machines, you should be covered!

Specialty Printers

Aside from dot-matrix and laser printers, which have a lot of variety in price and performance between them, there are other types of printers you can hook up to your PC. Some of these were introduced as interim solutions; offering better quality than dot-matrix printers or being cheaper than laser printers for a time. Others offered specialty features for certain edges of PC computing.

Four additional types of PC printers are:

◆ Color and Ink Printers

◆ Plotters

◆ Thermal Printers

◆ Daisy-Wheel/Impact Printers

You can still find these printers around. But if you don't need their special features, you'll probably find a better dot-matrix or laser printer for a comparable price.

Color and Ink Printers While *color laser printers* exist, they're usually so high priced that only top-line graphics arts houses can afford them. The alternative is the ink printer.

Ink printers work like dot-matrix printers. However, they lack a ribbon and print head. Instead, the image is formed on the paper by a series of nozzles. The nozzles shoot, or more accurately, lob a blob of ink on the paper. It's not as messy as it sounds, and these printers are whisper quiet—the quietest of the lot.

The majority of ink printers contain reservoirs for a number of differently colored inks. Those colors combine on the paper to produce color printouts from your PC. On color dot matrix and ink jet printers, this is the only way to print color graphics.

For the price, ink printers and dot-matrix printers generally offer the same features. But if you need to print in color, or prefer the quiet approach to using a printer, they can't be beat.

Plotters *Plotters* are specialty types of printers, used primarily in the design fields. Instead of operating like a traditional computer printer, which forms an image composed of dots, the plotter uses a pen to draw an image.

The pen moves across a flat surface. Or sometimes, paper is held snug between two rollers that position it under the pen (which moves left and right). The pen can then draw smooth lines to create drafts of architectural plans or circuitry drawings that look hand-made—but perfect.

The advantage of a plotter for an architect is phenomenal. Using a CAD program, blueprints can be updated and re-drawn in a matter of minutes. But outside of that and other specialty fields, a plotter is too high priced for most people. Few word processors support plotters, and they aren't set up to deal with multiple letter-sized pages as dot-matrix, ink, and laser printers are.

Thermal Printers Thanks to their light weight and low battery requirements, you'll often find portable thermal printers for use with laptops. A thermal printer works along the same principle as a dot-matrix printer. However, instead of using a ribbon and ink, the pins in the printer's head are heated. A special waxy paper used with the printer is affected by the heat and turns black at the point of contact. That's how the image is created.

Thermal printers are good for getting quick hard copy in some situations. They're quiet, so you could use them in a library or courtroom without disturbing anyone. But the image doesn't last. If the waxy paper is exposed to sunlight, it will turn black. And, even if the image does last, waxy paper doesn't impress anyone.

A common example of a thermal printer is your fax machine. Faxes use thermal printing and waxy paper to produce their image. So while they are appropriate in some instances, thermal printers will have their place only as temporary or secondary printers.

Daisy-Wheel/Impact Printers Long before laser printers became available, popular, and affordable, the *daisy-wheel* or *impact* printer was the standard for business correspondence.

An impact printer is basically a keyboard-less typewriter. It works on the same principle: a device with fully formed characters would impact with the ribbon and paper to create a character on the paper. The term "daisy-wheel" comes from the shape of the device containing the characters: some were shaped like flowers with the characters on the petals. The daisy-wheel would then spin 'round until the desired character was on top. A hammer then impacted with the character, ribbon, and paper to create the image.

Daisy-wheel printers weren't the most elegant things. Most were very expensive and quite large. And they were loud. Very loud. A daisy-wheel printer running at top speed (which was only about 40 characters per second, extremely slow by today's standards) sounded like a string of firecrackers in a Chinese New Year parade. And thanks to all those moving parts, they broke more often than anything else.

Eventually, dot-matrix printers fell in price to the point where they were competitive with daisy-wheel printers. Today, the daisy-wheel printer is a relic. It offers no support for graphics, it's slow, awkward to use, and loud. Laser and dot-matrix printers are just a much better deal.

How Printers Are Judged

The previous section contains information about the different types of PC printers. But specifically speaking, each printer by itself is judged by certain qualities, including:

- ◆ Type Quality
- ◆ Speed
- ◆ Fonts
- ◆ Miscellaneous Items

You use these characteristics to compare individual printers.

Type Quality

Type quality refers to how good the characters look on paper. But it's not judged by subjective values. Instead, the quality of type depends on how the printer produced the image.

For example, dot-matrix printers come in both 9- and 24-pin configurations. A 24-pin dot-matrix printer is capable of producing some very well-formed characters. The type quality is said to be *near letter quality* (NLQ), or roughly equivalent to what you'll get with a typewriter.

 Some 9-pin dot-matrix printers are also tagged as NLQ. However, the way they achieve it is to print the same line three times. Each time, the paper is advanced just a tad through the printer, which creates the illusion of NLQ. But keep in mind that a 9-pin printer achieves its NLQ look by cheating (and that NLQ will take longer on a 9-pin than on a 24-pin printer).

With laser printers, type quality is measured by the *dots-per-inch* (DPI) factor. The typical laser printer can slap down 300 dots on one inch of paper. (That's 300 × 300 dots per square inch.) This absolutely blows away dot-matrix printers as far as resolution is concerned.

There are option boards you can add to many laser printers to boost the resolution. Improvements from 600 to 1200 DPI are possible—but at a price. And there are some high-end laser printers that can go up to 1200 or 2400 DPI. These are covered in the last part of this chapter.

Speed

Another judge of a printer is its speed. The old daisy-wheel were judged by the number of characters per second (CPS) they could produce. Forty CPS was considered a top speed daisy-wheel printer. But it still took a few minutes to print one page of text. (And it sounded as if a small guerrilla army were staging a coup inside your printer.)

Dot-matrix printers are also judged by the number of characters per second they can print. A good printer may chug along at 80 CPS. Faster printers can manage 160 or even 240 CPS, which is fairly fast. But the quality drops at those high speeds.

Laser printers are the fastest of them all. Their printing speed is measured in pages per minute (PPM). The first laser printers could print four pages per minute. Today's models can manage up to 16. But real life performance will only rarely produce the same results.

Why? Because both of those values, CPS and PPM, are heavily optimized. Usually they're produced in a lab under ideal conditions. For example, to get a high CPS value, dot-matrix printer manufacturers will print only one long line of text. The amount of time taken for line feeds and form feeds is never factored in. So your speed will be less.

For laser printers, the high eight PPM figures are for printing the same page a number of times. When each page differs—and especially in high graphic or multiple font situations—printing will be slower. Use the CPS and PPM figures for comparison shopping only.

Fonts

The term *fonts* comes from typesetting and design. It was totally alien to computers until the Macintosh was introduced and threw in the conceptual font cud for computer users to chew on. Since then, fonts have become a part of word processing, desktop publishing, and just about any application that makes use of the printer. So printers are judged by the fonts they're capable of producing.

A font is a character set, a specific style of characters. For example, this book is typeset in the Stone Serif font. The headings in the book are in the Kabel Ultra font. There are dozens of popular styles of fonts, each giving a different look and appearance to the text. (And there are many books available to help you choose and use fonts for your desktop publishing and word processing efforts.)

Font Attributes Fonts have certain attributes used to describe how the font looks. The two most common font attributes are:

◆ Style

◆ Size

Style refers to the type style of the font: bold, italic, underline, outline, and so on. In traditional typesetting terms, a bold or italic style was a different font. You had Times Roman and Times Roman Bold and Times Roman Italic—three different fonts. But with computers, bold and italic are styles of one font. (Underline, outline and other special effects aren't traditionally parts of a font.)

The size of a font is measured using the typesetting term *points*. There are 72 points to an inch. A 72-point font has one-inch tall letters. More realistic sizes are 10, 12, and 14 points. Newspapers usually use 10-point fonts. Most correspondence is done in 12- or 14-point sizes.

Be careful not to confuse point size with *pitch*. Typewriters use pitch to refer to the number of characters you can fit on a line. Ten-pitch characters are called "Pica," and you can fit 80 of them on a line (ten to the inch). Twelve-pitch characters are called "Elite," and you can fit 96 of them on a line (12 to the inch).

Ironically, 10 pitch characters are usually 12 points high and 12 pitch characters are 10 points high. Don't let it confuse you; use points when referring to fonts.

Font Technology To produce fonts on a printer, a number of techniques are used. First, dot-matrix printers usually have a limited built-in font set if they have one at all. If they do, then you may find an italic, condensed, or expanded font available. But these aren't the traditional typesetting fonts and can be used by the printer only in a limited capacity.

With a PC, only a laser printer will give you any decent font output. Fonts in a laser printer can either be built into the printer (in the printer's ROM), added to the printer via an expansion slot or font cartridge, or "downloaded" to the printer via software.

Built-in fonts in a printer are best. They're either encoded into the laser printer's ROM or added via a font cartridge. Since the fonts are on chips and already a part of the printer's circuitry, producing them is fast and quick, and they don't gobble up the printer's processing time or RAM.

Downloadable fonts are fonts supplied to the printer via software you load into the PC or that is part of your word processor or some other application. When it comes time to print, the information necessary to produce the fonts is sent to the printer. The printer calculates the look of each font and creates its image as required on the page.

Downloadable fonts chew up either your PC's processing time or the printer's (depending on how smart the printer is). They definitely use up printer RAM, which slows down printing. And managing the fonts on a PC is a real chore. But they're available and sometimes the only way you can get different fonts with some printers.

PostScript and Outline Fonts   Two special types of fonts worth looking into are *PostScript* and *Outline* fonts. (Outline differs from the outline type style.) These fonts are also referred to as "scaleable." You can change the size of the font to just about any height or width and the characters look as good as the printer is capable of printing them.

Scaleable fonts will always give you the best printed results. This contrasts with bitmap fonts, which are created at specific point sizes and can print (or print well) only at those sizes. When you select a different size for the font, it either won't print or will take on a jagged, saw-tooth look.

Technically speaking, a scaleable font is produced by defining each character using vectors. The vectors specify direction and magnitude, creating the curves and lines that compose each character. Using complex mathematics (done by the printer, fortunately), the font can be scaled to any size with little loss in appearance.

The bitmap fonts are created using a pattern of dots. Those dots create a good looking font—but only at their original size. If you try to enlarge the font, you still get the basic dot-look, which will exaggerate itself as it gets larger.

The whole issue of fonts, points, and styles can easily be ironed out by purchasing a good desktop publishing book. But for your printer, note which ones are available and whether or not your word processor can access them. The latter is really important: Your printer can be bustling with fonts, but if your software doesn't know about them, they're of little use.

Miscellaneous Items

There are other standards you can use to compare and judge printers.
They're not as crucial as type quality, speed, and fonts, but still worth considering. Three of them are:

◆ Hardware Compatibility

◆ Carriage Width

◆ Feeding Mechanism

Hardware Compatibility As was mentioned earlier, PCs lack a printer-
hardware standard. IBM's printers are just lumped in there with the
bunch as far as the masses are concerned. But two issues of hardware-
compatibility do surface:

◆ Hewlett-Packard compatibility

◆ PostScript compatibility

Hewlett-Packard pioneered the PC laser printer with the HP LaserJet
(which is still the coolest name for any piece of computer hardware). The
LaserJet, and its descendants, use a printer control language called PCL.
It's a good sign if your printer understands PCL, or provides any compatibility with the LaserJet.

Of course, if LaserJet compatibility concerns you, you should always buy a
LaserJet. However, there are software LaserJet emulators you can purchase,
one of which is discussed later in this chapter.

PostScript is a page description language from Adobe Systems, Inc. Post-
Script fonts and graphics are a standard in the PC industry. So if your laser
printer supports them, you have access to a wealth of fonts and graphic
programs that support PostScript.

But PostScript is expensive. Since only Adobe makes it, you pay extra for
it. Apple's LaserWriter printers all incorporate PostScript and can use Post-
Script's scaleable fonts. But that feature adds $2,000 to the price of Apple's
PostScript-compatible printers. (And you can hook them up to a PC if you
so desire.)

Remember that the final word in compatibility comes from your software.
Even if your printer supports PCL or PostScript, it will be of use to you
only if your software can take advantage of it.

Carriage Width A moot point with laser printers, *carriage width* comes into play only with dot-matrix printers. The carriage width will tell you the largest size of paper you can run through the printer.

Standard dot-matrix printers have a letter-sized carriage width. They can accept paper only in standard 8½×11" format. (Though some printers will let you insert the long side first.) A wider format allows for 14" long paper to be inserted. This paper is ideal for printing wide spreadsheets.

With a laser printer, paper is usually of either legal or letter size. However, using software, the laser printer can print sideways on the page. This orientation is referred to as *landscape*. The standard orientation (up and down) is called *portrait*. If you think of a painting of a landscape or a picture portrait of someone famous, it helps to keep the two straight in your head.

Feeding Mechanism Paper for a laser printer is supplied either manually, one sheet at a time, or automatically through a paper tray. The paper tray holds letter or legal sized paper and feeds it to the printer one sheet at a time—just like a copy machine.

Dot-matrix printers can have three types of paper feed mechanisms. Sometimes these are built into the printer. But often they're options. If so, remember to buy one when you buy the printer—or buy one now if that's the part you've been missing.

The three types of feeding mechanisms for a dot-matrix printer are:

◆ Platen or "friction feed"

◆ Pin feed

◆ Tractor feed

Platen, or *friction feed*, works the same as a typewriter. You insert the paper into the printer, in between two platens (rubber cylinders), roll the knob forward, and position the paper just under the top of the print head. This method is best for printing one sheet at a time or envelopes.

Both *pin* and *tractor* feed mechanisms are used to feed long, continuous sheets of paper into a printer. This is the paper that comes with rows of detachable holes on the side. The holes match up with pins in the printer that are used to move and guide the paper through the printer.

A pin feed mechanism sits behind the printer's platen. It pulls the paper up and then pushes it through the printer. A tractor feed mechanism sits on top of the printer; it pulls the paper through the printer and around the platen.

 A printer's design will include either a pin or tractor feed mechanism, so you won't have a choice between them on a single machine. (You will have a choice, of course, in the type of printer you buy—pin, tractor feed, or the platen.) However, between the two, tractor feed works the best. Pin feeds sometimes jam because they push the paper into the printer.

Printer Paper

Printers need paper. People who buy a printer and leave the store without any paper suddenly figure this out. And contrary to the myth of the paper-less office, you need a lot of paper for a computer printer.

In the early days, printer paper lacked variety. You had paper rolls (which make for very unimpressive business correspondence) and the traditional green-bar paper, which is almost acceptable if every other inch of paper wasn't colored green. True, for program listings, it was fine. But for today's applications, it doesn't cut it.

Dot Matrix

For dot-matrix and other standard printers, you can use either single sheets of paper, such as your letterhead, single envelopes, or fanfold paper.

Fanfold paper is all connected, with every other page folded over to create a single stack. The paper also has the famous holes on each side, which give the tractor and pin feed mechanisms something by which to grab and pull the paper. (I call the holes "tractor food.") The holes can be detached, as can each sheet from each other, to give you individual sheets when you're done printing.

Fanfold paper is available in a number of sizes, weights, and options. There's wide fanfold for wide-carriage printers, but most of it is narrow, the size of a standard sheet of paper. Fanfold paper also comes in parts or forms, where one or more sheets are separated by carbon paper (for making duplicates). And you can still pick up the greenbar paper, as well as other color varieties and specialty papers.

The most common fanfold paper for dot-matrix and other printers is 20 lb. bond paper with "laser perfs." This paper is thick, as opposed to the cheaper stock. Each sheet is separated by a tiny row of dots (the laser perfs). When you separate a page, you don't get the frayed look produced with inexpensive printer papers. Laser perf paper is usually the preferred paper for business and professional documents.

Laser Printers

Laser printers and impact printers with single sheet-feed capability take just about any type of paper, though some thick papers (mostly art stock) won't fit. You just put the paper into the printer tray and print. Nothing could be easier.

As far as stocking up on laser printer paper, most people use standard copy machine paper. It comes in different weights and stocks, and you can get colored, bond, and cotton paper for printing special items. Printing on your letterhead can be as easy as putting a sheet in the printer.

Specialty printer stock is available for laser printers. One of the best for reproducing art is commonly called "laser paper." It's a special stock that almost resembles photographic paper. One side is smooth and holds an image a lot better than plain paper. The other side has blue markings, which tell you to print on the first side of the paper.

Many graphics arts houses and magazines that use laser printers will print on laser paper when the typesetting machine is busy, or for quick mock-ups. It's more expensive than plain copier paper, but the results are impressive.

Another specialty paper item you might consider is pre-punched paper. Some copy paper comes with three holes punched in it, making the paper immediately useful in a three-ring binder. This saves you from the extra step of punching the holes in afterward.

Three-hole paper doesn't come in the varieties of plain paper, but it's perfect for creating booklets, plays, or school reports that must be placed into a three-ring binder.

Finally, though a laser printer will accept high-quality paper, note that such paper is usually coated with a fine talc. That talc will collect inside the laser printer, building up a lot faster than dust ever will. It's a good idea to clean this talc from a laser printer after printing several pages on high-quality paper. (Those instructions are offered in Chapter 15.)

Your PC and the Printer

Printers are interesting devices. But they're *device-independent*, meaning they will work with a variety of computers. To deal with this situation, your PC, your software, and DOS all have to be flexible enough to deal with a variety of printers. Sometimes they do, usually they don't. That can cause one of the biggest headaches a PC owner—even "old hands"—can ever get.

This part of the printer chapter deals with your PC and the printer. There are three sections that cover all the valuable information:

◆ The Printer Port

◆ Your Software and Printers

◆ DOS and the Printer

The Printer Port

Your PC communicates with the printer via a cable, commonly called a *printer cable*. One end of the cable plugs into your printer. The other end plugs into the PC. Where it plugs into the PC is commonly referred to as the printer port.

PC Printer Ports

What is a port?

A *port* is often a socket on the back of your PC where you can plug in communications devices. Your PC talks to a printer, mouse, or external modem via a port. There are other kinds of ports; for example, the microprocessor has ports that it uses to communicate with other chips in the system. But for now, let's focus on ports that communicate with printers.

Printer ports go by a number of names:

◆ Parallel ports

◆ Serial ports

Only old timers will recall a parallel printer port a Centronics port. *Centronics* was the name of a company that used to manufacture a lot of computer printers. They set the standards for printer cables and hooking up computers and printers. So today, we still use Centronics-compatible printers and cables (though Centronics itself has long since left the scene).

The word "parallel" refers to how the information travels between the computer and printer—how the port operates. Each byte you send to the printer, which eventually forms a printed character on the page, is composed of eight bits. In a printer port, those eight bits are sent through the cable side-by-side—as if they were walking eight abreast in a parade.

A parallel port is also a one-way communications line in a PC. Information is sent only to the printer. While the printer may fire off a few messages back to the PC (such as the "I'm out of paper" and "I'm not ready" wires), it doesn't send any bytes back. The communication goes only one way.

Parallel port and printer port are interchangeable terms (with Centronics being the left-field term). However, a printer can also be hooked up to a serial port. In that instance, you can still call the port a printer port (because it's hooked up to the printer), but it's really a serial port.

Serial ports, discussed in Chapter 10, deal with a variety of different devices. The reason they're much more versatile than parallel ports is that communication works both ways in a serial port. For example, information is both sent to and received from a modem.

The term "serial" refers to how information is sent out the port. Unlike a parallel port, where the bytes are fed out in rows of eight, a serial port squirts all the bits in a byte through one of the printer cable's conductors, one after the other. They travel in a straight line, as opposed to eight abreast.

The standard with PC printers is a parallel interface, meaning most print-ers are hooked up to a parallel printer port. But a few printers are serial. (Nearly all plotters are serial.) Most of the older daisy-wheel printers were serial, or supported both ports. And the early laser printers were all serial, though today they too support both ports.

Which is better?

Serial is better over longer distances. A serial port's signal can travel quite a few yards before it begins to fade away. And while parallel is faster than serial, its signal fades after about 20 feet or so. This is all really moot if you have the printer hooked up to a network. But keep in mind that parallel is the standard printer port for all PC printers, and you can hook just about any printer up to it.

It's always a good idea to have both a parallel and serial port in your com-puter, a minimum of one each.

Where to Find It

Unfortunately, there are no labeling standards for PC printer ports. Some computers, high-end models mostly, will label their built-in serial and par-allel ports. (The Macintosh has tiny pictures above each port.) Yet, finding a parallel port on the back of a typical PC can be frustrating.

A printer port's connectors are what's commonly known as *D-shell 25-pins*. Sadly, there are a number of D-shell 25-pin connectors on the PC, one of which is probably a serial port. If you plug in the printer and it doesn't work, what you've probably done is plugged it into a serial port, or into a secondary printer port.

In about 1985 or so, serial ports started coming with only nine pins in a D-shell connector. (Of the 25 pins in the older D-shell connectors, maybe four were being used with the typical serial device.) If you have a newer system, especially an AT-level system, it probably sports a 9-pin serial port. This leaves the printer ports alone in the 25-pin D-shell category. Then the only hassle is trying to find out which port is which number if you have more than one. Unless you installed the ports yourself, trial and error seems to be the only way to go about it.

Your Software and Printers

Imagine a world where you have a PC *and* a printer *and* software that understands them both. Erase the term "printer driver" from your mind, forget about incompatibilities, forget about output looking one way on the home computer's printer and totally different at the office. Imagine...

What you're imagining in the above paragraph is a philosophy of computing we commonly refer to as the "Macintosh." But on the PC side, you have variety and lower prices, but you also have difficulties to solve, which is what this section is about.

Printer Drivers

Earlier in this book, we mentioned that the PC is a collection of off-the-shelf parts. This gives you a tremendous advantage as far as configuring a flexible system is concerned. You get competition and low prices, and in the end (providing you have enough money), there's a PC perfectly fit to your needs. But this also leaves your software utterly confused.

Video standards and memory are two things most software packages have little trouble dealing with. Monitors and display adapters have variety, but they're still standards more-or-less defined by IBM. Printers are off by themselves.

When an application concerns itself with good looking output, it really needs to know how to control your printer. If you want different type styles, sizes, or graphics, your software needs to know precisely which printer you have. Only then will it be able to speak to the printer in the printer's own language, and get the printer to do what you want it to do. This communication is made possible via a software device known as a *printer driver*.

 Printer drivers aren't the same as device drivers loaded into CONFIG.SYS. Device drivers are for DOS—which could really care less about which printer you have.

A printer driver is a custom part of an application or a separate program that provides for direct communication to a *particular* printer. For example, the commands to print italic text are different for the HP Laser-Jet, Epson LQ 1500, and Panasonic 1080i printers. But using a driver for each printer, an application can simply say "print in italics." The driver will then translate that instruction into the printer's code for producing italic text.

When you deal with printer drivers, you must contend with a few things.

Are There Drivers Available for Your Printer? Some software applications support only a limited range of printers, while there are hundreds on the market place. Is yours one of the ones supported? If not, are there any similar printers that have printer drivers available you can use?

Information on supported printers isn't normally listed on the side of the software box. To get it, you usually have to call up the developer's support line and ask Someone Who Knows.

Software Compatibility

Any application that produces complex printed output will need some type of printer driver. While drivers are available for most common printers, the sad part is that you need to install a different driver for each application. There is no common, once-installed-that's-it driver to use for everything. But the makers of printers are working on solutions.

One solution is available to PCs that run special computer environments, such as Microsoft Windows or OS/2. Windows has you choose a printer when you first install the program. With OS/2, you choose a printer when you first install the operating system. From that point on, any program that's compatible in that environment will be able to use the printer—without your having to install a printer driver.

Some integrated software packages will let you use a single printer driver with a number of packages. But the problem here is that individual pieces of integrated software are often poor performers when compared to better designed and more capable stand-alone products.

Printing to Disk

A printing option some applications offer (but seldom explain) is the print-to-disk option. This option sends output that would normally go to the printer to a file on disk instead. The disk file could contain one of two forms of the printed output:

◆ A formatted ASCII file

◆ Pure printer output

The first type of output is simply an ASCII or text file. Characters that would have normally been printed are sent to disk instead. Since you can't have underline, italics, or whatnot, the text is just plain text. However, some applications may format the disk file with margins, page breaks and so forth.

The second type of print-to-disk file is simply redirected printer output. All the codes, printer and formatting information are simply stored on a disk file instead of printed. Unlike the ASCII file, this type of printed file will probably be unreadable.

What you can do with these print-to-disk files varies with your needs. An ASCII file printed to disk makes for excellent on-line documentation. A user can TYPE the file to the screen to view its contents. Or, since it's text, they can load it into their own word processor for editing. (Though it's better to save a file in a plain ASCII format for editing by other word processors.)

A file composed of pure printer output seems rather useless. But, it's still a valuable file. Suppose, for example, that your printer is in the shop. Rather than wait to print something, simply print a document to disk and store it there until the printer returns. Or suppose you're working at home but want to print on the office printer. You set up your home software for the office printer (even though you don't personally own one), and then print the output to disk. Take the disk to the office and then "copy" it to the printer. The result will be the same as if you worked on the document at the office and printed it directly to the printer.

To print a file saved as print-to-disk, you copy it to the printer using the COPY command. For example:

```
COPY PRINT.DOC PRN
```

PRN is the name of your printer according to DOS. (It's a device in your system, which is described in detail in the following section.) Since your application sent the printed output to disk instead of the printer, all you're doing is creating a floppy disk "spooler." When copied to the

printer, the file on disk sends all the proper codes and formatting informa-tion—a delayed print job.

Simple formatted ASCII files created by a print-to-disk function can be copied to the printer in the same way. In a sense, they're more generic be-cause the formatting is pure text. The second type of print-to-disk docu-ment is printer specific. Copying it to a printer other than the one it was created for will doubtless yield wild and crazy results.

DOS and the Printer

DOS uses your printer in the so-called "dumb" mode. There's no need for DOS to print anything other than text characters on the printer. DOS doesn't underline, do bold or italics, provide margins or text formatting, nor will it print graphics (there's no need to). Your applications handle most of the complex printer chores, which is one reason why DOS falls short as an operating system. But it is possible to use a printer under DOS, and there are some interesting things you can do with it.

This section covers using a printer under DOS. There are three sections:

◆ The Printer as a DOS Device

◆ Using a Printer under DOS

◆ The PRINT Program

Since DOS isn't really a program requiring a printer, most of what you can do with a printer under DOS isn't impressive. But it is useful, and the in-formation here will help you be a more productive PC user.

DOS uses the printer in a fairly straightforward manner. The only time you may find incompatibilities with your printer and DOS is when you print some of the those weird characters that don't appear on your key-board (extended-ASCII characters), particularly the line drawing charac-ters. Not every printer supports these characters. On those printers that don't the printed results will be unpredictable. (For example, the Epson printers will display italics characters instead of the line drawing characters.)

Most printers do offer support for the line drawing characters. If a printer doesn't innately, then it supports them via some DIP switch settings that make the printer IBM printer compatible. In those modes, the graphics characters will print, but the results aren't always what you see on the screen.

The Printer as a DOS Device

As an operating system, DOS is flexible because it deals with all parts of the computer on an equal basis, treating everything on your PC as a *device*. The traditional devices are your disk drives. Other devices are serial ports, keyboards, monitors, and the printers.

DOS assigns a name to each of its devices. Disk drives are named with letters: A, B, C, and so on. The keyboard and screen are named CON, the keyboard being the input CON device and the screen providing output. The serial ports are named COM1, COM2, COM3, and COM4. And the printer ports are named LPT1, LPT2, and LPT3 for up to three printers attached to your PC. The first printer, LPT1 can also be called PRN.

Even though DOS treats the printer as a device, it still doesn't require a device driver in CONFIG.SYS. Those device drivers supply information to the PC and your programs for devices that DOS doesn't know about.

In the previous section, you saw an example where a file was copied to the printer using the traditional COPY command. This is a good illustration of how DOS uses devices. Since the printer is a device, it's possible to copy a file there, just as you'd copy a file to a disk drive.

The device name used for the printer in the previous section was PRN. PRN is the standard printing device, the one DOS will always use unless you tell it otherwise. The PRN device is usually the same as LPT1, the first printer. However, using DOS's MODE command, it's possible to reassign PRN to another device, most often the first serial port. This is done to make serial printers usable under DOS and by all your programs as the standard PRN device.

To set up a serial printer as the PRN device, you need to know two things:

◆ Which serial port the printer is hooked into

◆ The speed at which the printer is communicating

Serial ports are numbered like printer ports: COM1 for the first, COM2 for the second, COM3 for the third, and COM4 for a fourth. As with printer ports, serial ports don't have numbers on the back of your PC. So you won't know exactly which serial port you're plugging a printer into unless they're labeled or you know which is which.

Unlike parallel ports, a serial port must be configured. There are four attributes to set: the speed, measured in bits-per-second (BPS or *baud rate*); the data word size; the parity; and the number of stop bits. Typically, a serial printer will be set up to communicate at 9600 BPS, with an 8-bit word size, no parity, and one stop bit. This is abbreviated as 9600, 8, N, 1.

To setup a serial printer as PRN under DOS, the MODE command is used in two steps: First the MODE command is used to set the PC's serial port to match the speed and format of the printer's serial port. Next, the serial port is reassigned to the PRN port. Continuing with the previous example, the two MODE commands you would use under DOS are:

```
MODE COM1:9600,N,8,1,P
MODE LPT1=COM1
```

A *P* follows the first MODE command to let DOS know it's a printer you're configuring. The next command reassigns the first printer, LPT1, to COM1, the serial port. Since the PRN device is linked to LPT1, all commands made to it or LPT1 will now refer instead to your serial printer.

Note that this conversion will work only under DOS and other applications that use DOS to print. Using the COPY command with PRN and a serial printer under DOS will work just fine. But some applications require you to directly install the serial printer from within the program (or during its installation). Those applications bypass DOS to use the serial port's hardware directly. Be aware of them, so you don't suddenly think DOS forgot about your new PRN device.

To reset the printer device back to LPT1, you use the following:

```
MODE LPT1=LPT1
```

Driving Your Printer with DOS

There are times when you need to get a printout from DOS—a hard copy of a directory, a file listing, or just need some way to access the printer while you're working in DOS. There are three ways to do this:

◆ The Print Screen Key

◆ The DOS Echo-to-Printer Function

◆ Redirecting Output to the Printer

The Print Screen Key The Print Screen key isn't as much a function of DOS as it is of the PC's BIOS. but it works well in DOS, so it's covered here.

Print Screen, or Print Scrn or PrtSc (depending on which keyboard you have), is the old, fabled "screen dump" key nearly all microcomputers have had since Day One. Pressing the Shift key and the PrntScrn key reproduces a copy of the text on the screen on the printer. That's it! There's no form feed, and the action usually stops everything in progress while printing goes on.

Print Screen can be a blessing or a curse, depending on when it's pressed. As a curse, Print Screen can do a lot of damage. First, if you're already printing something, Print Screen will attempt to send the current screen to the printer at the same time. The end result is garbage. (Since Print Screen is part of your system's BIOS, there is no checking for other applications currently printing; it doesn't wait.)

Second, Print Screen will sometimes lock up a computer, waiting until you turn on your printer. If a printer isn't around, then you can't get any work done until after you've desperately hunted down some other printer, hooked it up to your system, and hope that nothing crashes in the mean time. Recent BIOSs, however, will detect that the printer isn't turned on and they'll skip printing the screen. But some older systems may lock up and wait for the printer.

As a blessing, Print Screen is a quick and dirty (which makes it not so blessed) way to get a hard copy of information on the screen. But note that Print Screen only "dumps" text characters. Pressing Print Screen during a graphics display definitely won't print your graphics screen. In fact, what it prints is unpredictable at that point. But for quick screen shots, it's a lifesaver.

Don't forget that not every printer will display the PC graphics character set.

Redirecting Output to the Printer   The final way you can get DOS to use the printer is by *output redirection*, or *I/O redirection*, as the diehards call it.

All output in DOS normally goes to the screen, technically referred to as the "default output device." However, by using DOS's output redirection symbol, > (the greater-than sign or right angle bracket), you can send a copy of printed output to the printer.

For example, to print a directory listing you can type the following on the command line:

```
C> DIR > PRN
```

This command sends the output of the DIR command to the printer, the PRN device. Since output is redirected, you won't see the directory listed on the screen. But you will see your printer spew out the directory listing. Output redirection has sent that text to the printer instead of to the screen.

You can redirect output to the printer from just about any DOS program or utility that produces output. Again, since most major applications don't use DOS to display information, output redirection won't work with them. But for DOS, it's ideal.

The PRINT Program

Since version 2.0, DOS has come with a program that's thrown many users for a loop. It's the PRINT program and what it does varies, depending on whom you ask. But note that few users bother with PRINT. It's a good idea, but never really perfected.

PRINT is a print spooler. A print spooler program collects output (documents, spreadsheets, etc..) destined for the printer, and feeds that output to the printer at the speed that the printer can accept it. By using a Print Spooler, you free your software for other jobs. Windows Print Manager is a good example of a popular print spooler program.

Unlike a traditional print spooler program, you must tell PRINT what to print. Because of that, PRINT works only with files on disk—files that may have been printed to disk or just text files you want to print.

Once you tell the PRINT program what to print, then it will sit in the background and spool them off to the printer. It works rather efficiently, but the extra step of printing to disk is required to make PRINT useful. This is why most people ignore it, opting for some of the better print spoolers on the market.

Since PRINT isn't useful unless you have a bunch of text files to print, there's no use explaining it in any detail here. However, there are two programs worth looking into if print spooling is something you seriously want to do. They are: The PC-Kwik Power Pak Print Spooler from PC-Kwik Corporation, and NOR Software's Printer Genius. Both will give you print spoolers in software that will really boost printer performance—and they blow the DOS PRINT command out of the water.

Additional information on using software to boost printer performance is covered in the final part of this chapter. But DOS does offer the PRINT command. Personally, I've used it to print several program source code files while the computer was busy doing something else. Aside from that, it's really nothing to get excited about.

Boosting Printer Performance

The printer is a reliable, trusty peripheral that you should know a lot about. There are ways to supercharge a printer, giving it abilities far beyond those of mere mortal printers. That's the subject of this part of the chapter.

Boosting printer performance is possible by both software and hardware means.

Software

There are three software solutions you can use to boost your printer's performance. They are:

- ◆ Printer Spoolers
- ◆ Font Management Software
- ◆ Emulation Software

Print Spoolers

A *printer spooler* is a software program in your computer. (This is opposed to a *printer buffer*, which is hardware.) The spooler will monitor and intercept all printer activity, saving that activity to disk as a file or keeping it in spooler memory. Then, every so often, the spooler will dish out a handful of characters to the printer. It does this while you're doing other work on the computer. So printing is done "in the background" while you're getting other work done at the same time.

A term often heard in connection with printer spoolers is *queue*. A queue is a line. In Commonwealth countries, the word *queue* is used instead of *line* to refer to a line of people at a movie theater, buying groceries, waiting for a bus, etc. A spooler's queue is simply a list of files that are waiting to be printed by the spooler.

Some sophisticated printer spoolers save the information to be printed to a file on disk. The files are kept in a special spooler subdirectory to keep them separate from other files. Each file is then queued to the printer while you're doing something else. This type of spooler gives you the advantage of deleting or "killing off" certain jobs to be printed. Some will even let you print documents at given times, or redirect printing to another printer.

Printer spoolers were touched upon briefly in the middle part of this book, as well as in the chapter on upgrading RAM. There are two types of print spooler products:

◆ DOS Print Spoolers

◆ Windows Print Spoolers

DOS Print Spoolers DOS print spoolers are usually intended to work with a particular word processor. For example, if you're a WordPerfect for DOS user, you'll find dozens of print spooler software products out there that will vary in feature sets somewhat. They basically do the same job, though.

Windows Print Spoolers Print Spooler products for use with Microsoft Windows or IBM's OS/2 will vary from DOS print spoolers in one big way. The standardization of the Windows and OS/2 environments make using a single print spooler for all applications possible. It's a lot like using Windows fonts versus fonts made to be used with WordPerfect or Microsoft

Word for DOS. Font software made for DOS products is normally application-specific. You usually can't expect to use either a print spooler or a font management tool for more than one DOS application. OS/2 and Windows are different. All OS/2 or Windows applications can share a single print spooler utility because these environments allow only a single print spooler to be used at one time.

Make sure you specify which type of environment you are working with when you buy a print spooler software product. Tell the seller if you're going to use the product with DOS, Windows, OS/2, etc.

Font Management Software

Font Management software is used to make more fonts available to your applications. If you're using a DOS word processing or desktop publishing application, you will want to check out fonts intended to work with a specific application, under DOS. If you're using Windows or OS/2, you'll want to look at font management products that are designed to work with all applications in either environment.

Font management software (also called *type management software*) is essentially an add-on product that works directly with your text-creation application so you can add fonts as you get more proficient or as you find you need more neat fonts.

There are two parts to each font management software product:

◆ The management software

◆ The fonts themselves

When you buy a font management package, you usually get the management software and some selection of fonts, popular or otherwise. Most software products in this vein offer from a half-a-dozen fonts to a library of hundreds of fonts. Since most of the demand for fonts comes from the desktop publishing industry, most font management software makers are bundling their management software with hundreds of fonts on CD-ROM.

Most professional or at least serious DTP folks already have a CD-ROM drive in their computer. They get to take advantage of some incredible

font software deals because CD's are cheap for the manufacturer to make and distribute.

When you install this software, either from floppies or from CD's, you install one of two types of products:

◆ Additional software that is required to enable the added fonts

◆ A set of fonts that is managed by your application

When you add a font management software package to your computer, you are essentially installing another program that must run all of the time just to make your add-on fonts available to your application. Adding a font manager takes memory space away from to your applications because these font managers must use some memory too!

When you add fonts intended for use by your application, you are just adding more fonts to your existing library. You use far less additional memory when you just add fonts and avoid additional font management software. Adding additional fonts can in some cases use up more memory, but it's barely noticeable when compared to font management software that can use up to 200K of your valuable conventional memory.

Regardless of whether you use DOS, Windows, or OS/2, always avoid add-on products that replicate your current font management software's abilities. If you're a Windows user, buy additional TrueType fonts for Windows to manage. If you're a WordPerfect for DOS user, buy extra fonts intended to be managed by WordPerfect. If it ain't broke, don't fix it!

Emulation Software

The issue of printer compatibility will crop up occasionally as you try to interface your particular printer with some software that doesn't support it. Though your printer may have a nationally known name, and there may have been twenty boxes of it stacked up at the store, some software won't recognize it. Also, some printers are too new for older applications to recognize them and support all their features. When this happens, you can do one of three things:

◆ Use your printer in the dumb mode

◆ Select a compatible printer

◆ Buy emulation software

The "dumb" mode is where your printer just prints simple text. You'll get no fancy fonts, no italics, and no graphics. Even though your printer may support such things, the software doesn't no how to make the printer work, hence everything is run in the dumb mode.

A compatible printer may be your same model, but manufactured under a different brand name. The old NEC 8023 printers were the same model manufactured and sold by C. Itoh as the ProWriter and by Apple as the ImageWriter. If an application supported any of those printers, your model was compatible.

If your printer isn't compatible, and it doesn't have any DIP switches to make it compatible with anything else, and you don't want to waste time writing a printer driver, your only other choice is to buy *emulation software*.

Usually top notch software developers will try to support every printer on the market. But it's an endless task. Some printers may even come with a bunch of diskettes containing printer drivers for various applications. But when all your luck runs out, emulation software is the way to go.

Hardware

On the hardware side, developers are constantly looking for new ways to boost printer performance. But unlike the software techniques covered in the previous sections, these methods here are often expensive, specific solutions for high-volume printer situations. It would be nice if there was this $29.95 gadget you could plug into a printer to get more power out of it. But that's sadly not the case.

There are five hardware solutions you can use to boost printer performance:

◆ Adding Printer RAM

◆ Using a Printer Buffer

◆ Font Cartridges

◆ Rasterizing Cards

◆ Fax Cartridges

Adding Printer RAM

As with a PC, a good way to get more performance from a printer is to add more RAM. With a dot-matrix printer, the RAM is simply used as a buffer to store incoming characters. Adding RAM to a dot-matrix printer means you don't have to wait as much for the printer. But unlike adding RAM to a PC, a special printer RAM board needs to be purchased for each individual printer, and it usually isn't cheap.

Laser printers use RAM as well, usually to store information you send to the printer. But because some laser printers are really computers in their own right, they use the RAM to make calculations and to prepare images for printing. This takes up much more RAM than the simple character storage for which RAM is used on a dot-matrix printer. PostScript printers in particular require lots of RAM for their images, from 1.5 upwards to 12 megabytes.

Again, you can add RAM to just about any printer, but usually it's in the form of some proprietary (and expensive) upgrade option available only from the printer's manufacturer. Some PC add-on boards will assist with extra RAM for the printer. They're covered near the end of the chapter.

Using a Printer Buffer

A *printer buffer* works like a printer spooler. But instead of using the PC's RAM, the buffer holds its own RAM. This gives you more memory to run DOS programs, and it eliminates the mess sometimes caused by memory resident print spoolers.

A printer buffer (as an add-on product) is one of those famous black boxes you hook up to your PC. It plugs into the printer cable between your PC and the printer. Basically, it's just packed full of RAM. So all characters sent to the printer are first stored in the buffer's RAM space. The buffer also contains electronic circuitry that monitors the printer, sending off characters as the printer is able to print them.

A printer buffer will save you printing time, but that's about all it does. (In fact, it can be viewed as simply a way to add more RAM to a printer without buying a proprietary RAM upgrade.) But printer buffers are limited by how much control they give you over what's printed. Usually, the only way to stop a buffer is to unplug it, which means all the information stored in the buffer is lost (as is anything that was in RAM when you shut off the power).

Font Cartridges

Another way to boost the performance of your printer is to buy *font cartridges*. A font cartridge is basically a ROM chip on a special, user-installable expansion card. The card plugs into a custom slot on the printer, and then gives the printer and your software access to the fonts encoded in the ROM. There are even font cartridges available for dot-matrix printers.

The problem with font cartridges is their price. Typically, you'll pay from $150 up to $450 for a cartridge of different fonts. This is rather drastic when you compare it with $150 for software "downloadable" fonts. But the advantage to a font cartridge is that you don't need the downloading software and the font takes up no extra RAM in the PC.

Rasterizing Cards

Finally, to give your laser printer more power, you can add a *laser printer assistant card* into your PC. It's basically an expansion card that boosts the printer's power, or assists the printer's circuitry in some way, for example, by boosting its resolution.

Most laser printers print at a resolution of 300 dots-per-inch. That's an impressive figure, and apparently an acceptable one because few laser printers have ever bothered to improve upon it. While it would be possible to buy a printer with a higher resolution, they're expensive and best suited for professional environments such as publishing, graphics arts houses, and advertising.

So one of the jobs of a laser printer assistant card is to boost the performance of a laser printer's controller. The card installs in your PC and then you connect the laser printer to the card. The laser board then takes over the job of controlling the printer's laser beam, increasing its resolution to 600 dots per inch or more. All of this is possible with a single expansion card that costs under $300.

In addition to boosting the laser printer's resolution, the laser board may also add its own RAM to the printer's RAM, add fonts, or give it PostScript or PostScript-like scaleable fonts and graphics. But the downside is that the add-on card may also suck up a lot of your PC's RAM and processor

time to do the job. For high capacity printing though, nothing can beat this upgrade.

The type quality on a laser printer is said to be "near typeset quality." These days, the newest standard to match is that set by HP's LaserJet IV. This machine will produce paper with a graphics resolution of 600 dpi!

The industry is scrambling to emulate the performance of this printer. There have been printers out there for some time that have offered 800 dpi for Windows users.

LaserMaster offers a printer called the WinJet 800. This printer's "brains" are located on a card that lives in one of your system slots. This card processes (rasterizes) output from Print Manager by using your computer's CPU! It doesn't even have it's own processor. And it does all of this faster than a conventional 300 dpi printer can because the odds are that your PC's processor is more powerful than the one provided in most laser printers.

You can just buy rasterizer cards that will boost the performance of your own printer under Windows. There's a catch, though. Most of them require you to have a video port on your laser printer. A video port on your printer is a special connector located somewhere on the outside of your printer, if your printer has one at all. Unless your printer is an HP II, HP III, or HP IV, you might not have a video port on your printer! The P series of HP printers can't make use of these add-on rasterizing cards because they don't have one of these video ports, which is one reason why the P series of HP printers costs less than the non-P series.

 Make sure your laser printer is the right type to make use of one of these performance-increasing rasterizing cards before you buy one. It's always a drag to be disappointed by a new toy.

Fax Cartridges

Add-on product makers are finding new ways to use the cartridge slots on your laser printer. At first, we were happy to get extra fonts (what a price, though), then PostScript capability, then bingo! someone figured-out how to get your laser printer to receive and print faxes.

These cartridges intercept a phone call originated by a fax machine and send the pages to the printer. You can't send a fax with these cartridges, but they are a great way to receive inbound faxes for an entire work group with only one phone line.

Let's say you have a group of folks using Windows for Workgroups. They are all using one shared printer. If you plug in this cartridge, all of the people can receive faxes with just one phone line.

The drawback to this approach is that you tie up a cartridge slot. If you need to use a cartridge with your printer to do the occasional PostScript job, then you may have to pop out the fax cartridge and insert the Post-Script cartridge. Of course, then fax machines would get no answer while you are using the cartridge slot for something else.

The Multimedia PC

Multimedia seems like such a flashy new buzzword. The truth is that multimedia has been around for a long time, but until now, it has been too expensive to use. Powerful new computers, combined with wide availability of multimedia hardware (and upgrade kits), bring the power and potential of multimedia to everyone.

But what exactly is multimedia? It's actually short for "multiple-media." A single media uses one sense, such as video or audio; when you combine senses, such picture and sound on a computer, you've got *multimedia*.

A History of Multimedia

As PCs standardized and became a popular sight on even the home desktop, hardware and software vendors did their best to sell us multimedia products at prices that kept us, well, uninterested. The multimedia industry has always been in a crunch to validate itself to the corporate customer, let alone end users like ourselves. We could all thrill at the marvels of multimedia, while the common expression among potential customers was, "Fine, but what does it *do* for *me*?"

What's the benefit of a multimedia PC in the home? An information kiosk for your teenager's location? A fancy way for the computer to play games? Is there a justification?

The PC industry struggled with finding reasons for buyers to purchase Multimedia products until the advent of Windows 3.1. Microsoft's Windows 3.1 has the ability to drive several types of multimedia devices. No longer was there an excuse—Windows 3.1 *came* with multimedia capabilities. You had it whether you wanted it or not.

Windows 3.1 and NT versions come with special drivers that allow Windows to do exciting things such as send sounds to your PC's speaker and work with MIDI (musical instrument) software and hardware. This allowed dealers to set up sound systems and play CD-ROM disks in the stores to dazzle and entice users. Overnight multimedia transformed from an abstract concept to "Windows can now play funny noises when it does things." People clamored for it. (Though the Macintosh has had this ability since day one, PC users were delighted that "multimedia" finally meant no more dreadful bleeping of the PC's speaker.)

The real key to the recent proliferation of multimedia products is really two-fold. First, everyone has been deluged with enough marketing dollars so that we should all (by now) feel lacking if our PCs don't play sounds and music. I think it might be part of the He-Who-Has-the-Most-Toys-Wins syndrome for many people who invest in the hardware and the software needed to join the multimedia rampage. Secondly, for the saner members of society, there is the notion that multimedia can make our jobs easier, faster, and simpler. It may be true, but wasn't that the promise of the PC to begin with?

A Short Survey of What Multimedia Can Do for Your PC

If you're itching to get on the multimedia bandwagon, you might consider any of several reasons for enjoying the benefits of an upgrade:

◆ With a sound card and CD-ROM drive installed in your PC, you'll have the ability to play audio CDs while you use your PC.

◆ You can make your PC into a complete CD-quality (16-bit) stereo system, complete with FM stereo, CD player, music recorder, and dedicated speakers, or just use headphones.

◆ Your games can be heard (and not just seen), even in stereo.

◆ You can use a CD-ROM drive as an extension of your hard drive. CD-ROM disks hold hundreds of megabytes of information and are as removable as floppy disks. More software applications appear on CD-ROM disks every day: references, games, massive programs that would otherwise take hours to install, graphics clip art libraries, sound files, and on and on.

◆ You have the ability to watch TV on your PC. You don't have to keep a TV set in your work area.

◆ You can create your own software applications that talk, play sounds, and display moving pictures.

◆ You can use a large-screen TV monitor to display software for presentations or training purposes.

◆ You're able to record audio segments from movies played on your VCR or TV and save them as .WAV files on your hard drive.

◆ You're able to use your PC as a sound mixer to create multitrack recordings of music.

◆ You can use your PC to compose music, and you can print it out on scoring sheets.

◆ You have the ability to use your PC to control several musical instruments that utilize the MIDI interface.

◆ You can use Microsoft Windows Object Linking and Embedding feature to add your own voice to electronic mail or documents that you create and send to others, and you can also hear others speak to you in voice-mail and documents.

◆ Use your PC to create professional-quality video productions, or if you're in the field, you can replace expensive equipment with your multimedia PC.

◆ You can have your photos, home movies, and home videos converted to CDs so you can store them easily and view them with your PC or TV.

◆ You can use a camera that captures pictures *electronically*, instead of the traditional method that requires chemical processing and printing.

◆ You can even use your PC as a Karaoke machine (though count me out on your first Karaoke party).

The list seems awfully long, but this is only the beginning! As hardware and software vendors line up to sell us products that truly talk to *each other*, you'll find uses for multimedia that aren't even imagined today.

Multimedia Hardware Options for Your PC

If you want to get involved in multimedia, you'll have to add hardware. Depending on what you want to do, you may not have to add any additional software. This next section is devoted to talking about the kinds of upgrades you can undertake for your PC. Generally speaking, you can't do multimedia "stuff" unless you add at least a sound card and speakers. Below I discuss these basic elements of a multimedia PC separately, because you'll most likely buy these items separately. Here are some of the issues this section covers:

◆ Audio upgrades

◆ CD-ROM upgrades

◆ Visual upgrades

◆ Device drivers

◆ Network considerations

Choosing multimedia hardware and software for your PC can be pretty intimidating. You run headlong into terms such as "Business-quality sound" and "CD-quality sound." To help you get through the process of upgrading to a multimedia PC, here are a few terms and their meanings.

Sampling Size: This specification found on the boxes of most sound cards determines how dynamic the sound will be. 8-bit cards offer 256 points of access to adjusting the sound level; 16-bit cards offer 65,636 points of access. A higher number is better, but it has the downside of requiring more disk space if you're making your own recordings.

Sample Rate: This determines the overall frequency range that can be handled by the card. There's a basic algorithm used to figure out which sample rate is needed. If you want to record a musical instrument in the 10KHz range, you need a sample rate of over 20KHz. The rule of thumb is: The sample rate needs to be twice the actual frequency of the sound you're processing. A higher number is definitely better.

Signal to Noise Ratio: 8-bit cards usually offer a ratio of about 60db; 16-bit cards offer up to a 95db ratio. A higher number is better because it means less background hiss.

Frequency Response: This determines whether you can hear all of the sounds recorded by the artist. Studio-quality hardware and software will record broader ranges of sound than the human can hear. Bass guitars will produce sounds below 100Hz. Brass instruments like cymbals and triangles usually make some of their sounds in the range of hearing above 12KHz. As a guideline, the average adult can't hear sounds below 100Hz or over 15KHz. Children however, can hear sounds up to 22KHz.

Business-Quality Sound: This term refers to a level of sound quality used for voice annotation. It is also called 8-bit sound.

CD-Quality Sound: This refers to the level of sound quality found on CD recordings and other *digitally processed* works. CDs are capable of storing and delivering sound at the level of quality of the original musical instruments. Business-quality sound is not.

MPC: This is an acronym for Multimedia Products Council. It is a set of standards for multimedia hardware and software intended for use with personal computers. Without getting into the nuts and bolts of the standard, rest assured that hardware and software products marked as being *MPC compliant* by their manufacturers will be able to work correctly with other multimedia products with the MPC logo.

Audio Upgrades

Audio upgrades consist of hardware and software additions that give your PC the ability to play and record sounds. This is primarily accomplished by adding a sound card to your system, which allows your computer to do more than just beep. In this section, you'll read about the multimedia upgrades that allow you to take advantage of the power of audio when computing.

Adding a Sound Card to Your System

There are essentially two types of sound cards. Even though most sound cards are marketed as being all things to all people, they generally fall into one of two categories based on the quality of sound that they are capable of delivering:

- Business-quality or 8-bit sound cards
- CD-quality or 16-bit sound cards

Business-Quality or 8-bit Sound Cards Business-quality sound cards are the cheaper than CD-quality cards. A business-quality sound system is suitable if you want to send voice-annotated mail messages to your buddies on the network or you want to embed their voices in documents as a running commentary. Business-quality sound cards will generally come with some sort of 8-bit sound card, software to record and playback audio files, and a microphone or telephone handset.

You'll have to assign an IRQ (Interrupt Request Line) and DMA (Direct Memory Access) channel to this category of sound card. IRQs are a direct channel to the CPU via the system bus. DMA channels are direct connections to your system's memory banks. You can usually buy business-quality sound cards for less than $100.

What you will need: an 8-bit slot for the audio card and a recording device such as a microphone (if it's not included with the card). You will also need a free IRQ, I/O base port address, and DMA channel. You may need to use a text editor (DOS EDLIN or EDIT will do) to add a device driver statement to your CONFIG.SYS file if you want to use the card under DOS. These device drivers allow the board to work under either DOS or Windows.

CD-Quality or 16-bit Sound Cards This level sound card allows you to play CDs—with all their clarity—through a set of speakers attached to your PC or through a separate stereo system. This type of card is ideally suited to users who demand the best consumer electronics can provide for a realistic sum.

A CD-quality sound card is referred to as a *16-bit* sound card. It offers audio mixing, built-in stereo music synthesis, and many other features.

There are several standards in the audio card business and most 16-bit cards do cover them all. Most of these cards will emulate the popular Sound Blaster and MediaVision sound cards. If a 16-bit card emulates two completely different standards from one board, you may find yourself having to assign two different IRQs to the board in order for that board to emulate more than one audio card standard. CD-quality or 16-bit sound cards go for less than $200 on the street. Business-quality sound cards can usually be had for less than $100. (Refer to Chapter 15 for more information on IRQs and why you should hate them.)

What you will need: a 16-bit slot for the audio card and a recording device such as a microphone (if it's not included with the card). You will also need a free IRQ, I/O base port address, and DMA channel. You may need to use a text editor (again, DOS EDLIN or EDIT will do) to add a device driver statement to your CONFIG.SYS file.

Adding Speakers to Your PC

Most sound cards have output jacks or connectors to attach a small set of speakers using the card's built-in audio amplifier or to send a stereo signal to an outside audio amplifier so you can play your CDs. Most 16-bit sound cards offer you the option of doing one or either, depending on your needs.

Most speakers designed to be used on a PC have special shielding inside them that keeps speakers and monitors from interfering with each other. If you're going to attach your audio speakers to the sides of your monitor, then make sure the speakers you buy are shielded. If you're not going to hug-a-monitor to hear your speakers, then don't sweat it; two or three feet of distance between your speakers and monitor will not create interference.

You can buy basic (self-amplified) speakers for your PC for $15. If the speakers have the means to power themselves (or you have a separate stereo amplifier), you can use any speakers that you wish, including expensive home audio speakers.

What you will need: a set of amplified or unamplified speakers, depending on your sound card's ability to drive either type. If the speakers have amplifiers built in and you intend to use them instead of the amplified output on your sound card, then you'll need batteries or a power supply to power your speakers.

Adding an FM Stereo Card

If you're one of those purists that must do everything from within Windows, there's a radio out there with your name on it! Actually, there are now several stereo FM tuners that are mounted on an expansion card. Most come with Windows software so you can change the channel, adjust the volume, and do other radio-like things like press the loudness switch, etc.

What you will need: an 8- or 16-bit slot (depending on the card's make and model) for the audio card. You will need to attach some sort of antenna for the card, which may or may not be included with the card. You will also need to install the software included with the card that's used to tune radio stations. Depending on the make and model of card used, you may also need a free IRQ, I/O base port address, or DMA channel.

Adding Sound to Your Notebook

Notebook and laptop users have been barking for at least business-quality sound capabilities, and the industry has responded with a type of device that plugs into a port on the back of a laptop or notebook. Fact is, these devices plug into any parallel port, regardless of the type of PC.

These devices look kind of like the modems that are plugged into the serial ports of portable PCs. They even have a speaker built into the device so you can hear WAVE files and embedded audio in both documents and electronic mail from other network users.

Business-quality, external audio devices sell for less than $200 on the street.

What you will need: an enabled parallel or serial port jack. You may also need to purchase batteries of some sort. As is often the case, you may also need a free IRQ, I/O base port address, or DMA channel.

Audio Input Devices

Depending on the ability of your particular sound card, you may be able to use a microphone or other audio input on your sound card. Some business-quality sound cards actually come with a microphone or telephone handset that can be used to record voices.

Check mail-order catalogs for microphones that are offered for use with sound cards, but keep this in mind: any high-impedance microphone will work well with any sound·card that will accept anything but an RJ11 (telephone) jack. Most microphones intended for a specific market underperform for the money when compared to a microphone intended for use by a performer or musician. It's not quite as bad as NASA's $25,000 toilet seat, but you get the point.

If you're recording your own voice because you like to listen to it, buy a mike at a music store with name brands like Shure or AKG. The quality will be much better and the mike will give you years of trouble-free service.

What you will need: a sound card (either business or CD-quality). The type of plug on the microphone or handset's cable must be the same type as the input or microphone jack on your sound card. If it's not, you may need to buy and additional plug-to-jack adapter. Your microphone (depending on the type) may also require batteries that may not be included.

CD ROM Upgrades

Adding a CD-ROM drive (it's also called a *reader*) to your PC is an upgrade of great scope. It opens a whole new world of information: a CD-ROM drive will not only give you file-based information just as though it were a massive floppy disk, but it will play your audio CDs as well. The multifaceted design and multiple purposes of a CD-ROM help to justify the cost.

Simply put, CDs are cheap to manufacture and virtually impossible to damage. A CD costs a software vendor about $3.00. When we all have CD-ROM drives in our PCs, then the cost should be about half of that! A CD holds up to 600MB of data, compared to 1.44MB for high-density diskettes. It's the cost, capacity, and the virtual indestructibility of a CD that will deliver the promise of home-use software for less than $40, and business-use software for less than $100.

Any way you cut it, by investing less than $400, you can open a whole new world of information and usability by adding a CD-ROM drive. This particular upgrade is bound to be one of the most popular ones of the early nineties.

CD-ROM drives get cheaper and perform better all the time. When CD-ROM drives first gained popularity, they had an average access time of around 850 milliseconds. A technology barrier was later broken to allow access times of around 600 milliseconds—for the same price! The next major improvement was an average access time on the same brand names for the exact same street price.

At this time, the best CD-ROM drives (without controller cards) are selling for less than $500 on the street, with the least expensive selling for under $200.

How to Choose a CD-ROM Drive

Your first decision in choosing a CD-ROM drive is to decide whether or not you need a controller card to run it. Every CD-ROM drive requires a controller card, just like your floppy and hard drive. In the case of a CD-ROM drive, however, the controller card is the standard SCSI controller card—which is even more popular with hard drives (and also goes to prove how handy the SCSI controller can be).

If you're now using a SCSI hard drive or a sound card with a SCSI port, then you don't need a separate controller to run a CD-ROM drive. If you're not using a SCSI hard drive, or your system lacks a SCSI controller expansion card, you'll definitely need to install one. Fortunately, controllers come with most CD-ROM drives.

The other two things you need are an empty drive bay if you want to mount the CD-ROM internally, and the CD-ROM drive itself. If you don't have an extra drive bay, then you'll need to get an external CD-ROM.

Once you decide where your CD-ROM drive is to reside, then the considerations are as follows:

◆ If you already have a SCSI controller card installed, then be sure to buy a drive that uses a "true" SCSI controller. Some drive makers manufacture SCSI controllers that are not compatible with other maker's SCSI CD-ROM drives, requiring you to upgrade your controller when you upgrade your CD-ROM drive in the future.

◆ If a SCSI controller card isn't installed now, then you can either upgrade your entire system to SCSI at this time, or plan to use a controller that handles the CD-ROM drive exclusively. The first option is more expensive, but it is the best investment in the long run since you can buy the faster and higher-capacity hard drives that SCSI controllers support in addition to enjoying a CD-ROM drive. If cost isn't an issue, then go the upgrade-to-SCSI route. If you're out for a bargain, then just get a SCSI card that controls the CD-ROM drive only.

If your PC has a SCSI card installed now, you don't need another interface card for a CD-ROM drive; however, you'll have to make sure that the drive you buy will run with the SCSI interface card you now own. Some drives need their own proprietary interface cards (mentioned earlier) regardless of your system's configuration. Welcome to the wacky world of DOS incompatibilities.

The External CD-ROM Drive To use an external CD-ROM drive, you'll need to buy a drive/controller combination. This combo will come with a controller, a cable, and a drive mounted inside its own case. It will cost about $50–100 more because of the additional circuitry, power supply, and the extra packaging required for external drives.

Remember, if you're out of horizontal drive bays, you must buy an external drive. The inner workings of a CD-ROM drive (things like motors and their related moving parts) are designed to spin disks in a horizontal fashion. Both hard drives and CD-ROM drives are designed to be mounted in a horizontal bay for the same reasons.

The Internal CD-ROM Drive Intalling an internal CD-ROM drive can be simple—very much like installing another floppy drive. Essentially, you take the faceplate off an empty half-height 5¼" drive bay and plunk your

CD-ROM drive into it. Then you connect the drive's cable to the drive's controller and install a device driver in your two boot files and away you go.

What you'll need: a drive bay that opens to the outside of the PC. (Some drive bays are "internal" for hard drives only; CD-ROM drives, like floppy drives, need to see the outside world so you can change disks. Refer to Chapter 8 for additional drive bay information.) Virtually all CD-ROM drives fit snugly into a half-height, $5\frac{1}{4}$" drive bay, just like a floppy drive.

The SCSI Controller Some CD-ROM drives require an interface card made only by the drive's manufacturer. If the drive maker *could* say the drive were SCSI compatible, they probably *would!* Many drive makers don't tell you this on the outside of the box! Double-check before you buy, and if you can't, don't buy that drive!

Performance and Cost Issues Now that you know what you want regarding internal versus external, and SCSI versus proprietary, you'll have to choose a drive based on performance and cost issues. CD-ROM drives fall into two general categories: double-spin and conventional single-spin drives.

Double-spin drives are the most expensive. These drives usually offer an average access time of 200–300ms *or faster* (faster means a smaller number in milliseconds). This access time is fast compared to most other CD-ROM drives, but they're still slower than your floppy drives. Double-spin drives achieve these faster access times by spinning the CD twice as fast as most other CD-ROM drives. The drives transfer data at a rate of 300K per second. Non-double-spin (conventional) drives transfer data at only around 150K per second. You'll also find that double-spin drives such as those made by NEC can also sport a 256K cache on the CD-ROM drive itself. This cache helps the drive transfer data more smoothly and reduces the number of times that you may have to access the CD-ROM drive. On CD-ROM drives as well as hard drives, the bigger the cache, the better the drive will perform for you.

As a general rule of thumb, cheap CD-ROM drives are slow and have proprietary interface cards bundled with them (though some are sold separately). If the drive will only run with the drive maker's expansion card, then you know that you can't use a standard SCSI drive controller to run that CD-ROM drive.

Expensive CD-ROM drives are SCSI-run, name-brand, and fast. Your question should be, "How bad do I want a CD-ROM drive?" Only if you're desperate and cash is low should you opt for the cheap CD-ROM drive. While I won't go out on a limb and recommend the most expensive model, the cheaper ones will do you a disservice; they'll be too slow to handle the demanding needs of animation and audio with the multimedia software of the future. Don't sell yourself short if you can avoid it.

Other Drive Differences The CD is loaded into the CD-ROM drive in two distinctly different ways. One way, and the most popular, is to place the CD into a *caddie* that acts as an interface between the CD and the drive. You then load the caddie into the slot in the front of the drive. Proponents of the caddie approach claim that if you use a caddie, the CD will last longer and is less likely to be improperly handled and damaged by the drive itself.

The second method of loading a CD is without a caddie device. Some drives accept CDs just the same way many audio CD players do. You press a button to make the drive slide out of the PC, then you open a door to drop your CD onto a spindle—sort of like playing a 45 RPM record.

Adding a CD-ROM Drive

The general instructions for installing any type of disk drive in your system are in Chapter 8. You can treat your CD-ROM drive just as you would a floppy-disk drive. The following are some pointers for installing CD-ROM drives.

◆ Never install a CD-ROM drive in a vertical (up-down) drive bay. CD-ROM drives spin their CDs at very high speeds. If you mount a drive vertically and it runs a lot, it will wear out one side of the spindle's drive bearings, dramatically shortening the life of your CD-ROM drive.

◆ Choose a caddie-based loading system if the drive is around airborne materials. Dust and grime will kill a CD-ROM drive faster than anything else except a direct strike by lightning!

The Multimedia PC

◆ Don't expose CDs or a CD-ROM drive to direct sunlight. Even the seemingly indestructible CD can melt or warp if it gets too hot! A CD damaged by heat may also damage a CD-ROM drive.

◆ Some CD-ROM drive makers claim that their drives are SCSI, but the drive will only work on their own proprietary "SCSI" standard.

Installing the Interface Card

IRQs or *interrupts* are a little like railroad tracks—they can only accept one train at one time. If you assign more than one train (expansion card) to a set of tracks (IRQ or *interrupt*), you're bound to witness a collision and system crash sooner or later.

Once you've installed the CD-ROM drive unit and interface card, you'll want to configure the controller card so that your new CD-ROM drive doesn't conflict with other hardware in your computer. There are three possible settings to make on a CD-ROM's controller card:

◆ The Interrupt (IRQ) setting

◆ The Base Port or I/O setting

◆ The DMA setting

Each of these settings may be selectable on your CD-ROM's controller card. Many modern controller cards for CD-ROM drives allow you to change these settings with software.

The Interrupt (IRQ) Setting You must give the CD-ROM drive access to the microprocessor whenever it needs that access. You do that by opening a direct channel to the CPU. On a PC, that channel is called an IRQ (also referred to as an *interrupt*).

On the average PC, you can assign one of several interrupts to a device. Your hard drive controller is using one interrupt, and your modem is using another. Your CD-ROM drive will also need an interrupt for its own use.

The Base Port Address or I/O Setting The base port address, or I/O setting, works with your computer's memory. Hardware devices use dedicated areas in your computer's RAM in which to work. On an IBM compatible computer, a base port address is a location in memory. The locations are usually given as combinations of letters and numbers (hexadecimal), such as C000 or B280. Without getting into a lot of malarkey about the PC's memory addressing system, let's just say that only one piece of hardware can work with the same piece of memory at any one time.

The DMA Setting   If your CD-ROM drive uses DMA channels, you'll need to assign an unused set of DMA channels to the drive's controller if you expect to use the drive for playing audio CDs. DMA or Direct Memory Access allows your hardware to move data directly to and from your system's main memory. This is the fastest and best way to set your CD-ROM drive for playing audio CDs.

Changing These Settings   If your CD-ROM drive works OK with the factory settings, you won't have to mess around with this stuff at all! If your CD-ROM drive doesn't work right (and you've physically installed the hardware according to the manuals), you probably have a hardware conflict of some kind. That means that you'll need change one of these settings to resolve it.

When you set an expansion card for IRQ, DMA, or I/O base address, write down your settings in the device's manual for future reference. Then when you install another piece of hardware that needs these settings made, you'll know what you've already doled out!

Visual Upgrades

For a few hundred pesos you can view and then save your home movies to files on your hard drive. You can watch CNN in a window while you work with Word for Windows. You can even return to your idle computer to see your screen savers displaying TV-quality, moving images instead of those boring old bitmaps.

As the computer industry further develops the technology to more efficiently compress images and sounds, we're finally able to record movie clips as files on our home PCs—and they're just a few megabytes in size. CD-ROM drives allow us to store up to 600MB of information on a single disk. There's a whole new generation of video controller cards that can capture part of a movie being recorded on your video cassette camera and save the images on your hard drive. You can then edit those images with special software at your leisure to create family albums made up of video

photography. There are a lot of exciting things that you can do with your PC when it comes to video, audio, and the artful combination of the two.

If you want to play or work with video or audio, you'll need to invest in some pretty specific hardware and software. Choosing just which hardware and software you'll need depends on want you want to do with it. Here are just a few of the upgrades you can perform and the hardware you'll need to work with:

◆ **Photo CD**   In a nutshell, Eastman Kodak has found a way to copy your still photographs to a CD, so you can display them on your computer's monitor. The process works like this: you use your usual camera and take pictures. Process your film at a photo lab, and then ask the photo lab to copy your processed film onto a special CD. Next, you take your CD home, and play the CD on your internal or external *Photo CD-compliant* CD drive. Photo-CD is a registered trademark of Eastman Kodak.

What you will need: a camera that uses 35mm film, access to any film processing service, access to a Photo-CD processing service, a Kodak Photo CD-compatible CD drive (a drive that can recognize Kodak's Photo CD format), and Kodak's Access viewing software.

◆ **Full-Motion Video**   The level of video *quality* you see when you watch a movie is called 24-bit or photo-quality video. Up until recently, moving pictures haven't been practical on the PC because the amount of hard drive space needed and the speed at which these images must be played. The cost has been in the thousands of dollars until 1992, and that cost has limited this type of video upgrade to just video professionals. In 1992, the cost of Full-Motion Video expansion cards dipped below the $500 mark. These cards can provide moving images that appear to be as clear and colorful as they do on your TV. These Full-Motion Video cards cost around $300.

What you will need: a video expansion card that will allow you to capture and control moving pictures from a VCR, laser disk player, or other NTSC video source (your cable TV is an NTSC source). You'll need a VCR, laser disk player, video camera, or cable TV tuner as well as a cable to run between one of these devices and the input jack on your full-motion video expansion card. You'll need DOS 3.0 if you intend to run this card using just DOS, and Windows 3.1 if you intend to use this expansion card with Windows software. Most full-motion video cards require a computer with an ISA (AT) bus, 386DX processor, 4MB of RAM, a VGA video controller that has a feature connector, and a free 16-bit slot. You'll need software designed to work with video signals during both record and playback, using either Windows or DOS (you need to specify one of the two when you buy). Full-motion video cards may also require you to install a device driver in your CONFIG.SYS file, if you intend to use the card without Windows. If you're using Windows, you may need to install a video driver with Windows' Control Panel utility. Full-motion video cards selling for less than $500 may not have audio and video outputs, requiring you to have a sound card installed in your PC in order to hear the sound in your movies.

◆ **Video Still Cameras** This technology has been around for some time. There are really two levels. High-quality cameras used by professionals take color images and transfer them to computers for further processing. These cameras cost several thousands of dollars and this cost places them in the professional marketplace, so we'll skip them in this book. The message here is that video still cameras that take color images cost thousands, while cameras that capture gray-quality (black-and-white) images cost hundreds.

The video still cameras, which are designed for use by us PC people, store a gray-quality copy of the image you see in the camera's viewfinder in the camera's RAM chips. Simply put, you point this camera at your subject, press the button and a copy of what you saw through the camera's viewer is stored in the video still camera's RAM.

You can store up to 32 images in these cameras at one time. When you're ready to copy those images to your PC, you connect the camera to your PC's serial port with the special cable provided with the camera. You then use the software that came with the camera to download and view the captured images on your PC. If you want to save any of the images you're viewing, you can save them a hard drive or floppy disk in TIFF, PCX, BMP, or EPS file formats.

The cameras come with a rechargeable battery, a battery charger, a built-in flash, a camera stand, and a neutral-density filter for the camera's lens. These cameras can be bought for about $400 to $700 on the street. You can buy additional lenses for these cameras from the camera's manufacturers. So much for dragging your film down to the drugstore!

What You Will Need: a video still camera, a cable to download your captured images to your PC, and software to receive/manage the images once they're in your PC (these three items usually come as a package). Your PC must have a 286 (or higher) processor, at least 1MB of RAM (2MB recommended), Microsoft Windows 3.0 and MS-DOS 3.1 (or higher on both), and a VGA video card/monitor. You'll also need a free serial port on your PC to accept the cable that's used to download the images from your camera to your PC.

◆ **TV-to-PC** There are half-card products out there that will hook-up to your current video card via the feature connector and display TV in a window—either in DOS appendices or in the world of Windows. You simply plug in the cable that runs between the video card and the TV card, then unplug your monitor from your VGA card and plug it into the TV card instead. You then install the TV card's software and watch TV, change channels, and adjust the volume and tone using the software provided with the card. TV-to-PC cards are currently selling for $200-$400 dollars on the street.

What you will need: an expansion card that will display TV on your computer's monitor. A VGA card with a feature connector and a VGA monitor are required. Your PC needs to be using an ISA bus with a free slot in order to accommodate most of these TV-to-PC cards. Your system needs to have at least 2MB of extended memory installed. DOS 3.1 for DOS users and Windows 3.0 for Windows are required. Most of these cards have a headphone output jack, which you can cable into an input on your sound card if you want to feed your multimedia PC with movie sound.

◆ **PC-to-TV** This hardware product runs any TV as though it were a PC monitor. Some of these products are sold in the form of internal expansion cards, taking an 8-bit or 16-bit system slot. Other PC-to-TV hardware products are sold as external products (little black boxes) intended to plug in between your TV and a VGA card's output jack. The more expensive products will display on both your computer's monitor and your TV at the same time. The cost of these products will vary, but swing from $300–$1500 on the street, depending on features.

What you will need: a VGA graphics card. An 8- or 16-bit slot will be required if the PC-to-TV hardware product is housed inside your PC. If the PC-to-TV hardware product is kept outside your PC, it will use your VGA graphics adapter's output jack. You'll need a TV that's defined by the maker as a TV/monitor combination (that means that the TV has video and audio inputs) with an S-VHS cable input. A 75 ohm cable or an RCA cable will be needed (and may be included with the product) to run between the TV and the PC-to-TV hardware. You may need a special cable adapter to couple your 75 ohm cable to your PC-to-TV card, though this item is normally included with the internal expansion card-type of PC-to-TV hardware product. Some PC-to-TV expansion products also require your VGA graphics card to have a pass-through feature connector. Check the manual for your VGA card to determine if the card has this connector in the event it's required by the internal-type of PC-to-TV expansion card.

About Device Drivers

A CD-ROM drive relies on a controller and a device driver to run it. DOS was never intended to run CD-ROM drives because CDs have more sectors on the disk than DOS can handle. So the solution is a device driver that pinch-hits between DOS and the CD-ROM drive so that DOS thinks that it's just another disk drive in your system.

A second device driver must also be installed so that your CD-ROM drive will play audio CDs. The software that comes with your CD-ROM drive will install both a CD-ROM driver program and a driver that will allow audio to be sent by your drive to your PC.

These drivers are called *multimedia extensions*. One is installed in your CONFIG.SYS and one is installed in your AUTOEXEC.BAT file. Be sure to use the latest and greatest versions of these files at your disposal. MS-DOS and Windows both come with updated versions of these two files: MTMCDD.SYS and MSCDEX.EXE. MTMCDD.SYS makes the drive work like any other DOS drive and MSCDEX.EXE allows you to hear audio CDs.

Network Considerations

If you're on a network and you want to use a shared CD-ROM drive instead of one installed in your own PC, you need to consider the following.

◆ You can't use someone else's CD-ROM drive if their PC isn't turned on.

◆ If you intend to share your CD-ROM drive with others on your network, the statement that loads the multimedia extensions must appear *after* the statements that load your network drivers in your AUTOEXEC.BAT file. This is true of both Windows for Workgroups and LANtastic for DOS (and Windows), as well as other popular networking software.

◆ If your network doesn't support the sharing of CD-ROM drives, there are new products available that can give you that ability without changing your network software. Have your network administrator dig up a software package that's designed to overcome the problem. These add-on software products are now advertised through all of the major channels, especially the catalog mail-order vendors such as Tiger, PC Connection, and Micro Warehouse, to name just a few.

◆ A few words on Windows NT: It's possible to buy a CD-ROM drive that NT can't recognize. If you intend to use a CD-ROM drive with NT as your operating system, make sure that both the CD-ROM drive and the drive's controller card are guaranteed "NT-compatible" before you buy. The good news is that you install a CD-ROM driver for your CD-ROM drive while NT is running. The process is similar to installing a Windows video driver—so you don't have to mess with CONFIG.SYS and AUTOEXEC.BAT files at all.

Multimedia Software Options for Your Computer

If you have the slot, the software, a VGA monitor, a little spare memory, and hard-drive capacity, you can work with multimedia on your PC. You can use multimedia software to create and edit demonstration materials or—why not be fun?—create works of art, mesmerizing cartoons, animate your old Super 8 movies, and let your creative juices flow using any of several visual and sound sources.

You may have a multimedia PC once you've upgraded to a CD-ROM drive, a sound card, and some audio speakers. However, to truly *create* in the world of multimedia, you might need to go one step further than using the simple editing software that's usually bundled with your sound card.

Here are a few suggestions on the general directions you can go in if you want to get creative with multimedia software:

◆ Videographer's software

◆ Authoring software

◆ Video editing software

◆ Music creation software

◆ Karaoke on CD-ROM

Videographer's Software

Videographer's software manipulates audio and video signals to create a single work in both audio/video. No longer limited to simply editing-in and editing-out, the Videographer software can combine virtually every available source of video and audio information into your creations.

What you will need: software designed to mix several video and audio inputs and outputs. A professional-quality full-motion video card (pro-quality full-motion video cards have outputs as well as inputs), a 16-bit sound card, a VGA graphics card (and monitor), and speakers that will accept output from your sound card. You'll also need DOS 3.0 or higher if you want to work in the DOS environment, or Windows 3.1 and DOS 4.1 or higher if you want to work within Windows. You'll also need at least 2MB of system RAM and a mouse.

Authoring Software

Authoring software is a class of software that is designed to help individuals or organizations create multimedia software applications, tutorials, and training aids using both audio and video. There are many products out there that give the multimedia author the ability to create interactive products.

These products start in the price range of around $300 to thousands of dollars, depending on the platform you're creating upon and the number and type of hardware devices with which you'll be working.

What you will need: software designed create multimedia software applications. A business-quality sound card is required. A VGA graphics card (and monitor), and speakers that will accept output from your sound card.

You'll also need DOS 3.0 or higher if you want to work in the DOS environment, or Windows 3.1 if you want to work within Windows. You'll also need at least 2MB of system RAM. A mouse may also be required. Depending on the type of audio and video sources used, you may need additional hardware and software.

Video Editing Software

These products allow users to edit the contents of an NTSC video tape while it's playing on a VCR. First, you play a tape on your VCR and capture individual images to your PC—either singly or in groups that appear to be in full-motion. The software part of the product allows you to organize these clips in any order you choose, and then save your work back to the same tape or another video tape. Video editing products go for less than $200 on the street.

What you will need: the products require you to use a VCR, a cable that runs from your VCR to your PC's serial port, and some software installed on your PC. Some video editing software products may require you to use a specific brand of VCR to use the software's more advanced features. A mouse may also be required. Some video editing software products offer software that runs with DOS, Windows 3.1, or both. Check the product's specific requirements before you order to get the right software for DOS or Windows.

Music Creation Software

Musicians have been able to create and record music with the Macintosh for some years now, but the multimedia capabilities of the latest version of Windows have provided a platform for a whole new group of music creation tools. Traditionally, music creation has been limited to using outboard synthesizers or keyboards that were hooked up to a computer via an interface known as MIDI (Musical Instrument Digital Interface).

The street cost of music authoring or creation software starts at around $400, and can be gauged based on the number of instruments and recording devices supported.

What you will need: a 16-bit sound card (to take full advantage of the potential sound quality), speakers (high-quality headphones are a popular substitution for speakers), and a VGA video card and monitor combination. If you want to use outboard musical instruments, additional hardware and cabling may be required to connect MIDI musical instruments to your sound card. You'll also need a recording device (like a tape deck) if the music creation software of your choice doesn't support recording music on your hard drive. As always, check on the DOS and/or Windows version requirements, and the memory and mouse requirements for the product you're thinking of buying. These last requirements can greatly vary between products.

Karaoke on CD-ROM

It had to happen. All would-be rock stars can now rehearse their shot at Karaoke stardom at home with your PC. It works like regular-old Karaoke.

You place the Karaoke CD into your PC's CD player, crank up the software, and select one of several tunes in the categories of rock, standard, country, pop, classic rock, and Motown, as well as songs from the '50s and '60s. You select one tune to play and then sing along into the supplied microphone as the voiceless music on CD plays through your PC's sound card and speakers. You can even buy an additional CD containing hundreds of additional songs. Somehow, I wouldn't expect these tunes to be the original renditions of the actual hits, but if you're a Karaoke fan with a multimedia PC, you'll probably have fun with this PC multimedia product.

What you will need: software to perform Karaoke on CD-ROM. A 16-bit sound card (to take full advantage of the potential sound quality), speakers (high-quality headphones are a popular substitution for speakers), and a VGA video card and monitor combination. You'll need an MPC-compliant CD-ROM drive. You may also need a microphone if it's not included with the Karaoke software on CD-ROM. Again, check on the DOS and/or Windows version requirements, and the memory and mouse requirements for the product you're thinking of buying.

Maintenance and Troubleshooting Tips

Keeping a PC in top notch condition requires knowledge and effort on your part. A lot of that knowledge will come from performing upgrades and getting a feel for the inside of your machine. No two PCs are alike—even if they're the generic varieties. So troubleshooting your own system well depends upon your familiarity with it.

This chapter is about maintenance and troubleshooting—recognizing problems and knowing what to do with them. But more important than that is preventing problems before they surface. On a PC, this involves fairly routine operations. Unfortunately, not everything that goes wrong with a computer can be explained in a few sentences. But if the problem can be narrowed down and evaluated, you will eventually find a solution.

Test Driving Equipment

One of the best troubleshooting techniques you can do is to run the equipment you upgrade or add to your PC! By this we mean to run it above and beyond the normal, routine use you'd give the equipment, but not as severe as a torture test.

Testing the Warranty

All PCs come with a *warranty*. The warranty states (generally) that if something goes wrong in a given duration after the date of purchase, the developer (or dealer) will fix or replace that something for a nominal charge.

The decision to buy a *service contract* or *extended warranty* is really up to you. But if you test the parts of your computer covered under the warranty as part of your basic troubleshooting, you'll probably never need to waste your money on a service contract.

The odds are fairly good that any marginal part inside the computer will go within the first two weeks of activity. So during that time, do the following.

Keep the PC Running 24 Hours a Day

Even if you're not using it, leave the computer on to keep the juice flowing through all the circuits. Once a day, turn the system off and on to check the power supply. At night, turn off the monitor—or better still, invest in a screen-saving program.

After Two Weeks, Stop Torturing the Computer

If parts were going to fail, they would have done so by now. A flaky RAM chip or suspect hard drive will show signs of stress under the two-week torture test. But odds are fairly good that you'll see anything questionable by the second day.

What Might Go Wrong?

After your initial torture test (which you should also do after a hardware upgrade), continue to use your PC as you normally would. But what might go wrong? Things do break. Things that worked only moments ago don't work now. What's high on the priority list?

Floppy Drives

Floppy drives fail because they have the most moving parts. They can also get knocked out of alignment just through everyday use. Since the front of the floppy drive is open, it's used as a vent by the power supply's fan to suck in air—which contains all kinds of nasties that can accumulate inside a floppy drive.

Old drives can be replaced by newer drives, often of higher capacity. (And the cost of a new floppy drive is well below that of a service contract.) Note that if your only floppy drive breaks, you'll have no way to back up the hard drive before the floppy replacement.

The Power Supply

Having a power supply pop can stop your heart. But rest assured, the PC will survive it. Power supplies go because there's too much drain being put on the system, or because of the many deaths that can be inflicted by the power line (surges, spikes, etc.).

When you're buying a surge protector, find one that advises you of its status. It's great to be able to tell if, while you're away from the PC, a surge has removed the security blanket normally provided by your surge protector. (Some products don't let you know they have saved your PC and been fried in the process, they just fail to save it the next time!)

The Hard Drive

Hard drives will and do fail after several years of use. The bearings wear out (they get louder) and sometimes they'll just stop altogether. When that happens, you'll need to replace the drive. (And you'd better have a recent backup of your data handy.)

Sometimes, all that's needed to "repair" a bad hard drive is a reformat— this can be a quick fix for a seemingly nonfunctional drive. Suspect sectors and read/write and seek errors, will start to accumulate on some drives. It may be a sign that the drive has the wrong interleave factor.

Expansion Cards and Devices

Expansion hardware must have the use of "channels" that move data to and from your system's memory and microprocessor. In the PC, there are many different ways to manage the movement of data.

One of the biggest problems caused by the installation of an expansion card (like a sound card, for example) is that the new addition conflicts with another piece of hardware already trying to use one of the same "channels". If two hardware devices (like a CD-ROM drive or sound card) try to use the same channels at the same time, they may work erratically or not at all.

There are three different "channels" that can cause a conflict of use between hardware devices. Each of these three possible scenarios for conflict should be checked if hardware or software fails to operate properly.

Interrupt Request Lines (IRQs) Of the three big PC killers, the IRQ conflict problem is the most common. An IRQ (Interrupt Request Line) is a wiring connection from your motherboard's slots to your CPU. On an ISA computer there are sixteen of them. When you plug an expansion board into a slot, it needs to talk to the CPU. The only way a CPU can tell if an expansion card needs to talk to the CPU is when the plugged-in expansion card issues an interrupt to get the CPU's attention. Most expansion cards use an IRQ to make that communication.

If more than one hardware device is set up to use wiring with the same addresses (or IRQs) the CPU won't know who it's supposed to be talking to, and the result can be a seemingly faulty hardware device or even a system crash.

PCs have 16 interrupt "channels" for use by hardware. Some of them are dedicated to running the motherboard, some are dedicated for floppy and hard drives, and some are left available for use by expansion hardware. If you have a mouse, you are probably using an IRQ to run that mouse. Most mice use COM1 or COM2. Depending on your own particular hardware setup, COM1 is probably using IRQ4 and COM2 is most likely using IRQ3.

There's a simple way to figure out which IRQs are available for use by expansion devices. If you've added a piece of hardware that uses an IRQ and something has gone wrong, you should first turn to Microsoft's *MSD.EXE* software tool to find the culprit.

MSD (short for Microsoft Diagnostics) comes with MS-DOS 5.0 (and higher) and Microsoft Windows 3.1 (and higher). It's a software program that looks at your computer and tells you what it finds. It checks your memory, tells you what's inside that big box of yours, and it also tells you something about what your computer is doing. We ran MSD on our computer and told it to check-out the IRQs. The results are shown in Table 15.1.

The IRQ number is shown in the far-left column. The lowest memory address being used by each hardware device is given in the second column. The third column provides a description of what MSD found "hooked-up" via each of your computer's interrupts. The fourth column shows whether MSD found a device using the IRQ.

Here's a breakdown of what MSD learned about one of our computers:

◆ The computer is using IRQ0 for its own internal functions.

◆ IRQ1 is being used by the keyboard to send letters and numbers to the CPU.

TABLE 15.1:   What MSD Had to Say about Our Sample System

IRQ	ADDRESS	DESCRIPTION	DETECTED
0	334D:0000	Timer Click	Yes
1	2BA4:185A	Keyboard	Yes
2	0BD0:0057	Second 8259A	Yes
3	0BD0:006F	COM2: COM4:	COM2:
4	0BD0:0087	COM1: COM3:	COM1:
5	0BD0:009F	LPT2:	No
6	0BD0:00B7	Floppy Disk	Yes
7	0070:06F4	LPT1:	Yes
8	0BD0:0052	Real-Time Clock	Yes
9	F000:EECF	Redirected IRQ2	Yes
10	0BD0:00CF	(Reserved)	
11	0BD0:00E7	(Reserved)	
12	0BD0:00FF	(Reserved)	
13	F000:EED8	Math Coprocessor	Yes
14	0BD0:0117	Fixed Disk	Yes
15	F000:FF53	(Reserved)	

◆ IRQ2 is being used by the microchip on the motherboard that handles the transfer of data to COM ports. The COM ports are being used by the modem and mouse.

◆ IRQ3 is being used by either COM2 or COM4 (only one COM port can be used at any one time on any IRQ). In this case, the modem is using COM2 and IRQ3.

◆ IRQ4 is normally used by either COM1 or COM3. In this system the mouse is hooked-up to COM1, so it's using IRQ4.

◆ Our computer has two parallel ports most commonly used by printers. IRQ5 is normally used by a printer that's connected to LPT2. We're using LPT1 (and its own IRQ) for the printer, so we've told the CD-ROM drive it can use LPT2 and IRQ5.

◆ IRQ6 is being used to manage the floppy-disk controller and floppy-disk drives.

◆ IRQ7 is dedicated for use with the printer using the LPT1 parallel port. Since parallel ports move data a lot faster than serial ports can, we use parallel ports for printing whenever possible.

◆ IRQ8 is being used to keep this computer apprised of the time and date supplied by the system's real-time clock.

◆ IRQ9 is being used by this computer for its own internal purposes, just like IRQ2.

◆ IRQ10 is reserved. That means that you can use it to run an optional piece of hardware. We're using IRQ10 to run a network card. (Most network cards come configured for use with IRQ10, by the way.)

◆ IRQs 11 and 12 are also "reserved". When MSD says an IRQ is re-served, it really means that it is OK to use that IRQ to run an expan-sion device, and that your computer does not need for its own operation. We're not using IRQ 11 on this machine for anything right now.

◆ IRQs 13 and 14 are used in this system to run a math coprocessor and hard drive. We can't set any other cards to use these IRQs or we may have problems computing or using the hard drive.

◆ IRQ15 is normally reserved (available). We're using IRQ15 on this computer to run a 16-bit sound card, so we'd better not try to hand it out to any other hardware device.

That's the line-up on this computer. When you look at the list of information provided by MSD and our assessment of it, you have to come to two conclusions:

◆ Yes, we're using all of the IRQs except 11 and 12.

◆ MSD can't tell exactly what kind of device is using some of the IRQs. It just tells us that they're reserved (or available) and maybe it will sense and report some piece of hardware using that IRQ (that last column of YESs).

Take another look at that list. MSD can't tell us if IRQs 10, 11, 12, and 15 are in use at all, let alone assigned to a piece of hardware! That's because we are using an ISA computer for this example, and ISA computers aren't set up to identify the cards plugged into the slots. EISA and MCA motherboards and expansion cards are set up so that a special software program can learn what the card's settings are without taking the case off your computer.

Since MSD can't tell you if you've got a card plugged into a slot and using a certain IRQ, it's up to you to keep track of which IRQs are in use by your expansion cards and devices. Even though MSD seems like a bit of a "load" at this point, it does tell you which IRQs are definitely not available. You need to figure out which of the available ones are already in use, and which of the still available IRQs are usable by the card or device you want to add to your system. Then set the card, plug it into a slot, and away you go!

The best way to keep stock of your computer's IRQ usage is to keep some sort of log, or to mark down each IRQ used on the outside of each card. The outside of the card is the part you can see when you look at the back of the computer.

Direct Memory Access lines (DMA) The *direct memory access* (DMA) line is another kind of channel used by your computer and your expansion cards or devices. If your expansion card is up to the task, it may use a DMA channel to send data to and from your system's memory. CD-ROM drives, sound cards, and other devices that move audio and video will often use DMA channels.

Take a look at the documentation for your motherboard. It will probably tell you that you have seven DMA channels that can be assigned (used) by

any hardware devices. Check your other cards to learn if they're already using any DMA channels and avoid using any that are already assigned.

If you make a mistake and assign a DMA channel to two devices, your new device may work erratically or not at all. A typical problem on most ISA computers is in the assignment of a DMA channel to a sound card and separate CD-ROM controller. If you try to use the same IRQ for a sound card and for a CD-ROM controller, your CD drive may start up when you play a Windows .WAV file prompted by a Windows system event. If you have this problem, change the DMA setting on either card so these cards are not sharing the same DMA channel.

A good general rule of thumb is this: *If an expansion card or device will use the higher DMAs (4, 5, 6, and 7), go ahead and assign the DMAs from seven on down as you need them for expansion cards or devices.* Since some cards will use only DMA channels 1, 2, or 3, it's best to use those higher DMA channels first (if possible) in order to leave the lower ones free for future use.

Base Port or I/O Base Addresses Another problem people have when installing a new expansion card or other device is with the *base port* or *I/O base address*. An I/O base address is simply the portion of your system's memory (located geographically with the actual address) that is the lowest part of the memory used by the expansion card or device.

Since the type of card or device determines how many settings you are allowed to make, you can't expect to find all three of these setting types on any single card or device. Some cards simply take the I/O address by default, and you can't change the address. These cards are the toughest to troubleshoot.

Most expansion cards or devices require you to select an I/O base port address and then set hardware switches and pin blocks or change these settings with the card's configuration software. You normally set the base port address when you install the card, but you might need to change the address if an installed card conflicts with a new hardware addition.

Follow these steps to properly set the I/O address on a new expansion card or device:

1. Read the manual. Check the card or device's manual to determine if the card has a configurable I/O address. (If it doesn't, don't sweat it any further. It's not an issue).

2. Use the default setting. If the card or device's I/O address has been set by the factory, don't change it before you install the card or device. The card's manufacturer will have done some of your homework in setting the I/O base port address for you, so if it ain't broke...don't fix it!

3. Check your own records. If you're one of those folks who write the I/O base port address on the outside of each expansion card, check the currently-taken I/O base port addresses against the factory setting for your new card or device. Don't use an address that's already taken by an installed card for your new card.

4. Finish installing the hardware. Follow the other installation instructions provided by the manufacturer of the card or device.

5. Perform any post-installation procedures. Some hardware products require you to software-select an I/O base port address after installation. If they offer a default I/O address for you to use, take them up on it. If they don't and require you to choose from a list of I/O addresses that your hardware can use, choose the first one on the list and then use the card or device to make sure your selection is OK.

If your newly installed card or device works erratically, try selecting a different I/O base port address once you have made sure that the problem is not caused by an IRQ or DMA conflict.

It's very easy and human to want to try to race through a troubleshooting session to get it over with sooner! Most people who have problems with newly installed hardware have simply failed to set the hardware switches correctly because they've rushed that part of the installation process.

 Don't make any changes at all until you've verified that you've done the switch set-up work correctly. And by all means, don't make more than one setting change of any type until you've taken the steps to find out if that single change did the trick!

Identifying Problems

Knowing how to deal with a problem is only half the battle. More important is being able to recognize that a problem exists, and locate the source.

This section will assist you in doing that. Here are some rules of the road that will help you track down nasty problems that may occur with your hardware. But first, here are some problem prevention tips you should try.

Keep Food, Drink, and Smoke Away from the PC

Food naturally goes with a PC. But while most of it will end up in your mouth, a few bits will always fall into the keyboard. (Of course, dust, lint, and hair also find their way into the keyboard.)

Drinking and computing don't mix. Spilling a soft drink into a keyboard is a common faux pas. If you power off the PC right after that, the keyboard will probably dry up and continue to work. But it may be sticky. This can all be avoided, of course, if you keep drinks away from the PC.

Use the POST

That boring memory test (the noticeable pause when your PC boots up) is important. It's the *POST*, your computer's Power-On Self Test. And it's one of the first clues you'll have that something's amiss in the PC. Generally you will get a message to the effect that the POST has failed, and you go from there.

Sometimes the failure of items unrelated to memory will throw you. For example, your AT's battery going out at the same time you do a RAM upgrade could really give you a heart attack. Or you may have unplugged your video adapter to install a hard drive and then forgotten to re-install it before you powered on the PC. These are common occurrences. So consider everything before you bail out to the PC Doctor for help.

When you get a POST error, or if you smell trouble-a- brewin', take a few moments to panic. (Personally, I become frustrated—but never depressed.) Remind yourself that whatever has happened isn't your fault. Then check through the items listed in the next two sections.

External

When something goes wrong, start by checking over the following external items on your PC.

The Power Cable Is the computer plugged in? Is the cord plugged into both the wall and the PC? It's funny how many people will remember to plug the cord into the wall socket or power strip, but forget to stick the other end into the PC. (Funny, that is, when it happens to someone else.)

The Power Switch Is the power switch on? Some people run their PCs from power strips or devices that have master switches. If you were extra careful and turned off the master switch in addition to the PC's power switch, re-check the PC's power switch.

Missing Pieces Always check for anything missing. This includes absent cables, loose cables, a printer out of paper, a boot disk, and so on.

Software Configuration Some upgrade items need to be configured via software before you use them. A new hard drive must be formatted; drivers must be installed in CONFIG.SYS; SETUP programs need to be run; and so on.

Check the Display Make sure the brightness and contrast are properly set on the display. Make sure the monitor is plugged in and turned on. Also, keep in mind that not all software will work with a monochrome system. Often people believe their system has crashed when in fact they're trying to play a color game on a monochrome PC.

Internal

After your external inspection, look over the following items inside your PC.

DIP Switches and Jumpers Have they all been set properly? Were any accidentally set or reset? Refer to the installation manual to make sure all the switches are set properly for your PC's configuration.

Cables and Connectors Sometimes cables get pulled from drives or expansion cards when you replace the PC's lid. Sometimes you'll forget to re-attach a cable after an upgrade (this is very common). Check all the computer's cables and connectors—even if they're nowhere near the item upgraded.

Disk Drives A disk drive contains the only moving parts in your PC. As such, it will experience more wear and tear than anything else and will

probably be the first item to fail. If you experience disk errors on all of your disks, then your drive has probably failed.

Chips Some chips just love to wiggle out of their sockets. To undo this, first ground yourself, then press down gently on each chip using your thumb or forefingers. (This is called "reseating" the chips.)

The Battery The battery that keeps the clock alive in a PC/XT or backs up the CMOS RAM in an AT system will last only so long. Usually, they're good for four years or so. You'll either get a low battery message before it fails (if your PC is smart enough), or one day you'll turn on the computer and it will say that you don't have a hard drive. (The battery backed-up RAM is gone, and so is the hard drive definition.)

If you should happen to tap your battery with something metallic—like an expansion card or screwdriver—you'll discharge the battery and cause your PC to fail the next time you turn it on. It's a good idea to print out your CMOS info and keep it near the PC so you can re-enter those weird hard-drive parameters should your battery either be accidentally discharged or wear out.

When the battery goes, you should replace it with a same or equal sized battery. The best source for this is the dealer from whom you bought the computer. Some mail-order houses also offer battery replacements. Make sure you get one of the same size and type.

If the battery goes out, you can "bump start" the PC by rolling it down an incline and popping the clutch once it gets under way. (—Not!)

Clean and Reset Your Expansion Cards Sometimes the connectors on those expansion cards can have a build up of an oxidation by product if the card has been in service for some time. If you keep the case off your PC, dust and other junk can settle in your slots, preventing proper connections the next time you plug a card into a slot.

Evaluation

If you're still experiencing problems and need further help. Consider the following questions before you contact the experts. You might find that going over these questions will help you pin down the problem even further.

Is the Problem Consistent?

When does it happen? Is it that your hard drive comes on-line only after the PC has warmed up for five minutes? Or is the behavior more erratic? Does the modem always go off-line when someone else in the house picks up the line? Does the error occur just after running some piece of software?

Has the Problem Surfaced Only After a System Upgrade or Enhancement?

Are you getting odd-looking characters on the screen after having installed your mouse card? Did the printer stop working after you installed the new video card (a sign of printer contention)?

Can You Determine Whether the Problem Is Hardware or Software Related?

Remember that upgrading hardware requires a change in your software. If some program no longer works after an upgrade, you might want to re-install it. Or maybe you need to install a device driver in CONFIG.SYS to make the new hardware work. Sometimes, when you're in a rush to play with some new toy, you forget details like that.

Trace the Steps

Finally, you should trace all the steps up to the point you encounter the failure. This will help immensely in narrowing down the possible origins of the problem.

If there is a glitch between your keyboard and the PC, then the problem may be with the keyboard or a keyboard extension cord. Keyboards do fail

and can easily be replaced (or simply plugged back into the PC, if that's the problem!)

Also, remember to check your software. In the final section of this chapter, some software troubleshooting techniques are offered. Software can be picky and on a PC, it has to be. With all the different configurations, getting software to match your hardware is often more trying than upgrading a power supply.

Troubleshooting Tips

This section offers some good troubleshooting tips. Each part deals with a different aspect of your PC, discussing possible problems and suggesting solutions.

External Cables

Competition has forced the price of computer cables down. Where an official IBM printer cable (from IBM) used to cost $75, you can buy a generic one today for $20.

Aside from the regular cables, there are benefits to using non-standard cables and certain specialty cables, as discussed in the following sections.

Do-It Yourself Cables

The home-spun cable industry is really dead. Back in the old days, it paid to buy a coil of cable and some end connectors to build your own computer cables. But the price of manufactured cables is just too cheap today to make the effort worthwhile for anyone but the hobbyist.

There is, however, some benefit to making your own serial cables. Serial cables are seriously nonstandardized in that they don't all have a male connector on one end and a female connector on the other end. Some are male-male, some are female-female, and some are male-female. Add this to the confusion of the serial cable ports and connectors on the back of modems and other serial devices, and you can work up one heck of a headache.

One end of the serial cable goes to your PC. So when you buy a cable, make sure one end matches whatever style of port you have: male/female or 25-pin/9-pin. Make the other end of the cable a 25-pin male or female. The "gender" doesn't matter, but most serial devices use a 25-pin D-shell type connector.

If you need the opposite gender, you can buy a small connector. When you get the extra connector, attach it to the end of your serial cable. Position it back about 2" from the end of the cable. Locate line 1 on the cable (the line on the outside that's colored) and match it up with pin 1 on the connector. Then attach the connector to the cable.

You now have a serial cable that can accommodate either a male or female serial device.

 This connector procedure will work properly only with a ribbon cable. If you have any other type of cable, you can buy a short ribbon extension for it and then attach the dual connector. The only caveat with this setup is that you shouldn't plug a device into both connectors at once.

The Null Modem

A null modem—a well-known yet misunderstood doo-hickey—is a special type of serial cable, or a "black box," that allows two computers to communicate. A null modem is required with some printer setups.

What the null modem does is to swap a few lines in the serial cable. The lines usually swapped are 2 and 3, then 8 and 20. When these lines are reversed (twisted) by the null modem cable, two devices can communicate directly using their serial ports.

Hooking Two PCs Together

The art of hooking PCs together is officially called *networking*. But what's covered in this section is far more primitive than full-fledged networking. It's the direct communication between two PCs—even of different ilks—using a null modem cable.

You can do this to communicate between two computers, to transfer files, or just to goof around. For example, if you need to send files to a Macintosh or laptop computer and lack a network or disk transfer program, then the null modem cable is the only option left to you. It's crude, but it works.

To make the connection, both computers will need a serial port, a null modem cable or a null modem connector for both their serial cables, and communications software.

First, Fire Up the Communications Software on Both Machines
Set both systems' speeds (BPS or Baud rate) to the same value. Since it's a direct connection, faster speeds are possible. Try 19,200 or at least 9,600 BPS. Then set each system's data word format (word length, stop bits, parity) to the same value.

Second, Hook Each System into the Null Modem Cable
This is where you plug each end of the null modem cable into a serial port on each machine (one that both is enabled on your PC, and is the port you've configured your communications software to use).

Third, Type Away
What you type on one system will appear on the other's screen. At this point you can send files back and forth using the file sending routines supplied with the communications programs. Text files can be sent by just typing them on one computer and capturing them with the other. Binary, .COM, .EXE, or data files should be sent using a protocol transfer: Xmodem, Ymodem, Zmodem, Kermit, etc.

Floppy Drives

There are two subjects worth troubleshooting with floppy-disk drives.

Head-Cleaning Disks

The debate over using so-called *head-cleaning disks* to clean floppy-disk drives shall rage onward. On one side, you have the "use them often" group. On the other are those that say only a professional should clean your disk drives. After all, they are delicate mechanisms. An abrasive scrubbing by a head cleaning disk can sometimes do more damage than good.

The truth is that magnetic oxide can rub off a floppy disk and build up on your drive's read/write head. Dust, and especially cigarette smoke, can also accumulate there. A quick and easy way to remove it is via a head-cleaning disk. Sometimes this will resurrect a formerly dead drive back to life.

The danger with head-cleaning disks comes when people treat them like a magic charm: "The drive is acting flaky, I think I'll use the head-cleaning disk." This is a bad thing to do. If you feel you must use a head-cleaning disk, then do so perhaps once a year—if at all. Otherwise, always take your floppy drives in to be professionally serviced.

Bad Disks

Don't forget that disks have only so long to live. People wonder why the same disk they've been using for three years suddenly won't work. Nothing's forever. Blaming a drive for a bum disk is a common mistake.

If you use a disk every day, then you should also constantly back it up. Use DOS's DISKCOPY command to make an exact duplicate of that disk. (A disk used every day may last for about three months.)

Also, formatting low-density disks in a high-capacity drive is asking for trouble. Unless you specifically tell the FORMAT command to format the disks as low-capacity (with the /4 switch), they will be formatted as high-density and you can expect errors on your disks.

Hard Drives

For hard disk advice and troubleshooting, there are three considerations.

Back Up Your Hard Drive!

The best preventive maintenance you can do in your computer is to back up your hard drive. Period. I could go on and on with finger wagging and example citing, but you should know by now. Back up the hard drive!

The Low-Level Format Solution

Some problems with hard drives can be fixed with a simple reformat of the drive. To do this, follow these steps:

1. Back up the hard drive (if possible).
2. Use your drive's low-level formatting routine or your computer's SETUP program.
3. FDISK the drive.
4. Reboot.

5. Perform a high-level format using the DOS FORMAT command on each of the drive's partitions.

Additional information on this procedure is covered in Chapter 9. You should also check the drive's interleave factor. Sometimes setting the interleave factor too low on a slow drive will lead to drive failures as well as general sluggishness.

Before Moving

Before moving your computer, do the following.

1. Back up the hard drive (if possible).

2. Park the hard drive (if needed).

3. Insert cardboard floppies or old disks into the floppy drives.

Backing up is obvious. Parking the hard drive is necessary (on some hard drives) in case you drop or bump the computer in transit. And the cardboard or old disks in floppy drives will keep their heads from banging together as well.

 "Before moving" in this case means moving the PC from one table top to another, down the hall, or across the country. It's also a good idea to back up the hard drive before upgrading your PC.

Run a Disk Compaction Utility Often

Since I make a living with my PC, I notice when it slows down. It will slow down when files become *fragmented* or spread out across my hard drives, forcing my drives to use more time when looking-up and working with these files.

I run CHKDSK/F on each drive (or partition) at least once each week, then I run a disk compaction utility even if that utility tells me that the drive is not awfully fragmented. It keeps my hard disks performing at maximum capacity. On drives with Stacker, I run SDEFRAG even if Stacker tells me I don't need it. You'd be amazed how much of a difference attention to detail will make on hard drives! Besides if you do it often, it takes a lot less time to compact each drive!

DOS 6 comes with a licensed, scaled-down version of the Norton Utilities disk compaction program. Another good reason to upgrade to DOS 6!

Internals

Internally, there are five different areas you can check for routine maintenance or troubleshooting.

Upgrade the ROM

Sometimes your PC will become suddenly incompatible with components or software. It may not recognize VGA graphics. A new hard drive won't boot. Or you may have gotten a deal on an old, original IBM PC, only to find that can have but 576K of RAM in it. To solve those problems, upgrade your ROM.

Often, the upgrade won't do anything crucial to your PC's performance. But if one's available, you should consider ordering it.

Reseat Chips

If you're just poking around inside the CPU (with the power off, of course), you should check all chips on the motherboard and expansion card. Gently pushing them down with your thumb is called "reseating" the chips. Though chips jumping out of sockets isn't something that happens often, sometimes after a move you'll see a chip start to wiggle free. Just reseat it.

Check the Cables

Anytime you're mucking about inside the CPU, you should always do a quick check of your cables and connections. Like unplugging a computer and forgetting to plug it back in, a loose cable is one of those problems some people overlook all too often.

Check DIP Switches

When re-affirming that everything is properly set up in your PC, check your DIP switches to make sure they're set the way they should be.

Look for Cracked Solder

A major cause of component failure in a computer is cracked solder, due to the heat changes in a PC. If you start your PC on a cold morning then run it all day, it gets hot. Do the same thing five days a week and you're cooking and freezing your PC's solder. That causes it to crack over time, which causes whatever the solder is holding down to fail.

One way around this is to leave your computer on all the time.

Keyboard

The keyboard is an important peripheral, but one that is prone to cause problems (especially if you like to touch type and hate the PC's keyboard!). There are two suggestions I can provide to make working with your keyboard easier.

Replace the Key Caps

A great joke tossed around by the computer elite is the need for a keyboard to have an "Any" key. (A key with *Any* stenciled on top.) This would satisfy the great need that neophytes have for wanting to "Press any key to continue."

On the same vein, there are replacement key caps available. The new key caps can give your keyboard color, but most likely they'll display command words for use with some applications. For example, WordPerfect's commands are often put on replacement key caps. Some also offer the Lotus 1-2-3 command set.

Vacuum the Keyboard

Cleaning the crud from your keyboard is an important part of keyboard troubleshooting. A sticky key usually means that the key has something under it to which it's adhering. (It's probably a piece of a pizza roll you were eating late one night.)

Monitor

Monitors are often a source of problems, but the solutions can be quite simple. The biggest problem is the infamous blank screen. There are three things to check with your monitor to make sure it's working properly. A fourth section here also covers some software troubleshooting.

Check Cables

Is the monitor plugged in? Is it turned on? Are all the cables properly connected. Note that there may be several monitor-port-sized connectors on the back of your PC. Make sure you're connected to the proper one.

Check Brightness

Turning the brightness down on a monitor is a good way to save the picture tube from the perils of phosphor burn-in (where an image is permanently etched on the screen). Check the brightness before you assume the monitor is out.

Check DIP Switches/SETUP Program

Finally, check to make sure your system's DIP switches or SETUP program is properly configured for your type of monitor. This includes DIP switches on the display adapter card as well. Note that some older PC/XT systems have to be set for "no monitor" if they're using an EGA or VGA display.

Software

On the software side, you can try the following things when you're faced with a suspect monitor:

Tap a Key Sometimes a screen saving program has taken over and dimmed the monitor. Usually a tap on the keyboard will bring the image back.

Note that Most Games are in Color Most games use color graphics only. If you run them on a monochrome system—even one with a Hercules or monographics card—you probably won't see anything. Some simulation programs are available that allegedly translate color graphics into Hercules-compatible graphics (one such program is called SIMCGA). But these programs are unreliable solutions at best. If you want to play games, you should upgrade to a color system.

Power Supply

The power supply is probably the most hearty beast in your computer. Still, there are two items to note for troubleshooting and maintenance with a power supply.

Ventilation

One of the PC's worst enemies is heat buildup. That's why the power supply has a built-in fan and one of its jobs is to circulate air through the PC. However, you can help by positioning the PC in an open area. Don't obstruct the vents on the front of the system unit, and keep the back of the PC's exhaust fan a good 5" away from the wall.

Line Conditions

If you're distressed because you flipped the power switch and PC won't come on, don't immediately blame the power supply. You may be experiencing a brown out. Several other electronic appliances may not function either. Call the power company if you believe you're in a brownout just to be sure.

If not, check all your power cables and the power strip (if you have one). Otherwise the nasty finger of death does point at the power supply.

Printer

Troubleshooting and maintaining a printer can get quite involved. But most of the major items are covered in the following sections.

Printer Contention

Printers *contend* when two or more of them are hooked up to a PC, each assigned to the same printer port.

A PC can have up to three printer ports, LPT1 through LPT3. Each time you install another printer port, you must make sure it doesn't conflict with an existing port. If they do conflict, and say you have two LPT1s in your computer, then the end result is no LPT1. Since DOS can't arbitrarily decide which is the real printer, it gives you a "no printer" message. (The conflicting circuitry would result in nothing being printed in any event.)

Ribbon Replacement

The only routine maintenance you'll need to perform on your impact printer is the replacement of its *ribbon*. This sounds trivial, yet too many people let the ribbon deteriorate for no good reason. Ribbons, which are $10 at the most, are too cheap not to have a fresh one on hand.

In addition to ink, the ribbon also contains a special lubricant for the print head. Without that type of ribbon, or when the ribbon dries up, you could be causing excess wear on the print head.

Finally, with the advent of laser printers, dot-matrix printers need all the help they can get. A fresh ribbon in a dot matrix printer really does a lot for the output. As the ribbon gets older, the characters will regain their "dottiness," which leaves a lot to be desired when you're trying for impressive correspondence.

Toner Recharging

Just as dot-matrix printers have ribbons, laser printers have *toner cartridges*.

A toner cartridge is a black box you insert into your laser printer. It contains this nasty black (or whatever colored) dust that's used to create the image on paper. The dust, or toner, is transferred to a drum depending on how the printer's laser beam has charged the drum. Then the toner is heat-welded to the sheet of paper, and it comes out of the printer looking like ink on the page.

When the toner gets low, you can remove the toner cartridge, rock it from side to side (short ways—not from end to end), and then put it back in to get a few dozen more pages out of it. But when the "Toner Low" warning light comes on again, it's time to either replace or recharge the toner cartridge.

Toner recharging is a popular upstart business, thanks to the low prices, high quality, and popularity of computer laser printers. Basically some outfit will take your old cartridge and repack it with fresh toner. Included with the price is lubrication and maintenance of the toner cartridge. And best of all, the cost is less than half that of new cartridges (about $30)!

You can recharge a toner cartridge only so many times. Maybe once or twice, but that's it. The better recharging outfits will tag older cartridges so you won't make the mistake of resubmitting one too often.

Printer Diagnostics

Every printer has built-in diagnostics. On a primitive level, these will print characters in succession until you turn the printer's power off. More advanced diagnostics will print complex graphics and "dump" their character sets. For example, some laser printers will cough up a sheet detailing their graphics prowess as well as a list of their full complement of fonts.

What you should look for in the diagnostics is completely formed characters (and having a good ribbon helps). If you notice that a row of dots is missing, that means a pin is out in the print head. Sometimes this pin is one of the crucial lower pins that prints the *descenders* on characters. (Any letter that dips below the baseline of text is a descender; *Egypt* has three descenders: *g*, *y*, and *p*.)

Double Spacing

An occasional problem with dot-matrix printers is that of *double spacing*. This can be rectified by checking the single DIP switch that determines whether the printer is to supply the line feed character or whether that character is sent from the computer, and switching it to the correct setting.

Cleaning the Printer

Since printers deal with ink (or worse, toner), they'll get grungy before anything else in your PC. Even your fingers will get inky after you change a ribbon. To avoid that you can wear plastic gloves while changing ribbons. Or you can just use some of those "moist towelettes" (we call them "Wipe–Dipes") to clean your fingers.

As far as printer internals go, nothing helps keep the printer clean like blowing through it with a can of air. Paper particles and dust accumulate in a printer very rapidly. You can pick up some of the dust with a keyboard vacuum.

Software

Finally, there are two things you should note about software when you troubleshoot a PC.

Software Is Buggy

Why is it when something goes wrong on a computer, people always blame themselves? No one stops to think that the program may not be working because it just can't do the job.

If you have problems with your software, you have a number of choices. The first is to call the developer's support line. You paid for the support when you bought the software, so you might as well use it.

The second source of support is your local dealer. Note the order here: developer and then dealer. Don't let the developer shuffle you off to the dealer. if they do, return the software and get your money back. Buy something else that works.

The final source of support is from local organizations known as *computer user groups*. These are usually meetings where computer owners get together and offer each other mutual support. Listings for user groups are often provided by local computer dealers, computer magazines, or sometimes local papers.

Manuals Are Bad

Everyone loves to complain about computer manuals, though complaining about them seems to be more popular than reading them. Manuals have a lot of good information in them. But the problems with computer software manuals are many. Consider the following.

Software Manuals Are Written before the Software Is Finished
Often the manual is completed (and *must* be completed) before the software is done. This means information in the manual might not be completely accurate.

Manuals Are Limited in Their Size The limit in size of a computer manual is based on packaging design. Packaging design is based on the size of the shelves at your local Egghead discount software store. Software boxes can be only so big (and this actually depends on the software

company's clout). The manual can take up so only much of that space, hence you often get a skimpy manual.

Manuals Are Written Offhandedly Usually the manual writer is directly on the software development staff. Sometimes he or she is the software project manager, who devotes as little of his or her time as possible to writing the manual.

Manuals Are Written by Those Intimate with the Program Since someone on "The Team" is writing the manual, he or she knows the program inside out. But you don't. Those details the manual author assumes "everyone" knows are lost when the manual's author starts describing things. (In a computer manual we have that was written in 1981, the description of the Control-Q command was: "The function of this command is obvious." —That was it!)

Manuals Are for Reference With the abundance of books written on computer software, manual writers will sometimes attempt to provide a reference only. They'll rely upon outside, professional writers to provide tutorials and decipher the program's intricacies in trade computer books.

Even still, some books on software are written before the software is released. This gives the publisher the advantage of having "The First Book on X" out there, but it usually means the book isn't accurate. The best books on software come out months after the software has been released. Only then will an author be intimate enough with a program to tell you how it works in the best way.

Bad Computer Manual Syndrome Sad but true: The long-time acceptance of mediocre computer manuals means we'll probably never see any improvement. But occasionally an exceptional manual is produced, so don't discount them all because it's popular to do so. You may stumble across a very good manual any day now.

Adios

That's about it! If you've actually read into this book far enough to find this good-bye section, then you deserve kudos for your interest and effort. All joking aside, if you got this far, you'll probably have great luck upgrading your PC because you've simply got the panache to go after the something new and unfamiliar—and that's the stuff of pioneers of any era!

Thanks for thinking of us (in buying the book). We're flattered that you found the book useful enough to purchase. As a last gasp, we promise to keep this book updated in subsequent printings. With the changes occuring in our world of PCs, it takes a great deal of time and effort to make sure that a book like this (that covers so much) is up-to-date.

Old PC upgrade books will provide you with the best of times and the worst of times. Some hardware devices (like floppy drives) become so standardized that they are permanently etched into any upgrade book of the present and the future. Other devices—like the 3270 emulator expansion board (a formerly popular PC upgrade option in the '80s)—are doomed to disappear as though the fell into the tar pits.

It's not very sensible to keep an old upgrade book around, because you're missing out on what's new and improved! Obsolescence means change, and PC upgrade books like this one are always being upgraded themselves.

It seems only fair.

Diagnostic Error Codes

This appendix contains three sections, each of which contains a list of specific types of POST errors your PC may produce.

The lists have been compiled from a number of sources. There is no indication as to which types of PCs produce these errors, or whether your own computer will produce them at all. Most are standard POST errors on the original PC, PC/AT, and PS/2 systems.

Beeping Errors

The PC will and should beep once before it attempts to load DOS from disk. Anything other than that indicates a problem.

The beeping error codes are used to detect problems with the power supply, motherboard, and video system. The POST checks those three systems first to make sure everything's okay. Any later POST errors will be displayed on the screen, but if the screen doesn't work, all the computer can do to alert you is beep.

Beep Pattern	Device at Fault
No beep	Power supply, Motherboard bad
Unremitting beep	Power supply bad
Short, repetitive beeps	Power supply bad
Long beep, short beep	Motherboard bad
Long beep, two short beeps	Video bad
Long beep, three short beeps	Video bad
Two short beeps	Video bad (with displayed error code)
Short beep, long beep	Video, disk drive, controller, cable bad
No beep	The speaker is bad or missing
Short beep	Everything's okay

General POST Error Codes

POST error codes fall into categories, with each category specific to some device being tested. The device is given a range of values, each of which are covered in the following list.

Error Code	Device that Failed the POST
2x	Power Supply
1xx	Motherboard
2xx	Memory (specific location listed)
3xx	Keyboard (specific key may be listed)
4xx	Monochrome video
5xx	Color (CGA) video
6xx	Floppy drive

Error Code	Device that Failed the POST
7xx	Math coprocessor
8xx	Not presently used
9xx	Printer adapter card
10xx	Secondary printer adapter card
11xx	Serial (RS-232) adapter card
12xx	Secondary serial adapter card
13xx	Game, A/D, controller card
14xx	IBM Graphics printer
15xx	SDLC communications
16xx	Not presently used
17xx	Hard drive
18xx	Expansion unit
19xx	Not presently used
20xx	Binary synchronous communications (BSC) adapter
21xx	Alternate BSC adapter
22xx	Cluster adapter
23xx	Not presently used
24xx	EGA video
25xx	Secondary EGA video
26xx	Not presently used
27xx	Not presently used
28xx	PC/XT 3278/79 emulation adapter
29xx	IBM color graphics printer
30xx	Network adapter
31xx	Secondary network adapter
32xx	Not presently used

Diagnostic Error Codes

Error Code	Device that Failed the POST
33xx	IBM compact printer
34xx	Not presently used
35xx	Not presently used
36xx	IEEE 488 adapter
37xx	Not presently used
38xx	Data acquisition adapter
39xx	PGA video
48xx	Internal modem
49xx	Alternate internal modem
71xx	Voice communications
73xx	3½" external floppy drive
74xx	VGA video
85xx	IBM expanded-memory adapter
86xx	PS/2 mouse ("pointing device")
89xx	Music feature card
100xx	PS/2 Multiprotocol adapter
104xx	PS/2 ESDI hard drive

If a device passes the POST test, then no value is reported.

A general failure is indicated by "01" replacing "xx" above. Other specific errors can be located in the section that follows this one.

 Your PC may not display these alpha-numeric codes—instead, it may display explicit messages indicating exactly what's wrong.

Detailed POST Error Code List

Again, this list is culled from a variety of sources. The POST will not necessarily produce these errors in such detail. Some of these error numbers result from running the tests that come on diagnostic disks.

Code	Description
101	Main system board failure
102	PC/XT ROM BIOS checksum error
103	PC/XT BASIC ROM checksum error
104	PC/XT interrupt controller error
105	PC/XT timer error
106	Main system board error
107	Main system board or math coprocessor or adapter card error
108	Main system board error
109	Direct memory access test error
121	Unexpected hardware interrupts occurred
131	IBM PC-1 Cassette wrap test failed
151	Battery-backed-up RAM or clock error
152	Main system board error
161	Battery/CMOS power error
162	Battery-backed-up RAM checksum error
163	Invalid date and time
164	Memory size incorrect (after adding extended memory)
165	System options not set (PS/2s)
166	MicroChannel adapter timeout
199	User-indicated configuration not correct

Diagnostic Error Codes

Code	Description
200	Memory passed all tests
201	Memory test failed
202	Memory error (address lines 0 to 15)
203	Memory error (address lines 16 to 23)
300	Keyboard passed all tests
301	Keyboard software reset failure, or stuck key
302	User-indicated error from the keyboard test
303	Keyboard locked
304	Keyboard error
305	PS/2 Keyboard fuse
365	Bad keyboard
366	Bad keyboard cable
367	Enhancement card or cable bad
400	Monochrome display passed all tests
401	Monochrome memory test, horizontal sync frequency test, or video test failed
408	User-indicated display attributes failure
416	User-indicated character set failure
424	User-indicated 80×25 display mode failure
432	Parallel port test failed
500	Color display passed all tests
501	Color memory test, horizontal sync frequency test, or video test failed
508	User-indicated display attribute failure
516	User-indicated character set failure
524	User-indicated 80×25 display mode failure
532	User-indicated 40×25 display mode failure

Code	Description
540	User-indicated 320×200 graphics mode failure
548	User-indicated 640×200 graphics mode failure
556	Light-pen test failure
564	Screen-paging test failure
600	Floppy-disk adapter passed all tests
601	Disk power-on diagnostics test failed
602	Disk test failed
603	Disk size error
606	Disk verify function failed
607	Write-protected disk error
608	Bad command—disk status returned
610	Disk initialization failed
611	Timeout—disk status returned
612	Bad adapter card—disk status returned
613	Bad Direct Memory Access (DMA)—disk status returned
614	DMA boundary error
621	Bad seek—disk status returned
622	Bad Cyclic redundancy Check (CRC)—disk status returned
623	Record not found—disk status returned
624	Bad address mark—disk status returned
625	Bad adapter seek—disk status returned
626	Disk data-comparison error
627	Disk change line error
628	Disk removed
700	Math coprocessor passed all tests

406

APPENDIX

A

Diagnostic Error Codes

Code	Description
701	Math coprocessor failure
900	Parallel printer passed all tests
901	Parallel printer adapter test failed
1000	Alternate printer adapter passed all tests
1001	Alternate printer adapter failure
1000	Asynchronous communications (ASC) adapter passed all tests
1101	Asynchronous communications adapter test failed
1110-1157	Individual errors within the ASC adapter, as reported by the diagnostic disk
1200	Alternate ASC adapter passed all tests
1201	Alternate ASC adapter test failed
1210-1257	Individual errors within the alternate ASC adapter
1300	Game control adapter passed all tests
1301	Game control adapter test failed
1401	Color printer test failed
1500	Synchronous data link control (SDLC) passed all tests
1501	SDLC test failed
1510-1549	Individual errors within the SDLC, as reported by the diagnostic disk
1600	Display station emulation adapter (DSEA) passed all tests
1604	DSEA or network error
1608	DSEA or network error
1624	DSEA test failed

Code	Description
1634	DSEA test failed
1652	DSEA test failed
1658	DSEA test failed
1662	Defective DSEA, or switches set wrong
1664	DSEA test failed
1668	Defective DSEA, or switches set wrong
1669	Older diagnostic disk error
1674	Older diagnostic disk error
1684	Invalid feature, switches set wrong, or DSEA error
1688	Invalid feature, switches set wrong, or DSEA error
1700	Hard-drive adapter passed all tests
1701	Hard drive not ready, adapter test failure
1702	Hard-drive timeout
1703	Hard drive error
1704	Hard-drive controller error
1705	No record found
1706	Write fault
1707	Track 0 error
1708	Head select error
1709	Bad error checking and correction
1710	Read buffer overrun
1711	Bad address mark
1712	Bad address mark or undetermined error
1713	Data compare error
1714	Drive not ready

Code	Description
1730	Hard-disk adapter failure
1731	Hard-disk adapter failure
1732	Hard-disk adapter failure
1780	Drive 0 fatal error
1781	Drive 1 fatal error
1782	Drive controller failure
1790	Drive 0 nonfatal error
1791	Drive 1 nonfatal error
1799	Time to buy a Macintosh (just kidding)
1800	Expansion unit passed all tests
1801	Expansion unit failure
1810	Enable/Disable failure
1811	Extender-card wrap test failed (disabled)
1812	High-order address lines failure (disabled)
1813	Wait-state failure (disabled)
1814	Enable/Disable could not be set
1815	Wait-state failure (enabled)
1816	Extender-card wrap test failed (enabled)
1817	High-order address lines failure (enabled)
1818	Disable not functioning
1819	Wait request switch set incorrectly
1820	Receiver-card wrap test failure
1821	Receiver-high-order address lines failure
2000	Bisyncrounous communications (BSC) adapter passed all tests
2001	BSC adapter failure
2010	8255 port A failure

Code	Description
2011	8255 port B failure
2012	8255 port C failure
2013	8253 timer 1 did not reach terminal count
2014	8253 timer 1 stuck on
2016	8253 timer 2 did not reach terminal count, or timer 2 stuck on
2017	8251 Data Set Ready failed to come on
2018	8251 Clear to Send not sensed
2019	8251 Data Set Ready stuck on
2020	8251 Clear to Send stuck on
2021	8251 hardware reset failed
2022	8251 software reset failed
2023	8251 software "error reset" failed
2024	8251 Transmit Ready did not come on
2025	8251 Receive Ready did not come on
2026	8251 could not force "overrun" error status
2027	Interrupt failure—no timer interrupt
2028	Interrupt failure—transmit, replace card or planar
2029	Interrupt failure—transmit, replace card
2030	Interrupt failure—receive, replace card or planar
2031	Interrupt failure—receive, replace card
2033	Ring Indicate stuck on
2034	Receive Clock stuck on
2035	Transmit Clock stuck on
2036	Test Indicate stuck on

Diagnostic Error Codes

Code	Description
2037	Ring Indicate stuck on
2038	Receive Clock not on
2039	Transmit Clock not on
2040	Test Indicate not on
2041	Data Set Ready not on
2042	Carrier Detect not on
2043	Clear to Send not on
2044	Data Set Ready stuck on
2045	Carrier Detect stuck on
2046	Clear to Send stuck on
2047	Unexpected transmit interrupt
2048	Unexpected receive interrupt
2049	Transmit data did not equal receive data
2050	8251 detected overrun error
2051	Lost Data Set Ready during data wrap
2052	Receive timeout during data wrap
2100	Alternate BSC adapter passed all tests
2101	Alternate BSC adapter failure
2110-2152	Alternate BSC errors (same as codes 2010-2052)
2200	Cluster adapter passed all tests
2201	Cluster adapter failure
2400	Enhanced Graphics Adapter (EGA) passed all tests
2401	EGA display adapter error
2408	User-indicated display attributes failure
2416	User-indicated character set failure

Code	Description
2424	User-indicated 80×25 display mode failure
2432	User-indicated 40×25 display mode failure
2440	User-indicated 320×200 graphics mode failure
2448	User-indicated 460×200 graphics mode failure
2456	Light pen failure
2464	User-indicated screen-paging test failure
2500	Alternative EGA passed all tests
2501	Alternative EGA test failure
2800	3278/79 emulation adapter passed all tests
2801	Emulation adapter failure
2900	Color/graphics printer passed all tests
2901	Color/graphics printer test failure
3000	Local Area Network (LAN) adapter passed all tests
3001	LAN failure
3100	Alternate LAN adapter passed all tests
3101	Alternate LAN adapter failure
3300	IBM compact printer passed all tests
3001	IBM compact printer test failure
3600	IEEE 488 adapter passed all tests
3601	IEEE 488 adapter test failure
3602-3698	Various tests and failures for the IEEE 488 adapter
3800	Data acquisition adapter passed all tests
3801	Data acquisition adapter failed
3810-3844	Various tests and failures for the Data acquisition adapter

Diagnostic Error Codes

Code	Description
3900	Professional Graphics Adapter (PGA) passed all tests
3901	PGA adapter test failure
3902-3995	Various tests and failures for the PGA
4800	Internal modem passed all tests
4801	Internal modem failure
4900	Alternate internal modem passed all tests
4901	Alternate internal modem failure
7100	Voice communications adapter passed all tests
7101	Voice communications adapter failure
7300	3½" disk drive passed all tests
7301	Disk-drive/adapter-test failure
7306	Change line error
7307	Drive error (disk is write-protected)
7308	Bad command
7310	Track 0 error
7311	Timeout; drive error
7312	Bad drive controller
7313	Bad Direct Memory Access (DMA)
7314	DMA boundary error
7315	Bad index
7316	Speed error
7321	Bad seek
7322	Bad Cyclic Redundancy Check (CRC)
7323	Record not found
7324	Bad address mark
7325	Bad controller seek

Code	Description
7400	Video Graphics Array (VGA) adapter passed all tests
7401	VGA test failure
8500	Expanded memory adapter passed all tests
8501	Expanded memory adapter failure
8600	PS/2 mouse passed all tests
8601	PS/2 mouse error
8602	PS/2 mouse error
8603	PS/2 mouse error/system board error
8900	Music feature card passed all tests
8901	Music feature card failure
10000	PS/2 multiprotocol adapter passed all tests
10001	PS/2 multiprotocol adapter failure
10002-10056	Various diagnostic errors for the PS/2 multiprotocol adapter
10400	PS/2 ESDI hard drive passed all tests
10480	ESDI hard-drive 0 failure
10481	ESDI hard-drive 1 failure
10482	ESDI hard-drive controller failure
10483	ESDI hard-drive controller failure
10490	ESDI hard-drive 0 error
10491	ESDI hard-drive 1 error

Drive Types

After you install a new hard drive in an AT-level system, you'll need to tell the computer's battery-backed-up RAM which type of hard drive it is. Do this by finding the drive type and entering that information during the running of your AT's SETUP program.

The drive type is identified in the installation manual or on the drive itself. Some computer manufactures will supply their own lists of drive types. When they don't, you can select a drive type based on the drive's description. The following table lists several popular drive types.

Drive Types

Drive Type	Cylinders	Heads	Write Precomp	Landing Zone	Sectors	Mega-bytes
1	306	4	128	305	17	10
2	615	4	300	615	17	20
3	615	6	300	615	17	30
4	940	8	512	940	17	62
5	940	6	512	940	17	46
6	615	4	1	615	17	20
7	462	8	256	511	17	30
8	733	5	1	733	17	30
9	900	15	1	901	17	112
10	820	3	1	820	17	20
11	855	5	1	855	17	35
12	855	7	1	855	17	49
13	306	8	128	319	17	20
14	733	7	1	733	17	42
15						
16	612	4	0	663	17	20
17	977	5	300	977	17	40
18	977	7	1	977	17	56
19	1024	7	512	1023	17	59
20	733	5	300	732	17	30
21	733	7	300	732	17	42
22	733	5	300	733	17	30
23	306	4	0	336	17	10
24	830	10	1	830	17	68
25	1024	9	1	1024	17	76
26	918	7	1	918	17	53

Drive Type	Cylinders	Heads	Write Precomp	Landing Zone	Sectors	Mega-bytes
27	1024	8	1	1024	17	68
28	918	7	1	918	17	0
29	1024	4	1	1024	17	34
30	820	6	1	820	17	40
31	969	9	F1	969	34	144
32	615	8	1	615	17	40
33	1024	5	1	1024	17	42
34	1024	15	1	1024	17	127
35	1024	15	1	1024	26	195
36	1024	8	1	1024	26	104
37	697	5	128	696	17	28
38	980	5	128	980	17	40
39	966	16	1	966	17	128
40	809	6	128	852	17	40
41	1024	4	1	1024	34	68
42	966	5	1	966	34	80
43	966	9	1	966	34	144
44	776	8	1	776	33	100
45	925	9	1	926	17	69
46						
47	1024	5	1	1024	35	87

Index

In this index, **boldface** numbers are references to primary topics and explanations that are emphasized in the text. *Italics* indicate page numbers that reference figures.

A

accelerator cards, 55, 245, **290**
access times
    of CD-ROM drives, 358
    of hard-disk drives, 215
activity lights, disk, 59–60, *61*, 168–169, *169*
A/D (analog-to-digital) ports, 89
adapters. *See* display adapters
address space, **122**
advantages in doing it yourself, **2–5**
air, compressed, 16
air vents, location of, 64, *65*
alignment of floppy-disk drives, 372
amplifiers for speakers, 353–354
analog monitors, **292–293**
analog-to-digital (A/D) ports, 89
ANSI.SYS screen driver, 109
anti-glare screens, 294
anti-static bags, 240
ASCII files, printing, to disk, 331–332
assistant cards for laser printers, 247,
    343–344
AT-command set, 245
AT systems, 21
    case for, 58–59, *59*
    drive bays in, *177*
    expansion cards for, 237, *238*
    features of, **30–33**
    floppy-disk drives for, 186–187
    hard-disk drives for, 223
    keyboard for, **68**, *69*
    power supplies for, 272
    slots in, 249

attributes of fonts, **319–320**
audio. *See* sound
audio CDs, 348, 353
authoring software, **367–368**
auto-cooling power supplies, 272
AUTOEXEC.BAT file
    with hardware upgrades, 113
    for multimedia extensions, 365
    skipping commands in, 108
    in startup, 39
    working with, **110–112**

B

background printing, 338
backup power supplies, 280
backups, file, **232–233**, 387
    tape systems for, **212**
    before upgrades, 92
bad floppy disks, **387**
bad sectors, 216
bandwidth of monitors, 295
banks of memory, 123, *124*, 146–147
bar-code readers, 245
base port addresses
    for CD-ROM drives, 360–361
    for expansion cards, **378–379**
Basic Input/Output System. *See* BIOS (Basic
    Input/Output System)
batch files, 40
    AUTOEXEC.BAT, **110–112**
    running, **112–113**
batteries
    in backup power supplies, 280

for CMOS RAM, **32–33**, 50–51, **82**, *82*, 382
baud rate
of modems, 245
of printers, 334
bays, disk drive, 64, *65*, **176**, *177*, 357–358
beeping in POST, 36
for errors, **41–42**, **399–400**
for power supply problems, 276
bent legs on memory chips, **164–165**, *164*
bent paper clips, 15, 48
bezels on hard-disk drives, *203*
BIOS (Basic Input/Output System)
DOS for, 30
functions of, **26–27**, 35
location of, *75*, **77**
in UMA, 132
upgrading, 389
bits in memory chips, 146
bits per second (BPS) setting
for modems, 245
for printers, 334
blank screens, troubleshooting, **390–391**
bold font style, 320
books, 24, 396
boot sector, 229
bootable floppy disks, **39**
bootable partitions, 228
bootstrap loader, 27
boxes, 24
BPS (bits per second) setting
for modems, 245
for printers, 334
brackets. *See* mounting and mounting brackets
brand names for floppy-disk drives, 186
breadboards, 247
brightness control, 391
brownouts, 267, 392
buffers. *See also* caches
on hard-drive controllers, 207
memory for, 108–109
for printers, **342–343**
BUFFERS command in CONFIG.SYS, 109
bugs, 103, 395
built-in diagnostic programs, 45
built-in fonts, 320
bulk erasing of floppy disks, 199

bus, 28, 55, 76, 235, **248–252**
bus edge connectors, 174
bus mouse, 242
business-quality sound, **351–352**
buttons, mouse, 88, 242
buying
display adapters, **298**
floppy-disk drives, **185–188**
floppy disks, **183–185**
hard-disk drives, **214–216**
memory, **152–153**
monitors, **298–299**
bytes, **121**, 213

C

cables
checking, 46, 381–382, 389
for expansion boards, 254, 257–258
for floppy-disk drives, **71–73**, **170**, **174–175**, 189–191
for hard-disk drives, **71–73**, 205–206, *205*, **208**, **210**, 221
labels for, 16
for monitors, 391
POST beep error message for, 42
for power supply, 71, 195
for printers, **309**, 326
screwdrivers for, 13
snagging cover on, 98–99
troubleshooting, **384–386**
for video still cameras, 363
caches. *See also* buffers
for CD-ROM drives, 358
for disks, 115, **130**
for hard-drive controllers, 207
SRAMS for, 145
caddies for CD-ROM drives, 359
cameras, electronic, 350, **363–364**
capacity
of floppy disks and drives, 175–176, **180–181**, **196–198**
of memory chips, **146–150**
card guides, *253*
cards. *See* expansion cards
carriage returns for printers, 311
carriage width of printers, **323**

cartridges
for fonts, **343**
for printers, **311**
cases
and floppy-disk drives, 187
for PS/2, **63**, *64*
putting covers on, **98–100**
removing covers from, **94–96**, *96*
screws for, *66*, **67**, 95
tower, **61–63**, *62*
for XT and AT, **58–59**, *58–59*
cautions, **7–9**
CD-quality sound, 351, **353**
CD-ROM drives, **211–212**, **355–356**
for audio CDs, 348, 353
benefits of, 349
device drivers for, 109
for fonts, 339–340
installing, **359–361**
positioning, 70
selecting, **356–359**
Centronics ports, 327
CGA video memory, 137, *138*
character-recognition software, 88
characters, 121
characters per second (CPS) for printer
speed, 318–319
cheap products, **8–9**
Chips & Technology chip sets, 78
chips for memory
bent legs on, **164–165**, *164*
buying, **152–153**
capacity of, **146–150**
checking, 382
identifying, **148–150**
inserting, **155–156**, **159–163**
installing, **153–156**
removing, **156–159**
reseating, 389
selecting, **147–148**
speed of, **147–150**, 153
tools for, 15, 157, 160
types of, **144–146**
CHKDSK command, **126**, 388
classic AT bus, **249–250**, *249*
cleaning
compressed air for, 16
expansion cards, 382

floppy-disk drives, 17, **386–387**
keyboards, 390
printers, **394**
clones, licensing fees for, 34
clusters
on floppy disks, **181–183**
on hard-disk drives, 213
CMOS RAM
batteries for, **32–33**, 50–51, **82**, *82*, 382
printing information in, 382
setup programs for, **50–51**
codes for memory chips, **148–150**
coffee, 10, 380
color monitors, 70, **283–284**, **292**
color printers, 86, **315–316**
colors
with display adapters, **283–284**, 288,
291, 298
of floppy-disk drives, 186
in graphics mode, 286
COM devices, 333
.COM drivers, 109
combination expansion cards, 241
COMMAND.COM file
in CONFIG.SYS, 108
copying, 230
in startup, 39–40
compaction utilities, 388–389
compatibility, 21
of CD-ROM drive controllers, 357–360,
366
of data files, 106
of display adapters, 296, 298
of EISA bus, 251
of graphics cards, 283
of hard-disk drives and controllers, 21,
207, 220
of mice, 243
of modems, **245**
of monitors, 296, 298–299
of printers, 308, 310–311, **322**, **330**
components, handling, **22–23**
composing music, 349
compressed air, 16
compressing hard-disk files, **230–231**
computer tool kits, 17
CON device, 333

CONFIG.SYS file
    editing, **110**
    and hardware upgrades, 113
    for multimedia extensions, 365
    skipping commands in, 108
    in startup, 39
    working with, **107–110**
configuration
    checking, 381
    CMOS RAM for, **32–33**
    for display adapters, 300
    for expansion boards, 261–262
    for floppy-disk drives, 194
    for hard-disk drives, 211, 220, 223
    for memory upgrades, 156, 161, 163
    for monitors, 303
conflicts
    with CD-ROM drives, 361
    with expansion cards, 374
    with hard-drive controllers, 206
    on ISA bus, 250, **262–263**
    with printers, 392
connectors
    checking, 381
    for display adapters, 290–291
    for expansion cards, 236–237, *236*, 239
    for floppy-disk drives, **170**, *172*,
        173–175
    for hard-disk drives and controllers,
        204, 206, 208, 221
    for LEDs, **79**, **81–82**, *82*
    location of, **65–67**, *66*, *75*, **79**
    for power supplies, *268*, **269–270**,
        274–275
    for printer port, 328
consistency of problems, 383
console device, 333
consoles, differences in, **63–67**
contention. *See* conflicts
contiguous memory, **122**
control panels in printers, 87, **309–310**
controllers, 81
    cables for, **71–73**, 205, *205*
    for CD-ROM drives, 356–360, 366
    compatibility of, 21, 207, 220, 357–360
    connectors for, **170**, *172*
    for floppy-disk drives, **172–175**, *173*,
        190, 194–195, 240

    for hard-disk drives, **204–207**, *205*,
        215, 220, 241
    for laser printers, 343
    location of, 73
    POST beep error message for, 42
controls on monitors, 294
conventional DOS memory, **131–132**,
    132, *134–135*
converting extended memory to ex-
    panded, **135–136**
cooling. *See* fans
coprocessor expansion cards, 231, 245–246
coprocessors, math, location of, *75*, **76**
COPY command, 331
covers
    putting on, **98–100**
    removing, **94–96**, *96*
    for slots, *66*, **67**, 81, *253*, 256
CPS (characters per second) for printer
    speed, 318–319
cracked solder connections, checking for,
    390
cylinders
    on floppy disks, **181–183**
    on hard-disk drives, 203, 213, **416–417**

D

D-shell connectors, 328
daisywheel printers, 85–86, **317–318**
data cables
    for floppy-disk drives, 189, 191
    for hard-drive controllers, 205, *205*
data files, compatibility of, 106
data word size for printers, 334
date, CMOS RAM for, 50
daughterboards, 239
dealers, **19–20**, 395
/DEBUG switch with MEM, **127–129**
debugging cards, 246
deleting old software versions, 106
density of floppy disks, **183–185**
descenders, 394
desk space for working, 18, 93
desktop publishing
    fonts for, 321, 339
    laser printers for, 314
DEVICE command in CONFIG.SYS, 109

device drivers
    for adapter cards, 304
    in CONFIG.SYS, **108–109**
    for disk drives, **115–116**
    for mice, 243
    for multimedia, 348, **365**
    for printers, **329–330**
    UMA for, 139
device independence, 326
DEVICEHIGH command in CONFIG.SYS,
    109
devices, printers as, **333–334**
diagnostics, 45
    for adapter cards, 304
    beeping codes messages for, **399–400**
    for printers, **394**
    visual messages for, **400–413**
differences in computers, **57**, **81–82**
    in disk drives, **70–74**
    in keyboards, **67–69**
    in models, **58–63**
    in monitors, **69–70**
    in motherboards, **74–81**
    in peripherals, **85–90**
    in power supplies, **73–74**
    in system units, **63–67**
    in tower configurations, **83–85**
digital monitors, **292–293**
DIP (Dual Inline Package) memory chips,
    145, *145*
DIP switches, **47–48**, *47*
    for bus conflicts, 262
    checking, 381, 389
    for display adapters, 291, 300
    for expansion cards, 239
    location of, *75*, **78–79**
    for monitors, 391
    in printers, 86, **310–311**, 332–333, 394
    setting, 15, 48
direct-drive monitors, 293
direct memory access (DMA) channels and
    settings
    for CD-ROM drives, 361
    for expansion cards, **377–378**
    for sound cards, 352
directories
    for printer queues, 338
    search paths for, 111

    for software, 107
disk drives. *See also* CD-ROM drives; con-
    trollers; floppy-disk drives; hard-
    disk drives
    activity lights on, 59–60, *61*, 168–169,
        169
    bays for, 64, *65*, **176**, *177*, 357–358
    caches for, 115, **130**
    checking, 381–382
    device drivers for, **115–116**
    differences in, **70–74**
    external, **90**
    floptical, 176, 180–181, **197–198**
    location of, *71*, *72*, 97
    power cables for, 74
    printing to, **330–332**
    software for, **29–30**, **115–116**
    in tower configurations, 83
    types of, **415–417**
diskettes. *See* floppy disks
display adapters, 81, **281**. *See also* monitors
    accelerator cards for, **290**
    buying, **298**
    color, **283–284**, 298
    companion diskettes for, **304**
    compatibility of, 296, 298
    expansion cards for, 241
    installing, **299–302**
    memory for, 123, *124*, 132, **136–137**,
        138, 286, **289–290**
    modes for, **284–286**
    monochrome, **282–283**
    POST beep error message for, 42
    POST test for, 37
    strategy for, **297–298**
    types of, **286–289**
    VESA connectors for, 290–291
displayable colors, 286
DMA (direct memory access) channels and
    settings
    for CD-ROM drives, 361
    for expansion cards, **377–378**
    for sound cards, 352
documentation
    printing, 331
    storing, 24
documents, sound in, 349, 352

door latches on floppy-disk drives, 168–169, *169*

DOS, 56
functions of, **29–30**, 35
installing, **224–230**
memory for, **126–129**, **131–132**, *132*, *134–135*
partitions for, 228
for printers, **332–337**

DOS 6, CONFIG.SYS and AUTOEXEC.BAT files with, 108

DOS kernel, 39

dot-matrix printers, 85, **312–313**, *312*
carriage width of, 323
DIP switches in, 310
feeding mechanisms for, **323–324**
memory for, 342
paper for, **324–325**
speed of, 318–319
type quality of, 318

dot pitch of monitors, **295**, 299

dots on memory chips, 148, 154, *155*

dots-per-inch (DPI) for type quality, 318

double-density floppy disks, **183–184**

double-sided floppy disks, 183

double spacing, correcting, 394

double-spin CD-ROM drives, 358

DoubleSpace program, 230

downloadable fonts, 320–321

DPI (dots-per-inch) for type quality, 318

DRAM (dynamic RAM) chips, 144–145, 153

drinking, 10, 380

drive-hub holes, 178, *182*

drive spindles, 171

drive units
for floppy-disk drives, **168–171**, *172*
for hard-disk drives, **204**

DRIVER.SYS device driver, **116**

drivers. *See* device drivers

drives. *See* CD-ROM drives; controllers; disk drives; floppy-disk drives; hard-disk drives

DTK computers, 78

Dual Inline Package (DIP) memory chips, **145**, *145*

dual-speed PCs, turbo mode light in, 60, *61*

dust, compressed air for, 16

dynamic RAM (DRAM) chips, 144–145, 153

E

edge connectors
for expansion cards, 236–237, *236*, 239
for floppy-disk drives, **173–175**
for hard-disk drives, 204, 208

EGA (Enhanced Graphics Adapter), **287–288**
display modes for, 285
video memory for, 137, *138*, 289

8-bit slots and expansion cards, 22, **31–32**, 237, 249, *249*

8-bit sound, **350–352**

EISA (Enhanced Industry Standard Architecture) bus, 237, **250–251**

eject buttons on floppy-disk drives, 168–169, *169*

electricity. *See* power supplies; static electricity

electromagnetic interference (EMI), 279

electronic mail, sound in, 349, 352

electronics swap meets, 8, 20–21

electronics tool kits, 17

Elite pitch, 320

EMI (electromagnetic interference), 279

EMM.SYS driver, 140

EMM386 memory manager, 140

EMS (Expanded Memory Specification), 109, 115, 133, *134*, **139–141**

emulation of printers, **340–341**

Enhanced Graphics Adapter (EGA), **287–288**
display modes for, 285
video memory for, 137, *138*, 289

Enhanced Industry Standard Architecture (EISA) bus, 237, **250–251**

enhanced keyboard, **68–69**, *69*

enhanced small device interface (ESDI) drives and controllers, 207
cables for, 72–73, 208
interleave factor for, 208
parking heads with, 233

environment variables, 111

equipment. *See also* hardware
diagnostics in, 45
sources of, **18–21**
types of, **21–22**

erasing floppy disks, 199

error maps for hard-disk drives, 216
errors detected by POST, 36
    beeping codes for, **41–42**, **399–400**
    after hard-disk drive installations, 211, 223
    after memory upgrades, 164
    after monitor installation, 303
    visual messages for, **43–44**, **400–413**
ESDI (enhanced small device interface) drives and controllers, 207
    cables for, 72–73, 208
    interleave factor for, 208
    parking heads with, 233
European power switch, 269
expanded memory, **132–134**, *134*
    converting extended to, **135–136**
    using, **139–141**
Expanded Memory Specification (EMS), 133, *134*, **139–141**
expanding, upgrading for, **54**
expansion cards, 28, 235
    base port addresses for, **378–379**
    cleaning, 382
    compatibility of, 21
    contents of, **236–237**, *236*, **239**
    DIP switches on, 48, 239
    direct memory access for, **377–378**
    examples of, **245–247**
    handling, **240**
    installing, **256–258**, **260–261**
    IRQs with, **374–377**
    location of, **80–81**, *80*, 97, **253**, *253*
    modem, **244–245**
    mouse, **242–243**
    multifunction, 241
    removing, **254–256**, **258–259**
    size of, **237**, *238*, 252
    slots for, **248–252**
    software setup for, **261–262**
    standard, **240–241**
    strategies for, **252–254**
    in tower configurations, 83
    troubleshooting, **373–379**
    types of, **240–247**
expansion slots, 28, 81
    in AT systems, **31–32**
    and case designs, 58
    covers for, *66*, **67**, 81, *253*, 256
    for expansion cards, **248–252**
    location of, *71*, *75*, **76–77**
    in MCA systems, 33–34
    for memory, 151, 153
    size of, 22
expansion units, **90**
extended-ASCII characters, printing, 332
extended-density floppy disks, **185**
extended DOS partitions, 228
extended memory, **132–134**, *134–135*
    in AT computers, **31**
    converting, to expanded, **135–136**
    for Windows, 31, 136, **139**
extended system checks, 37
extended warranties, 372
extensions on slots, 76–77
external CD-ROM drives, **356–357**
external differences in computers, **57**
    in keyboards, **67–69**
    in models, **57–63**
    in monitors, **69–70**
    in system unit, **63–67**
external disk drives, **90**, 176
external inspections, **380–381**
external modems, 88, 244

F

faceplates, **168–169**, *169*, 187, 195
fanfold paper, 324
fans, 266, 268–269, *268*, 272
    checking, 46, 392
    output from, 65–66, *66*
    in tower configurations, 83
fax cards, 246
fax cartridges, **344–345**
fax/modems, 244
FDISK utility, **225–228**, *227–228*
fear, 5
features, software upgrades for, 103
feeding mechanisms for printers, 87, **323–324**
files
    backing up, 92, **212**, **232–233**, 387
    compatibility of, 106
    compressing, **230–231**
    memory for, 108–109
FILES command in CONFIG.SYS, 109

filters, noise, 279–280
5¼-inch floppy disks and drives, 175–176,
    178, 186
5¼-inch hard-disk drives, 210, 212
flashlights, 15–16
flat-head screwdrivers, 12–13, *12*
flat-screen monitors, 296
floppy-disk drives, **167–168**, *172*
    abrasion in, 181
    buying, **185–188**
    cables for, **71–73**, **170**, **174–175**,
        189–191
    cleaning, 17, **386–387**
    controllers for, **172–175**, *173*, 190,
        194–195, 240
    disks for. *See* floppy disks
    drive units for, **168–171**, *172*
    full-height, replacing, **194–195**
    installing, **188–193**
    location of, *71, 72*, **176**, *177*
    mounting brackets and rails for,
        186–188, *188*, 195
    orientation of, **169–170**
    POST beep error message for, 42
    POST test for, 38
    problems in, **372–373**, **386–387**
    removing, **193–194**
    sizes of, 186
    software considerations for, **195–199**
    types of, **175–176**
floppy disks, **177**
    bad, **387**
    buying, **183–185**
    capacity of, 175–176, **180–181**,
        196–198
    erasing, 199
    formatting, **181–183**, **195–198**, 387
    operation of, **180–181**
    parts of, **178–180**
    tracks and sectors on, **181–183**, *182*
floptical disk drives, 176, 181
    formatting, **197–198**
    speed of, 180
FM stereo cards, **354**
Font Management software, **339–340**
fonts for printers, **339–340**
    attributes of, **319–320**

cartridges for, **343**
    PostScript and Outline, **321**
    technology of, **320–321**
food, 10, 380
footprints, 63
form feeds for printers, 87, 310
FORMAT command, **196**, 229–230
formatted disk-drive capacity, 175–176
formatting
    floppy disks, **181–183**, **195–198**, 387
    hard-disk drives, **213–214**, **224–226**,
        229–230, 373, 387–388
fragmented disks, **388–389**
frames, page, 133, *134*
frequency response in multimedia, 351
friction feed mechanisms, 323
front mounts for expansion boards, 256
front panels
    on printers, **309–310**
    on system units, **59–61**, *61*, 64, *65*
FSECT program, 225
full-height floppy-disk drives, **194–195**
full-height hard-disk drives, 204, 210, 212
full-length expansion cards, 80, 237, *238*
Full-Motion Video expansion cards, 88,
    362–363
fun software for expansion boards, 262

G

games
    stereo sound for, 349
    troubleshooting, 391
    turbo mode for, 60
good-to-have tools, **13–15**, *14*
graphics
    color for, 284
    displays for, **283–284**
    printing, 314, 335
    software for, 105
graphics mode, **284–286**
graphics tablets, 88
greater-than signs (>) for redirection, 336
grounding and grounding wrist straps, 8,
    16, 22, 153, 159

H

half-cards, 80, 237, *238*
half-height faceplates, 187
half-height hard-disk drives, 204, 210, 212
handling
    components, **22–23**
    expansion cards, **240**
hard buffers, 207
hard disk cards, **211**, 246
hard-disk drives, **201–202**
    backing up, 92, **212**, **232–233**, 387
    buying, **214–216**
    cables for, **71–73**, 205–206, *205*, **208**,
       210, 221
    compressing files on, **230–231**
    controllers for, 21, **204–207**, *205*, 215,
       220, 241
    drive units in, **204**
    formatting, **213–214**, **224–226**,
       229–230, 373, 387–388
    fragmented, **388–389**
    installing, **219–222**
    interleave factor for, **208**, *209*
    location of, *71*, *72*, **212–213**
    managing, **231–232**
    moving, **233–234**
    operation of, **202–204**
    parking heads on, 92, 215–216,
       233–234
    partitioning, **226–228**
    POST visual error message for, 44
    preventive maintenance for, **232–234**
    problems in, **373**, **387–389**
    removing, **217–218**
    repairing, 23
    software considerations for, **222–231**
    types of, **210–212**
hardware, **25–29**, **56–57**, *56*
    CONFIG.SYS for, **108–109**
    for multimedia, **350–351**
    for printers, **341–345**
    and software, relationship between,
       102, 106–107, **113–116**
    at turn-on, **35–38**
Hayes-compatible modems, 245
hazards, 9–10, 380
HD (high-density) floppy disks, **184**

HDSETUP program, 225
head slots, *182*
heads, 203, *203*
    actuators for, *203*, 204, 215, 233
    for floppy-disk drives, 171, *172*
    for hard-disk drives, 203–204, *203*, 213,
       416–417
    head-cleaning diskettes for, 17, **386–387**
    parking, 92, 215–216, **233–234**
heat, checking for, 46. *See also* fans
height
    of expansion cards, 237, *238*
    of fonts, 321
Hercules graphics cards and monitors, 283,
    289, 292
Hewlett-Packard compatibility, 322
high-capacity floppy disks, formatting,
    197–198
high-density (HD) floppy disks, **184**
high-density-media detection holes, 179
high-level formatting, **229–230**
High Memory Area (HMA), 133, *134–135*
hissing in multimedia, 351
holes on floppy disks, 178–179, *182*
home movies, 349, 361
hooking PCs together, 385–386
horizontal scan rates, 296
HP LaserJet printers, 315, 322
HSECT program, 225
hub holes on floppy disks, 178, *182*

I

IDE (integrated drive electronics) drives
    and controllers, 204, 207
    cables for, 72–73, 208
    interleave factor for, 208
    low-level formatting of, 224–225
    parking heads with, 233
identifying
    memory chips, **148–150**
    problems, **379–380**
impact printers, 85–86, **317**
improvements, software upgrades for, 103
incompatibility. *See* compatibility
index holes on floppy disks, 178
Industry Standard Architecture (ISA) bus,
    249–250, *249*, **262–263**

ink jet printers, 86–87, 311, **315–316**
ink packs, 87
input devices for sound, **355**
inserting memory chips, **155–156**,
 159–163
INSTALL programs, 109
installing
 CD-ROM drives, **359–361**
 display adapters, **299–302**
 DOS, **224–230**
 expansion cards, **256–258**, **260–261**
 floppy-disk drives, **188–193**
 hard-disk drives, **219–222**
 memory, **153–156**
 monitors, **300**, **302–303**
 power supplies, **275–277**
 software, 105–107, 232
integrated drive electronics. *See* IDE
 (integrated drive electronics)
 drives and controllers
interfaces
 for CD-ROM drives, 360
 DOS for, 30
 low-level, 27, 39
 for printers, 310
interference, 279
interlaced monitors, **295**
interleave factor, **208**, *209*
internal CD-ROM drives, **357–358**
internal differences in computers
 in disk drives, **70–74**
 in motherboards, **74–81**
 in power supplies, **73–74**
 in tower configurations, **83–85**
internal inspections, **381–382**, **389–390**
internal modems, 88, 244
interrupt request lines (IRQ)
 and bus, 251
 for CD-ROM drives, 360
 for expansion cards, **374–377**
 for hard-drive controllers, 206
 for sound cards, 352
"Invalid configuration information"
 message, 223
"Invalid Drive Letter" message, 225
I/O addresses for expansion cards,
 378–379
I/O redirection, **336**

IO.SYS file, 38–39
IRQ. *See* interrupt request lines (IRQ)
ISA (Industry Standard Architecture) bus,
 249–250, *249*, **262–263**
italic style for fonts, 320

J

jackets for floppy disks, 178
joysticks, **89**
jumpers, 15, **48–49**, *49*, **75**, **79**
 and bus conflicts, 262
 checking, 381
 for expansion cards, 239
 for floppy-disk drives, 186, 194
 for hard-disk drives and controllers,
 204, 206, 218, 221
 removing, 14, 49
 for video cards, 291

K

K (kilobytes), **121**
Karaoke players, **369**
Kb (kilobits), 146
kernel, 39
keyboards, 29
 connectors for, **66–67**, *66*, *75*, **79**
 device for, 333
 differences in, **67–69**
 maintaining, **390**
 POST error message for, 44
 POST test for, 37
keys and locks, 59, *61*
kilobits (Kb), 146
kilobytes (K), **121**
knock-outs, 66, **253–254**

L

labels
 for cables, 16
 for floppy disks, 178
landing zones for disk drives, **416–417**
landscape monitors, 296
landscape orientation, 323
laptops, **63**, **354–355**

large screen monitors, **89–90**
laser-perforated paper, 325
laser printers, 86, **313–315**, *314*
    DIP switches in, 310
    fax cartridges for, **344–345**
    memory for, 314, 342
    paper for, 323, **325–326**
    rasterizing cards for, **343–344**
    speed of, 319
    toner for, 86–87, 311, 313–314,
        393–394
    type quality of, 318
LaserJet printers, 315, 322
LaserWriter printers, 322
latches on floppy-disk drives, 168–169, *169*
LEDs, **59–60**, *61*, 64
    connectors for, **79**, **81–82**, *82*
    on floppy-disk drives, 168–169, *169*
    on printers, 87
legal size paper, 323
length of expansion cards, 237, *238*
letter size paper, 323
letterheads, printing on, 325
licensing fees, 34
lids
    putting on, **98–100**
    removing, **94–96**, *96*
light pens, 88, 246
lighting for working, 18
lights, **59–60**, *61*, 64
    connectors for, **79**, **81–82**, *82*
    on floppy-disk drives, 168–169, *169*
    on printers, 87
LIM EMS, 133, **139–141**
line conditions, checking, 270, 392
line drawing characters, printing, 332
line feeds for printers, 87, 310–311
line-noise filters, 279
liquids, 10, 380
local bus motherboards and slots, 32, 55
Local Bus Video, 55, 81, **251–252**
    connectors for, 290–291
    expansion cards for, 237
    monitors for, 289
local dealers, **19–20**, 395
locks, 59, *61*, 95, 99
logical drives, partitioning, **226–228**
loosening screws, 18

low-capacity floppy disks, formatting,
        197–198
low-level formatting, **224–226**, 387–388
low-level interfaces, 27, 39
low-profile expansion cards, 80
LPT devices, 333

M

magnetic migration, 198
magnetized screwdrivers, 17
magneto-optical disk drives, 211–212
mail, sound in, 349, 352
mail order houses, **20–21**, 187
mainframe communications cards, 246
maintenance. *See also* troubleshooting
    of hard-disk files, 231
    of keyboards, **390**
    of printers, **392–394**
major software releases, 103
manuals, 24
    for printers, **311**
    problems with, **395–396**
mapping memory, **123**, *124*
master status for hard-disk drives, 218
math coprocessors, location of, *75*, **76**
Mb (megabits), 146
MB (megabytes), **121**
MCA (Micro Channel Architecture), **33–34**,
        250
MCGA graphics standard, 289
MDA (monochrome display adapters),
        282–283, 292
media-detection holes, 179
media in floppy disks, 178–179
MediaVision sound cards, 353
medium screwdrivers, 12–13
megabits (Mb), 146
megabytes (MB), **121**
MEM command, **126–129**
memory, 119, 143
    and address space, **122**
    in AT systems, **31**
    for base port addresses, 360–361
    battery-backed-up. *See* CMOS RAM
    buying, **152–153**
    chips for, **144–150**
    contiguous, **122**

for disk caches, **130**
for DOS, **126–129**, **131–133**, *132*, *134–135*
for downloadable fonts, 321
expanded, **132–136**, **139–141**
on expansion cards, 239, 241
extended, **132–136**, *134–135*, **139**
for files and buffers, 108–109
inserting, **155–156**, **159–163**
installing, **153–156**
for laser printers, 314, 342
location of, **77–78**, **150–151**, 153–154
mapping, **123**, *124*
for memory-resident programs, **130**, 138–139
POST error message for, 44
POST test for, 36–37
for print spoolers, **130–131**
for printers, 86, **342**
problems after installing, **163–165**
for RAM disks, **130**
RAM vs. ROM, **122–123**
removing, **156–159**
report on, **126–129**
for software, 107
speed of, 133, **147–150**, 153
types of, **131–136**
UMA, **131–132**, *132*, *135*, **138–139**
uses for, **114–115**, **120**
for video, 123, *124*, 132, **136–137**, *138*, 286, **289–290**
for video still cameras, 363
memory-resident programs
in AUTOEXEC.BAT, 111
memory for, **130**, 138–139
MFM (modified frequency modulation) drives and controllers, 207
cables for, 72–73, 208
parking heads with, 233
Micro Channel Architecture (MCA) bus, **33–34**, **250**
microphones, 355
microprocessors, **26**
accelerator cards for, 245
address space for, **122**
location of, **75–76**, *75*
POST test for, 37
upgrading, **55**

mid-length expansion cards, 237, *238*
MIDI (Musical Instrument Digital Interface) cards, 88, 246–247
minor software releases, 103
minus screwdrivers, 12–13, *12*
mirrors, 16
missing parts, checking for, 46, 381
MODE command, 333–334
models, external differences in, **57–63**
modems, 88
buying, **244–245**
null, **385–386**
modes
for display adapters, **284–286**
Real and Protected, 31, 134–136
modified frequency modulation (MFM) controllers, 207
cables for, 72–73, 208
parking heads with, 233
modularity of computers, 3–4
money, saving, **4**
monitors, 29, **281**, **291–202**. *See also* display adapters
buying, **298–299**
checking display on, 381
differences in, **69–70**
installing, **300**, **302–303**
monochrome vs. color, **292**
phosphor burn-in on, 6, 279
power for, *268*, 269
repairing, 23
second and large-screen, **89–90**
strategy for, **297–298**
technical information on, **294–296**
troubleshooting, **390–391**
types of, **292–293**
monochrome adapters and monitors, 70, **282–283**, 292
motherboards, **74–75**, *75*, 97
BIOS on, **77**
bus on, **248–252**
DIP switches on, **78–79**
expansion cards and slots on, **76–77**, **80–81**, *80*
jumpers on, 49, **79**
keyboard connectors on, **79**
LED connectors on, **79**
location of, *71*

math coprocessors on, **76**
memory on, **77–78**, 123, 125, 151, 153–154
microprocessors on, **75–76**
POST beep error message for, 42
power cables and connectors for, 74, **79**, *268*, 270, 274–275
swapping, 55
in tower configurations, 83
mounting and mounting brackets
for CD-ROM drives, 359
for expansion cards, 81, 236, *236*, 239, 254–256
for floppy-disk drives, 170, *172*, **186–188**, *188*, 195
mouse, **87–88**, **242–243**
MOUSE.COM driver, 243
MOUSE.SYS driver, 108, 243
MOVE'EM program, 138
moving
computers, **388**
hard-disk drives, **233–234**
MPC (Multimedia Products Council), 351
MS-DOS. *See* DOS
MSCDEX.EXE file, 365
MSD.EXE program, **374–377**
MSDOS.SYS file, 39
MTBF (mean time between failure) ratings, 216
MTMCDD.SYS file, 365
multifunction expansion cards, 241
multimedia
benefits of, **348–350**
device drivers for, 348, **365**
hardware for, **350–351**
history of, **347–348**
network considerations in, **365–366**
software for, **366–369**
sound, **352–355**
visual, **361–365**
multimedia extensions, 365
Multimedia Products Council (MPC), 351
multiple CONFIG.SYS files, 108
multiscanning monitors, **293**
music
composing, 349
software for, **368–369**
synthesizers for, 88

Musical Instrument Digital Interface (MIDI) cards, 88, 246–247
must-have tools, **12–13**, *12*

N

names for devices, 333
nanoseconds, 147
near letter quality (NLQ) printing, 313, 318
near-typeset quality printing, 314, 344
needle-nosed pliers, 14, 49
networks and networking, **89**, **385–386**
adapters for, 247
with multimedia, **365–366**
new features, software upgrades for, 103
9-pin printers, 313, 318
9-pin serial ports, 328
NLQ (near letter quality) printing, 313, 318
noise filters, 279–280
non-interlaced monitors, **295**
"Non-System disk or disk error" message, 38
notches
on floppy disks, 179, *182*
on memory chips, 148, 154, *155*
notebooks, sound for, **354–355**
null modems, **385–386**

O

Object Linking and Embedding feature, 349
OEM (original equipment manufacturers) sources, **19**
on/off issue, **278–279**
on-line control for printers, 87, 309–310
on-line documentation, printing, 331
on-the-fly disk compression, **230–231**
open architectures, 53
operating systems, partitioning for, 226
optical media. *See* CD-ROM drives
optical mice, 243
organizing hard-disk files, 231
orientation
of floppy-disk drives, **169–170**
of memory chips, **154**, *155*
of printers, 323

original equipment manufacturers (OEM)
  sources, **19**
OS/2 operating system
  extended memory for, 31, 136
  printers with, 330
  spoolers in, 338–339
Outline fonts, **320–321**
output redirection, **336**

P

page-display monitors, 296
page frames, 133, *134*
pages per minute (PPM) for printer speed,
  318–319
palettes, 286, 288
paper clips, 15, 48
paper for printers, **323–326**
paper-white monitors, 292
parallel ports
  device for, 333
  location of, 66, *66*
  for printers, 327
  for sound, 354–355
parity errors, 163–164
parity setting for printers, 334
PARK program, 233
parking heads, 92, 215–216, **233–234**
partitioning hard-disk drives, **226–228**
PATH command in AUTOEXEC.BAT, 111
patience, importance of, 16, 23, 46
PC-DOS. *See* DOS
PC-Kwik Power Pak Print Spooler, 337
peer-to-peer networking, 89
pen lights, 15–16
pens with plotters, 316
performance. *See also* speed
  of CD-ROM drives, **358–359**
  of printers, **337–345**
peripherals, **29**, **85–90**
permanent storage. *See* CD-ROM drives;
  controllers; disk drives; floppy-disk
  drives; hard-disk drives
Phillips screwdrivers, 12–13, *12*
phosphor burn-in, 6, 279
Photo CD product, **362**
photographs, 349, **362**
Pica pitch, 320

piggyback cards, 239
pin blocks. *See* jumpers
pin feed mechanisms, 87, **323–324**
pins in print heads, 313
pitch for fonts, 320
pixels, 283
planning, **23–24**
platen feed mechanisms, 87, 323
platters in hard-disk drives, 203, *203*
pliers, 14, 49
plotters, 86, **316**
plus screwdrivers, 12–13, *12*
pointing devices, **87–88**
points for fonts, 320
poor products, **8–9**
portrait orientation of printers, 323
ports
  analog-to-digital, 89
  cables for, **384–385**
  conflicts with, 263
  device for, 333
  expansion cards for, 241
  location of, 66, *66*, **328**
  for mouse, 88, 242
  for printers, **326–328**, **333–334**
  for sound, 354–355
  for video still cameras, 363
POST (Power-On Self Test), **27**, **35–36**
  errors reported by, 36
    beeping codes for, **41–42**, **399–400**
    after hard-disk drive installation,
      211, 223
    after memory upgrades, 164
    after monitor installation, 303
    visual messages for, **43–44**, **400–413**
  tests in, **37–38**
  troubleshooting with, **380**
PostScript fonts and compatibility, **321–322**
power cables and connectors, 71, 195, *268*,
  269–270
  checking, 381
  connecting and disconnecting, 274–275
  location of, 65, *66*, *75*, **79**
  for printers, 309
Power Good line, 270
power light, 59, *61*, 64
Power-On Self Test. *See* POST (Power-On
  Self Test)

power protection strips, **279–280**
power supplies, 29, *73*, **265**
    cables for. *See* power cables and
        connectors
    checking for, 46
    duties of, **266–267**
    for expansion boards, 248
    fans in, 65–66, *66*, 266, 268–269, *268*,
        272
    for floppy-disk drives, **170**, *172*,
        189–190
    for hard-disk drives, 204
    installing, **275–277**
    location of, *71*, **73–74**, 84, 97, **267**
    parts of, **268–270**
    POST beep error message for, 42
    problems in, **373**, **392**
    protecting, **278–280**
    ratings of, 74, 268, **270–272**
    removing, **273–275**, **277**
    screws for, *66*, **67**
    in tower configurations, 83
power switch, location of, 65
powering down, **92**
PPM (pages per minute) for printer speed,
    318–319
precautions, **7–9**
pre-formatted floppy disks, **185**
pre-punched paper, 325
preventive maintenance for hard-disk
        drives, **232–234**
price
    of CD-ROM drives, **358–359**
    of display adapters, 298
    of floppy-disk drives, 186
    at local dealers, 20
    of monitors, 299
primary DOS partitions, 228
print heads, 312–313, 394
PRINT program, **336–337**
Print Screen key, **335**
Printer Genius spooler, 337
printer units, **86**
printers, **307–309**
    buffers for, **342–343**
    cables for, **309**, 326
    carriage width of, **323**
    cleaning, **394**

color, 86, **315–316**
compatibility of, 308, 310–311, **322**, **330**
as devices, **333–334**
diagnostics for, **394**
DIP switches in, 48, 86, **310–311**,
    332–333, 394
DOS for, **332–337**
dot-matrix, **312–313**, *312*
drivers for, **329–330**
emulating, **340–341**
evaluating, **317–324**
fax cartridges for, **344–345**
feeding mechanisms for, **323–324**
fonts for, **319–321**, **339–340**, **343**
front panel switches for, **309–310**
hardware for, **341–345**
impact, 85–86, **317**
laser, **313–315**, *314*
maintaining, **392–394**
manuals for, **311**
memory for, 86, 314, **342**
paper for, **323–326**
parts of, **86–87**
performance of, **337–345**
ports for, **326–328**, **333–334**
rasterizing cards for, 247, **343–344**
redirecting output from, 331, **336**
ribbons and cartridges for, **311**, **393**
software for, **329–332**, **337–341**
speed of, 314, **317–319**
spoolers for. *See* spoolers
thermal, **316–317**
type quality of, **318**
types of, **85–86**
printing
    CMOS information, 382
    to disk, **330–332**
    screen, **335**
PRN devices, 331, 333
problems. *See* troubleshooting
processor direct slots, 32
program switchers, 126, 141
programs, memory for, **126–129**
proprietary memory systems, **32**, **77–78**,
    125, 151, 153
Protected Mode, 31, 134, 136
protective shutters on floppy disks, 179
prototype cards, 247

PS/2 computers, **33–34**, **63**, *64*
pulled chips, 152
punching holes on floppy disks, 179, 198
purchasing. *See* buying
putting on covers, **98–100**

Q

QEMMB program, 135, 138, 140
QRAM program, 138
quad-density floppy disks, 184
quality of printing, 313–314, **318**, 344
queues, printer, 338

R

radio, cards for, 354
radio frequency interference (RFI), 279
RAM (Random Access Memory), **27–28**.
        See also memory
RAM disks, **115**, 139
   CONFIG.SYS for, 109
   memory for, **130**
RAMDRIVE driver, 115, 139
rasterizing cards, 247, **343–344**
ratings for power supplies, 74, 268,
       270–272
read/write heads
   in floppy-disk drives, 180
   in hard-disk drives, 203–204, *203*
read/write windows on floppy disks, 178
reading before doing, 92
Real Mode, 31, 134–135
reasons
   for doing it yourself, **2–5**
   for not doing it yourself, **5–7**
   for upgrading, **54–55**, **103–104**
recharging toner cartridges, **393–394**
redirecting printer output, 331, **336**
reference materials, 24
reformatting hard-disk drives, 373, 387–388
refresh rate of monitors, 296
refreshing of memory chips, 144–145
removable hard-disk drives, **211**
removing
   covers, **94–96**, *96*
   expansion cards, **254–256**, **258–259**

floppy-disk drives, **193–194**
hard-disk drives, **217–218**
memory chips, **156–159**
power supplies, **273–275**, **277**
replacement keyboard keys, 390
replacing
   full-height floppy-disk drives, **194–195**
   power supplies, **271–277**
reseating chips, 389
reset switch, 60–61, *61*
resistors for floppy-disk drives, 194
resolution
   of display adapters, 288–289, 298
   in graphics mode, 285–286
   of monitors, **295–296**
   of printers, 318, 343–344
   in text mode, 285
RFI (radio frequency interference), 279
RGB monitors, **292–293**
ribbon cables, 71–72
ribbons, printer, 87, **311**, **393**
RLL (run length limited) drives and
      controllers, 207
   cables for, 72–73, 208
   parking heads with, 233
ROM (Read Only Memory), 86, **122–123**,
      343
ROM BIOS (Basic Input/Output System)
   DOS for, 30
   functions of, **26–27**, 35
   location of, *75*, **77**
   in UMA, 132
   upgrading, 389
run length limited (RLL) drives and con-
      trollers, 207
   cables for, 72–73, 208
   parking heads with, 233

S

/S switch with FORMAT, 230
sample programs with adapter cards, 304
sample rates and sizes for multimedia,
      350–351
scaleable fonts, **321**
scan rate of monitors, **296**
scanners, 88

screen. *See also* display adapters; monitors
    device for, 333
    printing, **335**
screen savers, 279
screwdrivers, 12–13, *12*
    magnetized, 17
    for removing memory chips, 157
    using, 18
screws
    for case, *66*, **67**, 95
    for floppy-disk drives, 189
    for power supplies, *66*, **67**, 267, 273
SCSI (small computer system interface)
    cards and controllers, 207, 247
    cables for, 208
    for CD-ROM drives, 356–360
SCSI-2 controllers, 245, 251
search paths in AUTOEXEC.BAT, 111
sectors
    bad, 216
    boot, 229
    on floppy disks, **181–183**, *182*
    on hard-disk drives, 213, **416–417**
    and interleave factor, **208**, *209*
security
    backing up files for, **232–233**
    locks for, 59, *61*
    removable hard-disk drives for, 211
segments of memory, 123, *124*
self-amplified speakers, 353–354
self-diagnostics, 45
serial interfaces for printers, 310
serial mouse, 242
serial ports
    cables for, **384–385**
    conflicts with, 263
    device for, 333
    expansion cards for, 241
    location of, 66, *66*
    for mouse, 88, 242
    for printers, **327–328**, **333–334**
    for video still cameras, 363
serial printers, setting up, **333–334**
service contracts, 372
SET command in AUTOEXEC.BAT, 111
setup programs, **50–51**
shadow RAM, 125
sheet feeders, 87, 325

SHELL command in CONFIG.SYS, 108
shielded speakers, 353
shipping
    boxes for, 24
    with mail order houses, 20
shutters on floppy disks, 179
signal to noise ratio for multimedia, 351
SIMM (Single Inline Memory Module)
    memory chips, **145–146**, *146*
    capacity of, 147
    inserting, 156, **161–163**
    packaging of, 152
    removing, **158–159**
single-spin CD-ROM drives, 358
SIP (Single Inline Package) memory chips,
    146
16-bit slots and expansion cards, 22, **31–32**,
    76–77, 237, 249, *249*
16-bit sound, 350–351, **353**
size
    of disk drives, **416–417**
    of expansion cards, *237*, *238*, 252
    of expansion slots, 22
    of floppy disks, 176
    of fonts, **320–321**
    of hard-disk drives, 210
    of monitors, **296**
    of power supplies, 272
    of printer paper, 323
    of screwdrivers, 12–13
slave status for hard-disk drives, 218
slot 8 adapter cards, 77, 81
slots on floppy-disk drives, 168, *169. See*
    also expansion slots
small computer system interface (SCSI)
    controllers, 207, 247
    cables for, 208
    for CD-ROM drives, 356–360
small footprint machines, **63**
small screwdrivers, 12–13
smart expansion slots, 33–34
smoking, 9, 380
software, 26, **101**
    for adapter cards, 297, **304–305**
    adding, **106–107**
    AUTOEXEC.BAT for, **110–112**
    color for, 284
    CONFIG.SYS for, **107–110**

configuration of, 261–262, 381
for disk drives, **29–30**, **115–116**,
  195–199, **222–231**
and hardware, relationship between,
  102, 106–107, **113–116**
installing, 105–107, 232
for multimedia, **366–369**
for printers, **329–332**, **337–341**
running automatically, **111–112**
troubleshooting, **391**, **395–396**
at turn-on, **38–40**
upgrading, **102–105**
solder connections, checking, 390
soldering, 5
sound, 349, 351
  FM stereo cards for, **354**
  input devices for, **355**
  for notebooks, **354–355**
  sound cards for, 89, 246–247, **352–353**
  speakers for, **353–354**
Sound Blaster sound cards, 353
sources of equipment, **18–21**
space for working, 18, 93
speakers, 81, *82*, **353–354**
speed
  accelerator cards for, 245
  of CD-ROM drives, 358
  of floppy-disk drives, 180
  of hard-disk drives, 215
  and interleave factor, 208
  of memory, 133, **147–150**, 153
  of microprocessors, 76
  of modems, **245**
  of monitors, 295
  of printers, 314, **317–319**
  of serial ports, 334
  shadow RAM for, 125
  upgrading for, **54–55**
spindle motors for floppy-disk drives, 171
spindles in hard-disk drives, 203
spoolers, **115**, **336–339**
  CONFIG.SYS for, 109
  memory for, **130–131**
  PRINT program, **336–337**
  in Windows, 336, **338–339**
SRAM (static RAM) chips, 144–145
Stacker program, 230
standards for multimedia, 351

standby power supplies, 280
static electricity, **8**, 22
  and expansion cards, **240**
  tubes for, 153
static RAM (SRAM) chips, 144–145
stepper motors
  in floppy-disk drives, **171**, *172*, 180
  in hard-disk drives, 204, 215, 233
stereo sound, 349, **354**
stop bits setting for printers, 334
styles of fonts, **320**
sunlight and CD-ROM drives, 360
Super VGA adapters, **289**, 297
SuperStor program, 230
support, 20, 395
support hardware, **28**
surge suppression, **279–280**, 373
swap meets, 8, 20–21
switchable power supplies, 269
switches. *See* DIP switches
synthesizers, 88
SYSINIT program, 39
system files, 230
system test in POST, 37
system units
  differences in, **63–67**
  putting cover on, **98–100**
  removing cover from, **94–96**, *96*

T

tablets, 88
talc in laser printers, 326
tape systems
  for backups, **212**
  installing, **192–193**
temporary storage. *See* memory
terminate-and-stay-resident (TSR) programs
  in AUTOEXEC.BAT, 111
  memory for, **130**, 138–139
terminating resistors, 194
testing. *See also* POST (Power-On Self Test)
  equipment under warranty, **371–372**
  upgrades, 93
text, adapters for, 283–284
text files, printing, to disk, 331–332
text mode, **284–285**
thermal printers, **316–317**

third-height hard-disk drives, 210
32-bit slots and expansion cards, **32**, 76–77, 125, 237
32-bit video cards, 291
3270 emulation cards, 246
3½-inch floppy disks and disk drives, 175–176, 178–180, 186
3½-inch hard-disk drives, 210, 212
386 systems, features of, **30–33**
386MAX program, 135, 138, 140
tightening screws, 18
time
    CMOS RAM for, 50
    saving, **4**
tiny screwdrivers, 12–13
toner and toner cartridges, 86–87, 311, 313–314, **393–394**
tools, **11–12**
    to avoid, **17**
    good-to-have, **13–15**, *14*
    kits for, 17
    must-have, **12–13**, *12*
    useful, **15–16**
    using, **18**, 93
tower cases, **61–63**, *62*, *84*
    drive bays in, *177*
    hard-disk drives in, 213
    location of parts in, **83–85**
TPI (tracks per inch), 184
tracing problems, 383–384
trackballs, **243**
tracks
    on floppy disks, **181–183**, *182*
    on hard-disk drives, 203, 213
tracks per inch (TPI), 184
tractor feed mechanisms, 87, **323–324**
training aids, software for, 367–368
troubleshooting
    cables, **384–386**
    evaluating problems, **383–384**
    expansion cards and devices, **373–379**
    floppy-disk drives, **372–373**, **386–387**
    hard-disk drives, 373, **387–389**
    identifying problems, **379–380**
    keyboards, **390**
    after memory upgrades, **163–165**
    monitors, **390–391**

    with POST, **380**
    power supplies, **373**, **392**
    printers, 392
    software, **391**, **395–396**
    start-up problems, **40–45**
    testing equipment, **371–372**
true displayable colors, 286
TrueType fonts, 340
TSR (terminate-and-stay-resident) programs
    in AUTOEXEC.BAT, 111
    memory for, **130**, 138–139
TTL (transistor-transistor logic) monitors, **292–293**
tubes, static-free, 153
tuners, cards for, 354
turbo mode light, 60, *61*
turbo switch, 60–61, *61*
turning off computers, **278–279**
turning on computers
    hardware events after, **35–38**
    POST after, **35–38**
    problems in, **40–45**
    software events after, **38–40**
tutorials, software for, 367–368
TV expansion cards, 349, **364–365**
20 lb. bond paper, 325
24-bit video cards, 291
24-pin printers, 313, 318
type management software, 339
type quality of printers, 313–314, **318**, 344
typewriter printers, **317**

U

UMA (Upper Memory Area), **131–132**, *132*, *135*, **138–139**
underline font style, 320
uninterruptible power supplies (UPS), **280**
UNIX systems, extended memory for, 31, 136
unplugging power before upgrades, 92
upgrading, **53–54**
    reasons for, **54–55**, **103–104**
    strategy in, **91–94**
Upper Memory Area (UMA), **131–132**, *132*, *135*, **138–139**

UPS (uninterruptible power supplies), **280**
used parts, **20–21**
utilities
    for adapter cards, 304
    for expansion boards, 262

V

variable frequency monitors, **293**
variables, environment, 111
VCRs, editing tapes for, 368
VDISK driver, 115, 130
vectors for fonts, 321
ventilation, 65–66, *66*, 98, 266
    checking, 46, 392
    in tower configurations, 83
vents, location of, 64, *65*
versions of software
    deleting, 106
    numbers for, 104
vertical positioning of desktops, **84–85**
vertical scan rates, 296
VESA local bus, 55, 81, **251–252**
    connectors for, 290–291
    expansion cards for, 237
    monitors for, 289
VGA (Video Graphics Array) adapters,
        33–34, **288–289**, 297
    display modes for, 285
    video memory for, 137, *138*, 289–290
VGA monitors, paper-white, 292
VGA Wonder cards, 242
video. *See* display adapters; monitors
Video Feature Connectors, 290–291
Video Graphics Array (VGA) adapters,
        33–34, **288–289**, 297
    display modes for, 285
    video memory for, 137, *138*, 289–290
video still cameras, **363–364**
Videographer's software, **367**
Virtual Mode, 140
visual error messages, **43–44**, **400–413**
visual multimedia, 88, **361–365**, **368**
voice-annotated mail messages, 352
voice-coil actuators, 204, 215, 233

W

"WARNING, ALL DATA ON NON-
        REMOVABLE DISK WILL BE
        LOST!" message, 229
warnings, **7–9**
warranties, **6–7**
    with mail order houses, 20
    for monitors, 299
    testing equipment under, **371–372**
wattage ratings for power supplies, 74,
        268, 270–272
.WAV files, 247
width of fonts, 321
Windows NT, CD-ROM drives with, 366
Windows program
    accelerator cards for, **290**
    with EISA bus, 251
    extended memory for, 31, 136, **139**
    hard-disk drives with, 215
    print spooler in, 336, **338–339**
    printers with, 330
    TrueType fonts for, 340
    with VESA bus, 251–252
WinJet 800 printer, 344
wire cutters, 15
word size for printers, 334
work space for upgrades, 18, 93
wrist straps, 8, 16
write-enable notches, 179, *182*

X

Xenix systems, extended memory for, 136
XT systems, 21
    case for, 58, *58*, *177*
    disk drives in, 72, *72*, 186–187
    expansion cards for, 237, *238*
    features of, **30–33**
    keyboard for, **68**, *68*
    power supplies for, 272

Y

Y splitters for power supply, 71, 195

FREE BROCHURE!

Complete this form today, and we'll send you a full-color brochure of Sybex bestsellers.

Please supply the name of the Sybex book purchased.

_____

How would you rate it?

_____ Excellent   _____ Very Good   _____ Average   _____ Poor

Why did you select this particular book?

_____ Recommended to me by a friend

_____ Recommended to me by store personnel

_____ Saw an advertisement in _____

_____ Author's reputation

_____ Saw in Sybex catalog

_____ Required textbook

_____ Sybex reputation

_____ Read book review in _____

_____ In-store display

_____ Other _____

Where did you buy it?

_____ Bookstore

_____ Computer Store or Software Store

_____ Catalog (name: _____)

_____ Direct from Sybex

_____ Other: _____

Did you buy this book with your personal funds?

_____ Yes   _____ No

About how many computer books do you buy each year?

_____ 1-3   _____ 3-5   _____ 5-7   _____ 7-9   _____ 10+

About how many Sybex books do you own?

_____ 1-3   _____ 3-5   _____ 5-7   _____ 7-9   _____ 10+

Please indicate your level of experience with the software covered in this book:

_____ Beginner   _____ Intermediate   _____ Advanced

Which types of software packages do you use regularly?

_____ Accounting	_____ Databases	_____ Networks
_____ Amiga	_____ Desktop Publishing	_____ Operating Systems
_____ Apple/Mac	_____ File Utilities	_____ Spreadsheets
_____ CAD	_____ Money Management	_____ Word Processing
_____ Communications	_____ Languages	_____ Other _____
		(please specify)

Which of the following best describes your job title?

_____ Administrative/Secretarial   _____ President/CEO

_____ Director   _____ Manager/Supervisor

_____ Engineer/Technician   _____ Other _____
                                                          (please specify)

Comments on the weaknesses/strengths of this book: _____

_____

_____

_____

_____

Name _____

Street _____

City/State/Zip _____

Phone _____

PLEASE FOLD, SEAL, AND MAIL TO SYBEX

SYBEX, INC.
Department M
2021 CHALLENGER DR.
ALAMEDA, CALIFORNIA USA
94501

SYBEX

Audio Error Codes

BEEP PATTERN	DEVICE AT FAULT
No beep	Power supply
Unremitting beep	Power supply
Short, repetitive beeps	Power supply
Long beep, short beep	Motherboard
Long beep, two short beeps	Video
Long beep, three short beeps	Video
Two short beeps	Video
Short beep, long beep	Video
No beep	Speaker

Technical Data for the Four Popular Floppy-Disk Formats

	360K	720K	1.2Mb	1.4Mb
Disk Size	5¼"	3½"	5¼"	3½"
Tracks	80	160	160	160
Sectors	9	9	15	18
Tracks Per Inch	48	135	96	135
Sides	2	2	2	2
Cylinders	40	80	80	80
Density	Double	Double	High	High
Total Bytes	368,640	737,280	1,228,800	1,474,560

Recommended Minimum Specifications for Maximum Performance

	PC/XT	AT 286	AT 386	AT 486
RAM	640K	1Mb	4Mb	8Mb
Memory Access Time	120 ns.	100 ns.	80 ns.	70ns.
Hard-Drive Capacity	20Mb	80Mb	120Mb	250Mb
Hard-Disk Access Time	65 ms.	28 ms.	18 ms.	12ms.
Power Supply	150 watts	200 watts	220 watts	250 watts